'The Body for the Lord'

Sex and Identity in 1 Corinthians 5–7

Alistair Scott May

T & T CLARK INTERNATIONAL
A Continuum imprint
LONDON • NEW YORK

Copyright © 2004 T&T Clark International
A Continuum imprint

Published by T&T Clark International
The Tower Building, 11 York Road, London SE1 7NX
15 East 26th Street, Suite 1703, New York, NY 10010

www.tandtclark.com

British Library Cataloguing-in-Publication Data
A catalogue record for this book is available from the British Library

ISBN 0-567-08096-X

Typeset by Data Standards Ltd, Frome, Somerset BA11 1RE
Printed on acid-free paper in Great Britain by MPG Books Ltd

JOURNAL FOR THE STUDY OF THE NEW TESTAMENT
SUPPLEMENT SERIES
278

Editor
Mark Goodacre

JOURNAL FOR THE STUDY OF THE NEW TESTAMENT
SUPPLEMENT SERIES

278

Editor
Mark Goodacre

Editorial Board
John M.G. Barclay, Craig Blomberg, Kathleen E. Corley,
R. Alan Culpepper, James D.G. Dunn, Craig A. Evans, Stephen Fowl,
Robert Fowler, Simon J. Gathercole, John S. Kloppenborg,
Michael Labahn, Robert Wall, Steve Walton, Robert L. Webb

CONTENTS

PREFACE

This work is the product of research undertaken at Glasgow University between 1997 and 2001. As an undergraduate and postgraduate through the 1990s, I found Glasgow to be an inspirational place to work, and my heartfelt gratitude is due to Professors John Barclay, John Riches and Joel Marcus who instilled in me a passion for the study of the New Testament.

In particular, I owe a debt to John Barclay who supervised this research and without whose friendship, patience and stimulation it would never have come to be. It is impossible to acknowledge all the points at which his comments and criticisms have improved this work. I am also grateful for the supplemental supervision of Dr David Horrell of Exeter University. Additionally, I would like to thank those colleagues who made the tedium of research bearable: in particular, Susan Miller, Jonathan May (no relation), Karen Wenell and Angus Paddison. Over many a welcome coffee break, they always managed at least to appear interested in my project. However, my greatest thanks are to my wife, Elaine, without whose support, sacrifice and tolerance it would all have been impossible. I dedicate this book to her.

This study asks questions about sex and Christianity. What is the relationship between Christian belonging and Christian ethics? What are to be the attitudes of Christians to marriage, singleness and forbidden sexual behaviour? What does the Church do when individuals do not conform to sexual norms? Do (and, if so, how do) Christian ethics differ from those of non-Christians? Standing behind these questions are questions about the relationship between the Church and the social and moral environment in which it finds itself. How different, how 'sectarian', should the Church be?

In this study I am asking these questions of Paul and his first-century Christian community, and doing so as a New Testament scholar. But, as a Christian minister, it would be futile to pretend that these questions would command the same interest if they were not questions that the twenty-first century Church is urgently asking itself today. If I have a disappointment with this work, it is that I have had no opportunity to develop suggestions as to if and how answers to the first-century questions might impinge on those questions of our own day. But perhaps that exploration can be left to others.

ABBREVIATIONS

BAGD	W. Baur, W.F. Arndt, F.W. Gingrich and F.W. Danker, *A Greek-English Lexicon of the New Testament and Other Early Christian Literature* (Chicago: University of Chicago Press, 2nd edn, 1958)
BibInt	*Biblical Interpretation: A Journal of Contemporary Approaches*
BJRL	*Bulletin of the John Rylands University Library of Manchester*
BT	*The Bible Translator*
CBQ	*Catholic Biblical Quarterly*
EQ	*Evangelical Quarterly*
ExpTim	*Expository Times*
HR	*History of Religions*
HTR	*Harvard Theological Review*
ICC	International Critical Commentary
Int	*Interpretation*
JAAR	*Journal of the American Academy of Religion*
JBL	*Journal of Biblical Literature*
JR	*Journal of Religion*
JSNT	*Journal for the Study of the New Testament*
JTS	*Journal of Theological Studies*
KJV	King James (Authorized) Version
LCL	Loeb Classical Library
NCB	New Century Bible
NETR	*Near Eastern Theological Review*
NIGC	New International Greek Commentary
NIV	New International Version
NJB	New Jerusalem Bible
NovT	*Novum Testementum*
NRSV	New Revised Standard Version
NTS	*New Testament Studies*
RB	*Revue Biblique*
RSV	Revised Standard Version
SBLDS	SBL Dissertation Series

SJT	*Scottish Journal of Theology*
ST	*Studia Theologica*
Str-B	H.L. Strack and P. Billerbeck, *Kommentar zum Neuen Testament aus Talmud und Midrash*
TDNT	G. Kittel and G. Friedrich (eds.), *Theological Dictionary of the New Testament*
TLG	*Thesaurus Linguae Graecae* (Irvine: University of California)
TTod	*Theology Today*
TynBul	*Tyndale Bulletin*
USQR	*Union Seminary Quarterly Review*
VC	*Vigiliae Christianae*
WBC	Word Biblical Commentary
WTJ	*Westminster Theological Journal*
ZNW	*Zeitschrift für die neutestamentliche Wissenschaft*

Introduction

1. *Beginnings*

1 Corinthians 5–7 is the most extensive discussion of sexual ethics in the entire New Testament. Chapter 5 opens abruptly with an accusation of sexual immorality, levelled at the Corinthian church (5.1). Paul then demands that the community exclude one sexual offender (5.8), before clarifying the implications of a misunderstood previous demand that the community disassociate itself from sexual offenders in general (5.9–13). Believers need not completely withdraw from outsiders.

Chapter 6 begins with the only section not explicitly mentioning sex (6.1–8). However, once more the concern is with the relation of insider to outsider (outsiders should not be called upon to settle disputes between insiders). The passage proceeds (6.9–12) to divide humanity into two groups (those who will, and those who will not, inherit the kingdom), and to do so on the basis of ethics (and especially sexual ethics). Once again we are concerned with sex, boundaries and behaviour. Finally, in 6.12–20, Paul demands that the 'body is for the Lord' and from this draws the conclusion that sexual union with a πόρνη is unacceptable for believers. Πορνεία is here presented as a particularly grievous breach of Christian ethics. But how this discussion of πορνεία connects with the expulsion of 5.1–8 is not immediately clear.

Chapter 7 famously discusses marriage. What are the implications of Christian identity for those who are, or would be, married? Can and should a believer marry? What is the attitude of the believer towards this crucial social institution to be? The discussion appears to draw Paul into a wider consideration of the believers' attitude to various social activities (mourning, rejoicing, buying, owning, dealing with the world, 7.30–31) and the relation of, and compatibility between, Christian identity and various other social identities (circumcision/uncircumcision, slavery/freedom, 7.17–24). The question also arises as to whether Christians are to remain in (7.12–16), or are free to contract (7.39), marriages with outsiders. Throughout this chapter then we have again a concern with the norms and boundaries of the Christian group. Where are Christian attitudes to marriage, divorce and other social institutions to differ from those of outsiders – outsiders who also engage in the same social practices? How are believers to relate sexually to outsiders? But again, whether and how this connects to 1 Corinthians 5–6 is not immediately clear.

The object of this study is to explore the part played by sexual ethics in the formation of Christian identity. (1) How far are Christian sexual ethics and behaviour viewed as different from those of the outside world? How far does this create a distinct sense of Christian identity? (2) How do Christian ethical convictions govern attitudes to and relations with outsiders? (3) How are Christian sexual ethics related to internal regulation (discipline)? (4) How are Christians to relate to those social institutions (marriage and divorce) that normally govern sexual relations? (5) Further, what is the significance of Paul's discussion of the body for these questions? How does the construction of the body govern its sexual use, and what might this indicate about the relationship between the individual, the Christian group, and the wider community? To answer these questions we shall need to carefully exegete 1 Corinthians 5–7. We shall need to define our understanding of identity. We shall also need to explore some resources, which might aid our understanding of the relationship between the behaviour of individuals and their belonging to a social group, and how such a belonging might affect the individual's relationship to the wider society. Here we shall look to the social sciences. But there is perhaps a prior question. Can 1 Corinthians 5–7 be read as a sustained Pauline discourse on sexuality, in which we might find coherent answers to our questions?

2. Unity or Disunity?

From the outset, the problem that confronts any consideration of 1 Corinthians 5–7 as a unit is that, despite its common theme of sexual behaviour, few commentators consider these chapters as a whole. Most separate 5.1–6.20 from 7.1–40, and this for two reasons. First, 5.1–6.20 is viewed as the culmination of the first part of the epistle, where Paul responds to what has been reported orally to him from Corinth (1.11; cf. 5.1), while 7.1–40 is viewed as the beginning of the epistle's second part, where Paul is answering a letter from the Corinthian congregation.[1] But secondly, and perhaps more significantly, commentators postulate separate situational backgrounds for 5.1–6.12 and 7.1–40. 5.1–6.12 is seen as Paul's criticism of a libertine faction within the Corinthian church (whose slogan is πάντα μοι ἔξεστιν), while 7.1–40 is seen as his response to a marriage-denying ascetic tendency (whose contention is καλὸν ἀνθρώπῳ γυναικὸς μὴ ἅπτεσθαι). These separate backgrounds are presented as key to the understanding of the parts. Often, rather than explore the contours

---

1. E.g. Barrett 1971: 28 and Fee 1987: 21–22.

of Paul's theology of sexuality as revealed in 5.1–7.40 as a whole, the scholarly energy has largely been taken up with reconstructing the separate situational backgrounds. Little attention is given to reconstructing a coherent Pauline ideology or rhetorical strategy.

The first of these contentions, that Paul responds first to an oral report and then to a letter, would seem to be correct. However, its significance for the understanding of 5.1–7.40 should perhaps not be overplayed. Paul's decision to connect his response to the oral report and the issues raised by the letter, even if only sequentially, may well indicate that the form of 5.1–7.40, although responsive, is *his* construct for *his* own reasons. The second of these contentions requires further exploration. How far does the situational background serve to shape Paul's writing? How plausible is it that two so diverse attitudes to sexuality could coexist within the one (small?) congregation? We shall return to both these questions in due course. However, be that as it may, preliminary justification for reading 5.1–7.40 as a block can be offered. Perhaps more links these chapters than Paul's desire to respond to the variously communicated sexual issues of the Corinthian church.

1. Our chapters are concerned with the construction of the body. As we have seen, the construction and boundaries of the body politic (that is, the Christian community) are constantly in view (esp. 5.1–6.11). (Although here Paul does not apply the body metaphor to the church as in 12.12–26.) There is also a concern with the boundaries of the physical body (6.12–20, 7.4 and possibly 5.5 and 7.28), which is to be viewed as a member of Christ and 'for the Lord'. As we shall see, studies of both anthropology and ancient rhetorical discourse suggest that ideas of the physical and social bodies are closely related.

2. A linguistic and conceptual link can also be found in the discussion of authority (ἐξουσία) exercised over the believer by a sexual partner. Paul's response to the contention πάντα μοι ἔξεστιν is οὐκ ἐγὼ ἐξουσιασθήσομαι ὑπό τινος (6.12), stressing the illegitimacy of allowing someone or something extrinsic to hold an ἐξουσία over the believer. This is an implied argument against intercourse with a πόρνη. However, 7.4 refers to an ἐξουσία held legitimately over the believer by a spouse.

3. There is another linguistic and conceptual link between 6.(19-)20 and 7.23. Paul uses the same argument (ἠγοράσθητε τιμῆς) to argue against entering into πόρνη-union and slavery respectively. Since 7.17–24 must somehow relate to the discussion of marriage, we again find a connection between marital and πόρνη union.

4. More controversially, many commentators have observed that Paul's reasoning in 6.12–20 logically goes beyond prohibiting

πόρνη-union.[2] For if πόρνη-union is prohibited as those who are
'one spirit' with the Lord cannot become 'one flesh' with the πόρνη,
then arguably this implies that no believer should become 'one
flesh' with any other – even within marriage. We need to explore
whether the discussion of the legitimacy of marriage in 1
Corinthians 7 could be connected to 6.14's observations on the
compatibility of sexual and spiritual unions?

3. Previous Studies of 1 Corinthians 5–7

Commentaries aside, there is a positive abundance of monographs,
articles and other works that focus on (parts of) these chapters. Perhaps
the largest number have their interest either in providing an historical
reconstruction of the situation in the Corinthian church that lies behind
the discourse, or in using the discourse as evidence for a more general
reconstruction. In particular, those who have sought to construct a social
profile of the Corinthian congregation have found many clues in 1
Corinthians 5–7 (for example, in the existence and nature of the lawsuits).[3]
Others, seeking to reconstruct the social dynamics of the congregation,
have used aspects of 5–7 as a test case for their theories.[4] Other studies
have focused more particularly on reconstructing the peculiarities of the
various parts of 1 Corinthians 5–7 itself. Effort has been made to identify
the nature of the offender's relationship with the γυνὴ πατρός of 5.1,[5] to
uncover the precise issue of the lawsuits of 6.1–8,[6] to detect a particular
historical referent for the ἀνάγκη of 7.26,[7] and to recover the reasons why
a woman is divorcing her husband in 7.10–11.[8] However, perhaps the
greatest effort has been committed in reconstructing the identity of the
supposed ascetics, whom Paul addresses in 7.1–40. Here, studies abound
which seek to establish whether these are women or men (invariably the
former), how they relate to Paul, and what might be their position with
regard to the congregation and its wider social environment.[9]

Historical reconstruction is not the main purpose of this study.

---

2. E.g. Héring 1962: 45; Burkill 1971: 116; Boyarin 1994: 170–72.
3. E.g. Theissen 1982: 97; Meeks 1983: 66; Meggitt 1998: 122–25.
4. E.g. Clarke (1993 esp. 59–72 and 85–88) who suggests that the normal (secular)
leadership patterns of ancient Corinth have been preserved in the Corinthian church, and
then offers this as an explanation of the internecine lawsuits, and the failure of the
community to expel the incestuous man. (See also Chow [1992 esp. 123–41] who does much
the same with the notion of patronage.)
5. E.g. De Vos 1999.
6. E.g. Winter 1991 and Richardson 1983.
7. Winter 1989.
8. Murphy-O'Connor 1981.
9. E.g. Fiorenza 1983: 220–26; Gundry Volf 1994a, 1996; M.Y. MacDonald 1990;
Scroggs 1972 and Wire 1990.

However, in order to understand Paul's discourse, we shall be required to consider the historical situation from which it arose. What is it about Corinthian practice and belief that Paul seeks to modify or confront? What prior discussions of the issues have there been between church and apostle? Although we shall address such questions, our focus shall remain on the text itself, and what it says about *Paul's* construction of Christian identity in general, rather than on the precise views of the Corinthian congregation (as far as these might be reconstructed).

Many studies have sought to place 1 Corinthians 5–7 within the history of religions. Some have argued for a direct influence on Paul: for example, Rosner seeks to show Paul's debt to the language and motifs of Hebrew Scripture.[10] Others have, less ambitiously, attempted to draw cultural parallels between various aspects of the text and other phenomena: for example, Forkmann compares 1 Corinthians 5 to the practice of expulsion within Rabbinic Judaism and Qumran.[11] Some have sought to compare the language and sentiment of 1 Cor. 5.5 to curses in Graeco-Roman magical papyri.[12] However, again, most interest has been devoted to 7.1–40. Wimbush has sought to situate Paul's response to the world (encapsulated in the ὡς μή of 7.29–31) within Graeco-Roman asceticism.[13] Yarbrough has attempted to compare Paul's marriage rules with those of Judaism and ancient philosophy.[14] Deming and Balch have tried to situate the entire thesis of 1 Corinthians 7 within the Stoic-Cynic marriage debates.[15] Gundry Volf has attempted to compare the motivations of the supposed ascetics with notions of inspirational asceticism in Graeco-Roman religion.[16]

In contrast to the above, the focus of this study will not be upon the search for parallels to, or influences upon, Paul from the history of religions. Our focus is on how Paul's sexual ethics serve to inform Christian identity, rather than where they may have come from, or to what they might later lead. That having been said, some comparison of Paul's ethos and that of his Graeco-Roman contemporaries will be of interest, particularly where this helps to explain where Paul would stand out as different.

Dale Martin

Because of its interest in the body and its significant observations on 1 Corinthians 5–6, perhaps the single most significant work for our

---

10. Rosner 1994 (also 1998 and 1999).
11. Forkmann 1972.
12. A.Y. Collins 1980 (cf. response by South 1993).
13. Wimbush 1987.
14. Yarbrough 1984.
15. Deming 1995; Balch 1983.
16. Gundry Volf 1994a.

purposes is Dale Martin's *The Corinthian Body*. Martin's basic thesis is
that 'the theological differences reflected in 1 Corinthians all resulted from
conflicts between various groups in the local church rooted in different
ideological constructions of the body'.[17] However, this is not perceived as
a mere conflict of ideologies, for Martin, following the work of Theissen
and Meeks, holds that with regard to these issues, 'the Corinthian church
was split along social status lines'.[18] Here a wealthy and (importantly)
educated minority in the church (the 'strong') differ in outlook from the
low status minority.

As to these ideological constructions of the body, Martin is at pains to
ensure that we situate our discussion of such matters as body, pneuma,
self and sexuality in an ancient context, rather than reading modern
notions into it. Martin contends that the ancients viewed the body as a
microcosm of society, and did not clearly distinguish the individual as a
unit from society or nature. 'Rather than trying to force ancient language
into our conceptual schemes, we would do better to try to imagine how
ancient Greeks and Romans could see as "natural" what seems to us
bizarre: the nonexistence of the "individual", the fluidity of the elements
that make up the "self", and the essential continuity of the human body
with its surroundings'.[19] Thus the ideology of the body, cosmology, and
constructions of society are all to be identified.

Martin argues that the elite minority in the Corinthian church holds, in
common with most of the educated minority in antiquity, a hierarchical
view of the body. The healthy body must be structured, balanced and
united. Internal disruption and imbalance are the principal threats to the
ordered body, and the appropriate remedial action is to restore equilibrium within that body. This is the concern of both the medics in treating
physical aliments, and the politicians in addressing social unrest. (The
homonoia or *concordia* speech is a common example of an appeal for the
restoration of social harmony by each component of the body politic
accepting its place within the social hierarchy.) The promotion of such an
ideology, naturally, supports the social status quo and favours the elite.

However, Paul and the uneducated majority in the Corinthian church
hold to a more popular understanding of the body. This interprets illness
not as lack of equilibrium in the body (an aetiology of balance), but as a
pollution of the body by some extrinsic element (an aetiology of invasion).
Such a pollution fear results in an emphasis on the maintenance of the
boundaries of the body from external threat. Foreign bodies must be
identified and expelled. For Paul, this aetiology of invasion is pictured in
terms of an apocalyptic war between pneuma and sarx. The purity of the

---

17.   D.B. Martin 1995: xv.
18.   D.B. Martin 1995: 86.
19.   D.B. Martin 1995: 21.

pneuma is constantly in danger of pollution from the corrupt outside world (the sarx). Thus the boundaries of the body stand in constant need of definition and protection. For Paul 'potentially both eating and sexual intercourse are boundary transgressing activities',[20] whereas the Corinthian 'strong' 'show little concern that bodily activities, whether eating meat offered to idols, or visiting prostitutes, will pollute either themselves or the rest of the church'.[21]

True to his insistence that the individual and corporate bodies are to be identified in Paul's thought, Martin collapses talk of the body of Christ, the body of the believer, and the church as body, into a discussion of the pollution of *the* body and the threat to *its* pneuma from that which pertains to the outside world. For instance, in 1 Corinthians 5, Martin sees Paul arguing for the expulsion of the immoral man, for without such 'the pneuma of Christ's body will become polluted by the corrupting presence of the sinful sarx'.[22] 'Since no secure boundary separates the offender's body from the church's body, the offender's presence in the church represents an invasion of the sarx into the church itself.'[23] Although social contact with outsiders does not pollute (1 Cor. 5.9–13), the body of Christ 'may be polluted if its boundaries are permeated and an element of the cosmos [i.e. the immoral man] gains entry into the body'.[24] Martin's insistence that that 'no ontological dichotomy between the individual and the social can be located in Paul's logic in 1 Cor. 5',[25] allows him to read every reference to the body as simultaneously a reference to the community and the individual.

1 Cor. 6.12–20 is read in much the same way. The πόρνη is now 'not a person in her own right ... but a representative of the cosmos that is estranged and opposed to God and Christ', whereas the believer shares the same pneuma as Christ, so that 'the man's body is therefore an appendage of Christ's body'.[26] Thus as the man penetrates the prostitute, the body of Christ is penetrated by the corrupt cosmos, and the divine pneuma stands in danger of pollution.

Noting that some of the medical writers express concern that excess intercourse or sexual desire can unbalance the body, Martin postulates that some of the Corinthian 'strong' have valued abstinence for similar reasons. Paul's fear, however, expressed in 1 Corinthians 7, is again for the pollution of the body either by πορνεία or by sexual desire itself. Whereas most of the medics seek to moderate sexual desire by recom-

20. D.B. Martin 1995: 175.
21. D.B. Martin 1995: 71.
22. D.B. Martin 1995: 169.
23. D.B. Martin 1995: 174.
24. D.B. Martin 1995: 170.
25. D.B. Martin 1995: 173.
26. D.B. Martin 1995: 176.

mending self-control and a balanced (non-excessive) exercise of sexual intercourse, Paul seeks to eliminate sexual desire altogether. Those who experience such should marry, as, for Paul, marriage is the prophylaxis of desire.[27]

The overall structure of Martin's thesis, however, is dependent on a number of polarities, each of which is open to question. First, he relies heavily upon Meeks's and Theissen's reconstruction of the Corinthian church as divided between the rich minority and poor majority: a scenario that has recently been challenged.[28] However, be that as it may, Martin has also polarized ancient views of the body between a hierarchical understanding with its attendant aetiology of balance held by the educated elite, and a more popular understanding of the body as a permeable entity with an attendant aetiology of invasion, held by the rest of the population. But do these two understandings constitute mutually exclusive alternatives?[29] Paul himself seems to use both, in his understanding of the relation between spiritual gifts (12.28–31), and (as even Martin concedes) in his understanding of relations between the sexes. If Paul can hold both together, why cannot others?[30]

Here our central interest is, however, in Martin's contention that Paul (and ancient thought in general) does not distinguish between the individual and society, and the properties of the physical body and those of the body politic. Certainly there is a relationship between the two. Constructions of the physical body are socially constructed and socially shared. Social anthropology would affirm that how we view the body and its boundaries is directly related to how we view society and its boundaries. Classicists would agree that in ancient thought the body is a microcosm of the state. Additionally, the notion of the autonomous individual may be thought distinctly modern, notions of identity in the ancient world being more related to belonging to a social group. Within the field of New Testament studies, the work of Bruce Malina has constantly contended for this[31] (we shall return to this in section 1.2). But does a *relationship* between body and society, necessarily imply an *identity*? Does Paul perhaps distinguish between the social body and the physical body and between these and the body of Christ more clearly than Martin suggests? This question is important for our study because we are interested in both the Christian community and the individual, and how

27. Cf. D.B. Martin 1997.
28. See Meggitt 1998.
29. A criticism of Martin often raised by the reviewers (e.g. Horrell 1996b: 626 and M.M. Mitchell 1997: 291).
30. When we examine the rhetoric of the Roman moralists in Chapter 2 of this volume, we shall observe that these elite and educated writers certainly exhibit a concern for the boundaries of the body politic.
31. Cf. Malina 1981: 51–68; Malina and Neyrey 1996: 1–18.

belonging to the community impacts on the identity and social behaviour of the individual.

Martin has made a number of important claims about how Paul's ideology of the body influences his instruction on sexual matters, and in particular how Paul's logic of invasion influences his view of how a believer should relate to the outsider. In answering our questions about sex, Christian identity and social behaviour, we shall require to explore Martin's views. A central weakness of Martin's approach is that he does not engage in detailed exegesis of the texts that he discusses. We shall do just this, and evaluate his findings in the process.

4. *1 Corinthians and the Social Sciences*

Questions concerning the relationship between individuals, social groups and the wider society perhaps obviously take us into the field of the social sciences. In recent years, many scholars have applied insights from the social sciences in the study of biblical texts,[32] and there are a number of clear advantages for us in such an approach. First, it demands the reading of the ideas of the text in social context, remembering that ideas (and perhaps particularly those of a community builder like Paul) produce, and are (at least to some degree) produced by, a society. Secondly, analysing the social dynamics of the text using explicit models or theories developed by the social sciences helps to avoid the danger of using the implicit models of the interpreter's own experience (which are liable to be ethnocentric and anachronistic) to understand Paul and his social world. We are helped to remember that Paul and his world are radically dissimilar to us and ours.

Studies of this nature abound, many of them bearing on 1 Corinthians and a few directly on chs 5–7. For instance, Harris, in a study of 1 Corinthians 5, has made use of the deviance theory of Himmelweit to analyse the Corinthian attitude to incest, and a model of the millenarian sect developed by Burridge to consider the differing attitude to norms of Paul and his audience.[33] Gordon, in a study of Paul's dealings with Corinthian factions in 1 Corinthians 7, has made use of Turner's model of social drama.[34]

However, perhaps most significant for our purposes is the application of the work of anthropologist Mary Douglas to our texts.[35] This is because Douglas's theories are concerned not only with the relation of the individual to society, but also with how this relates to language about the

---

32. For a survey see Horrell 1999.

33. Harris 1991. It is rather worrying that Harris cites only one short and dated dictionary article by Himmelweit.

34. Gordon 1997.

physical body. Douglas sees an analogous relationship existing between the human and social body. The human body is a microcosm or symbol of society. When concern for bodily orifices is exhibited (to prevent pollution) this symbolizes a concern to mark and guard the boundaries of society.[36] Further, Douglas contends that body symbols 'represent condensed statements about the relation of society to the individual'.[37] Where strong pressure is placed upon the individual by society, this manifests itself in strong control over the body.

Douglas also presents four ideal-types of culture: each either high or low in regard to the variables group and grid. 'Group' measures the level of participation in the social group. Low group societies exhibit a high level of individualism, little pressure to conform to social norms, and a resultant view of the body as a porous flexible entity. In high group societies collective belonging is important; personality is dyadic; conformity, order and control are stressed; and there will be concern for the boundaries of physical body. Society exerts control over the individual by demanding that the body conform to communal norms. Broadly speaking, 'grid' is the measure of acceptance, by the individual or the group, of the prevailing symbol system. High grid indicates an acceptance of a public system of classification: the individual's experience of the world fits society's evaluations, and the world is seen as coherent. Low grid means a rejection of this in favour of a private system of cosmological interpretation: the cosmos will tend to be seen as a dangerous and unpredictable place.

Using Douglas's models, Neyrey and Carter label Paul's ideals as high group.[38] 1 Corinthians shows the apostle's concern for the integrity and conformity of the church. This would lead us to an expectation that Paul would be concerned with the integrity of the physical body, and seek to regulate it. This is found to be confirmed by the text, where Paul regulates the use of the genitals (1 Cor. 5–7), the head (1 Cor. 11), and the mouth in eating (1 Cor. 8–11) and speaking (1 Cor. 12–14). The Corinthians, on the other hand, less concerned for the integrity of the church, or the control of the body, are to be classed as low group.[39]

Criticism and Grounds for Proceeding
Since the use of social-science resources will form an important part of this study, it is worth making a few critical remarks on previous studies at

35.   E.g. Gordon (1997) applies Douglas to 1 Cor. 7. Neyrey (1986) and Carter (1997) apply her work to 1 Cor. as a whole.
36.   Douglas 1973: 88–99.
37.   Douglas 1973: 195.
38.   Neyrey 1986; Carter 1997.
39.   Carter, however, disputes Neyrey's attribution of high grid to Paul, arguing that Paul refuses to give assent to the cultural norms and values of the surrounding society.

this juncture. We should learn not only from the strengths of these studies, but also from their weaknesses. First, there is the danger of using social science to fill in gaps in the evidence, or to replace careful historical-exegetical study.[40] The study of human behaviour is simply not a science where it may be assumed that people conform to rules. Secondly, the relevance to the textual situation of the social-science model chosen needs to be considered. Invariably social-science models are developed as generalizations from observations made in sociological or anthropological fieldwork: they are not (as good social anthropology recognizes) universal rules applicable in every social situation.[41] However, there is the danger that models are inappropriately applied as universal rules – without due consideration of the *differences* between the cultural contexts.[42]

To give an example, which will prove pertinent to our study, we need look no further than the application of Douglas's social theory to the Corinthian congregation. Neyrey and Carter are concerned to relate the anthropology and cosmology of the Corinthians to their position in regard to 'grid' and 'group': a relationship made explicit in Douglas's theory. However, Douglas's theory is derived from fieldwork completed among tribal groups. In these groups there is generally one relevant 'group' and one relevant 'grid' – that of the tribe. But for the Jewish-Christian Paul, operating in urban Corinth, this is clearly not the case. Paul's relationship to the 'group' and 'grid' of Judaism, Graeco-Roman society, and formative Christianity all fall to be considered. Further, if some in Corinth exhibit a low degree of commitment to the congregation, can they be said to be 'low group' without further qualification? In truth they may exhibit a high degree of commitment to other groups – kinship group, social network, the *polis*, or even a particular church faction, which may serve to weaken their commitment to the congregation. Thus we must speak of a variety of possible 'group' relations. But which should we attempt to correlate with their construction of the physical body (or indeed cosmology)? The problem here is with forgetting that Douglas's

40. E.g. Harris uses the millenarian model to reconstruct a progression from 'old rules', through 'no rules' (where the Corinthians are), to 'new rules' (where Paul is), without proper consideration of the textual evidence. (Whether Paul had a 'no rules' phase from which he passed, as Harris implies, is at least historically debatable. It should not be *proved* merely from a model!) See also Horrell's critique of aspects of Esler's use of models (2000: 90–92).

41. Horrell (2000: 84) warns, 'a model based approach can lead to historically and culturally variable evidence being interpreted through the lens of a generalised model of social behaviour'.

42. E.g. when Harris applies the model of the millenarian sect to the Pauline community, he recognizes the danger of applying a model derived from observations of a twentieth-century social phenomena, but comments that he does so 'on the basis that Pauline Christianity can be classified as a millenarian movement' (1991: 12). This is simply a circular argument.

theory – as much as it appears to offer universal rules – is a model of society developed in particular cultural contexts. The question of its relevance to a first-century urban context must be considered, just as with the millenarian sect model. Perhaps we require a model more appropriate to an urban context, which is able to take account of the multiple social identities that coexist there.

However, despite the dangers, it is difficult to see how sociological modelling can satisfactorily be avoided. Scholars who have rejected the use of social-scientific resources entirely can rightly be criticized for naiveté.[43] One cannot simply interpret historical data in an empirical manner without the use of some form of theory – all data is theory laden. Those who refuse the use of explicit sociological models are perhaps doomed to use implicit models, for instance, from their own experience of twentieth-century society as a framework for analysis. We may grant that such may be as valid as any cross-cultural model provided by the sociologist, but its danger lies in its implicit character – its pretence to objectivity, and its impunity to the theoretical critique, to which the explicit model may be subjected.

Nor can the dangers of modelling be avoided by eschewing a model-based approach in favour of another more general theoretical one. Criticizing both Esler's use of models, and his application of the term to cover almost any form of sociological approach to the text, Horrell suggests that there can be a non-model sociological approach (a 'research framework'), which does not depend on simplifications of the results of empirical studies. Such approaches, he suggests, serve better as heuristic devices.[44] But Horrell seems to imply that the use of such frameworks protects the scholar from the dangers that the 'model user' runs of reading observations specific to the culture from which the model is developed into the text.[45] However, even if certain social anthropological approaches can be more sophisticated than others, and their theories have been developed in wider cultural contexts than, say, the millenarian sect model, they still inevitably remain theories that have grown out of specific cultural contexts and fieldwork. To this degree they remain *models*. Indeed, it is perhaps precisely where observations on human activity are *claimed* as cross-cultural universals (a claim Horrell appears to be making for his frameworks), that there lies the danger of forgetting the specifics of the context from which the observations are taken.

In our consideration of identity, we shall be examining the work of the anthropologist Frederik Barth and the social psychologist Henri Tajfel. We shall be using these as models for understanding the relationship

43.   E.g. Clarke 1993; cf. Horrell's criticism (1996a: 27–28).
44.   Horrell 1996a: 9–18; 2000: 83–105.
45.   Horrell 2000: 90–92.

between individual and group. We shall use social-science resources because it is doubtful whether there is any other satisfactory means for a proper consideration of human society. But we shall do so remembering that purely abstract social theory is simply impossible. Rather we proceed with our resources tentatively, making no grand claims. We will attempt to use our 'theoretical frameworks' (Horrell) as 'tools, heuristic devices, and not social laws' (Esler[46]) to define terms and to generate new questions. But we shall do so in the awareness of the dangers as well as the uses of our *models*, and by refusing to claim that our resources are immune from such dangers.

5. *Sex and Identity*

In recent years, there has been much discussion of the formation of early Christian identity. What identity markers distinguished the Pauline church? What similarities and dissimilarities defined the Christian church from its environment? Wayne Meeks in particular has contributed to the study of the 'factors that contributed to their [Pauline Christians'] sense of belonging to a distinct group and the ways in which they distinguished that group from its social environment'.[47]

In a chapter of *The First Urban Christians* entitled 'The Formation of the Ekklesia', Meeks catalogues these various factors.[48] There is the Christian 'language of belonging', which uniquely applies to insiders. Believers are designated 'saints' and those 'called' by God; they are referred to using kinship language: brother, father, children; they are said to be related as parts of the body. Then there is the 'language of separation', which serves to divide insider from outsider. Outsiders are associated with 'this world', are 'perishing' and are stigmatized as 'unbelievers' and by the vice lists. Then Meeks explores the boundaries of the community. Although Paul makes no use of Jewish boundaries such as circumcision and food laws, he retains a prohibition on idolatry and a sexual ethic that would differentiate his community from outsiders. In addition, the ritual of baptism establishes a boundary between the old and the new life. So too does participation in the Lord's Supper – a ritual open only to believers (and refused to those who will not conform to group norms: 1 Corinthians 5; 10.15–22; 2 Thess. 3.14?).

The particular interest of this study is in how sexual ethics contributes to the formation of Christian identity. We are interested in what Paul has to say, both in terms of the language (how the sexual rhetoric contributes to the sense of 'belonging' and 'separation') and in terms of the rules

---

46. Esler 1998b: 256.
47. Meeks 1983: 74.
48. Meeks 1983: 84–107 (essentially a restatement of Meeks 1979).

themselves (how far they divide insider from outsider). Although the relationships between sexual rhetoric and behaviour on the one hand, and construction of the individual and social body on the other have been of increasing interest to classicists over recent years, little parallel work has been done by New Testament scholars.[49]

So often Paul's sexual ethic is quickly dismissed as a Jewish hangover, and not part of his distinctive Christian theology. Brown speaks of Paul's desire to subject the Corinthians 'to what he evidently considered to be the ordinary decencies of Jewish life'.[50] Meeks observes of Paul's 'rules about sex' that 'the Jewish abhorrence of homosexuality and the equation of irregular sex with idolatry were *retained* by the Pauline Christians. Indeed, the way in which the general marriage rule was formulated, "not as the gentiles who do not know God," suggests strongly that this whole tradition had its origins in the diaspora synagogue.'[51] In terms of the origin of ideas Meeks is perhaps correct, but there remain two important differences between Paul's teaching and Jewish sexual ethics.

First, since Paul's converts were mainly Gentile, it is incorrect to say that Jewish rules were *retained* by Pauline Christians. Such would need to be learned anew. The social impact of such a process then requires exploring. What difference would the adoption of such codes mean to Gentiles in reality?

Secondly, a distinctively Christian ideology appears to underscore Paul's ethical argumentation. Christians are not told simply to do as Jews, and 'not as the Gentiles'. Rather the story of Christ's death (1 Cor. 5.7–8; 6.20) and resurrection (1 Cor. 6.14), and the believer's participation in Christ (1 Cor. 6.13, 15) and the Spirit (6.17, 19) through baptism (1 Cor. 6.11) appear integral to Paul's ethical reasoning. Might not this Christian rationale make an all-important difference to Christian self-understanding?

6. *Program for this Study*

What then does it mean for Paul to claim that 'the body is not for πορνεία but for the Lord' (6.13)? What are the connections between the believer's allegiance to the Lord (his Christian identity) and his sexual behaviour? How far is Christian identity viewed as transforming behaviour? What are the perceived differences between those whose bodies are 'for the Lord' and the rest of humanity? How does the perception of difference between

---

49. See particularly Foucault (1986) but also e.g. Rousselle (1988, 1989), Hallett and Skinner (1997) and Edwards (1993). P. Brown (1988) does explore these issues in Paul and early Christianity, but his focus is more widely on the first few centuries of Christian history.

50. P. Brown 1988: 51.

51. Meeks 1983: 100–101; emphasis added (cf. Meeks 1979: 13).

insider and outsider in regard to sexual ethics affect how the believer perceives and treats insiders and outsiders respectively? What type of worldview does it encourage?

We shall approach these questions in the following manner. First, in Chapter 1, we shall consider theoretical issues. We shall explore what we mean by identity. We shall use the work of the anthropologist Frederik Barth and the social psychologist Henri Tajfel to reflect on how social identities interact, both at the psychological level of the individual and at the sociological level of the group. In Chapter 2 we shall examine the lessons learned in Chapter 1 with a brief consideration of the discourses of some Roman writers. How do they use sexual ethics in the creation of identity? What parallels can we see with Paul's rhetoric? Here we are assisted by the interest of classicists in issues of sexual rhetoric and social identity.

In Chapter 3, we shall take an overview of 1 Corinthians. We shall examine the context into which Paul writes. What are Paul's objectives? In particular we shall look at how Paul constructs a dichotomy between insider and outsider in 1 Corinthians 1–4, and examine how this might aid his purposes in writing. Then we shall take an initial look at 1 Corinthians 5–7 and its ethical dichotomy between believer and outsider, considering the significance of this for Christian identity.

We shall then proceed to examine 1 Corinthians 5–7 in depth. In Chapter 4 we shall look at 1 Corinthians 5, examining how Paul deals with the immoral man. How are Christian ethical convictions affected by deviance? What is Paul's analysis of this deviance? How does he encourage Corinthian action? We shall also consider Paul's attitude to social relations with outsiders in 5.9–13.

Chapter 5 will examine the lawsuits. Although probably not concerned with sex as such, what does Paul's prohibition teach about his attitude to outsiders? How does Paul's treatment of believers who offend against their fellows compare with his treatment of the sexual offender in 5.9–13? Chapter 6 will examine 6.12–20. What do these verses teach about the nature of sexual sin and sexual relations with a woman labelled πόρνη? What are the implications of Paul's understanding of the 'body for the Lord' for the compatibility of sexual union and Christian identity?

1 Corinthians 7 is usually read with the assumption that Paul is reacting to Corinthian ascetics. As this reconstruction dominates interpretation of the chapter and separates its concerns from those of 1 Corinthians 5 and 6, we shall take time to consider its veracity. In Chapter 7 we shall assess various articulations of the ascetic hypothesis and explore possible objections. In Chapter 8 we shall develop this by considering the social implications of the renunciation of marriage and the attitudes to society that normally accompany such. We shall then compare these findings to

what 1 Corinthians as a whole reveals to us about the social attitudes of Paul and the Corinthians.

Our final chapter shall examine the text of 1 Corinthians 7 in depth. We shall explore its connections with 1 Corinthians 5–6. Does the understanding of the 'body for the Lord' in 1 Cor. 6.12–20 impact on Paul's view of the compatibility of sexual relations and Christian identity? We shall re-examine what the chapter reveals about Paul's attitude to marriage itself, and to divorce. What difference does Christian identity make to the believer's attitude to the social institutions that govern human sexuality in antiquity?

When we have considered all of this we shall be in a better position to understand the rhetorical and ideological impact of 1 Corinthians 5–7, and what part sex plays in the construction of Christian identity.

Chapter 1

IDENTITY IN THEORY

1.1. *The Sense of Belonging and Distinction*

As we have noted, 1 Corinthians 5–7 is repeatedly concerned with the boundaries of the Christian community. 5.9–13 denies the need for total withdrawal from outsiders, 6.1–6 prohibits using outsiders as judges, and 7.12–16 (and 7.40) negotiates the question of marriages to outsiders. This discussion of activity toward outsiders is juxtaposed with various comparisons between believers and outsiders. Eschatologically, believers will judge, while unbelievers will be judged (6.2). Outsiders are consistently denigrated as immoral (πόρνοι, ἄδικοι etc., 5.10–11 and 6.9–11), in contradistinction to believers who have been transformed by baptism (6.9) (although this moral comparison seems to be reversed at 5.1). But what might all this 'boundary language' indicate to us about Christian identity?

In his analysis of a group's existence and persistence and the language and activity that differentiates it from its social environment, Meeks contends that 'in order to persist, a social organization must have boundaries, must maintain structural stability as well as flexibility, and must create a unique culture'.[1] A question arises here. To what degree (if any) does a social group require a 'unique culture' or distinctive boundaries?

We might ask the historical question as to how 'unique' the culture of the Pauline church actually was. How much cultural overlap was there with its Graeco-Roman or Jewish environment? Do Christians live by a different set of moral rules? Or do they try to live by the same set, but demand a 'higher righteousness'? What happens if they commit sins 'not found among' outsiders? But there are more fundamental questions here about the nature of social groups. How 'unique' must its culture be for a group to form and persist? Does the 'uniqueness' of culture vary with the persistence and cohesion of social organization? Or are these the wrong

---

1. Meeks 1983: 84.

types of question? Do they relate too much to notions of the 'objective stuff' of the group's culture, and too little to the subjective disposition of its members: that is, the *sense* of belonging and distinction, as opposed to the supposed facts of similarities between members and their distinctiveness from their social environment?

1.1.1. *Barth on Ethnicity*

The relation of the group's existence and its culture has been a question considered by social anthropological studies of ethnic groups for some time.[2] Although the Pauline churches are not ethnic groups, some observations of the anthropologists may still be illuminating.[3]

Traditionally, studies of ethnicity have taken the existence of ethnic groups and their cultural difference for granted, and focused on how these 'things' interacted. However, Fredrik Barth[4] forcefully critiqued the tendency to assume that 'cultural variation is discontinuous: that there are aggregates of people who essentially share a common culture, and interconnected differences that distinguish each such discrete culture from all others'.[5]

Barth suggests that ethnic groups are subjective 'categories of ascription and identification by the actors themselves, and thus have the characteristic of organizing interaction between people'.[6] These socially agreed categories are generated and preserved in the process of social interaction. Thus the sharing of a common culture is not the primary determinant of the social group, but rather 'an implication or a result' of the group and its interactions.

Indeed the studies Barth is introducing serve to suggest that the barriers between groups can be somewhat permeable. Individuals may even change their ethnic identity.[7] However, despite this movement of individuals, the social category persists: 'boundaries persist despite a flow of persons across them'. Thus the focus of ethnology should be upon the 'social processes of exclusion and incorporation whereby discrete social categories are maintained *despite* changing participation and membership in the course of individual life histories'.[8]

---

2. For examples see the studies in Sollors 1996.
3. On the application of Barth's studies to other than ethnic groups see Jenkins 1996: 100.
4. For an assessment of Barth's importance to anthropology see Jenkins 1996: 90–103.
5. Barth 1969: 9.
6. Barth 1969: 10.
7. See particularly the study by Haaland (1969) of how members of the Fur communities of Western Sudan may adopt a nomadic lifestyle and eventually become members of Baggara communities.
8. Barth 1969: 10.

For Barth, the group is produced and maintained in intergroup activity. The 'social construction of (external) difference generates (internal) similarity rather than vice versa'.[9] Thus external difference is not primarily one of culture but of people, for indeed the identity markers that symbolize the conviction of difference may alter over time, and context. That which signifies (say) Jewish identity in the first century is not identical with that which denotes a contemporary Jew. Difference then is socially organized. Further, relations across the boundary, rather than weakening identity, may be carried out on the basis of the very dichotomy itself. Group norms may not only *proscribe* certain interaction with outsiders; they may also *prescribe* such activity.

This is not to suggest that the ethnic group is unrelated to *any* notion of 'objective' difference. However, it is to suggest that there is 'no simple one-to-one relationship between ethnic units and cultural similarities and differences. The features that are taken into account are not the sum of "objective differences", but only those which the actors themselves regard as significant... some cultural features are used by the actors as signals and emblems of differences, others are ignored, and in some relationships radical differences are played down and denied.'[10]

Taken together, these findings indicate that the group dichotomy, the sense of 'us' and 'them' (or belonging and distinction), does not depend on the separation of the relevant cultures or lack of interaction between the actors. Even where cultural difference is minimal, this does not necessarily correlate to a reduction in the relevance of the group identity to the individual actors or to a breakdown in the group boundary.

1.1.2. *The 'Narcissism of Minor Difference'*

> It is precisely the minor differences in people who are otherwise alike that form the basis of feelings of strangeness and hostility between them ... it would be tempting to pursue this idea and derive from this 'narcissism of minor differences' the hostility which in every human relation we see fighting against feelings of fellowship and the overpowering command that all men should love one another.[11]

Freud perhaps overstates, and yet he again brings out the notion that it is not the quality or quantity of the difference but the decision to place value upon it, that is determinative in alienation and cohesion. It is the *feeling* of

---

9. Jenkins 1996: 93.
10. Barth 1969: 14. Barth has been criticized for overemphasizing individual choice (see Jenkins 1996: 97). However, since our interest is in voluntary groups, where individual choice is particularly important, such criticism may be less relevant.
11. Freud, *The Taboo of Virginity* (1917) as quoted by Ignatieff 1998: 48.

strangeness and hostility that determines the evaluation and perception of cultural differences.

Michael Ignatieff has taken up this Freudian concept of 'narcissism of minor difference' to explore the dynamics of group identity in the recent Serbo-Croatian War. He contemplates, but then rejects, the 'nationalist myth' that Serbs and Croats are different people with nothing in common, and that ethnic tension (indeed ethnic identity itself) rests on 'objective' difference. He notes that other social identities were previously pertinent to the individual actor, so that 'before the war, he might have thought of himself as a Yugoslav or a café manager or a husband, rather than a Serb'. Thus 'nationalism does not simply "express" a pre-existing identity: it "constitutes" a new one'.[12]

According to Ignatieff, the nationalist takes the sheer neutral facts about people – 'language, habit, culture, tradition, and history' – and turns these facts into an identity based upon 'a narrative, whose purpose is to illuminate the self-consciousness of a group, to enable them to think of themselves as a nation with a claim to self-determination'. The nationalist creates a narrative that accentuates similarities among members and difference from outsiders, and suppresses factors that operate in the opposite direction.

Ignatieff then argues that 'the less substantial the differences between two groups, the more they both struggle to portray these differences as absolute', i.e. to assert a 'unique culture'. Moreover, Ignatieff states that:

> the aggression that is required to hold a group together is not only directed outward at another group, but directed inward at eliminating the differences that distinguish individual from group. Individuals ... pay a high psychic price for group belonging. They must turn the aggressive desire to conform against their own individuality. In order to dissolve his identity in Serbdom, for example, the foot soldier must repress his own individuality, and his memory of common ties with former Croatian friends. He must do a certain violence to himself to make the mask of hatred fit.[13]

One might with some justice contend that Ignatieff's own mask slips at this point, to reveal his personal disdain for nationalism: disdain that somewhat colours his analysis. But perhaps more significantly Ignatieff reveals that he shares the Western notion that the 'true self' is the autonomous individual: and that the assertion of the group is to the detriment of the individual's identity. However, it will not do simplistically

12.   Ignatieff 1998: 38.
13.   Ignatieff 1998: 51.

to oppose group allegiance to individuality, as if nationalism were different in kind from any other social identity, or as if the previous concepts of identity held by Serb or Croat ('Yugoslav or café manager or husband') were not also *social* identities. The emergence of a new social identity, or the increasing pertinence of an existing one, is at the expense, not so much of the 'individual' as it is of alternate social identities. As Serbian or Croatian social identity becomes salient in an increasing number of social encounters, other identities that would serve to divide the ethnic group (e.g. occupation, social class, political affiliation) will diminish in importance. Similarly, those identities that would unite members of the competing groups (e.g. as members of a mixed-ethnic local community, Yugoslavs or Balkan residents) become untenable. The only social identities likely to grow in relevance are ones that serve to reinforce the dichotomy between the two emerging identities (e.g. adherence to either the Orthodox or the Roman Catholic Church).

However, leaving aside Ignatieff's misplaced emphasis on the individual, the greater point of his observations remains: that the level of 'objective difference' or 'unique culture' is not what is all-important in the creation of social identity. Rather the pre-existing differences and similarities are manipulated and prioritized by the actors themselves (or new ones are constructed) in order to reinforce their sense of belonging and distinction.

1.1.3. *The Difference Christianity Makes*
In terms of sexual norms, if we were to seek for a 'unique culture' among Paul and his converts, we may encounter some difficulties. It is at least arguable that the content of Paul's sexual ethic differs little from Judaism or indeed aspects of Graeco-Roman values. Paul condemns incest: but then such, as even Paul notes, 'is not found/condoned among pagans' (1 Cor. 5.1). Paul condemns sexual union with a πόρνη: but Jews habitually condemned prostitution. As for Paul's *Lasterkataloge* (1 Cor. 5.11, 6.9–10), such have parallels both in Hellenistic Jewish and certain Graeco-Roman literature.[14] But then, Barth and Ignatieff indicate that it is not a uniqueness of culture that allows the group to persist. Indeed, it is perhaps only from the viewpoint of the actors themselves that culture is unique.

We must proceed bearing two things in mind. First, we must pay attention to the importance of the *sense* of belonging and distinction to the ways that individual actors construct social reality from the similarity

---

14. R.F. Collins (1999: 218) describes them as 'well known rhetorical devices in the ancient world' used in the Stoic-Cynic tradition and adapted by Hellenistic Judaism (e.g. 1QS 4.9–11).

and difference that surrounds them: the psychological *feeling* of differ-ence, which evaluates even 'minor' difference as significant for identity. Since group differentiation does not depend on 'objective' difference, even where groups are 'objectively' similar – and perhaps especially here – small differences can be stressed. Boundaries are as much psychological as physical. Thus, if Paul is a community builder, we must examine how he creates and enhances this sense of belonging.[15] What narrative of identity does he (like Ignatieff's nationalist) offer his converts?[16] Since an understanding of psychology and not simply culture is key to under-standing group identity, we need a framework for evaluating the psychological aspects of social identity.

Secondly, we must take seriously the contention that identity is created in interaction between groups. We must examine the ways in which Paul seeks to regulate (by proscribing or prescribing) intergroup activity. Areas where the group norms allow but *prescribe* interaction on the basis of group membership may be as important as symbols of distinction as areas where interaction is *proscribed*. Thus we need a framework that allows us to explore intergroup activity and its relationship with the identity of the individual actors. Our contention is that the social identity theory developed by the social psychologist Henri Tajfel meets both of these requirements.

1.2. *Social Identity Theory*

> The central tenet of this approach is that belonging to a group ... is largely a psychological state which is quite distinct from that of being a unique and separate individual, and that it confers social identity, or a shared/collective representation of who one is and how one should behave. It follows that the psychological processes associated with social identity are responsible for generating distinctly 'groupy' behaviours, such as solidarity with one's group, conformity to group norms, and discrimination against outgroups.[17]

15. In fairness to Meeks, despite his remarks on 'unique culture', he shows considerable interest in what we would term the psychological aspects of group belonging. He examines 'aspects of language, practice, and expressed sentiments and attitudes that gave the group cohesion' (1983: 85) and in particular the 'language of belonging and separation'. Our problem is that he regards this language as part of the 'unique culture'. Although such language may assert uniqueness, it is not in itself unique.

16. We use the term 'narrative' loosely here to denote whatever stories are told within a group (coherent or otherwise) concerning its origins, properties or destiny, which serve to enhance and legitimate its self-identity. In the case of 1 Cor. we might include Paul's references to the call and transformation of believers (e.g. 1.26, 6.9–12), their possession of the Spirit (e.g. 6.19) or their role and fate at the Eschaton (e.g. 6.2–3).

17. Hogg and Abrams 1988: 3.

1.2.1. *Social Identity*

Developed by Henri Tajfel,[18] social identity theory[19] is a diffuse but interrelated group of social psychological theories concerned with when and why individuals identify with, and behave as part of, social groups. It is also concerned with what difference it makes when encounters between individuals are perceived as encounters between group members. Social identity theory is thus concerned both with the psychological and sociological aspects of group behaviour.

Reacting against both individualistic explanations of group behaviour and tendencies to reify the group, Tajfel sought an account of group identity that held together society and individual.[20] Tajfel differentiates between those elements of self-identity derived from individual personality traits and interpersonal relationships (personal identity) and those elements derived from belonging to a particular group (social identity). Each individual is seen to have a repertoire of identities open to them (social and personal), each identity informing the individual of who he or she is and what this identity entails. Which of these many identities is most salient for an individual at any time will vary according to the social context.

Tajfel then postulated that social behaviour exists on a spectrum from the purely interpersonal to the purely intergroup. Where personal identity is to the fore, the individual will relate to others in an interpersonal manner, dependent on the character traits and personal relationships of individuals. However, under certain conditions 'social identity is more salient than personal identity in self-conception and ... when this is the case behaviour is qualitatively different: it is group behaviour'.[21]

1.2.2. *Group Behaviour*

Tajfel suggests that at the 'intergroup' end of the behavioural spectrum social behaviour will be largely:

1.   independent of individual differences either in the ingroup or in the outgroup

---

18.   Since we have protested that theory is borne of social context, Tajfel's biography may be relevant. A Polish Jew, he fought for France in 1939–45 surviving capture by the Germans by pretending French nationality. After the war he naturalized as French, before emigrating to the UK. Thus his work is borne out of an experience of both intergroup conflict and personal variations in social identity (see Turner 1996: 2–6).

19.   In what follows, I am indebted to Philip Esler for demonstrating the possibilities of social identity theory for the study of New Testament texts. See in particular his analysis of ethnic identity in Galatians (Esler 1998a) but also Esler 1996b and 2000.

20.   For comparisons of Tajfel to prior theories of the group see Turner *et al.* 1987: 1–17.

21.   Hogg and Abrams 1988: 25; cf. Tajfel and Turner 1979: 34.

2. independent of personal relationships which may exist in other situations between individual members of different groups
3. unaffected by the temporary motivational states of the individuals.[22]

(We might also add that social behaviour would be less determined by the other possible social identities of the individuals.)

At the intergroup end of the spectrum, we can then expect a greater uniformity in behaviour towards members of outgroups, and a stronger tendency:

> for members of the ingroup to treat members of the outgroup as undifferentiated items in a unified social category... This will be reflected simultaneously in a clear awareness of the ingroup-outgroup dichotomy, in the attribution to members of the outgroup of certain traits assumed to be common to the group as a whole, in value judgments pertaining to these traits, in the emotional significance associated with these evaluations, and in other forms of behaviour associated with the ingroup-outgroup categorization.[23]

When then does interpersonal behaviour become intergroup behaviour? Tajfel suggests that:

> there is a reciprocal (or 'dialectical') relationship between social settings and situations on one hand, and the reflection or expression in them of subjective group membership... The number and variety of social situations which an individual will perceive as being relevant in some ways to his group membership will increase as a function of: (1) the clarity of his awareness that he is a member of a certain group; (2) the extent of the positive or negative evaluations associated with this membership; and (3) the extent of the emotional investment in the awareness and the evaluations.[24]

We can thus now define the psychological element, which we have argued throughout to be primary, not simply as the 'sense of belonging and distinction', but more precisely as the *cognitive* (the awareness of belonging), the *evaluative* (the value of membership) and the *emotive* (the emotional investment in membership) responses to membership. Further we can see that where the cognitive, evaluative and emotive elements are greatest, group belonging will be most determinative of both individual identity and individual behaviour.

22. Tajfel 1978: 44.
23. Tajfel 1978: 45.
24. Tajfel 1978: 39.

1.2.3. *Social Competition*

Tajfel challenged the assumption that competition and conflict between social groups had a purely objective rationale. Objective conflict of interest (i.e. competition for scarce resources) was not a *necessary* condition for intergroup rivalry.[25] Rather, competition between groups was an intrinsic psychological fact of social identity. Social categorization itself produced group behaviour – and group behaviour was competitive in nature.

This claim was advanced from the 'Minimal Group Paradigm'[26] experiment. In this experiment all objective variables that might cause intergroup competition were removed so that only the bare social categories remained. Anonymous individuals were assigned to ad-hoc meaningless groups; they had neither knowledge of, nor previous interaction with, any other participants and no group goals were set: thus there was no individual self-interest in the success of the group. Participants were then asked to allocate financial resources to other subjects, in such a way that they could choose between maximizing the total allocation, maximizing the allocation to members of their own group, or maximizing the differentials between members of the two groups. What the experiment revealed was that individuals responded to non-identifiable members of their own group in a discriminatory form, tending either to maximize allocation to ingroup members, or maximize differentials between the groups. It was taken from this that merely imposing social categories on actors produced discriminatory behaviour.[27]

Thus social categorization is all that is required for psychological group formation. This bears out what we argued earlier, that 'unique culture' is not a prerequisite for the existence of the group. The group produces effects even when it has no 'real' existence. 'Group cohesion is the effect rather than the cause of group formation'.[28] But, if a psychological group has formed, why should individuals discriminate in favour of their group?

Tajfel suggested that comparisons between groups were focused on the establishment of *positive social identity*. Individuals have a psychological need to obtain a positive self-identity relative to others. Since part of self-identity is social identity – given by membership of a social group – it can be expected that where social identity is pertinent there will be a desire to

25. Tajfel and Turner 1979.

26. Sherif in fact first carried out the experiments (cf. Turner 1978: 101–40).

27. See further Turner 1987: 26–35 and Tajfel and Turner 1979: 38–42. It may be noted that in the experiment the groups were already artificially manufactured. In reality, perceived differences and similarities may be required in order for new groups to form.

28. Turner 1987: 28.

secure a positive social identity from the group. Thus the social group requires being able to distinguish itself from others in ways that give it a relatively positive social identity.

The need to establish a relatively positive social identity can cause a number of differing reactions, depending upon the structure of the relations between social groups.[29] Where the social structure is such that the group is (believed to be) fixed in an inferior social position, but individual identity change is (believed to be) possible, individuals may attempt to join the higher status group. This is a strategy of *social mobility*.[30] Alternatively, where the change of individual identity is (believed to be) impossible, the group may adopt a collective response. First, if it is believed possible, the group may adopt a strategy of *social competition*: attempting to displace the superior group within the social structure. Secondly, where a challenge to that structure is seen as impossible or undesirable, the group may adopt a strategy of *social creativity*. Here the group may seek to:

1. Change the criteria of the social comparison to a more favourable dimension ('you may be richer than us, but we are more pious than you').
2. Force a re-evaluation of ingroup characteristics in the social consensus ('black is beautiful').
3. Compare themselves with other groups, against which they rate higher (poor whites stressing their social superiority over blacks).

Thus, where individual identity is viewed as fixed, then social identity theory suggests that we can expect intergroup behaviour to be more pronounced. This is because only collective responses have the potential to generate a positive social identity for group members.[31]

1.2.4. *Social Categorization and Stereotypes*
As was stated above, social identity theory contends that where social identity is more pertinent than personal identity, there will be a tendency 'for members of the ingroup to treat members of the outgroup as undifferentiated items in a unified social category'.[32] This is not simply related to behaviour, but also to perception. Where social identity is to the

---

29. See further Tajfel and Turner 1979: 35, 43–46.
30. Cf. Tajfel 1978: 65. This is an individualistic response, which does not endanger the dominance of the higher status group. Indeed the dominant group may foster the belief that social mobility is possible in order to discourage any desire to change the social structure (e.g. occasional manumissions help to safeguard slavery as an institution, by encouraging slaves to seek their own individual freedom, rather than the betterment of their social group).
31. Tajfel and Turner 1979: 36; Tajfel 1978: 51.
32. Tajfel 1978: 45.

fore, there will be a greater tendency to view members as conforming to the stereotypical picture of members of their social category.[33]

Social categorization, by its very nature, involves social stereotypes (distinct pictures of the typical member of the category). Indeed, stereotyping is part of the cognitive process. Unless we have a stereotypical picture of what membership of a certain group can be expected to entail then the category can have no cognitive value. There is no point in saying A is French, or B is a doctor, if we have no view of what membership of either group normally implies.

According to social identity theory, however, stereotypes are not simply the mean of the attributes of group members. Rather, the stereotype is created to maximize the social category's distinctiveness from the ingroup. (Thus, the more socially unusual members of the group are often the basis of the stereotype.) Once objects are categorized, Tajfel postulated that subjects tend both to accentuate similarities between members of the category, and to accentuate difference from members of other categories, even in dimensions other than that used for categorization.[34] Human cognition seeks clear distinctions between categories. However, social cognition is never neutral, for in establishing category distinction, actors are also concerned to establish their own positive social identity relative to other groups. Thus social groups will create stereotypical pictures of the other that differentiate them in ways that secure a relatively positive social identity for the ingroup.

Further, since categorizing the social world also means categorizing one's place within that world, the ingroup will establish not only a (relatively negative) stereotypical picture of the other, but also a (relatively positive) stereotypical picture of the ingroup member.[35] In a development of social identity theory, *self-categorization theory* explores the relationship between the process of self-categorization and group behaviour.[36]

---

33. That having been said, categorization may not totally determine the perception of the individual. Perception and stereotype exist in a dialectic of variable strength. A perceived failure of an individual to conform to stereotype will result in a cognitive confusion that may be resolved in a variety of ways, depending on the resilience of the stereotype. The stereotype may be strong enough to affect perception so that conformity is 'seen'. The individual may be classified as deviant (an aberration that does not bring the stereotype into question). The categorization of the individual may be rejected. Only lastly the stereotype may be questioned (this may require something of a Kuhnian 'paradigm shift' with many exceptions needed before the stereotype is revised).

34. Tajfel observed that where coins differed continually in size, in such a way that larger coins had a higher monetary value, subjects tended to overestimate the size of the larger coins, and underestimate the size of the smaller. Tajfel concluded that, where objects are of value to subjects, the act of categorizing on one dimension (by denomination) causes subjects to overestimate (accentuate) the differences between objects on another (size).

35. See Hogg and Abrams 1988: 21.

36. For a fuller statement see Turner 1987 esp. 42–67.

Self-categorization is responsible for assigning group identity to the self, and again it has perceptual implications, for one accentuates the differences between oneself and members of other categories (also playing down similarities), and one accentuates the similarities between the self and other ingroup members (also playing down differences).[37]

According to self-categorization theory, it is the positive ingroup stereotype that encourages group cohesion and conformity to group norms. Once a member accepts the shared stereotype of the group there is an incentive to conform to it, and to reject attributes and behaviour that are seen to characterize the outgroup. This is because any move away from the stereotypical group attributes towards those stereotypically regarded as belonging to the outgroup is perceived as a move in a negative direction by both other group members and the individual, as it is the attributes of the ingroup that give its members a positive social identity. To deviate is not simply to be untypical, but to risk one's positive social identity in the eyes of the group. Furthermore, it may be to jeopardise one's categorisation by others as a member of the positively valued group.

1.2.5. *Controlling Language*

We can perhaps extrapolate from social identity theory a few observations about power within the group, and how language relating to stereotypes and boundaries can be used as a means of exercising control over group members.

Although the stereotype is shared, its generation, or the power to influence it, is not necessarily fixed by consensus. Power to affect the stereotype is power over the group. It is power to define stereotypical behaviour in the expectation that members will be influenced to conform to such. It is power to determine which individuals constitute or best resemble the stereotype, and thus will be regarded as having the most positive social identity. Shifting the stereotype creates winners and losers and encourages the losers to conform to the amended stereotype.

Behaviour which those with power wish to discourage can be built into the group narrative: it can be portrayed as 'un-group' behaviour and attributed to the outgroup. Members of the group failing to conform may not only be labelled as deviant, but may also be compared with members of the outgroup. To fail to conform is to be less like 'us' and more like 'them'. Such a comparison is double edged, since it implies not only that the individual fails to conform to the positively valued stereotype, but that they are in pertinent ways comparable to members of an outgroup, which by definition is perceived as having a lower social identity. Implicit also is the threat that a persistent deviant may forfeit group identity.

37. See Hogg 1987: 101–104.

The hierarchy of ingroup/outgroup social identity may also be used as a symbolic model for social hierarchies within the group, ranking attributes and individuals according to their perceived value. Undesirable attributes and individuals are labelled as pertaining to the outside (and are thus inferior). To give some examples: where the social identity of the male is ranked higher than that of the female, disparaged males or undesirable male traits may be labelled 'womanish' or 'unmanly' – simply taking for granted that this is a pejorative label. Or in ethnic groups deviant behaviour may simply be labelled as foreign ('un-English' attitudes, 'un-American activity'), again on the assumption that such is a pejorative label.[38]

1.2.6. *Criss-Crossing Social Identity*

Social identity theory has made much of the spectra of personal/social identity and interpersonal/intergroup behaviour. As the salience of a social identity rises, personal identity and personal relationships are suppressed, and behaviour increasingly becomes intergroup behaviour, treating the other as an undifferentiated member of a group. However, the strength of social identity theory is that it does not analyse identity simply in the two dimensions of personal and social (for which we criticized Ignatieff). Rather it accepts that 'individuals belong to a number of different groups and different social categories and thus potentially have a repertoire of many different identities to draw on'.[39] Thus, when a particular social identity becomes salient, it is not simply at the expense of the actor's personal identity, but also of alternate social identities. Further, when interaction between actors becomes intergroup, this is not simply at the expense of personal relationships, which may exist between them, but of other social identities which might serve to divide and unite the same actors in different ways.

Given that we are dealing in this study with identity in the context of Graeco-Roman urban society, where there are a plethora of social groups and categories interacting and crosscutting, social identity theory may have certain advantages over other models. It recognizes not only the competition between social groups, but that this competition often occurs within the psychological processes of the individual, as he or she decides on which identity and group norms are most relevant in a particular context.

---

38. As Hospers comments 'When a word or phrase has already acquired a favourable emotive meaning, people often want to use the word or phrase to carry a cognitive meaning different from its ordinary use, so as to take advantage of the favourable emotive meaning that the word already has ... The same thing can happen ... with *un*favourable emotive meaning' (1967: 53–54). Hospers cites the example of the use of the term 'bastard'.

39. Hogg and Abrams 1988: 19.

We may contrast this with the limitations of Douglas's grid/group model which, although capable of considering the relation of the individual to the group, and the extent to which the group integrates the individual into the social (grid), is hardly able to account for conditions where there are several grids and groups available to the individual. We cannot satisfactorily model existence in a heterogeneous urban society by postulating one 'group' with its norms and worldview and considering all aberrations from this as examples either of deviance or of individualism. Such may provide an adequate etic description (from the stance of the ingroup), but never an emic one. Behaviour not heavily regulated by group norms may not evidence a 'low-group' or 'individualistic' attitude but may be conforming to an alternative social identity held by that individual. Whereas it may be said to be 'individualistic' *qua* that particular group, it may not be so in any 'objective' sense.

In recent years many New Testament scholars have sought to stress the differences between the concept of the individual in first-century Mediterranean society and personality in the modern West.[40] Whereas modern society is said to prize the autonomous individual, 'who acts alone regardless of what others think and say', in first-century society 'the person is ever aware of the expectations of others, especially significant others, and strives to match those expectations. This is the dyadic personality, one who needs another simply to know who he or she is.'[41] Thus, in first-century Mediterranean society, social identity is always more salient than personal identity.

However, leaving aside the question of whether such generalized pictures of ancient Mediterranean society can be sustained,[42] how helpful is such a contention? Even if the ancient personality is more 'collectivist' than 'individualist', how does this help us consider how a particular individual relates to a particular group? It does not explain why the individual identifies with one collective rather than another. How will a 'collectivist' behave when groups criss-cross? If Pauline converts are 'collectivist', will they be more prone to deriving social identity from the Christian collective, or from membership of other social groups that serve to divide them from fellow believers (such as kinship, client-patron network, or even church faction)? In the end such questions can only be answered by careful historical exegesis, and generalizations about the ancient personality are of little assistance.[43] However, social identity

40. See esp. Malina 1981.
41. Malina 1981: 67.
42. Cf. Horrell 2000: 89–91.
43. Esler is at great pains to justify the integration of Malina's models of Mediterranean anthropology in his use of social identity theory (1998a: 45–48). Regrettably this appears to preclude what otherwise might have been an illuminating exploration of conflicting and cross-cutting identities (Jewish–Christian–Gentile) at the level of the individual.

theory perhaps allows us to say something about what is likely to happen when social identities intersect in such a way that individuals must choose between multiple roles.

Deschamps and Doise postulated that, since in a simple group dichotomy subjects accentuated intragroup similarity and intergroup difference, if two such dichotomies were crossed then the accentuation effects would decrease or even cancel out. In an experiment they crossed the gender dichotomy with two arbitrary groups and found that 'the difference between the estimation of performance of subjects of the same sex and those attributed to subjects of the opposite sex is markedly smaller in the crossed than in the simple categorization'.[44] However, Brown and Turner questioned both this experiment and its conclusions. Using more nuanced experimentation, they argued that since accentuation of group difference was caused not just by the need for cognitive clarity, but also by the need to establish a positive social identity for the individual, in crossed categories the effect of ingroup bias would be cumulative. Individuals would increase the perceptual bias towards actors with whom they shared both categories, and against actors with whom they shared neither. Thus criss-crossing 'can intensify discrimination against certain individuals apparently through combining the biases due to simple dichotomies'.[45] The cumulation theory still allows for a reduction in bias towards individuals who are simultaneously both ingroup and outgroup from the subject.

More recently, Brown has returned to the issue, to explore how the interplay of alternate social identities might result in the reduction of intergroup conflict.[46] He argues that, despite the experimental evidence, there is a 'tendency for one categorical dimension to dominate in real life contexts'.[47] This is perhaps obvious, since in reality, few dichotomies are not criss-crossed by other social categories: indeed few actors share no social categories. However, it does not mean that crossing categories has no effect. For a start, if one categorical dimension dominates in a given context, it follows that other dimensions are subordinated or even effectively eliminated in that context. Social identities uniting ingroup and outgroup members, or dividing members of the same group, are suppressed or neutralized by the dominant identity. (Here we are back to Ignatieff's Serbian soldier!) Additionally, while Brown observes that cross-categorization will not eliminate ingroup bias (in the dominant dimension), all these studies clearly show that the effect may be weakened.

44. Deschamps and Doise 1978: 152.
45. Brown and Turner 1979: 381.
46. For an interesting use of Brown's analysis in biblical studies see Esler 2000.
47. R. Brown 1996: 172.

Where individuals have some reason to identify with members of the outgroup, and to differentiate between members of the same group, it will be more difficult to conduct social behaviour purely on the basis of the group dichotomy and to 'treat members of the outgroup as undifferentiated items in a unified social category'.[48] Social identities may not always present the actors with an either/or choice.

1.3. *Grounds for Proceeding*

In the following chapters, we shall be examining how Paul uses sexual ethics and rhetoric to construct Christian identity and community. Social identity theory serves as a heuristic device to generate the following observations and questions:

1. Understanding Christian identity in and against its social environment is not simply a matter of examining cultural differences between Christian ethics and those of outsiders. Rather, we must examine the *cognitive* (the awareness of belonging), the *evaluative* (the value of membership) and the *emotive* (the emotional investment in membership) elements of group belonging. Thus it is not simply a matter of whether Christian sexual ethics differ from those of outsiders, but how references to (or the allegation of) such differences might serve to enhance a sense of belonging.
2. We must look at the degree to which Christian identity serves to give its members a positive social identity relative to the outgroup. How successfully does it generate a group stereotype and differentiate this positively from the outgroup stereotype? How is sexual rhetoric used here?
3. We must examine how Christian social identity governs relations with outsiders. The strength of Christian social identity can be measured in the number of social encounters in which it is pertinent to perception and behaviour. Are encounters with outsiders seen as intergroup encounters, where other social and personal identities are suppressed, and relations governed by group norms and stereotypes? We shall want to examine attitudes exhibited towards relations with outsiders in 5.9–13 and 6.1–11, and we shall want to consider sexual encounters with outsiders both outwith and within marriage.
4. How is control exercised within the group and conformity demanded? Is a loss of positive social identity used to ensure conformity to the ingroup stereotype? Is deviant behaviour related to the negatively valued outgroup? We shall look particularly at how Paul deals with the immoral man of 5.1–8 and those involved in lawsuits in 6.1–11.

48.   Tajfel 1978: 45.

5. How does Christian identity interplay with alternate identities, which may be held by the same individuals? We consider here not just personal but other social identities. Do such serve to weaken Christian social identity, or is this always dominant? Specifically, what of a believer who is also a husband or wife? Does this alternative social identity weaken Christian identity, particularly where it creates a bond with one outside the Christian community?

However, before applying these observations to 1 Corinthians 5–7, we shall proceed to test their usefulness for our purposes by examining some Roman authors contemporaneous to Paul, who also show concern with sexual ethics and identity.

Chapter 2

SEX AND SELF-DEFINITION AMONG THE ROMAN ELITE
(A CASE STUDY)

The object of this case study is to test our observations about social
identity against the rhetoric of some Roman authors. We shall observe
how these authors manipulate gender and ethnic stereotypes to ensure and
legitimize the positive social identity of their ingroup, as well as to exert
control over its members. This will sharpen our focus before we move to
consider Paul's similar use of rhetoric in 1 Corinthians. The Latin writers
chosen are approximately contemporaneous with Paul, and the social
environment in which they operate (largely the city of Rome) is perhaps
not that different from Paul's (Roman Corinth). However, this is not the
principal point of our study. We are not arguing for literary influence or
cultural parallel between the respective rhetorical constructions. The
significance is rather sociological and socio-psychological. We are
attempting to explore how our theoretical observations, developed in
the observation of modern social interactions, might also operate in an
ancient urban culture.

2.1. *Social Competition*

Roman society left the elite Roman male master of all. Rome was the hub
of a multi-ethnic empire to which all the races of the Mediterranean and
beyond had submitted. She was dominant militarily, economically and
politically. Despite the (arguably) more liberated position of the Roman
woman in the early Empire than under the Republic, Rome remained an
unchallenged patriarchy.[1] The Roman man ruled over the women and
slaves of his household. As for the elite male's social superiority over the
mass of the urban plebs, it was also guaranteed not only by massive
wealth differentials,[2] but also by the very structure of the Roman legal
system, which ensured the pre-eminence of the elite class. Rome was most
certainly a stratified society. On nearly any scale by which an elite Roman

---

1. On the position of Roman women see G. Clark 1989.
2. Cf. Alföldy 1988 and Meggitt 1998: 11–74.

male might measure himself his social identity was superior to that of any relevant outgroup.

2.1.1. *Boundary Erosion*

Despite this stratified society, however, the Roman moralists had fears, either real or imagined, that the boundaries that defined their class and ensured its superiority were under siege – indeed perilously close to collapse. The rise of the Principate had to a large degree emasculated the power of the senatorial elite, eroding the rights to power and freedom it had long asserted. A threat was also perceived in the ubiquitous rise of new political and economic elites. The power and wealth of the imperial freedman and the *homines novi* was deeply resented by those who believed in their inherited right to rule.[3] Thus, the traditional barriers of wealth and privileged access to power could no longer serve to define those whom the moralistic writers regarded as 'us' from the encroaching 'them'.[4]

Furthermore, as the city of Rome exerted world mastery, she was increasingly becoming 'multiethnic, polyglot, and culturally fragmented, containing greater numbers of immigrants and foreign-born ex-slaves'.[5] The social rise of the foreigner could cause some alarm.[6] There was a real fear of the dilution and diminishment of what is presented as the 'real' Roman identity with its ancestral virtues.[7]

2.1.2. *Social Comparisons*

Social creativity need not only be a strategy adopted by an inferior group. Tajfel argues that, in response to social competition from the inferior, the dominant group may react 'either by doing everything possible to maintain and justify the status quo or by attempting to find and create new differentiations in its own favour, or both'.[8] In the moralists we can find an attempt at such a redefinition. If the *arivistes* now possess the prized attributes of wealth and power, then the traditional elite will differentiate themselves by taste and education. Consider, for instance, Petronius' *Satyricon*.[9] Here the freedman

---

3. On social mobility see Meeks 1983: 19–22. On Juvenal's resentment see Green 1999: 29–30 (cf. Pliny on Pallas, *Ep.* 8.8).

4. Observe how Juvenal laments the property qualification for theatre seats, which causes 'whoremongers boys' to take a 'knight's cushion' (*Sat.* 3.153–59); also his bitter cry that fortune raises the base for a joke (*Sat.* 3.38–40).

5. Skinner 1997: 4.

6. Witness Juvenal's scorn at the Egyptian Crispius becoming Praetorian prefect (*Sat.* 4.32), and the Jew Tiberius Alexander becoming prefect of Egypt (*Sat.* 1.136).

7. Cf. Juv., *Sat.* 3.58–80.

8. Tajfel and Turner 1979: 38.

9. See Walsh 1970: 111–40.

Trimalchio ostentatiously parades his wealth in the face of the better-born, although impoverished, narrator. But despite the fact that Trimalchio acts in ways that are designed to impress his guests with his new social status,[10] the freeborn narrator demonstrates the illegitimacy of Trimalchio's pretensions. The decor of his house, the food he serves and the coarse language he uses mark him out as vulgar. His pretensions to learning demonstrate his ignorance.[11] Trimalchio lacks both the education and the aesthetic appreciation of his social betters. Not only is wealth not the only criteria of social acceptability, the rule is turned on its head, and an inappropriate display of wealth is a mark of those who do not belong.[12]

The importance of the criterion on which a comparison is made can also be seen in Cicero's apology for writing philosophy in Latin. He begins by asserting Roman cultural superiority: 'it has always been my conviction that our countrymen have shown more wisdom everywhere than the Greeks, either in making discoveries for themselves, or else in improving what they had received from Greece...' But the proud boast fails even to convince its own author, who retracts by degrees. 'When it comes to our natural gifts *apart from book learning* they are above comparison with the Greeks or any other people.' Before conceding: 'In learning Greece has surpassed us and in all branches of literature, and victory was easy where there was no contest.' However, lest Rome be regarded as Greece's inferior, Cicero quickly selects a preferable way to differentiate between the two nations:

> For morality, rules of life, family and household economy are surely maintained by us in a better and more dignified way; and beyond question our ancestors have adopted better regulations and laws than others in directing the policy of government. What shall I say of the art of war? In this sphere our countrymen have proved their superiority by valour as well as in an even greater degree by discipline.[13]

Cicero effects an intergroup comparison, but when forced to concede the literary and philosophical high ground to his rivals, he asserts a different criterion, one in which his own Roman social identity can be seen as superior. Such is a strategy of social creativity.

---

10. Trimalchio argues, 'if you have a penny, that is what you are worth, by what a man hath shall he be reckoned' (Petronius, *Satyricon* 77).

11. Petronius, *Satyricon* 50.4; 59.4.

12. Cf. Rudd 1986: 151.

13. Cicero, *Tusc.* 1.1, LCL translation.

2.2. Controlling Language

2.2.1. A Positive Stereotype

The moralists present an ideal stereotype of the elite Roman male (the *vir*[14]). He exhibits the quality of *Romanitas*: perceived as self-control, *gravitas*, sexual morality, and in particular an abstention from the dangers of *luxuria* and *licentia*. This stereotype is often bolstered with a narrative portraying these as qualities of Rome's rustic ancestors (the *mos maiorum*), who by their superior virtue established Rome's greatness.[15] Deviance from these norms is presented as the cause of the city's present ills.

This stereotype also differentiates the ingroup from the relevant outgroups. The vices, which correspond to the Roman virtues, become the stereotypical attributes of the relevant outgroup (the foreign, the feminine, and the masses): groups inferior to the *vir*, and thus ruled by him.

The social inferiority of the female is simply assumed by the Roman writers. Virtues are for the greatest part male (courage, leadership and self-control are masculine)[16] while women are stereotypically susceptible to *luxuria* and *licentia*. The social and moral hierarchy is symbolized in convictions about sexuality. Active males demonstrate their superiority by penetrating passive females.[17] Sexual submission symbolizes political, moral and social weakness. This male/female, active/passive hierarchy can be transposed into other social comparisons. The foreigner and the slave have submitted to the all-conquering Roman master, thus demonstrating their inferiority both in strength and masculine virtue. The stereotypical 'unmanly' vices of women are then associated with other subordinate groups. As Edwards comments, 'feelings of contempt for sexual passivity, for slaves and for women were made mutually reinforcing by this elision'.[18]

We can see this mutually reinforcing stereotype in Roman attitudes towards their Greek subjects.[19] *Luxuria* and *licentia* are also proverbially Greek vices. The excess of the banquet, for instance, is presented as a

14. The term *vir* seems reserved for male adult citizens of a relatively high status (see Walters 1997).

15. Juvenal continually harps back to a golden age of virtue (1.94–95; 2.124–26; 4.1–20; cf. Green 1999: 28–30 and Winkler 1983: 23–59).

16. *Virtus* (Gk: ἀνδρεία) translates as courage or manliness.

17. See Walters 1997.

18. Edwards 1993: 72. As Skinner (1997: 20) comments, 'Dichotomies of same/other and active/passive are built into each of those three categories, leading to their inevitable conflation: thus an impoverished, freed, or slave individual of non-Italian, and especially Greek or Eastern Mediterranean, background will inevitably be feminised as well.'

19. On Roman attitudes to Greeks see Balsdon 1979: 30–58 (cf. the stereotypical pictures in Juvenal, *Sat.* 1.24–25, 1.104–106, 3.73).

typical Greek influence.[20] So too Greek influence is held responsible for
the perceived increase of pederasty in Rome. Greeks are seen as having a
higher propensity to homosexual activity.[21] Greek culture is thus the
antithesis of the rustic Roman ideal, and these Greek traits indicate the
softness (*mollitia*) of the race (i.e. its effeminacy).

However, our Roman writers are not so much interested in demonstrating their contempt for the outsider, as in regulating and assessing the
behaviour of their own elite class. Charges of effeminacy, sexual passivity
and (to a lesser degree) foreignness are continually levelled by the
moralists against their own peers. Thus the stereotype is not simply used
to secure the positive social identity of the ingroup or justify its political
dominance; it also forms the basis for political attacks where the targets
are accused of adopting un-Roman or unmanly behaviour, and thus
rhetorically associated with the negatively valued outgroup.[22]

2.2.2. Effeminacy Charges

The charge of sexual passivity (being a *cinaedus* or *pathicus*) is not a
charge of homosexuality per se, but an allegation that a man chooses to
submit sexually, to adopt the *feminine* role.[23] Passivity is described in
Roman literature as *muliebria pati*: i.e. 'having a woman's experience'.[24]
To accuse a man of submitting to such in his youth is a familiar insult,[25]
but worse to accuse him of continuing to do so. Either charge brings his
maleness into question. We might think of Suetonius' famous quip
(attributed to Curio) accusing Caesar of both adultery and submission to
sodomy by calling him 'a man for all women and a women for all
men'.[26]

However, it is not just sexual passivity that can bring on a charge of
effeminacy. A deviation from any stereotypically male behaviour can
bring a charge of acting in a womanly way.[27] Often writers move from
observation of the man's outward appearance (dress, poise, grooming or

---

20.   Greek banqueting excess threatens Roman *gravitas* (Edwards 1993: 186–88).
21.   Cf. Cicero, *Tusc.* 4.70 (of course, this may simply be another instance of 'attempting
to humiliate one's rivals by likening them to women, sometimes in specifically sexual ways',
Edwards 1993: 94).
22.   See further Edwards 1993 and Corbeill 1996.
23.   Romans were as horrified by men playing the passive role in relations with women
(H.N. Parker 1997). As Edwards notes, 'men who took a "passive" part in homosexual
activity are … often portrayed as assimilating themselves to women – hence the frequency of
such terms as *effeminatus* in discussions of behaviour of this kind' (1993: 76–77); see further
Williams 1999.
24.   Walters 1997: 30.
25.   As Cicero (*Phil.* 2.44–45) accuses the boy Anthony of doing.
26.   Suetonius, *Iul.* 52.3; cf. 49.
27.   See further Corbeill 1996: 128–73.

voice),[28] or his indulgence in *luxuria*,[29] to making judgments as to his manliness, judgments that are then transferred into the moral sphere. 'For a Roman to suggest that a man was behaving like a woman was to imply that he was inferior to other men. Conversely, to suggest that a man was inferior to other men in that he was promiscuous, luxurious, lazy, or cowardly, was to imply that he was in some ways like a woman.'[30] To question masculine attributes is to question masculinity, and as a result the entitlement to the higher social status accorded that gender.[31]

The invective of effeminacy is, however, more than pure slander. Behind it 'lurks the possibility of a man undergoing a behavioural transformation' so that 'a preponderance of effeminate qualities in an adversary would allow an opposing speaker to suggest that an adversary not only violates the boundaries of social propriety but represents a failure within nature itself'.[32] This is because biological convictions underpinned the social hierarchy of the sexes. Bodies exist on a spectrum ranging from the ideal warm, dry, hard body of the man to the cold, moist, soft body of the female.[33] Without the proper care of the body and its behaviour, downward movement on this spectrum was possible, and although 'no man might actually become a woman...each man trembled on the brink of becoming "womanish"'.[34]

A more general anthropological study of cultural uses of gender, by Ortner and Whitehead, makes much the same observations that we have discerned from the Roman moralists. They state that 'very commonly the same axes that divide and distinguish male from female (and indeed rank male over female) also cross-cut the gender categories producing internal distinctions and gradations within them'. Further, and this bears out what we have said about the male/female divide mirroring other social rankings, 'many axes of gender distinction are not in fact unique to the domain of gender but are shared with (both derived from and exported to) other important domains of social life'.[35]

28. Cf. Juvenal, *Sat.* 2.65–81 and Cicero's attitude to male dress: whether one wears a long toga, or girds it up is a sign of effeminacy and merits a charge of passivity (Cicero, *Off.* 1.131; cf. Corbeill 1996: 161).

29. 'The stigma of convivial excess stems from anxiety over what constitutes and deconstitutes Roman masculinity' (Corbeill 1996: 129): hence the literary topos of the effeminate banqueter.

30. Edwards 1993: 78. We can also note how the rhetorical handbooks suggest how vices are interrelated: if an opponent can be shown guilty of one, then it is possible to implicate him in others (Cicero, *Inv.* 2.33).

31. Walters (1997: 32) terms this 'gender-as-social-status'.

32. Corbeill 1997: 109.

33. See Rousselle 1988: 4–46 and D. Martin 1995: 32–35.

34. P. Brown 1988: 11; cf. Corbeill 1996: 142–46.

35. Ortner and Whitehead 1981: 9.

2.2.3. Greek Behaviour

We can see this masculine/feminine social hierarchy being superimposed on that of Roman/Greek. Whatever virtues the Greek stereotypically possesses, the Roman surpasses him in morals, in courage, in discipline and in warfare, the stereotypically male attributes. Greek inferiority is symbolized in the contention that Greeks are more effeminate than Romans. But again, the charge of foreignness can also, like that of effeminacy, be levelled at Roman men themselves.

The whole dynamic can be illustrated by a discourse of the elder Pliny. Discussing avarice and other vices associated with gold, Pliny cites a number of supposed historical examples. First, he cites a Roman example: Gaius Gracchus, killed by a friend for the price on his head. After beheading him, the 'friend' filled his mouth with lead, since the price on the head was its weight in gold. But the next example, King Mithridates, explicitly 'not a Roman citizen', pours not lead but molten gold into the head of his prisoner, a Roman general. Thus the foreigner outdoes the Roman in *luxuria*.

Pliny then proceeds to note (almost as an aside) that:

> One is ashamed to see the new-fangled names that are invented every now and then from the Greek to denote silver vessels filigreed or inlaid with gold, niceties which make gilded plate fetch a higher price than gold plate, when we know Spartacus issued an order to his camp forbidding anyone to possess gold or silver: so much more spirit was there in one of our runaway slaves![36]

Thus the *luxuria* of gold is firmly associated with Greece, but even the lowest Roman, a rebel slave like Spartacus, shows his superiority to the Greeks by avoiding such vice. It is significant that Spartacus is owned here by Pliny as 'as one of *our* runaway slaves' (*fugitivis nostris*). Even this lowest one of 'us' knows better than the Greek and if he, how much more so his social betters.

However, at this point Pliny changes tack. He moves from an intergroup comparison, asserting the Roman superiority in regard to the desire for *luxuria*, to considering the case of one particular Roman: Mark Anthony. Unlike Spartacus, Anthony is compared unfavourably with the foreigner in regard to his use of gold.

> The triumvir Anthony used vessels of gold in satisfying all the indecent necessities, an enormity that even Cleopatra would have been ashamed of. Till then the record in extravagance had lain with foreigners – King Philip sleeping with a gold goblet under his pillow and Alexander the Great's prefect Hagnon of Troas having his sandals soled with gold

---

36.   Pliny the Elder, *Nat. His.* 33.50.

nails; but Anthony alone cheapened gold by this contumely of nature. How he deserved to be proscribed! But proscribed by Spartacus![37]

The rhetoric is devastating. The Roman ideal of the avoidance of *luxuria* built up in the previous section as existing in contradistinction to foreign vice is now turned ruthlessly against Anthony. 'Pliny emphasises the enormity of Anthony's behaviour by stressing that his luxury outdid the proverbial extravagance of women and eastern tyrants. Such behaviour is marked as undesirable by its association with the feminine and the foreign.'[38] Philip is outdone, and Cleopatra ashamed. But there is more than this: not only is Anthony portrayed as un-Roman and un-manly, but the mention of Cleopatra serves to remind the reader of the historical events surrounding Anthony's dalliance in the Greek East, his relationship with a foreign woman, and his opposition to the armies of Augustus. Anthony, despite his seeming greatness, is truly 'not one of us' – unlike *our* Spartacus. Anthony does that from which even the least of Romans would have refrained. Anthony is thus inferior to the feminine and the foreign, and proscribed by the lowborn Spartacus.

2.3. *Conclusion*

The language of the moralists serves to narrate a boundary between the *vir* and the other. It informs the (elite Roman) reader of who he is, and what it means to belong, and does so in process of defining the other. The narrative serves to create a positive social identity for the ingroup by claiming that the stereotypical ingroup member possesses a higher virtue than any outgroup member. Thus, the 'cognitive, evaluative and emotive' aspects of group belonging are raised. The reader is encouraged to know who he or she is, value that belonging, and invest emotionally in it. Belonging matters.

But this stress on the positive value of ingroup identity is not only a matter of group differentiation, but also of group control. For if ingroup identity matters for status, and if the outgroup is devalued, rhetoric that calls the identity of an ingroup member into question is likely to be effective. If belonging matters, then the accusation that one ceases in some way to belong is one that any ingroup member would seek to avoid. If the ingroup stereotype is positive in comparison to the outgroup, then the accusation that one's behaviour resembles that of the outgroup rather than ingroup stereotype (a deviance charge), will matter to the ingroup member. Social control can thus be asserted by attacking deviance by

---

37.   Pliny the Elder, *Nat. His.* 33.50. Cf. Cicero, *Phil.* 2.29, 2.67–68 for further charges of Anthony's *luxuria* and *licentia*.
38.   Edwards 1993: 25.

pejorative association with the outsider. The more negatively the outsider is valued, the more negatively non-conformity will be valued.

We shall proceed to examine how Paul's language might serve similar functions to that of these Roman authors. We shall explore how Paul's discourse serves to create a sense of Christian belonging, giving to the community a positive social identity, and doing so in the process of defining the other. We shall also examine Paul's use of controlling language: how is social control effected by relating deviance to the negatively valued outgroup?

Chapter 3

SOCIAL DYNAMICS AND RHETORIC IN 1 CORINTHIANS

3.1. *Introduction*

In the previous chapter, we examined the ways in which social identity is created by distinguishing ingroup from outgroup and creating for that ingroup a positively valued distinctiveness. We also examined how this charged group boundary can then be used to effect social control within the group: creating a distinct stereotype that influences behaviour, and associating non-conforming members and their characteristics with the relatively devalued outgroup. Now, before focusing directly on 1 Corinthians 5–7, it is our intention to analyse social identity in 1 Corinthians as a whole, and particularly in that part of the letter (chs 1–4) that precedes our area of interest.

First (3.2), we shall examine the context of the entire epistle (the situation it presupposes), that we might better understand the social dynamics of the Corinthian church, and Paul's goals in writing. Then (3.3) we shall examine the rhetoric of 1 Corinthians 1–4. We shall be asking how Paul constructs the social identity of the believing group and how he distinguishes it from the outgroup, looking particularly at the respective group stereotypes (3.3.1). How is a positive estimation of social identity encouraged? Then we shall examine the function of Paul's dichotomy (3.3.2). How does Paul's construction of Christian social identity and his manipulation of stereotypes serve to influence the social dynamics of the church? Then we shall examine Paul's explicit use of controlling language, that is, where he deliberately uses the values of the group dichotomy to control the behaviour and attitudes of ingroup members (3.3.3). Finally (3.4) we shall repeat the same procedure for the general function of the ethical dichotomy of 1 Corinthians 5–7, preparing the way for a closer examination in the rest of this study.

3.2. *The Context of 1 Corinthians*

3.2.1. *The Nature of the Problems*

When commentators generalize from the plethora of issues raised in 1 Corinthians to the underlying problem that Paul is attempting to address, they tend to stress either internal divisions in the church (and Paul's attempt to effect reconciliation) or a dispute between the church and Paul, over its relations with its social environment.

Mitchell, for example, forcefully argues the former case. The call for unity in 1.10 is the thesis statement of the epistle (πρόθεσις) and 'the entire letter of 1 Corinthians is indeed consonant with this thesis statement, the appeal to the church at Corinth to be unified and end its factionalism'.[1] For Mitchell, Corinthian party divisions underlie not only Paul's rhetoric in 1–4, but also the issues addressed in 5–16.[2] On the other hand, Barclay stresses how Paul and the Corinthians differ in their attitudes towards, and experience of, unbelievers. He points to 'the absence of conflict between [Corinthian] Christians and "outsiders"' and suggests that 'Paul is somewhat uneasy about the degree of [social] integration which the Corinthian Christians enjoy' and that Paul 'has a much more sectarian and separatist expectation of the social standing of the church'.[3] Adams goes further. 'The dominant issue of the letter is that of group boundaries. The Corinthians were defining the lines of demarcation between the church and the surrounding society far too loosely for Paul's liking... The Corinthian "aberrations" are largely failures in boundary maintenance.'[4] The question must be whether this is an either/or choice. We shall examine the textual evidence for internal division (3.2.2) and disputes over boundaries (3.2.3), before using social identity theory to make a number of observations (3.2.4).

3.2.2. *Internal Divisions*

Powerful evidence exists for internal divisions among the Corinthian believers.[5] The letter opens with the appeal of 1.10, and continues by citing the report of ἔριδες ἐν ὑμῖν (1.11) supplied by Chloe's people. Whatever the ἐγώ εἰμι slogans of 1.12 signify, they indicate divisions definite enough to be identifiable by such (caricatured?) shorthand. Furthermore the same shorthand is again cited at 3.1–4 as evidence of the ζῆλος καὶ ἔρις, which Paul holds to be a falsification of the Corinthians' claims to be πνευματικοί. In the body of the letter we find further

---

1. M.M. Mitchell 1991: 66.
2. Similarly Horrell 1996a.
3. Barclay 1992: 57–59.
4. Adams 2000: 87.
5. See Pickett 1997: 37–58.

evidence: believers are suing their fellows in the law-courts (6.1–11) and Paul criticizes their conduct at the Lord's Supper as pointing again to σχίσματα and αἱρέσεις (11.18–19).

However, the identification of these dissensions with defined 'parties' corresponding to competing theological positions can no longer be sustained. In Baur's classic reconstruction, the objects of the four slogans of 1.12 were reduced to two all-pervasive parties – a Jewish-Christian (Cephas-Christ) party and a Hellenistic-Christian (Paul-Apollos) party. Baur saw the battle between these movements as underlying the disputes of the Corinthian, as well as other, epistles. However, the thesis collapses when one considers the total absence of discussion of the characteristic issues of debates between Paul's gospel and that of the Jerusalem church.[6] In this epistle there are no more than echoes of disputes over the Torah, circumcision, or the relation of Gentiles to Israel.[7]

But other problems with this reconstruction make alternative attempts to analyse the disputes as theological struggles are also difficult to sustain.[8] Neither Apollos nor Cephas are denounced in this letter.[9] Nor can any precise theology be identified with them or their supposed adherents. Indeed, although divisions and the raising up of leaders are denounced, no faction is singled out for criticism.[10] This would be strange if the factions represented various theologies: would Paul really have no preferences among them? But Paul's attack is more general. The cross, which reveals true wisdom, true power, and a true estimation of reality, serves to critique both factionalism and a seeming Corinthian tendency to wrongly appraise Paul and his preaching (either by stressing allegiance to him, or by belittling his presentation, 2.1–5). Although it may well be that the Corinthians are divided in their attitude to Paul, and thus Paul is implicitly criticizing some more than

6.   See Munck (1959: 135–67) who argues that there are neither parties nor Judaizers at Corinth. Goulder (1991) revises Baur's thesis, but the same problems beset his suggestions. Goulder requires to see the discussion of Apollos as a veiled attack on Cephas, and links σοφία to Hellenistic Judaism. (For criticism of Goulder see Kerr 2000: 80.)

7.   Fee 1987: 57.

8.   Such as identifying the 'Christ party' with Gnostics (as Lütgert 1908 and Schmithals 1971). 'Theological party' reconstructions were questioned as early as Weiss (1910: 30–31) (cf. Welborn 1987: 89).

9.   Paul is keen to stress his unity with, even if superiority over, Apollos (3.5–9; 3.22; 4.6). Hostility to Apollos would make Paul's request that Apollos return to Corinth (16.12) unintelligible. Thus we may assume that Paul views Apollos as basically 'on message', even if his eloquence and willingness to accept financial support have been used against Paul (cf. Kerr 2000). Cephas plays a less important role, but twice out of the three times Paul makes mention of him it is to assure the Corinthians of their unity (3.22; 15.11).

10.   'Paul's rhetorical strategy is to combat the phenomena of factionalism itself, not each individual faction directly' (M.M. Mitchell 1991: 67–68).

others, there is no indication that there exists among any of the Corinthians a developed alternative theology of wisdom or the cross, which Paul is combating.[11]

Where there is no evidence of theological disputes dividing the Corinthian community, there are indications of socio-economic divisions. Even without the recent sociological studies of the Corinthian church,[12] Paul's words justify us taking such factors seriously. In ch. 11 he explicitly links the divisions at the Lord's Supper with the distribution of food and drink and to the fact that the Corinthians 'humiliate those who have nothing' (καταισχύνετε τοὺς μὴ ἔχοντας, 11.22).[13] This may or may not be due to Graeco-Roman dining practice (where the quantity and quality of food was sometimes allocated according to status),[14] but in any case it appears to represent discrimination against certain members of the church, on the basis of their social position.

Theissen, and those who have followed his sociological reconstructions, have discerned the same socio-economic issues lying behind other disputes in the Corinthian church: the immoral man,[15] food offered to idols,[16] and the lawsuits between believers.[17] However, even if we can extrapolate from what is explicit in 11.22 to what may be implicit elsewhere, the existence of socio-economic divisions (common to antiquity) within the Corinthian church is not in itself evidence of 'class' conflict. Although Paul at points 'takes the side of those members of the community who come from the lower strata',[18] this is an insufficient explanation for all the conflicts we find in the epistle, and particularly in chs 1–4.

First, although Paul may question the treatment of the poor by the rich, this does not necessarily mean that we have a dispute between two groups. Paul could be taking (and creating) the cause of the otherwise voiceless (and passive) poor to question the assumptions of the whole community. Thus, in effect, the critical division may really be between apostle and church. Secondly, as Welborn has shown, we cannot read all of Paul's rhetoric in 1 Corinthians as aimed against the rich, since some of those

---

11.   As Pickett 1997: 38.

12.   E.g. Theissen 1982; Meeks 1983; Chow 1992; Clarke 1993; D.B. Martin 1995.

13.   Meggitt (1998: 118–22) objects that οἱ μὴ ἔχοντας may simply mean those 'without the elements' rather than 'the have nots'. However, since the result of their lack is that they are hungry (11.21), it is difficult to escape the notion of division (even if not conflict) between the destitute and those (relatively) better provisioned.

14.   As Theissen 1982: 153–68; for variations see Fee 1987: 534 and Chow 1992: 111.

15.   Chow (1992: 113–66) suggests that the Corinthian pride in the man and his impunity from prosecution are best explained by his high social status (see also Clarke 1993: 73–88).

16.   Theissen 1982: 121–40.

17.   Theissen 1982: 97.

18.   Theissen 1982: 57, cited disparagingly by Welborn 1987: 98.

whom Paul commends are, under Theissen and Meeks's reconstruction, to be numbered among the rich minority.[19]

Thus although we may have a division (at least in Paul's mind) between 'those who have nothing' and the rest, this division cannot account for all the internal discord. The references to factions and disputes in 1–4, and probably the legal dispute of 6.1–11, seem better read as disputes among prominent members of the congregation. Paul then seems to see a variety of divisions within the Corinthian church: competition between rival cliques or power bases (which are obvious to the congregation) and a divisive discrimination against the poor (which may simply be taken for granted by the Corinthians). How, or if, these divisions are related must remain an open question.[20]

3.2.3. *A Boundary Dispute*
Not only does it appear that Paul is most often addressing the entire congregation rather than certain identifiable 'opponents', but there also appear to be strong disagreements between him and the congregation. Paul's tone is often aggressive (esp. 1–4),[21] and sometimes defensive (4.1–5; 9.1–27).

Of course, care must be taken not to read criticisms of Paul found in 2 Corinthians into this earlier period in the relationship. However, even from 1 Corinthians, it seems legitimate to 'mirror read' Corinthian accusations from Paul's defensiveness. Paul's comments on his personal presentation of the gospel at Corinth (2.1–5) would seem to be an apology for what the Corinthians have rated as weak and foolish (this may be borne out by Paul's comments in 2 Cor. 10.10). The pains Paul takes in 3.5–23 to stress his equality with, and pre-eminence over, Apollos, strongly suggest his status is being questioned. His exposition of his apostolic right to support (9.3–27), while it may primarily have other than an apologetic intent, is difficult to understand unless his status as an

19. E.g. Stephanus (16.15) and Gaius (Rom. 16.23); cf. Welborn 1987: 98 and Theissen 1982: 73–96.

20. Welborn (1987) postulates that the division is not between rich and poor, but that 'bondage of the poor to the rich is the breeding ground of faction' (99). Poverty allows the deployment of wealth to create supporters for the factions of the wealthy. Paul thus expresses solidarity with the poor in order to recruit them to his own cause. However, while the notion that the rich might seek the support of poor clients is historically plausible, there are significant problems with Welborn's reconstruction. First, there is no textual evidence of the rich competing in their patronage of the poor: rather Paul accuses the rich of humiliating them by refusing to meet their needs. Secondly, as for Paul competing for their allegiance, he appears more often to be appealing *to* the powerful *on behalf* of the poor, rather than directly for the support of the poor.

21. 'The language and style of 1 Corinthians are especially rhetorical and combative. Paul is taking them on at every turn. . . he is attacking and challenging with all the weapons in his literary arsenal' (Fee 1987: 5–6).

apostle, or his refusal of Corinthian financial assistance, are being questioned.[22] (It can hardly be coincidental that this issue also re-emerges 2 Corinthians!) Further, at least one of his previous instructions to the Corinthians (5.9) has been (we shall argue later) deliberately rejected and undermined.

If the Corinthians are unhappy with Paul, he is certainly perturbed by them. Continually he takes a stand against their conduct and attitudes. Thrice he cites reports of behaviour he finds unacceptable (1.11; 5.1; 11.18). He strives to correct their response to πορνεία, marriage, lawsuits, idolatry and idol food, the behaviour of women in worship, their practice at the common meal, their use of spiritual gifts, and more besides. It seems improbable that his instruction in such areas represents a mild response to questions asked in the letter of a devoted congregation. Rather, there appears clear disagreement between the parties.

It is difficult to escape the conclusion that this dispute largely concerns the boundaries of the community. In 5.1–8 Paul has to argue for an expulsion to preserve the ethical purity of the community. In 6.1–6 he chides the Corinthians for taking lawsuits before outsiders. 5.9–11 evidences previous debate between Paul and the Corinthians concerning relations with outsiders.[23] Further, as Barclay notes, the Corinthians seem to enjoy good relations with non-believers, and although Paul is far from demanding total withdrawal from the world, he does appear critical of these.[24] In 4.9–11 he bitterly contrasts the persecution and disrepute he has experienced with the honour in which they are held (presumably by outsiders). Paul's unhappiness with the Corinthian 'response to the world' might also be read in the fact that Paul seems to present the world, its wisdom, its assumptions and its rulers in a negative light throughout the epistle (1.18–2.8; 3.18–20; 7.31).[25]

3.2.4. *Conclusion*
It is not our purpose to offer a detailed reconstruction of relations within the Corinthian church, or between church and apostle. We simply wish to note that tension and disagreement characterize both relationships. There is, for our purposes, no need to choose as to which of these tensions most determine the tone and content of the letter. Indeed, if there are divisions

22.   *Pace* M.M. Mitchell (1991: 243–50), who denies that Paul is being defensive here (see the rebuttal by Horrell 1996a: 205–206).

23.   If socio-economic division or factional rivalry are common in Graeco-Roman culture, then one could characterize Paul's critique of such as a concern with boundaries: a call for the community to distinguish itself from cultural norms (as Adams 2000: 93). Such a characterization does, however, seem a little too broad. Does not *every* issue then become a boundary issue?

24.   Barclay 1992: 57–60.

25.   Cf. Adams 2000: 105–49.

or competing factions at Corinth then this is most likely to occur where there is weak regard for Paul's (or anyone else's) central leadership and authority. Similarly, if the founding apostle's status and teaching are questioned by some in the church, it is likely that this will be contentious with others.[26] In 1 Corinthians 5–7 we will see Paul simultaneously concerned with the outside world, and regulating conduct within the church; critical of the congregation's relations with outsiders and at pains to restore internal harmony (esp. 6.1–9).

Social identity theory would also support the notion that group cohesion and group boundaries are closely related. Where a social identity is important to self-identity, then in an increasing number of social situations behaviour will be intergroup behaviour. Here, group rather than individual relations will govern social behaviour (1.2.2) and outsiders will be perceived according to the group stereotype (1.2.4). The group boundary will be important. Further, other criss-crossing identities that serve to divide ingroup members, or identify ingroup members with outgroup members, will be suppressed (1.2.6). Ingroup members will also self-categorize, and tend to conform to the positively valued self-stereotype (1.2.4). Thus cohesion is likely to increase. An increase in the importance of a social identity is thus likely to increase both group cohesion, and the concern with boundaries. Conversely, where individuals do not regard a particular social identity as relevant, there will be little concern for boundaries, and little group cohesion.

A Pauline attempt to raise the importance of Christian social identity, by raising the 'cognitive, evaluative and emotive' aspects of group belonging is thus likely to increase both cohesion and attention to boundaries. We shall now examine how Paul undertakes this.

3.3. *Paul's Group Boundary in 1 Corinthians 1–4*

3.3.1. *Stereotypes and Identities*
The prevalence of language in 1 Corinthians 1–4 serving to create a sense of belonging and distinction is noticeable. A stereotype of the believing and non-believing groups is constructed and in such a way as to create both distinctiveness and a positive social identity for the believing group in absolute, rather than merely relative, terms.

From the beginning Paul addresses a community which he believes to

---

26. So Dahl 1967. Dahl argues that there were divided Corinthian reactions to Paul, and to the decision by the pro-Pauline leadership to write for his advice. Paul receives the official delegation from Stephanas with its 'polite and official letter, asking for advice' (325) but also separate reports of disputes about his status. Against Dahl, it appears naïve to believe that the Corinthian letter was so subservient. If the slogans Paul quotes originate from this letter, then its tone must have been assertive, if not defiant at points.

have been separated from the rest of humanity. He writes: τῇ ἐκκλησίᾳ τοῦ θεοῦ τῇ οὔσῃ ἐν Κορίνθῳ, ἡγιασμένοις ἐν Χριστῷ Ἰησοῦ, κλητοῖς ἁγίοις (1.2).

Paul describes a people called into existence by God, and designated ἅγιοι; that is, set apart from the rest of humanity for a particular relationship to God. Paul thus describes an ingroup set against a wider outgroup: a people called out of one community to become another. But his words also begin to create a positive social identity for the ingroup – they are uniquely in this special chosen position vis-à-vis the Divine.

However this 'coming out' is not simply a social separation – there is also an ethical separation of the group from the surrounding society. Believers are ἡγιασμένοις and κλητοῖς ἁγίοις. Sanctification is most probably here a conversion metaphor (as in 1.30 and 6.11), but it also implies a behavioural change.[27] Holiness is the unique purpose, predicate and designator of the believing group, which positively distinguishes both the community and its members from outsiders. From this point on the ἅγιος word group, and the notion of the ethical differential between the groups fades into the background until chs 5–7, where that dichotomy will become a controlling notion (6.1–2, 11, 19; 7.14, 34). Meanwhile other attributes distinguish the groups.

First, there is a soteriological dualism: an apocalyptic presupposition about the nature and the fate of each group. In the present, one is ἀπολλυμένοι, while the other is σῳζόμενοι (1.18). For the future, one is associated with the rulers of the world, who are doomed to pass away (καταργουμένων), while the other is associated with a predestined divine purpose for their glorification (πρὸ τῶν αἰώνων εἰς δόξαν ἡμῶν) (2.6–7).

Secondly, there is an epistemological dualism, based on σοφία. The outgroup seek and possess human wisdom (1.22; 1.26) which views the cross as folly (1.18; 1.23; 2.8). Believers, however, seek and possess a divine wisdom (2.6–7; 2.10), which correctly evaluates the cross as a divine act – the wisdom, power and salvation of God (1.18; 1.24) – and correctly discerns that what the world considers wisdom and power is in comparison foolish and weak. Only true wisdom can comprehend the divine paradox of the cross. This paradox means that preaching in general (1.21–23), and Paul's delivery in particular (1.17; 2.1–5), both of which seem folly by worldly standards, are the means by which God's power and wisdom are demonstrated. Only those who possess divine discernment understand this.

Thirdly, connected to the epistemological dualism is an ontological dualism. The believer possesses God's Spirit (2.12) and consequently may be called πνευματικός. This Spirit uniquely enables the believer correctly to interpret the truth Paul teaches (2.13) and the gifts that God gives to

---

27. As Fee 1987: 32.

believers. However, the unbeliever possesses the spirit of the world (2.12), and may be called ψυχικός (2.14). He neither receives the gifts of the Spirit of God, nor the ability to understand them (2.14). Thus again the believing community is given a positively valued distinctiveness over the outgroup.

Lastly there is an implied distinction of social status. Believers are stereotyped by their social weakness: they are said to be οὐ πολλοὶ σοφοὶ κατὰ σάρκα, οὐ πολλοὶ δυνατοί, οὐ πολλοὶ εὐγενεῖς (1.26). But God elects such social 'nobodies' precisely in order (ἵνα × 3) to nullify those of social status (1.27–28). The only outsiders in this narrative are also of a comparatively high social status: the σοφός, γραμματεύς and συζητητὴς τοῦ αἰῶνος τούτου (1.20) and the ἄρχοντες τοῦ αἰῶνος τούτου (2.6; 2.8) who have the power to crucify. The believing group is thus denoted by the social weakness of its majority, whereas the outgroup is denoted by the social power of its most illustrious members.

Whereas such a rhetoric of social status undoubtedly creates a feeling of distinctiveness, it may be objected that it hardly creates a positive social identity for the believing group. On this scale of assessment their position is inferior. However, as we have observed (1.2.3), groups faced with a negative social identity can be expected to attempt to change either the scale of comparison or the evaluation of the properties being compared. (Petronius admitted Trimalchio's superior wealth, only to portray wealth as irrelevant to true virtue. Cicero admitted Greek scholarly superiority, only to insist on Roman moral supremacy [2.1.2].) Here we find the same: the soteriological, pneumatic and (later) ethical superiority of the ingroup is protested, whereas superior wisdom (in society's eyes) and now social position are conceded to the outgroup. However, the concessions are made only to be subverted, because the paradox of the cross deprives human wisdom and social position of all positive value. Indeed, the negative of these, human weakness, folly and insignificance, are now declared to be highly prized attributes (the criteria for God's election). The 'nobodies' nullify the socially powerful (1.26–27). Thus the ingroup's superiority on every scale is assured.

Thus, chs 1–4 give us an overview of two different groups, with two different estimations of wisdom and the cross, two different fates, and two different concepts of power. Paul has created a dualism that splits all humanity in two, and endowed that division with such theological, eschatological and epistemological significance that it should not surprise us if it will govern everything on which Paul instructs his converts in the letter. Paul's language is both descriptive and evaluative, denoting two existing groups, but in such a way that everything that separates them serves to ensure the superiority of the ingroup in pertinent areas. These areas are so critical that the difference and opposition of the groups becomes fundamental to any understanding of reality.

3.3.2. *The Effect of the Dichotomy on the Divisions*

If Paul's attempt to resocialize his converts succeeds (and that is always an if) and they accept his narrative of who believers are and how they differ from outsiders, then we can expect that the 'cognitive, evaluative, and emotive' aspects of group belonging will increase. Believers will increasingly be aware of their new social identity in Christ, evaluating it positively, and investing emotionally in it (1.2.1). Further, as a high evaluation of Christian social identity, and a positive self-stereotype are accepted, a corresponding lower evaluation of the outside world, and a negative stereotype of the unbeliever is its inevitable corollary.

This new worldview will have social consequences. Social identity theory indicates that as the 'cognitive, evaluative and emotive' dimensions of a group belonging increase, we can expect that particular social identity to become salient for self-identity in an increasing number of situations. There will be an increase in the number of instances in which the individual will conceive of him/herself as a member of the group, and allow that identity, rather than any other, to govern his or her interaction with others (whether fellow members or outsiders) (1.2.2). Increasingly, perception of self and others will be informed by the group stereotypes. We are moving from the inter-personal to the inter-group end of the behavioural spectrum.

If there are divisions among the Corinthians, whether theological or socio-economic, they are likely to be lessened or eliminated by a rise in the importance of Christian self-identity. This rise in importance, and an increase in the extent to which behaviour is group behaviour, will be at the expense both of personal relationships (loyalties or enmities) existing between individuals, and other criss-crossing social identities. The relevance of self-categorization as a member of either church faction or socio-economic group will yield to the rise in the believer/unbeliever dichotomy.

If the boundary between church and world is, in Paul's opinion, too lightly regarded by the Corinthians, then any increase in the importance of Christian identity and group behaviour is likely to lead to more regard for the boundary. Christian identity and norms will increasingly govern relations with outsiders regardless of any individual relationships (1.2.2). Outsiders will increasingly be perceived as a 'unified social category' corresponding to their negative group stereotype (1.2.4). Similarly, alternate social identities, which might serve to link insiders with outsiders (shared kinship group, socio-economic group, or ethnicity) will suffer a diminution in salience (1.2.6). Thus, if Paul's group dichotomy and its attendant stereotypes are accepted, the Corinthians are more likely to accept a call, either to avoid certain social interaction with outsiders (proscription) or to carry out such interaction in the light of the group dichotomy (prescription).

We should also be alert to the nature of the ingroup stereotype or prototype, which Paul is creating, or rather manipulating. Much of it is at the theological level and not socially quantifiable (who has salvation, wisdom, the Spirit). But two aspects of it operate differently: socio-economic classification and estimation of the Pauline gospel. Paul stereotypes the believers as those without worldly wisdom, power and status, whereas the outgroup stereotypically includes the socially power-ful. Thus, if the stereotype is accepted, members of the community without social status will best conform – and thus paradoxically may be perceived as possessing the highest social identity within the community. Thus Paul's stereotype serves to raise their social identity at the expense of the better-born few.

Paul also sets himself up as the epitome of the group stereotype. In 2.1–5 he presents his own weak and fearful proclamation of the gospel as the ideal example of God's paradoxical wisdom. Then in 2.6–13 he defines the ideal group member (the mature) as one who understands this paradox (and therefore values Paul's presentation). Those who fail to do so reveal themselves to be ignorant of the true wisdom and power, which should be possessed by the believing community. Thus, whereas Paul's detractors appear to have created an ingroup stereotype by which he is poorly rated, Paul reverses this, creating a stereotype by which he, and those who value him, best conform to the highly prized ingroup attributes. The same occurs in 4.7–13 where Paul offers the painful apostolic experience of the world as a model for believers, therefore implicitly lowering the standing of those who devalue such social suffering, or experience a differing attitude from outsiders.

3.3.3. *Controlling Language*
As with the Roman moralists, we can also observe that Paul not only stresses the group dichotomy, but also uses the negative connotations of that dichotomy to ensure conformity among ingroup members.

For Paul, division within the community is an unacceptable phenom-enon. Whether μεμέρισται ὁ Χροστός (1.13) is a rhetorical question or statement of horror, it relates Paul's accusation of factionalism to the impossible theological notion of the body of Christ divided. The theological rejection of schism continues in the discussion of baptism (1.13–17). Baptism is a symbol of the essential unity of the church (ἐν πνεῦμα and ἐν σῶμα) which transcends other social divisions (12.13; cf. Gal. 3.28). That it should be used as a marker of division among the Corinthians is thus a blasphemous parody of its true intent. Unity is the mark of the church and disunity threatens its identity in Christ. As Fee observes, being spiritual (an ingroup characteristic) and being divided are 'mutually exclusive options'.[28]

---

28. Fee 1987: 122.

Thus, for Paul, the existence of divisions among the Corinthians calls into question their claim to believing identity. They are not conforming to the ideal-stereotype. Constantly Paul points to the existence of divisions in order to question Corinthian pride and in doing so deliberately relates them to the devalued outgroup. As we have seen, in 2.6–16 Paul sets up a group dichotomy on the basis of wisdom. Paul speaks true wisdom, revealed by God to the mature believer and not understood by the world (2.6–9). The believer has discernment, the Spirit, the gifts, and the true understanding (2.12–13). In both cases the first person plural is used, inviting the Corinthians to identify with Paul against the devalued outsider. But then in 3.1 Paul changes tack. The Corinthians are not πνευματικοῖς but σαρκίνοι, mere νήπιοι ἐν Χριστῷ. The second of these allegations is a diminutive, opposing the claim to maturity (τελείος) in matters of understanding (2.6). But the first can only be relating their behaviour to the outgroup, who, as Paul has already stated, lack the Spirit and understanding which is the predicate of the believer. As if to hammer the point home, Paul states in 3.2–4 that while the Corinthians exhibit ζῆλος καὶ ἔρις, they are σαρκικοί living κατὰ ἄνθρωπον. Thus, just as Pliny constructed a group dichotomy only to number Anthony among the devalued outsiders (2.2.3), so Paul constructs the dichotomy of wisdom and spirituality, only to compare the Corinthians with the outsiders. Paul does not state that their factiousness has entirely falsified their member-ship of the ingroup. They are, after all, *still* νήπιοι ἐν Χριστῷ (a description that may be intended to mitigate the worst implications of the charge). He merely suggests that they are exhibiting behaviour charac-teristic of the outgroup and thus to be negatively evaluated.[29]

3.3.4. *Conclusion*
Thus, as with the rhetoric of the Roman moralists, we can see two movements within Paul's writing. First, a group dichotomy is stressed: a narrative of who 'we' are and why we are both different from and superior to 'them' is offered. The narrative seeks to raise the 'cognitive, emotive and evaluative' dimensions of group belonging. It seeks to make this social identity matter, in order that that there might be an increase in

---

29. It would appear significant that Paul does not call the Corinthians ψυχικοί, which is the direct designator of the outsider in 2.14. Fee suggests that this is deliberate: the ψυχικός is one without the Spirit (an outsider) whereas Paul charges the Corinthians with being unspiritual 'not because they lack the Spirit but because they are thinking and living just like those who do' (1987: 123). However, it is certain that the meaning of the σάρκινος/σαρκικός charge is derived from the dichotomy of 2.14–16 (they cannot be addressed as πνευματικοίν, 3.1). 'The three terms ψυχικός (2.14), σάρκινος (3.1), and σάρκινος (3.3) all draw their semantic nuances from their mutual interaction with one another within a single semantic field in which the major contrast to all three is πνευματικός, *spiritual* or *pertaining to the Spirit*' (Thiselton 2000: 292; original italics).

group cohesion and conformity, and a corresponding increase in the number of social situations where that social identity might be regarded as salient.

Secondly, the narrative is an attempt to exercise social power. For it attempts to construct a group stereotype in ways that will manipulate behaviour and status within the group. The social identity of those members who conform to the stereotype will rise, while those who dissent are deprived of high social identity and associated with the identity of the outgroup, an outgroup that is being evaluated as foolish, unspiritual and perishing.

3.4. *The Ethical Dichotomy in 1 Corinthians 5–7*

3.4.1. *Ethical Stereotypes*

Having examined the nature and the function of Paul's group dichotomy in 1 Corinthians 1–4, we shall now take an overview of the same in 5–7, before considering these chapters in greater depth in the remainder of this study. In 1 Corinthians 1–4 we found that, not only did Paul differentiate the group in such a way as to ensure its *comparatively* positive social identity, but ingroup superiority was *absolute*: a difference of kind rather than degree. Not only is there no salvation found outside Christ,[30] neither is there true wisdom, discernment or spiritual power. When we turn to consider the ethical properties of each group, we see the same dichotomy operating. Or perhaps we had better speak here of a double dichotomy. For, in Paul's schema, there is not only an ontological dualism of two different peoples, related to their respective eschatological fate, estimation of values, and ethics, but there is also a temporal dualism between two stages in the life of the individual believer, pre- and post-conversion. Once they were members of the immoral world, but then they were called out to a different style of existence.

This double dualism can be seen most clearly in 6.9–11. Here the ἄδικοι stand opposed to the ἅγιοι: the two categories of humanity. The outgroup are characterized both by their eschatological fate (they 'shall not inherit the kingdom') and by their stereotypical vices (vices here used as personal labels for categories of people). However the ἅγιοι are reminded that they too were once numbered among the ἄδικοι.

Of course, perhaps few in the church would accept the appropriateness of such appellations as 'robber' or 'adulterer' to their pre-Christian lives, or for that matter to all of their non-Christian associates. Paul grants this in his τις qualifier. However, like all stereotypes, these may be informed by the most blatant examples. Further, as Chester has argued, the order of

---

30. According to 1 Cor. at any rate. The situation of non-believing Israel in Rom. 9–11 may prove to be an exception.

Paul's list perhaps invites Gentile believers to identify their previous lifestyles in Paul's description. Few may have been robbers, but what Gentile convert would not have learned to characterize his previous pagan existence as idolatrous and perhaps even pertaining to πορνεία by Christian standards.[31] At any rate, all of them required to be 'washed, sanctified and justified'; by baptism transformed in ethical nature and eschatological fate.

In each case the ingroup stands opposed to an outgroup; the believer to the unbeliever; and the believer as new creation to the believer in his previous life as an unbeliever. In each case the outgroup is stereotypically polluted and marked out by its innate vices. In each case the dualism implies a difference in kind rather than degree, such that believers are ἅγιοι and unbelievers ἄδικοι, terms which denote not just the status of individuals in regard to Christ, but also carry a behavioural inference.

It is also worth noting the logic of 5.11 here, for this verse also reveals the two mutually exclusive identities that Paul believes an individual may have. One may either be an ἀδελφός or an immoral outsider. The dichotomy is however somewhat obscured by inadequate translations of the verse, which serve to make Paul's list in 5.11b a list of sins rather than of sinners. Hence the μὴ συναναμίγνυσθαι ἐάν τις ἀδελφὸς ὀνομαζόμενος ἢ πόρνος ἢ πλεονέκτης ἢ εἰδωλολάτρης ἢ λοίδορος ἢ μέθυσος ... becomes 'not to associate with anyone who bears the name of a brother if he is *guilty* of immorality or greed, or is an idolater, reviler, drunkard ...' (RSV). This fails to translate πόρνος or πλεονέκτης as designations of people rather than of vices. The KJV's 'if any man who is called a brother, *be* a fornicator...' is preferable (although 'fornicator' is perhaps too narrow) as it preserves the sense of the personal, rather than merely behavioural, description.[32]

Two things follow from this. First, outsiders are being stereotyped not only as those who commit vice, but also as those who are denoted by that vice. They are πόρνοι, or εἰδωλάτραι. Thus when Paul previously wrote μὴ συναναμίγνυσθαι πόρνοις, this could be (wilfully?) misinterpreted as a command to avoid outsiders, but he writes 'νῦν' commanding them not to associate with a sub-class of πόρνοι, those πόρνοι who claim the name brother (ἀδελφός ὀνομαζόμενος). Secondly it follows that one can either be an ἀδελφός or a πόρνος, πλεονέκτης, εἰδωλολάτρης, λοίδρος, μέθυσος... The two are quite distinct.

31. Chester 2003: 135–36.
32. Fee (1987: 220) and Conzelmann (1975: 95) make the same error as the RSV, but Barrett preserves the sense in translating 'anyone known as a Christian brother who is a fornicator, or rapacious man, or idolater, or abusive man, or drunkard, or robber' (1973: 120).

All this expresses the conviction that the holy and ethical life of the church in Christ stands opposed to the evil age outside, whether this be seen in terms of those presently not in Christ, or the time when believers were once not in Christ. The people of the world are defined as those who are 'immoral, greedy, swindlers and idolaters' (5.10) whereas the believers, who were once, like all outsiders, immoral, are now 'washed, justified, and sanctified' (6.9–11). Ethics, and sexual ethics in particular, are just as much the boundary as faith, or justification. They define both insider and outsider. Πόρνοι is what the Christians were (6.11), πορνεία is the defining trait of the unbelievers around them (5.9–10) and the abstention from πορνεία is thus to be the visible difference between the community and the outside. Therefore it follows that the individual must flee πορνεία as being incompatible with his Christian status (6.18), and that the community must expel one who blatantly indulges in it.

3.4.2. *Conclusion*
The social function of the ethical dichotomy is identical to that of all the other Pauline dichotomies (wisdom, Spirit, power), which serve to differentiate insider from outsider and give the insider a positive social identity (3.2.2). They serve to raise the importance of group belonging, thus strengthening group cohesion, and the importance of that social identity in an increasing number of interactions.

Since in 1 Corinthians 5–7 Paul is dealing with both sexual ethics (5; 6.12–20; 7) and relations with outsiders (5.9–13; 6.1–11; 7.12–16; 7.39), the ethical dichotomy has a specific function in this context. First, a positive evaluation of the group will (as we have seen) encourage conformity to the positively valued group stereotype. The group stereotype includes adherence to certain ethical standards. Thus Paul's ethical dichotomy itself, if accepted, will serve to foster that ethical behaviour among the believers. Secondly, if the negative stereotype of the outsider is accepted (and perceptual accentuation will encourage this) it will be easier to control relations with outsiders. Even before the rules of engagement with outsiders are presented as an ingroup norm, the view of outsiders as immoral will encourage disengagement from them. Who wants to marry, or submit their legal case to, a person whom they categorize as morally corrupt? Thirdly, as we shall discover later, Paul uses association with the negative outgroup as 'controlling language' to encourage and discourage certain courses of action.

Chapter 4

PUTTING THE πόρνοι IN THEIR PLACE (5.1–13)

4.1. *Introduction*

4.1.1. *The Questions*

As we have just seen, Christian social identity is, for Paul, symbolized in assumptions about moral difference. 'We' differ from 'them' in regard to ethics, and particularly sexual ethics. Believers are ἅγιοι: unbelievers πόρνοι. Such a dichotomy not only creates a differentiation for the Christian ingroup, but it creates a positively valued distinctiveness: for there can be little doubt that morality must rate higher than its opposite. What then happens when this dichotomy is contradicted by facts? What happens when an insider's behaviour is inconsistent with the positive ingroup stereotype, indeed corresponds to the outgroup stereotype? The existence of the incestuous man of 1 Corinthians 5 raises just such a question. How can a moral boundary persist when so obviously transgressed? Must such an occurrence bring into question Paul's attempt to create a positive social identity for believers using the criterion of morality?

There are various questions that shall concern us as we examine this chapter. First, we are interested in Paul's social and theological account of the situation. How does the apostle analyse the facts reported to him? What type of social and theological remedy does this analysis generate? What, in Paul's view, are the implications of boundary crossing for transgressor and community? Secondly, we are interested in how Paul attempts to ensure Corinthian compliance with his analysis and solution (his use of controlling language). Given that the Corinthians have taken no action against the offender, how does Paul attempt to ensure future action? How does Paul make the situation matter to the congregation? Thirdly, we are interested in what Paul's demand for action, and the Corinthian failure to act, reveals to us about their respective understandings of Christian identity. Finally, we are interested in 5.9–13, where Paul, in the midst of the discussion of the immoral man, deals with relations with outsiders. What does this reveal to us concerning the social implications of the ethical dichotomy?

We shall allow the agenda for our study to be set by the text itself. First (4.2) we shall look at Paul's introduction of the matter in 5.1, and his attempt to shame the Corinthians into action. Secondly (4.3), we shall look at his theological and social solution in 5.2–8. Finally (4.4), we shall examine Paul's instructions on relations with outsiders in 5.9–13.

4.1.2. *Paul's Purpose*

Why does Paul raise objection to the immoral man? Mitchell contends that to secure the unity of the church Paul must first clarify its membership. The immoral man is expelled as he has become a 'cause of division' and is therefore 'not included in the unity to which Paul calls the Corinthian church'.[1] However, while Paul certainly wishes the community to take concerted action against the offender, there seems scant evidence that the Corinthians were divided in their attitude to the man. If they were, or if some did wish to expel him, such tensions are not, in Paul's opinion, significant enough to merit mention. Rather he appears to criticize the *entire* community for its inaction and pride (5.2). Fee suggests that 1 Corinthians 5 is the first of the 'test cases of the crisis of authority' (5.1–6.20),[2] where Paul confronts those 'puffed up' against him. Will the Corinthians obey Paul or their 'new prophets who are remaking the gospel into worldly wisdom divorced from truly Christian ethics'?[3] Fee thus takes seriously Paul's attempt to ensure compliance with his vision of the church. However, while Paul certainly attacks the Corinthians' pride and inaction, it is less clear that he is attacking an alternative articulation of the gospel.

Most obviously Paul raises this subject because his conception of the church as a moral community is threatened by the existence of a notoriously immoral man in its midst. He thus wants the church to expel such people. Certainly, if this is to occur, the church must unite in corporate action. The congregation must be cohesive enough for the behaviour of one individual to matter to the rest. The Corinthians must be made to care about the individual and his or her effect on the purity and reputation of the social unit. Such corporate responsibility was evidently a concept with which the Corinthians had some difficulty. As Paul has to reiterate later, 'if one member suffers, all suffer together; if one member is honoured, all rejoice together' (12.26).[4]

Contextually, Paul raises the issue of the immoral man *at this particular*

1. M.M. Mitchell 1991: 112.
2. Fee 1987: 194.
3. Fee 1987: 195.
4. Cf. Paul's teaching on concern for fellow believers (8.9–13; 9.19–23; 10.24–30; 11.17–22).

juncture to justify his threat of discipline in 4.18–21, a discipline threatened against the community as a whole.[5] Paul's argument is that the community's failure to act, demonstrated by their continued tolerance of the man, falsifies their positive view of themselves. However, corporate responsibility and falsification of pride stand or fall together. For if Paul cannot convince the Corinthians that corporate action is required, then the lack of that action will fail to shame them.

4.2. *Controlling Language: An Intergroup Comparison*

4.2.1. Ὅλως ἀκούεται ἐν ὑμῖν πορνεία

How Paul introduces the matter is significant. He narrates that he has heard, or rather that '*it* is heard' that πορνεία is ἐν ὑμῖν. The choice of ἀκούεται rather than ἀκούω is important. Paul is not simply indicating that he has received an oral report (and that implicitly the Corinthians did not see fit to mention it in their letter), but he implies that others are making the same observation as he. Something is being said of them, which ought not to be said. Their public reputation (positive social identity) is at stake.

This is one of three oral reports to which Paul refers in 1 Corinthians; but there are significant differences between 5.1, and the charges he brings against the Corinthians on the basis of the other reports. In 1.11 Paul accuses the congregation of factionalism with the words: ἐδηλώθη γάρ μοι περὶ ὑμῶν, ἀδελφοί μου, ὑπὸ τῶν Χλόης ὅτι ἔριδες ἐν ὑμῖν. Not only are these words less confrontational than 5.1; they suggest a private communication delivered to Paul's own ears, by the (trustworthy?) people from Chloe. That Paul's information (as summarized in 1.12) is so detailed probably indicates an inside source, and it is probable that this inside source is reporting out of concern for the community.[6] In 11.18 Paul introduces another charge of division, this time with the simple formula: ἀκούω. Here the verb (first person singular) implies only that *he* has heard the report, and, while it is probable that others are aware of the situation, that fact is not drawn out. Again, it is probable that the informants are members of the

---

5. Granted 4.18–19 refers to the arrogance of 'some' rather than the whole church. However, the charge of pride is quickly broadened out to include the whole community (5.2) and, in 4.18–21, the pride of the 'some' makes the discipline of the whole necessary (he will come ἐν ῥάβδῳ πρὸς ὑμᾶς), just as the πορνεία of the one is now the concern of all.

6. We have no way of knowing whether Chloe herself was a believer, but it is probable that those people to whom Paul refers were. Whether they were members of the Church in Corinth is less sure; Barrett (1971: 42) is agnostic, while Fee (1987: 54) argues against. In either case, they appear to be a source of information Paul trusts and that he thinks adds credence to his charge against the congregation.

community, as Paul is once more supplied with detailed information (concerning behaviour at the sacrament).[7]

The reference to the report in 5.1 is different. Not only is the charge harshly introduced (there is no mitigating ἀδελφοί μου), but Paul appears to be suggesting, by his use of ἀκούεται (the third person singular), that this negative report is reaching more than just his ears. Indeed mention of the ἔθνη might imply that it is circulating even outwith the church. These observations do not rely upon, but could be supported by, the taking of the adverb ὅλως with ἀκούεται to indicate that the hearing is being done generally or universally.[8] But even if we take the majority position[9] and translate ὅλως as indicating Paul's horror at what is ('actually') being heard, we cannot dismiss the idea that some of the horror is that such a thing is being said of the church, as much as at the content.[10]

In any case, Paul's purpose is to shame the Corinthians by repeating back to them the negative report which has circulated at least as far as his ears. Whatever the congregation should have done about the situation, whatever attitude they should have adopted, such things should not be being said of them. The situation is intolerable, and this is even before Paul points out that it is compounded by their simultaneous pride (5.2).

Our argument here is that Paul is attempting to ensure the acceptance of corporate responsibility for, and thus corporate remedial action towards, the situation. It is thus important to realize that before Paul cites the facts of the case, the inappropriateness of the Corinthians' attitude (5.2), the appropriate action (5.3–5), and the anticipated spiritual damage to the church (5.6–8), he draws the Corinthians' attention to the

---

7.   If the problem at the Lord's Supper was the adoption of status differentials in dining, it is improbable that any outsider would find such arrangements remarkable, if such practices were common in antiquity. Fee (1987: 537) plausibly suggests that although Paul certainly credits his informants, his remark μέρος τι πιστεύω is an admission that they are 'scarcely disinterested observers'. Fee also suggests that Paul's remark reflects a recognition of the sociological divide between the informers' 'view from below' and Paul's 'view from above' as he writes. This may be so, but overreaches the evidence. It need not necessarily be the poor who are objecting to their treatment; any believer who shared Paul's presuppositions on the nature of the community might make an objection.

8.   As KJV 'it is reported commonly'; Conzelmann (1975: 94) 'in general there are reports'.

9.   Barrett 1971: 120; Fee 1987: 199; Schrage 1991: 368; BAGD; RSV; and NRSV.

10.   Fee (1987: 199), denying the possibility of a locative meaning for ὅλως, insists that 'the horror lies in the fact that there is sexual immorality among them, but they are taking no action'. However, even without a locative meaning, there seems no reason to discount that the horror may be in that such a thing may be heard at all, regardless of how widespread is the report.

common perception of them as a group in the light of the existence of the immoral man and their failure to exclude him.[11] Rather than simply cite the instance of one immoral man, Paul begins by pointing to the perception of a community infested with immorality. Critically the ἐν ὑμῖν forces the πορνεία upon the community as a whole. This is an observation of a collective, which serves to diminish that collective on the ethical/immoral value scale, thus making the actions of one individual impact on the reputation (shared social identity) of all other members of the group. Paul thus defines a collective problem that requires a collective solution.[12]

4.2.2. καὶ τοιαύτη πορνεία ἥτις οὐδέ ἐν τοῖς ἔθςεσιν

Here Paul is still unspecific about the facts of the case. Before citing the full horror of the incest, he seeks rather to elaborate further on its seriousness, and its effects on the status of the Corinthian congregation. He does this by making an intergroup comparison. Such is the horror of this particular πορνεία that not even the ἔθνη would engage in it. Thus, by implication, the report that there is such πορνεία ἐν ὑμῖν serves to diminish the status of the congregation as against, and perhaps even in the eyes of, the outgroup. As Rosner notes, such a rhetorical device is often used in the Hebrew Scriptures.[13]

The selection of the term ἔθνη also has significance.[14] Although both the NT and the LXX can use the term neutrally for 'peoples', it most often stands as an outgroup designation. In the LXX ἔθνη stands opposed to λαός; denoting 'the rest' and the chosen people, while in the Gospels and Acts the majority of the references to ἔθνη denote Gentiles as opposed to Ἰουδαῖοι. For Paul, even although in some passages Gentile Christians are still to be numbered among the ἔθνη,[15] in 1 Corinthians its use always implies that the church now stands (with, or in the place of Israel) opposed to the outgroup ἔθνη. Ontologically, the church is divided from

---

11. Pascuzzi (1997: 104) demonstrates how the rhetorical handbooks affirm that an appeal to the emotions is correctly placed at the beginning of an argument. Shame, in particular, is noted by Cicero as an effective emotion for inducing change in thought or behaviour (Cicero, *Part. Or.* 26.91).

12. As Schrage (1991: 371) has it: 'Entscheidend im ersten Satz aber ist das ἐν ὑμῖν. Damit wird bereits signalisiert, daß es weniger um den Inzestfall des einzelnen korinthischen Christen als um die Heiligkeit und Verantwortung der Gemeinde geht' (cf. Harris 1991: 5).

13. 'The nations are used as a negative model for Israelite behaviour' (Rosner 1994: 84, citing Amos 1, 2; 2 Kgs 21.9, 11; Deut. 12.29–31; 1 Kgs 14.24).

14. Greek of the Hellenistic period used the term to denote foreigners as opposed to Ἕλληνες, thus 'when applied to non-Greek peoples, the word ἔθνος often has a disparaging sense rather like the unambiguous βάρβαρος' (Schmidt 1964: 371).

15. Mainly in Romans, e.g. 1.5; 1.13.

the outside ἔθνη (to whom the cross is folly, 1.23) and temporally they are no longer the ἔθνη whom they once were (12.2).[16]

Social identity theory suggests that every group requires a positive self-evaluation relative to the pertinent outgroup, so that members can receive a positive social identity through membership. By linking the case of the immoral man to a negative perception of the ingroup relative to the outgroup, Paul undermines the group's positive self-evaluation (their boasting) and at the same time insists that their corporate and individual social identity is connected to the moral integrity of the group. Thus he undermines any argument that would seek either to trivialize the effect of the offender being part of the church ('a *little* leaven'?) or deny the corporate responsibility, or corporate effects, which arise from his continued membership.

The impact of the negative intergroup comparison in 5.1 is intensified in that the outgroup's negative status has already been established. The ἔθνη are the outsiders that formed the foil to Paul's group comparison in chs 1–4. Therefore, as in 3.1–4, the congregation is being compared to a group that has already been dismissed as damned (1.18), foolish (1.21) and eschatologically impotent (1.28). However, the comparison of 5.1 is stronger than that of 3.1–4 as now believers are not merely being equated with outsiders, but unfavourably compared. The believers outdo outsiders in immorality (cf. Pliny's comparison of Anthony with the Greeks; see 2.2.3 above).

However, in all of this nothing should lead us to suppose that Paul holds that the believing group can hold an inferior position to the outgroup (see 4.3.1 below). Paul's dualism could not tolerate this. The device is rather rhetorical, seeking to use the ontological distinction to ensure that the Corinthians strive to maintain the ethical distinction, and the perception of that distinction.

To say that this πορνεία is οὐδὲ ἐν τοῖς ἔθςεσιν is not a comment on pagan morals. 'This does not contain a relative acknowledgment of the fact that they, too, have a certain moral standard. The pagans serve only as a foil for the sharpness of his judgment concerning the case in the community.'[17] Yet, for the rhetorical comparison to be effective, it must have at least some degree of descriptive relevance. What then is the relationship between the ἔθνη and this πορνεία?

The problem is the lack of a verb. Whether to supply 'occur' or

---

16. The only other possible use in 1 Cor. is 10.20 where it again designates outsiders, but the text is doubtful.

17. Conzelmann 1975: 96; see also Schrage 1991: 370: 'Er will damit den Heiden weder Komplimente machen noch die unverschütteten Reste oder die ungebrochene Höhe natürlicher heidnischer Moral hervorheben'.

'condoned' is a difficult decision.[18] If the implication is 'unheard of' then
the concept probably belongs as a contrast to the 'hearing' of such a thing
within the congregation. If the idea is that it is 'not condoned' then the
concept probably belongs with 5.2, and the observation that the
Corinthians appear to be condoning it. The former is probably to be
preferred.[19] However, Paul may have deliberately chosen ambiguity in
order to claim '... the greater ("not occur") ...' without making such a
(contestable?) assertion. At any rate Paul's point is that there is a
difference between the relationship of the congregation to incest (in its
occurrence or their toleration) and that of unbelieving Gentiles, and that
the church comes out in the inferior position.

4.2.3. ὥστε γυναῖκά τινα τοῦ πατρὸς ἔχειν

Finally, it is necessary to consider briefly the specifics of the case, and how
this might actually compare with Graeco-Roman morality. It appears that
we are dealing with a case of a marriage or concubinage[20] between a
believer and his stepmother. This is borne out by the fact that the term
γυνὴ πατρός in the LXX, and its Hebrew equivalent אֵשֶׁת אָב in
Rabbinical literature, designate the stepmother.[21]

If this is the case, it doubtless constituted a crime in Roman law.[22] But
to suggest, as de Vos does, that this implies that such an act could not
occur in Gentile society or, if it had, prosecution would necessarily follow,
seems somewhat unreasonable.[23] It is a fallacy to say that because
something is illegal it does not occur, and another fallacy to say that all
enacted laws are enforced. De Vos himself has to concede there is little

---

18. Translators generally favour verbs implying the non-existence of incest in Gentile
society: 'not occur' (NIV and Fee – although Fee also uses 'condoned' with little thought to
any significant difference), 'unheard of' (Conzelmann), 'not found' (RSV), 'not practised'
(Barrett), 'nicht vorkommt' (Schrage), but also 'not so much as named' (KJV).

19. Where, as here, there is an ellipsis, and the preceding verb (ἀκούεται) would make
sense, it would seem reasonable to imply it (Blass-Debrunner, §479).

20. Cf. Conzelmann (1975: 96). At any rate, by virtue of the present tense verb ἔχειν, it
would seem correct to see the relationship as ongoing. Schrage (1991: 369), also insisting on
an ongoing relationship, suggests that it must be other than marital since ἔχειν is *not* the
usual form for marriage. However the NT usage seems quite varied on this last point (cf. Mk
6.18; 1 Cor. 7.2; 7.29, but then also Jn 4.18).

21. Str-B 3.343–58. Its use in Lev. 18.8 must mean other than the natural mother as in
18.7 she is separately denoted as μήτηρ σου.

22. Gaius *Inst.* 1.63; Cicero, *Clu.* 5.14–6.15; cf. Clarke 1993: 77–79; R.F. Collins 1999:
206, 209–10.

23. De Vos 1998: 108, 'In light of this [legal] background, it is difficult to understand how
the couple involved in the case in 1 Cor. 5 could have escaped prosecution. It would mean
that all of their male relatives were dead, that they were not co-habiting and that nobody else
knew about it.'

evidence of trials on any sexual charges,[24] and he can cite none of son-stepmother incest.

On the other hand, despite the law and social disapproval, there is a small but significant amount of evidence that such unions did occur, even if it is in the number of instances of polemic against it.[25] Veyne asserts 'a Rome, l'inceste mère-fils ou frère-soeur n'était pas très rare'.[26] Indeed the high instance of remarriage, and the fact that women often married at an early age, would suggest a good number of step-relationships in antiquity, where stepmothers were of similar ages to stepsons.[27] Granted this, it is perhaps naïve to search far for a motive for such unions![28] Thus there seems little need to depart from the traditional interpretation. The very fact that such relationships were rare and universally condemned is precisely Paul's point.[29]

24. In a footnote! (De Vos 1998: 109 n. 25).

25. Martial writes to Gallus (*Epig.* 4.16) complaining of a rumour of incest (although the possibility of prosecution may be inferred). See also Apuleius, *Metam.* 10.2–12.

26. Veyne 1978: 48. He then remarks: 'il était, bien entendu, condamné, mais il ne soulevait pas d'horreur sacrée, comme chez nous: chez les satiriques, il est un thème de plaisanterie ou de sarcasme, un sujet de bons mots médisants; c'était plus grave que l'adultère, mais enfin, c'était une faute du même ordre, non un attentat contre la nature'.

27. See P.A. Watson 1995: 135 and various other commentators on Roman family life (cited fully in Deming 1996: 294 n. 16).

28. Chow (1992: 134) suggests that sexual desire itself is an improbable motive, as desire was not a high priority in Roman marriage. But this assumes that we are talking about a marriage, whereas the stepmother may be serving as a mistress to a son who was already married. Further, Chow's evidence that desire plays a low part in marriage comes from the philosophers, and Juvenal's *Satire* 6. It may be asked how representative these sources are (for examples of desire and affection in antiquity see Foucault 1986: 77–80), and how much they reflect the social reality for a young man free perhaps from a *paterfamilias*. Further, Chow's suggested material motives for the marriage (also Clarke 1993: 19–84) do not hold up. By virtue of the illegality and social unacceptability of such a relationship it is improbable that it would either protect the man's patrimony or satisfy the Augustine family legislation (for a full critique see Meggitt 1998: 150).

Cicero, in referring to a similar incest case, is only too ready to blame passion rather than avarice: 'The madness of passion broke through and laid low every obstacle: lust triumphed over modesty, wantonness over scruple, madness over sense' (*Clu.* 6.7–9). Apuleius also has the offending stepmother driven by uncontrollable lusts (*Metam.* 10.2–3).

29. Indeed de Vos's suggestion that the woman was the father's concubine falls foul of his own objections to the traditional interpretation. He states of marriage to a father's concubine: 'Although it was unusual, and possibly socially unacceptable, for a son to have taken as his *concubina* his late father's *concubina* at Rome, it may have been more acceptable at Corinth' (1998: 112). But this is surely special pleading, for the evidence mustered against the possibility of the relationship being with the father's wife is precisely its social unacceptability, and also assumes that what held good in Rome held good in Corinth!

4.2.4. *Corinthian Boasting*

Critically Paul's ploy assumes that πορνεία is a shaming term with which no one would wish to be associated, and that the crime cited constitutes such πορνεία. This has implications for 'libertine' hypotheses, which assume that the man had a Christian motivation/justification for his crime and that the community's pride was in him.[30] For, if the community would either fail to recognize this case as πορνεία or took some type of perverse pride in πορνεία, any attempt to falsify their pride by associating their standing with such an act would be a miserable failure. Elsewhere, when Paul attempts to deflate Corinthian over-confidence by pointing out communal failings (3.1–4; 11.17–22), he cites what he obviously believes to be incontestable evidence of community weaknesses. It would seem reasonable to believe that 5.1–6 operates in the same way. Further, Paul makes no attempt to argue for the sinfulness of the incest, nor for the shame brought by a charge of πορνεία. His strategy is focused on why the appearance of πορνεία is the concern of the whole church, in the attempt to ensure Corinthian compliance with his solution. This would appear very peculiar if Paul were consciously doing battle with those who would defend either the man's relationship or πορνεία in general. This brings libertine reconstructions into question (we shall return to this when we consider 6.12–20).

There is certainly a link between the pride of the community and the toleration of the immoral man, but we are suggesting that this link is made by Paul rather than by the Corinthians. Indeed, the failure of the Corinthians to make such a connection between their self-assured social identity, and the immoral man who they number among themselves, is precisely Paul's complaint. Like the factions and quarrelling, the toleration of the πόρνος is both unacceptable in itself, and indicative of a dangerous lack of cohesion in the community.[31]

4.3. *The Theological and Social Solution*

4.3.1. *Not* πορνεία *but a* πόρνος

Paul begins with the report of πορνεία and his intergroup comparison in an attempt to shame the Corinthians. In 5.2, however, he changes tack. As

---

30. E.g. Moffatt 1938: 54; Thiselton 1973: 211; 1977: 516; Barrett (1971: 120) suggests this may be the case and Fee (1987: 202) thinks it 'probable'.

31. As Harris (1991: 7) notes, in more cohesive groups there is more demand for conformity and greater rejection of deviant members. Harris then correctly comments that 'the congregation's reaction to the incest was accepting, and ... [this] ... suggests that the congregation was not cohesive'. However Harris also assumes that the incestuous behaviour has been adopted as 'an expression of a new norm'. But, if this were the case, then the lack of condemnation would say nothing about the cohesiveness of the group, as they may well have cohered around this new norm.

he begins to offer a solution, he gives an alternative analysis of the situation. Now crucially the problem is not to be seen as πορνεία ἐν ὑμῖν, but as ὁ τὸ ἔργον τοῦτο πράξας being ἐν μέσῳ ὑμῶν. The move is from the abstract notion of a vice being illegitimately associated with a group, to the concrete notion of an individual being illegitimately in a group. The perception of πορνεία ἐν ὑμῖν is for Paul caused by the reality of ὁ τὸ ἔργον τοῦτο πράξας being ἐν μέσῳ ὑμῶν. We shall argue that this analysis pervades Paul's thought throughout the remainder of the chapter.

Paul's opening thus focuses on two things, πορνεία and the community (ἐν ὑμῖν). Commentators in general note this and then insist that Paul's focus remains on the community, showing (apart from 5.5) very little interest in the man himself.[32] We are in agreement.[33] However the same commentators generally assume that having made mention of the man and his specific offence, Paul retains his focus on sexual vice in general and its relation to the community. Hence Zass argues that 'Paul's argument quickly moves from the condemnation of a specific vice [incest] to a denunciation of a general one, the vice of *porneia*'.[34] We are not in agreement. Our contention is that although Paul's focus remains on the community and not the specific individual, the danger to the community, which he is constantly discussing after 5.1a, is not sexual vice (specific or general) but individual moral offenders being in the community. He thus moves in 5.2–13 from the call to exclude one specific offender, to the more general call to exclude immoral (and particularly sexually immoral) people from the church.

For Paul's ethical dualism, it is impossible to contemplate the holy people having πορνεία in them. 5.1 may reflect public perception and the shameful report, but it is not the theological reality. Further, as we shall see, it is impossible for Paul that an ἀδελφός who is by definition a ἅγιος who has been 'washed, justified and sanctified', should behave like a πόρνος. That which is designated holy, be it individual or community, must be holy. Hence, for Paul, it is obvious that ὁ τὸ ἔργον τοῦτο πράξας should be removed ἐν μέσῳ ὑμῶν, since it is now obvious that he is not 'one of us'. (For the moment we shall leave open the question as to whether Paul considers that the man's acts reveal that he never held, or deprive him of, the status of insider.) Paul thus provides two motivations for the community to act. The first, as we saw, was the need to rectify the shameful perception of the church in the eyes of its observers. The second, given in the leaven metaphor of 5.6–8, is that outsiders do not belong in the church. Such is a pollution, not because there would then be πορνεία

32. E.g. Conzelmann 1975: 95; Fee 1987: 197.
33. *Pace* Barrett 1971: 127.
34. Zass 1984: 259.

in the church, but because there would then be a πόρνος among the holy people.[35]

This is why there is no need for the church to pronounce judgment on the man. Paul has already done so (5.3), as he has reclassified the man as the πόρνος, which his actions reveal him to be. The perceptual rectification being complete, all that is left is for the church to rectify the social position of the man in accordance with his status.

4.3.2. *The Leaven Analogy*

Paul's leaven metaphor supports our contention that the pollution with which he is primarily concerned is not πορνεία in the community but an outsider in the midst of the church. It is the πόρνος as an individual and not the πορνεία as a concept that is the leaven.

From the beginning it is necessary to insist that ζύμη be translated leaven and not yeast.[36] Some translators make this error, or assume that the two concepts are interchangeable, which they are not.[37] Yeast, in our modern understanding, is something wholesome and clean, added to dough to its benefit. If understood like this, Paul's metaphor would simply warn that a little thing can have disproportionate results upon the larger whole to which it is added. But, as we shall see, the metaphor is more intricate. In the ancient world yeast was not commonly available and so leaven was used as a readily affordable raising agent. Leaven, however, was made by retaining a piece of the previous week's dough, which when added to the new dough caused the whole to rise. Thus old dough was constantly being kept back, and new dough being brought into contact with it: an effective means of raising dough, but always with the danger that if one batch of dough became infected the infection would be passed to the next.

For the Jews the laws surrounding the Feast of Unleavened Bread broke the chain. Once a year the entire community destroyed all the old leaven. Whether the laws were intended, or were understood as being, for such a hygienic purpose is a moot point. The fact remains that the Jews viewed this 'clearing out' of leaven, this fresh start, as essential.

From this, Mitton suggests that there are four separate aspects to the metaphors of leaven in the New Testament:

1. It symbolizes something that has a vitality of its own and a power to affect whatever it touches [as does yeast].

---

35. As D.B. Martin (1995: 170) puts it, Paul is concerned lest the purity be spoilt by 'the disguised presence within the church of a representative of the outside, from the cosmos that *should* be "out there"'.

36. See Mitton 1973: 339–43.

37. e.g. NIV, NJB, BAGD.

2. It is a symbol for something that is to be destroyed as it has become tainted in itself, and threatens any dough with which it is mixed.
3. The Festival of Unleavened Bread saw all leaven ruthlessly destroyed, and a new start made with the baking of new unleavened dough. Thus it symbolizes the newness of the Christian life.
4. The association in the one festival of the clean newness of the unleavened bread with the slaughter of the Passover lamb is a ready symbol for Christians of the death of Jesus and the resulting new life of the community. [We shall return to this part of the analogy in 4.3.3].[38]

When this is considered, Paul's metaphor can be more readily understood. The apocalyptic event of the death of Christ has inaugurated the new age, and a new community. Just as at the Passover the old leaven is destroyed prior to the constitution of the new dough, so the death of Christ marks the end of the old way of life and the constitution of a new way, and a new people untainted by the old.[39] This necessitates the church being a community purely composed of those who are part of this new, clean, ethical life; it necessitates the church being a zone free of those who are still in the old age, still part of the old order.

The problem, for Paul, is that there is still 'old leaven' remaining in the church of the new order. There is a man out of place. In one sense this does not threaten the integrity of the church. It, unlike him, still exists in the new order. It and its true members are still ἄζυμοι. However, if it is to be fully what it should be, it must reconstitute itself as a νέον φύραμα[40] by cleansing out the old leaven (i.e. the man who belongs to the old age) from where it does not belong.[41]

All of this supports our contention that the immoral man is already considered by Paul to be an outsider. For, once the old leaven is put out (where it properly belongs) the church can reconstitute itself as a new unleavened lump – which it was from the beginning (καθώς ἐστε ἄζυμοι, 5.7). Thus Paul's argument assumes that the man and the church are two distinct and separable entities. It is not that the man's status has to be changed but that he is to be removed from the place which his status as

---

38. Mitton 1973: 340.

39. This is the point that Countryman (1988: 197) misses when he tries to insist that the 'yeast' in Passover language is not impure. This is not the point. Leaven is to be excluded from the bread during the feast, as being unfit for the celebration. If any remains, it is 'matter out of place', and the bread is not fit for the festival.

40. The fact that Paul does not call upon the believers to be 'new lumps' but 'a new lump' indicates again that community and not individual reform is in view (as Rosner 1994: 71).

41. Fee (1987: 215) rightly observes that the 'metaphors get slightly mixed (the church alternately is the purified house, the new batch of dough, and the celebrants of the feast)'. However, there is consistency in that the man is always leaven and the church is the place where he should not be during the feast (the bread, the house, among the celebrants).

an unreformed πόρνος indicates he has no right to occupy. 5.8 reiterates
the point: in light of the apocalyptic Christ event, which creates the new
life and divides it from the old, the church is to proceed only with those
who exhibit this new life, excluding the man marked by inappropriate
vice.

4.3.3. *Christ our Passover*

Having examined the leaven, we now turn our attention to the festival
metaphor of 5.7b-8. The mention of the church as unleavened already
alludes to a Passover allegory, and this is made explicit in 5.7b where
Christ is described as the Passover [lamb] (πάσχα ἡμῶν) who has been
sacrificed (θύω). The exclusion of leaven and the sacrifice of the Passover
lamb belong together in the Exodus account,[42] and the Festival of
Unleavened Bread is so closely related to the feast of the Passover that
Ezekiel can speak of the 'Passover of unleavened bread'.[43] Thus, there is
no need to see the drawing of a parallel between the death of Christ and
that of the Passover lamb as a second part of the analogy, as if it were a
separate theological grounding for Paul's imperatives. Rather, naming
Christ as the Passover lamb justifies Paul allegorically regarding the
church's present existence as the festival (the death of Christ has initiated
the time that is allegorically the Festival of Unleavened Bread). Only when
the crucifixion is regarded as the death of the Passover lamb can the call to
exclude leaven (5.7-8b) operate.

As leaven is excluded from the bread/house/community during the
Passover, so the immoral man is to be excluded from the zone demarked
by the sacrificed Christ. It has been suggested that the Lord's Supper is in
view here (believers after all have not to *eat* with such a man, 5.11).[44] But
it seems more likely that the reference is more general. The Passover lamb
has *been* sacrificed (aorist) and the festival is to *be* celebrated (present).
Thus the festival represents the new age, inaugurated by the death of
Christ, in which the church presently exists (as a *new* lump exists without
the *old* leaven). The man is thus to be excluded not only from the
Eucharist, but also from all that is within the domain of the sacrificed
Christ.

This may well be all that Paul intends to take from the equation of
Christ with the Passover lamb: a justification for the exclusion from the
church of that which the leaven represents. But it is at least possible that
there is a greater depth to the allegory, stemming from the purpose of the
sacrifice of the Passover lamb.

---

42. Exod. 12.15 and 12.6 respectively.
43. Ezek. 45.21 (cf. Deut. 16.1–8; Lev. 23.4–8).
44. E.g. Orr and Walther (1976: 187) and tentatively Fee (1987: 218). Conzelmann (1975:
102) denies such a possibility.

Fee sees the sacrifice of Christ presented here as expiation for sin.[45] But this would appear unlikely. There is nothing in this passage, or in the Passover allusion, which would serve to bring the forgiveness of sins into the allegory. Whereas, for instance, Rom. 3.24–26 and 2 Cor. 5.21 allude respectively to the sin offering and scapegoat of the Day of Atonement,[46] 1 Cor. 5.8 alludes rather to the Exodus narrative and the Passover commemoration, events connected with deliverance, but not with the expiation of sin(s).

In the first instance, the death of the Passover lamb in the Exodus narrative delivers the Israelites from the angel of death, who slays the first-born of Egypt. The blood of the lamb, placed on the doorposts and lintels of the Israelites' houses, separates them from the Egyptians and thus from the fate of Egypt.[47] Secondly, and perhaps more significantly, the annual Passover festival, of which the exclusion of the leaven and the killing and eating of the lamb are key elements, celebrates the Exodus deliverance as a whole: the event of Israel coming out of Egypt.[48] Thus the deliverance and separation of Israel from Egypt, rather than atonement for sin, are the key aspects of the Passover enactment.[49]

The Passover allusion thus provides no support for those commentators who wish to read 5.6–8 as an exhortation for individuals to avoid sinning in light of the atonement, but rather supports reading these verses as an injunction for the community to separate from outsiders.

4.3.4. *The Nature of the Exhortations*

The implications that Paul draws from the Passover allegory in 5.8 (implied imperatives) are thus something of a crux. How is the leaven metaphor to be understood: as a motivation for casting out sinners, or casting out sins? Barrett relates this command to the latter, with Paul concerned for the 'purity of character and conduct' of the believers in light of the feast.[50] Fee will have it both ways, arguing that as well as a reference to the exclusion of the immoral man it is:

> a command that ties the present broader imperative to the earlier specific one. This at least includes an elimination of the kinds of sexual immorality represented by the excluded man. But now the 'old leaven' is further qualified in terms of 'malice and wickedness'. These two words

---

45. Fee 1987: 218.
46. Lev. 16.15–22.
47. Exod. 12.13; cf. 12.27. This is the same significance drawn by Heb. 11.28.
48. Deut. 16.1, 3, 6.
49. It is also significant that no Gentile is permitted to celebrate the Passover but only such that are circumcised (Exod. 12.43–49).
50. Barrett 1971: 129; see also Moffatt 1938: 58.

are synonyms, which gather under their umbrella every form of iniquity.[51]

However, although this passage is generalizing from the specific case to the general rule, it is better understood as a call to remove sinners rather than sins from the life of the community. First, if it is understood in this light, our passage moves seamlessly from 5.1 through to 5.13 in its concern for where the boundaries are drawn between insider and outsider. The leaven metaphor first arose out of Paul's command for the expulsion of the immoral man (5.2, 5) and is best understood as an explanation of the need for such an action. Further, our metaphor moves us into Paul's call μὴ συναναμίγνυσθαι πόρνοις (5.9), which as Zass has observed[52] is probably a continuation of the idea of mixing, so prominent in the leaven metaphor, and is at any rate a further prohibition of συναναμίγνυσθαι (again v. 11) with immoral people inside the church. There is simply nothing in this passage that constitutes a call to ethical behaviour. The whole context is of a concern with the putting away of the sinner and with the purity of the community.

Secondly, nowhere in this passage is 'sexual immorality represented by the excluded man' (Fee). Indeed the contrary is true; vices represent and denote people. The man is a πόρνος. Thus even if κακία and πονηρία are 'umbrella terms' (Fee) for vices (which we shall contend they are not) one would suspect, on the basis of the usage of this passage, that these too would refer to people (as in 5.9–11) rather than possible sins of believers. Indeed to portray these two descriptions as a short vice list would seem unlikely since there are strictly speaking *no* corresponding vice lists in 1 Corinthians 5–7. All the supposed catalogues of vice in these chapters (5.10–11; 6.9–10) are lists of *individuals* denoted by their stereotypical vice, rather than of vice in the abstract.

Thirdly, we turn to consider the function of the four corresponding genitives in the statement μηδὲ ἐν ζύμῃ κακίας καὶ πονηρίας ἀλλ' ἐν ἀζύμοις εἰλικρινείας καὶ ἀληθείας. Like Fee, commentators have tended to view 'malice and evil' as a short *Lasterkatalog* and then discuss whether or not it is situation-specific. Does it refer to division among the Corinthians in general or perhaps specifically to the animosity stirred up by the immoral man? However, first and foremost κακία and πονηρία refer to the nature of the leaven, and strengthen the call to exclude it.[53] κακία can carry the sense of that which is of poor quality or defective, as can πονηρία. Examine, for instance, Mt. 6.23 where we find the ὀφθαλμός πονηρός – the bad eye that is to be torn out. Or take Mt. 7.17–19 where

---

51. Fee 1987: 219.
52. Zass 1988: 626 n. 2.
53. *Pace* Thiselton (2000: 406), who suggests κακία is what the leaven generates.

we find the καρποὺς πονηρούς – again denoting defective material that is to be destroyed.[54]

In the second instance these two terms refer to *those* who constitute the old leaven, who do not belong in the community that is reconstituted in Christ. Here πονηρία has a double function. First, it is used as a preparation for the citation from Deuteronomy in 5.13b: ἐξάρατε τὸν πονηρὸν ἐξ ὑμῶν αὐτῶν,[55] a citation that is evidently (in view of both its grammar and Scriptural context) commanding the removal of the sinner rather than of sin from the community.[56] Secondly, as Zass has noted, πονηρία/πονηρός is being used in a 'word play' with πόρνος, the exclusion of whom is the issue from which the whole episode begins.[57] So it would seem likely that the call to exclude the leaven labelled as πονηρία is a reference to a type of person who does not belong in the community, rather than a type of behaviour. κακία may well function similarly at this level as a cipher for a 'brother gone bad' – a defective insider who should be excluded.

The case is strengthened when we consider what is to be preferred to this type of old leaven. Paul commands that they celebrate the festival ἐν ἀζύμοις εἰλικρινείας καὶ ἀληθείας. Again these are primarily properties of the unleavened bread once the old leaven is removed. εἰλικρινεία can carry the sense of that which is unmixed, pure, separate and distinct: the bread with the leaven removed. Here it stands in opposition to that which is κακία or πονηρία – relating most obviously to the quality of the material, the quality of the bread when the leaven is removed. But at a second level εἰλικρινεία can refer to openness or straightforwardness, that transparency which is right and which is seen to be right.[58] This is the sense in which Paul uses it in 2 Cor. 1.12 and 2.17. When we combine this with the term ἀλήθεια, which introduces the notion of that which is true in opposition to the lie or the mere appearance, it looks likely that our reference is to the pure unleavened bread which has excluded that which on the face of it belonged, but in actuality did not, that is, the 'false' or 'so-called' brother who is rejected in 5.11.

---

54. Tuckett (2000: 415) insists that, since there is no direct correlation between the four terms and Paul's argument in 1 Cor. 5, they must emanate from the Christ-as-Passover tradition that Paul is using. However, recourse to such a hypothesis is only necessary because Tuckett insists they are ethical terms. If not, their relevance to Paul's argument is easier to see.

55. Deut. 17.7; 19.13; 21.21; 22.21; 22.24; 24.7.

56. However, there is some doubt as to whether there is a citation here (the case is argued by Rosner 1994: 61–62, but see Tuckett 2000: 412).

57. Zass 1984: 259.

58. Thiselton (2000: 407) suggests that its etymological root may be κρίνω and ἥλιος judgment in/by the sun.

Pollution language must be used carefully here. The old leaven is polluted, as indeed is the entire world outside the new age of Christ and his church. Believers transfer between the ages by baptism (they are washed, sanctified, justified, 6.11), leaving behind the life marked by vice. But the immoral man is in a sense doubly polluted; he is an outsider and thus by definition polluted by sin (as leaven), but he is also a man out of place, a usurper, false and insincere (as leaven is in unleavened bread). The polluting effect of the man is *not* caused by the fact that he is an outsider (mere contact with outsiders does not pollute for Paul) but by the fact that he is on the wrong side of the boundary: he is in the unleavened bread.

4.3.5. Conclusion

Thus, for Paul, the disgraceful and impossible notion of the sanctified community having πορνεία in its midst is solved. The problem of πορνεία ἐν ὑμῖν is reduced to that of a πόρνος ἐν μέσῳ ὑμῶν: an outsider out of place. Paul's intention throughout has been to ensure that the community accepts corporate responsibility, by excluding the offender from its midst. The existence of a πόρνος in the community is to matter to the community, and the purity of the community is to matter to its individual members. The call is not for an ethical reformation of members, nor of the offender, but that the offender is recognized as a πόρνος and that the community cease to mix with πόρνοι in this regard. They are to separate socially from that from which God has already made them ontologically distinct.[59]

59. Rosner (1992, 1994, 1999) has demonstrated the textual and conceptual debt that 1 Cor. 5 owes to Hebrew Scripture – and in particular with regard to the notion of corporate responsibility for sin. However, there appear to be two separate notions of corporate responsibility for sin in the Scriptures. First, there are instances where the sin of the individual is taken as being that of the community and the community is thus either punished or called to confess (e.g. Exod. 16.27–28; Ezra 10.6; Neh. 1.4; Dan. 10.2). Secondly, there are instances where the community is blameless providing it expels the offender (e.g. Deut. 13.5; 17.7; 19.19; Num. 16.20–24; Josh. 7.1). Here there is no call to repent, merely to expel. The second of these would seem closer to Paul's thinking (and the citation from Deuteronomy in 1 Cor. 5.13b points in this direction). Although Paul mentions mourning (perhaps over the offender's sin), there is no thought of communal punishment or communal confession. No sin attaches to the community except the sin of failing to expel the offender. Further, offences connected with the holiness of the cult always fall into the second category. On the basis of physique or descent certain individuals must not enter the assembly of the Lord (Deut. 23.1–8, which is taken up in the exclusion of foreign wives in Ezra 9.1–2 and Neh. 13.1–3). This motif is later expanded to include gravely offending Jews (Ezek. 44.6–9; Isa. 33.14–17). Nothing here associates the community with sin – it merely lays an obligation to exclude. Such exclusions are connected to the holiness of the Temple, which in the narratives of 2 Chron. (esp. 29–30; 34–35) is ceremonially cleansed prior to the Passover being celebrated.

4.4. *The Status of the Immoral Man*

4.4.1. *Already an Outsider*

By virtue of Paul's argument, the immoral man is *already* an outsider: he is leaven existing illegitimately in the unleavened bread. It is on this theological indicative that the sociological imperative to expel the man rests.[60] Prior to the church's act, Paul has already passed judgment (5.3), but even this judgment merely recognizes the state of affairs revealed by the man's action.

It is interesting to contrast the instruction to the church in 1 Corinthians 5 with that attributed to Jesus in Mt. 18.15–20. In Matthew the subject is again an ἀδελφός who commits a sin (this time unspecified). The ἀδελφός is to be rebuked, first privately, and then before the community: in each case being given opportunity to repent. If he repents the complainant has 'gained his brother'. If he will not listen to the church, then he is to be treated as a Gentile or tax collector. Thus, in Matthew, the church's act determines the status of the offender, deciding when he shall be treated as an outsider. The community's authority to determine the offender's status is then asserted with the promise that 'whatever you bind on earth shall be bound in heaven, and whatever you loose on earth will be loosed in heaven' (18.18). The church's act thus determines not only the membership of the (visible) church, but also an individual's status before God.

This is the opposite of 1 Corinthians 5. In 1 Corinthians 5 the ecclesiastical act is to reflect rather than determine the ontological status of the man. The man's sin, and status as a sinner, defines his status as an outsider. This ontological status is determined prior to the action of the church. He has already been 'bound in heaven', and so the church must now 'bind on earth'.

However, in saying that the man is already an outsider in 1 Corinthians 5, we leave open an important question: did the man forfeit his insider status by his action, or did his action merely reveal that he was never in fact a true insider? Gundry Volf, correctly contending that the man is not to be considered a true insider, has insisted that this is not a case of a brother 'falling away', but of a false Christian who has illegitimately entered the church.[61] Her assertion is certainly compatible with the text of 1 Corinthians 5, which can be read as an injunction to expel a man revealed to have made a false profession. However, there are no immediate textual grounds for dismissing the alternative hypothesis.

---

60. *Pace* Oropeza (2000: 224), who argues that 'expulsion from the social body ... is concomitant to being cut off from the elect community'.

61. Gundry Volf 1990: 113–20.

The question of whether a brother can 'fall away' must be decided on the exegesis of other texts. We shall return to the question later (5.4.2).

4.4.2. *The Hope of Salvation*

Paul's command that the man be expelled ἵνα τὸ πνεῦμα σωθῇ ἐν τῇ ἡμέρᾳ τοῦ κυρίου, is normally taken to mean that the purpose of expulsion is the eventual repentance and restoration of the offender.[62] Many commentators also see the command παραδοῦναι ... τῷ σατανᾷ implying not only that the man is to be ejected from the church (into the realm of Satan), but also that Satan is to be an agent of the man's chastisement (the ὄλεθρος τῆς σαρκός).[63]

Exegetical problems abound here and space prevents a full consideration. However, a few observations can perhaps be made. What does Paul mean by εἰς ὄλεθρος τῆς σαρκός? A literal reading seems to suggest the man's death; yet how this might contribute to his salvation is unclear.[64] The alternative is that some physical punishment short of death is envisaged; yet how this could be called 'destruction' is extremely problematic.[65] Further, the notion of Satan as an active agent of God's purpose, although not unparalleled in Pauline thought, would certainly be remarkable.[66] Additionally, our observations on 1 Corinthians 5 throw up a further problem. If the man has become, or has always been, an outsider, how is a remedial punishment appropriate to ensuring salvation? Outsiders surely require a change of identity and not merely a change of attitude or behaviour if they are to transfer from the people who are perishing to those who are being saved.

How might a solution be found? First, by insisting that salvation cannot be perceived as an automatic result of the church's act, but only as Paul's desire. Expulsion from the social group neither deprives the man of salvation (he has none to lose), nor effects salvation, but is a prerequisite if there is to be any hope that the man might (once again?) become a genuine

---

62. Some commentators, noting that πνεῦμα lacks the αὐτοῦ supplied by most translators, have argued that the Spirit to be saved is not that of the offender but the Holy Spirit in the community (D.B. Martin 1995: 169; Shillington 1998: 31–32). However, although such an interpretation would fit Paul's concern for the community throughout 1 Cor. 5, it is not to be accepted. It can do little justice to the references to 'salvation' or the 'day of the Lord'.

63. E.g. Barrett 1971: 126–27; Conzelmann 1975: 97.

64. The much-cited parallel of Acts 5 mentions neither excommunication nor salvation (see South 1993: 547–48).

65. Cf. South 1993: 556–59.

66. 2 Cor. 12:7 is the only instance where Satan is seen as God's agent; on all other occasions Paul presents him as the direct opponent of God's work and people (Rom. 16.20; 1 Cor. 7.5; 2 Cor. 2.11; 11.14; 1 Thess. 2.18; 2 Thess. 2.9).

ἀδελφός. His present false membership of the community precludes any hope of a legitimate future (re)entry.

Secondly – and here we must be more tentative – while we cannot exclude the possibility that Paul accompanies the expulsion with a curse intended to ensure physical suffering (or death), given the difficulty of connecting such to the hoped-for salvation, Fee's suggestion that the ὄλεθρος τῆς σαρκός might be a conversion metaphor merits serious consideration.[67] The man would thus be expelled in the hope of genuine conversion. The ὄλεθρος τῆς σαρκός would be the desired outcome rather than the necessary result of the expulsion, and would thus convey the same basic meaning as the salvation of the spirit, although appropriately stressing the moral transformation that would accompany genuine salvation.

However, even if Fee is not followed here, nothing in 5.5 contradicts our contention that the immoral man is held not to be a true insider, and that this is the basis of the call for the community to expel him. That expulsion may be necessary if any hope for the man's true salvation is to be held out, but, whatever its meaning the primary concern (5.6–8) is with the proper constitution of the church.

4.4.3. *The Nature of the Sin*

We have established then that the man's action either reveals or reconstitutes him an outsider. The commission of this act of πορνεία identifies the man as a πόρνος and thus not an ἀδελφός. But a question remains, is it *any* unethical act that identifies a false brother? Does an act of πλεονεξία make one a πλεονέκτης or an act of εἰδωλολατρία make one an εἰδωλολάτρη, and thus unfit for fellowship with believers (5.11)? Or, is the *particular* offence of this man different in kind from other sins? In which case, is this because he commits πορνεία? Or is this because it is a particularly offensive type of πορνεία (as incest)? As we cannot settle this question on the basis of this text alone, we shall return to it when we consider how Paul treats other offences committed by believers in 6.7–8, and what he has to say about the uniqueness of πορνεία in 6.12–20.

4.5. *The Significance of the Boundary*

Paul's treatment of the ambiguity of the immoral insider (by denying his status as insider, and insisting on his expulsion from the church) serves to

---

67. See Fee (1987: 209–14) for a fuller discussion. Paul's use of σάρξ to denote the sinful nature is well attested (Rom. 7.5; 8.1–13; Gal. 5.13–24). The use of ὄλεθρος would be unique (but this would be true of any of the interpretations of its use in 5.5). Similar verbal metaphors can, however, be found in Rom. 8.13 (θανατόω), Gal. 5.24 (σταυρόω) and Col. 3.5 (νεκρόω).

clarify the boundary and its attendant stereotypes. Believers are moral: outsiders immoral. We can expect that Paul's defence of the boundary, if accepted, will increase for insiders the importance of Christian identity. The clarity of the awareness of membership will increase with the clarity of the boundary, and the evaluation of any emotional attachment to that membership will increase as the positive social identity (morality) is established (in the minds of believers) over the outgroup.

Our consideration of Barth's work on ethnic boundaries (see section 1.1.1) suggested that the existence of a social group does not necessarily depend on the restriction of social relations across the boundary. Indeed such interaction often proceeds precisely on the basis of the group dichotomy. It is not only the prohibition of certain intergroup activities that may mark out the boundary; the regulation of interaction by the group can also be an effective mechanism for symbolizing and maintaining the group's distinct social identity. In terms of social identity theory, the question is not the level of social interaction, but whether social identity is salient in that interaction. Does the individual engage in the social situation in the awareness of his or her social identity, and of the social identity of other actors? Does this identity inform perception and behaviour?

4.5.1. *Relations with Outsiders*

In the midst of his attempt to persuade the Corinthians to expel the incestuous man, Paul additionally deals with the misunderstanding of his previous letter, and its injunction: μὴ συναναμίγνυσθαι πόρνοις (5.9–13). Unless Paul is being disingenuous, the purpose of that injunction was to command that believers separate themselves from those who professed Christian identity but were perceived to act in an unethical manner (like the immoral man). Yet the potential for μὴ συναναμίγνυσθαι πόρνοις to be misunderstood or deliberately misrepresented by the Corinthians as a call to withdraw from contact with outsiders altogether is rather obvious. Πόρνος is for Paul normally an outgroup designator.

However, Paul's response to the Corinthian misapplication of the command is significant, for it reveals to us something of Paul's attitude towards Christian relations with outsiders. Evidently, Paul conceives no need for a prohibition of social relations with outsiders.[68] Believers are not to withdraw from the world. But that having been said, the terms on which Paul permits such social interaction should make us wary of any conclusion that Paul's boundary between church and world is necessarily revealed here to be weaker than if he had prohibited such interaction.

Paul clarifies the misunderstood imperative μὴ συναναμίγνυσθαι

---

68. This is borne out by Paul's expectation that believers will receive and accept dining invitations from outsiders (10.27), and that outsiders may be present during worship (14.23).

πόρνοις by restricting its application to those πόρνοι who have once been called ἀδελφοί (5.11). Significantly, however, although Paul rejects the application of this imperative to all outsiders, he does not reject the application of the epithet πόρνοι to such people. The κόσμος is infested with πόρνοι, and to such an extent that any attempt to withdraw from the latter would necessitate a withdrawal from the former. Indeed the implication appears to be that if the designator πόρνοι in the injunction of 5.9 were to be taken in its unrestricted sense, it would not simply include sexual sinners who are numerous among unbelievers – but may well be taken to encompass all humanity outside of the believing community. 5.10 expounds who such an unrestricted application of πόρνοι would include: it would *include* the πόρνοι τοῦ κόσμου, but also the greedy, the robbers and the idolaters. So the command μὴ συναναμίγνυσθαι πόρνοις, if read in the unrestricted sense, not only *implies* a withdrawal from the κόσμος, but would *explicitly command* such a withdrawal. ὁ κόσμος and οἱ πόρνοι become referential equivalents.

The result is that although Paul countenances eating with outsiders, it is precisely *as* outsiders that the believer is permitted to interact with them. They are eating with the enemy: dining in full consciousness of the difference in social identity with its related ethical stereotype. Paul's social permissiveness thus does not diminish, but paradoxically reinforces the boundary. To use Tajfel's language, the salience of the group identity is raised, so that the inter-individual encounter, although permitted, becomes an intergroup encounter.

For Paul, however, group identity may prohibit some types of intergroup interaction. We shall later examine his attitude to interaction with outsiders as judges (section 5.2), or as marriage partners (section 9.5).

4.5.2. *Relations with Apostates*

Despite Paul's contention that the offender is an outsider, and despite the fact that both outsiders and such offenders are designated πόρνοι, 5.9–13 indicates that Paul does draw some distinction between the fallen brother and the regular outsider.

In 5.11 the so-called ἀδελφός is declared to be an unsuitable dining companion. Indeed anyone called a brother but shown by their unethical identity (as a πόρνος πλεονέκτης εἰδωλολάτρης λοίδορος ...) to be an outsider is to be denied table fellowship with believers.[69] Thus, the believer's relations with such people are not identical to his relations with

---

69. The command not to eat with such a person would certainly include the Lord's Supper (indeed it may possibly have such primarily in view). However, in view of Paul's concern to state that such an injunction does not apply to eating with outsiders in general, whom Paul would hardly wish admitted to the Lord's Supper, the call not to eat must have wider social implications.

outsiders in general. Although numbered among the outsiders, the false-brother is not simply treated as a 'sinner or tax-collector', but singled out for a particular type of social ostracism. We can only postulate why this might be the case. Perhaps since the baptismal division that divides insider from outsider has been violated by the pseudo-ἀδελφός, and can no longer divide this particular outsider from believers, a new boundary is required: a boundary unnecessary in the case of the πόρνοι τοῦ κόσμου.

4.6. *Conclusion*

We have demonstrated that the ethical dichotomy is crucial for Paul's construction of Christian identity. It both defines who believers are, and how they differ from outsiders, and does so in a manner that ensures the positive social identity of the Christian community. The fact that the Christian sexual ethic shares its condemnation of incest with the outside world matters little. The fact that one insider notoriously offends against this shared norm also fails to falsify Paul's dichotomy. Yet this offence matters, for it nevertheless endangers that dichotomy. This is evident in Paul's attempt both to end the aberration (by exclusion from the social group) and to explain the aberration (by insisting that this can be no true insider).

As we have seen, Paul's strategy for ensuring compliance assumes that that no believer would wish to be associated with πορνεία. The Corinthian toleration of the offender thus suggests that their individual social identities were not derived to any great extent from their membership of the believing community. As we observed in the previous chapter, Paul's rhetoric in 1 Corinthians 1–4 sets out to alter this situation. It attempts to increase the 'cognitive, evaluative and emotive' aspects of group belonging: to increase the awareness and the importance to believers of their Christian identity. 1 Corinthians 5 plays on this. Christian social identity matters and the immoral man endangers this. He associates the community, and its members, with πορνεία. He endangers the reputation of the church.

We have also generated questions that require to be answered. The incest is incompatible with Christian identity: but does it only reveal an offender as a false Christian, or does it deconstitute his Christian identity? What is it about the incest that declares the offender to be an outsider? Would any act of πορνεία have the same effect? Is πορνεία a unique sin? What difference does this dichotomy make to social interactions with outsiders? Such interaction may not necessarily be forbidden, but how might viewing insiders as stereotypically moral and outsiders as immoral affect such interaction? What types of interaction might it prohibit? We shall attempt to answer these questions as we proceed.

Chapter 5

Lawsuits before the ἄδικοι (6.1–11)

5.1. *Introduction*

At first glance 1 Cor. 6.1–11 appears to be a digression from the dominant theme of chs 5–7. There is no mention of πορνεία; indeed no mention of sexual ethics at all (except in the list of 6.9–10). Certainly, the placing of the discussion of lawsuits in the context of 1 Corinthians 5–7 may *prima facie* give some support to the suggestion that Paul is referring to litigation somehow connected to sexual relations. However, despite attempts by a number of scholars to generate reconstruction on this basis, no credible hypothesis has yet been offered.[1] Notwithstanding this, many of the themes that we have detected in 5.1–13 can be found in this passage.

This passage, like 5.1–13, has to do with the group dichotomy (6.1–6 and esp. 6.9–13). On its basis Paul prohibits believers having recourse to outsiders as judges (6.1–6). Indeed, on its basis, he discourages a believer seeking any redress whatsoever against his fellow ἀδελφός (6.7). (Presumably he may sue an outsider.) The identity of both the defendant and the adjudicator, as believer and outsider respectively, should determine the offended believer's attitude and relationship to them. We

---

1. Bernard (1917) suggested that the lawsuit was instigated by the father of 5.1, who sued his son for adultery. Deming (1996) suggested a similar prosecution, brought by a group within the church who have become frustrated by the community's failure to discipline the offender. Both of these suggestions are beset with difficulties. Against Bernard is the fact that Paul does not relate the incest to an offence against the father (who would need to be a believer) in 5.1–13. Against Deming is the lack of evidence that the Corinthians were divided in their toleration of the man. Against both stands the fact that Paul relativizes the issue of the lawsuit as βιωτικά: would he have described incest as such? Could Paul describe suffering incest (6.7) as better than bringing a lawsuit? It can hardly be thought so.

Richardson (1983; cf. Wire 1990: 75–76) has offered a variety of reconstructions that seek to link the lawsuit to ch. 7: thus he suggests some possible disputes between ascetic and non-ascetic believers over marriage or sexual duties. However, he fails to present a developed argument for any of these possibilities. Having rejected these suggestions, nonetheless, it is not impossible that the case does have some connection to family relations in general: many civil cases involved inheritance disputes (cf. Chow 1992: 125–26).

may contrast this with Paul's permissive attitude to social interaction with outsiders in 5.9–11.

In this passage, as in 5.1–13, Paul and the Corinthians (or certainly those involved in litigation) appear to have differing understandings of the social implications of Christian identity. Paul again has attempted to create a positive Christian social identity so that Christian identity becomes salient in a growing number of social relations (in this case legal relations) with insiders and outsiders. Again, as in 5.1–2, Paul uses the language of corporate failure (6.5, 6.7) to shame the Corinthians into compliance with his instructions.

But this passage has also to do with ethics. Ethics are the basis of the group dichotomy (quite obviously in 6.9–11). Further, we have in this passage once more to do with the ethical failure of some believers (6.8). We may compare and contrast this with Paul's treatment of the immoral man in the previous chapter.

Our study of this text will focus on the part played by ethics. In particular, what does 6.9–11 – with its insistence on the ethical difference between insider and outsider – contribute to Paul's instructions? How does Paul attempt to make Christian identity matter in the choice of judge and in the attitude to those who might offend against a believer? Further, bearing in mind the questions we left open at the end of the last chapter, we are interested in Paul's attitude to believers who have offended against their fellows. What impact might this have on their status as insiders? How does this compare with the fate of the offender of 5.1–13? Does the type of ethical breach, of which Paul here complains, serve either to falsify or destroy Christian identity, as πορνεία does for the offender of 5.1–13?

5.2. Objectionable Judges

5.2.1. Unjust or Unjustified?
Paul begins this section by prohibiting, or better (in view of the outraged τολμᾷ) condemning, the practice of ἅγιοι taking their disputes for arbitration before ἄδικοι. Most commentators view Paul's objection (and thus the basic meaning of ἄδικος simply to be that these judges are outsiders.[2] However, Winter has rejected the notion that the objection to the use of the local magistrate proceeds on the basis of the group dichotomy alone. He views a categorical rejection of the competency of the state authority as impossible for the author of Romans 13, which portrays the magistrate as the servant and instrument of God. Winter offers evidence that the Corinthian magistrates may be considered to be

---

2. E.g. Barrett 1971: 135; Conzelmann 1975: 104; Fee 1987: 232.

particularly corrupt and partial, and he suggests that this is the reason Paul labels them ἄδικοι, rather than because of their status as outsiders.[3] Paul's objection to the judges is thus limited to the moral character of these particular courts, rather than being a principled rejection of outsiders as judges.

However, two factors count heavily against Winter. First, Paul shows no apparent concern for the justice of the verdict that believers might receive in the courts. Secondly, the structure of 6.1–6 reveals conclusively that Paul is referring to outsiders as a class in 6.1. Having set up the ἄδικοι/ἄγιοι contrast (6.1), Paul proceeds to juxtapose the status of the ἄγιοι with that of the κόσμος (6.2–3).[4] It is difficult not to conclude that κόσμος is an outgroup designator. Then, in 6.6, he returns to state that ἀδελφόι litigate before ἄπιστοι. Here ἄπιστοι is most certainly an outgroup designator. 6.1 and 6.6 thereby form an *inclusio*, indicating that ἄδικοι is primarily a referent to the judges as outsiders.[5]

However, insisting that ἄδικοι does refer to outsiders does not mean that it is to be read merely as a synonym for ἄπιστοι as most commentators suppose. Barrett, for instance, argues that οἱ ἄδικοι and οἱ ἄγιοι mean no more than 'non-Christian' and 'Christian' so that ἄδικοι 'is to be taken not in a moral sense but in a religious sense – not justified, not rightly related with God through Christ'.[6] This appears extremely unlikely. The δίκαιος word-group is too closely associated with those moral properties required for the proper administration of justice for the choice of this particular term to be so incidental.[7] Significantly, other than in 1 Cor. 6.1–11, Paul never uses ἄδικοι to refer to unbelievers. Indeed, in all the attributed letters, there is only one other instance where Paul refers to anyone as an ἄδικος and that instance is significant. In Rom. 3.5 he asks the rhetorical question as to whether God is an ἄδικος in regard to his judgment of human

---

3. Winter 1991. Thiselton (2000: 419) suggests that the injustice of the local magistrates is a 'major factor' in Paul's objection. Winter's case is developed by Clarke (1993: 59–71) who suggests that the Corinthian courts were used by those of high status to protect and enhance their social standing, and that those of low status had little chance of justice.

4. Adams (2000: 128) notes, 'The distinction between οἱ ἄγιοι and κόσμος in v.2 mirrors the distinction between οἱ ἄγιοι and οἱ ἄδικοι in the previous verse. It can thus be inferred that ὁ κόσμος is contextually synonymous with οἱ ἄδικοι.'

5. As Robertson and Plummer (1914: 110), 'The term reflects, not on Roman tribunals, but on the pagan world to which they belonged.'

6. Barrett 1971: 135, similarly Conzelmann (1975: 104 n. 12) and Fee (1987: 232). The latter insists that Paul 'does not intend to demean the Roman courts'.

7. Especially when we consider the use of technical legal terms in this passage (πρᾶγμα, κρίνω, κριτήριον, καθίζω). (On which see Fee 1987: 231.)

wickedness. Being an ἄδικος is thus connected to the status of being an unjust judge.[8]

Further, as Rosner has shown, being δίκαιος is the basic qualification that Jewish scripture demands of the judge.[9] And, despite the widespread evidence of corruption and partiality among the magistrates of Graeco-Roman society, we can hardly imagine that any upstanding gentile would not consider such a quality desirable.

Thus ἄδικος is not simply a designation of the outsider (one who is unjustified), but it also carries ethical connotations (one who is unjust). These judges are being presented as members of a group that is inherently and stereotypically unethical, a point that is underlined in 6.9 where the ἄδικοι are both identified as those who lack eschatological salvation and as those defined by their sins. It is not only the membership of the outgroup category, but also the ethical stereotype of that category that functions to disqualify such people as arbiters. Who, after all, in their right mind, elects to submit their case to an unjust judge? Such a judge lacks the basic quality valued in a legal adjudicator: that he be δίκαιος.

5.2.2. The Shame of the Community

The prohibition, then, is based directly on the group dichotomy with all its ethical overtones. ἅγιοι and not ἄδικοι should arbitrate disputes between ἀδελφόι (6.1). This dichotomy is developed in 6.2–3, where the separate role of the ἅγιοι in eschatological judgment provides the rationale for their competency to judge βιωτικά in the present. Indeed, the eschatological role of believers is such that the notion that they are presently incompetent to judge can be ridiculed. Implicitly their competency is being asserted over and against that of the ἄδικοι judges. The future role of the ἅγιοι both gives competency to their judgment and renders the submission to worldly judges improper, as such judges lack this eschatological role, and are paradoxically the objects of the judgment. As Fee concludes: 'The absurdity of the Corinthian position is that the saints will someday judge the very world before whom they are now appearing and asking for a judgment'.[10]

The parallelism of 6.2 and 6.3 thus serves to build up the competence and status of the believers in future and present judgments in contradis-

---

8. ἄδικος is in fact a relatively rare term in the NT. Aside from Heb. 6.10 (which is akin to Rom. 3.5) and the three Pauline uses cited above, it appears only on seven occasions. Luke uses it once in a Pauline speech where it might just possibly be without ethical implications (Acts 24.15). However, his three other uses (Lk. 16.9–11; 18.11) simply refer to dishonest persons, who are not even necessarily unbelievers (also Mt. 5.45). Although it is used in 1 Pet. 3.18 and 2 Pet. 2.9 to denote outsiders, the ethical implication is clearly to the fore.

9.   Rosner 1994: 107, referring to Deut. 16.18–20a; Exod. 23.6–8; Lev. 19.25; 1 Sam. 8.3; Isa. 5.23; 32.1; Mic. 3.9.

10. Fee 1987: 230.

tinction to outsiders.[11] This leads directly into the irony of 6.4–5. Here Paul suggests that recourse to outside judges indicates that Corinthians regard none of their number fit to judge.[12] Implicitly he accuses the Corinthians of failing to understand their eschatological role and its current implications. (His three-fold ἢ οὐκ οἴδατε ὅτι question should be answered by them in the negative!) Explicitly he questions any claim they may have to σοφία.

Paul's move in 6.2–5 thus does two things. It attempts to instil in the Corinthians a high view of Christian identity, particularly in relation to their competency to judge. But it also claims that the Corinthian actions (in their recourse to unbelieving judges) bring their understanding of Christian identity into question. While their failure does not invalidate their eschatological position, it does invalidate their claim (presumably important to them) to have in their number any who possess sufficient σοφία.

The rhetorical strategy is akin to that employed in 5.1–8. Paul's high notion of the community and its ethical/eschatological status, and the Corinthians' failure to act in accordance with Paul's view of that status, are utilized to knock down the Corinthians' pride in their version of who they are, and what makes them important.

This shaming tactic also serves to turn what may be seen as a private dispute between two individuals into a community problem. For these individuals to use an outsider to judge, casts the whole community in a poor light. Not only are the actions of the parties inappropriate, but their occurrence indicates that none of the Corinthians are σοφοί.[13] The positive social identity offered by a true understanding of the group dichotomy (6.2–3) is called into question.

---

11. Whichever way we read τούτους ἐξουθενημένους ἐν τῇ ἐκκλησίᾳ τούτους καθίζετε (6.4) – whether as a question, an ironic suggestion or an accusation – it serves to reiterate the group dichotomy. Either it is stating that even those believers 'least esteemed by the church' are, by virtue of the eschatological role of the church, more competent to judge than the best pagan magistrate, or it is suggesting that the pagan magistrate, to which the brothers submit their dispute, is, by virtue of the outgroup's low eschatological status, lacking in any competence in the eyes of the church.

12. *Pace* Rosner (1994: 94–122) Paul's point here is hardly to appoint judges, but, taken in entirety, is to avoid lawsuits among believers, and particularly before outsiders. If internal arbitration is suggested it is a concession, the necessity for which still constitutes a defeat (6.7). It is not an 'attractive solution' (A.C. Mitchell 1993: 567). Paul's remarks in 6.4–5 are designed primarily to highlight the irony of believers using ἄδικοι judges rather than to provide a program for alternative interior adjudication.

13. Theissen (1982: 97) suggests that the claim to be σοφοί hints at the high status of the litigants, who consider themselves among the wise, but there appears no reason to limit the term in this manner.

5.3. Litigious Brethren

In 6.7–8 Paul goes further, and makes a separate observation on the community's failure: the very existence of lawsuits, regardless of the manner of settlement, is an indication of defeat (ὅλως ἥττημα) and should serve to shame the community. They are inappropriate in view of the common status and close relationship of the litigants. Paul underlines this by the shift of the designator from ἅγιος to ἀδελφός when he speaks either of the pursuer or defendant (6.1; 6.6; 6.8). Thus, just as it is categorically improper for ἄδικοι to judge ἅγιοι, it is improper for an ἀδελφός to sue an ἀδελφός.[14] Group membership again serves to control behaviour.

Even before the verdict of the court is pronounced, the lawsuit already amounts to a defeat. Why is this so? Perhaps 6.8 gives the reason. The instigation of lawsuits offends against the Pauline principle of forgoing one's rights for the sake of a fellow brother (8.9, 9.12).[15] Better to be ἀδικεῖσθαι or ἀποστερεῖσθαι than to seek legal redress at a brother's expense. Or possibly 6.7b is not the reason for the defeat, but merely the cost. Lawsuits are a defeat as they are a sign of the σχίσματα that Paul has previously claimed are an indicator of corporate weakness (3.3). Thus it is better to suffer injustice than for the community to be so defeated. In any case, the defeat would seem not only to be that of the individual litigants but of the community as a whole (ὑμεῖς), compounding the shame caused by inability to provide a suitable arbiter. Thus again Paul insists that the acts of the individual believer impact on the whole community and show up its corporate weakness.

There is, however, more here. As 6.8 indicates, the existence of lawsuits presupposes that believers commit ἀδικία and ἀποστέρησις. Probably Paul has in mind here the offence that provokes the suit (or possibly 6.8 is the corollary of 6.7b, indicating the suit itself is an offence against the defending brother). In any case believers are associated with vice. The use of the same verbs, first in the passive, then in the active, serves to show how the same lawsuit is a double defeat for the church; one brother is wronged (and doesn't suffer it) and another wrongs. In no way can such behaviour be regarded as a private matter.

14. Rosner (1994: 108) demonstrates the common biblical objection to feuds and disputes between brethren (e.g. Gen. 13.6–13; Ps. 113.1). However the notion of the dysfunctionality of families who engage in litigation seems too universal to require such a Scriptural background as an explanation.

15. Much is made by commentators of the possible allusion to the non-retaliation ethic of Jesus in Mt. 5.38–42 and Lk. 6.27–31 (e.g. Fee 1987: 241; Witherington 1995: 166). Be that as it may, there is a closer parallel to such non-action in Paul's own attitude in 1 Cor. 4.12–13 (cf. 1 Thess. 5.15; Rom. 12.17).

5.4. *The Function of 6.9–11*

5.4.1. *Who are the* ἄδικοι?

This leads us into 6.9–11. Taken alone these verses serve to rearticulate the group dichotomy, with its ethical and eschatological boundary (reiterating 5.7b-8 and 6.2–3). They serve both to remind the believers that at their baptism they were called out of one lifestyle, and corresponding fate, to another, and to point out the present difference between ingroup and outgroup in regard to eschatology and ethics. In the context of the surrounding ethical discussion (5.1–7.40) it is easy to see how such a reminder serves to underline the command to adopt a different mode of behaviour (the imperative for Christian ethics), and to regulate interaction with outgroup members (part of the content of Christian ethics).

However, many commentators seem to pay too little attention to the function of this passage in the specific context of 6.1–8, often preferring to concentrate on the origin of the vice list, or the theology of baptism, or the details of the sins themselves.[16] Our interest here is specifically in its contextual function. The natural question here is: who are the ἄδικοι to whom Paul refers? There seem to be two, perhaps not mutually exclusive, ways of answering that question, which will lead us to two, perhaps not mutually exclusive, ways of viewing the function of the passage.

First we may take ἄδικοι as a reference back to the ἄδικοι of 6.1 to whom Paul, at the outset, forbade believers to have recourse for judgment. If taken this way, the passage serves as a closing rationale for the avoidance of litigation before outsiders. After a digression to suggest even disputes settled internally are undesirable (6.7–8), Paul returns to the initial point of his attack – the transgressing of the group boundary by setting up outsiders as judges. The rationale for avoiding pagan judges is precisely the status that they have as members of the ἄδικοι group: outside judges lack the positive eschatological fate of the believers; they will not 'inherit the kingdom'. Thus just as the eschatological role of judging the world gave believers a competency to be judges of βιωτικά among fellow believers in the present (6.2–3), so the fact that unbelievers do not inherit the kingdom underlies their eschatological difference and thus their incompetence to be judges between believers. But Paul now additionally brings in the ethical boundary marker to underline the negative status of outsiders and to stress the differential between them and believers. He does so by pointing out that believers, as those who are 'washed, justified and sanctified', are set apart from both the ethical identity and the eschatological fate of the ἄδικοι. The terms chosen verbally echo the group designations: ἁγιάζω – made a ἅγιος; δικαιόω – unmade an ἄδικος. This introduction of the ethical boundary marker was prefigured

---

16. E.g. Barrett 1971: 139 and Conzelmann 1975: 106.

in the group designations that Paul selected in 6.1. ἄδικος/ἅγιος carries the same sinner/sanctified dualism as 6.9–11. Thus the group boundary underlies the proscribed inter-group behaviour (using pagan judges). Only believers have been made δίκαιος, the basic quality required for judging.

Secondly we may take ἄδικοι with reference to those who commit ἀδικία mentioned in the previous verse,[17] and thus the whole as a warning against this type of behaviour.[18] Thus Paul continues with the thought of 6.8 rather than returning to 6.1–6.[19] Paul now engages in a clever play with concepts and words where ἀδικέω ἄδικος and δικαιόω (6.8, 9, 11) are used to stress both group status and corresponding behaviour differences.[20]

The three verbs used to indicate the change of status are most revealing. Paul states ἀλλὰ ἀπελούσασθε, ἀλλὰ ἡγιάσθητε, ἀλλὰ ἐδικαιώθητε, terms almost impossible to translate into English without losing their function and semantic connections with other terms in the passage. Despite attempts to understand a theological significance in the choice and order of these verbs,[21] they are best understood as being selected for the particular context.[22] Although all three are conversion metaphors, all carry specifically ethical overtones. They are emphasizing the change of status which, in Paul's mind, is not here primarily eschatological (from those who will not inherit, to those who will inherit), but ethical (from being numbered among those indicated by the vice list, to being a new people set apart). Additionally, the last two terms are particularly remarkable. ἡγιάσθητε relates to the status of being a ἅγιος, and ἐδικαιώθητε to no longer being an ἄδικος. Hence Paul reminds the Corinthians that their identity as either an ἄδικος or ἅγιος is formed in behavioural change. This at the very least should warn us against reading ἄδικος and ἅγιος as static designations of identity or standing before God (unjustified/saints), which merely carry ethical imperatives. Rather these terms function as much as behaviour labels as do πόρνος, λοίδορος and so on. Thus if one commits ἀδικία one cannot be said to be ἡγιάσθηναι, or ἐδικαιωθῆναι, and one may be

17. As A.C. Mitchell 1993: 569; Fee 1987: 242; R.F. Collins 1999: 235. Barrett (1971: 140) insists that the term is used here in a 'strictly moral sense' unlike in 6.1.

18. If so, it would neatly parallel Paul's thought in 1 Cor. 10.1–13 where those who were 'overthrown in the wilderness' did not inherit the Promised Land. 10.1–13 is most explicitly given as a warning 'do not desire evil as they did'.

19. This is strengthened by the fact that grammatically 6.9–11 are integral to 6.1–8. The ἤ that begins 6.9 indicates that this is no new start.

20. Fee (1987: 246 n. 33) speaks of Paul's 'wordplay' with the three terms.

21. K. Bailey (1980: 29–30) attempts to see a Trinitarianism lying behind their selection: Christ washes, Spirit Sanctifies, God justifies.

22. With Fee (1987: 246) 'each of these verbs is chosen for contextual, not dogmatic, reasons; and their sequence is theologically irrelevant'.

said to be an ἄδικος and not a ἅγιος. Here is a grave warning to those engaging in such activity.

5.4.2. *The Perseverance of the* ἅγιοι

As Gundry Volf states: 'no doubt ... Paul intends vv. 9–11 to exercise a reforming influence on his readers' conduct'.[23] Paul links their behaviour to the status, ethical and eschatological, of the outside world from which they have been delivered. In doing so he shows how inappropriate it is. The question is: is Paul merely reminding them that they have been delivered from this status of vice and disinheritance, and that as such their behaviour is inappropriate and constitutes a defeat (an imperative flowing from a certain indicative)? Or is he warning them that there is a real danger that those (believers) who practise ἀδικία may actually revert to the status and fate of the ἄδικοι?

Gundry Volf objects to the notion that Paul is motivating the believers by hinting at the possible loss of salvation, for a number of reasons.[24] First, that this would have Paul, in the same passage, asserting that believers will judge the world (6.2), and putting that eschatological role in doubt. The eschatological superiority presupposes the triumph of the believer. This objection, however, does not hold up. Eschatological judgment is explicitly a property of the ἅγιοι which does not in itself preclude the notion that one could cease to be a ἅγιος.

Gundry Volf's second objection is that Paul does not actually say that the Corinthians are in danger of losing their eschatological inheritance, but that the ἄδικοι will not inherit the kingdom.

> The designation ἄδικοι belongs to conventional terminology used in vice lists (cf., e.g., Luke 18.11), where it denotes unbelievers. In keeping with this conventional usage, in the present context οἱ ἄδικοι is synonymous with οἱ ἄπιστοι ... The view that Paul warns the Corinthians indirectly not to become ἄδικοι, however, requires the term to change meanings in the context: whereas it refers strictly to unbelievers at 6.1, at 6.6 [*sic*] it would have to mean 'wrongdoers including believers'. Since such a change in meaning is doubtful, the Corinthians could be included in οἱ ἄδικοι only if they are not Christians at all but actually ἄπιστοι.[25]

There are a number of problems here. As we have seen, οἱ ἄδικοι is not 'conventional terminology' for unbelievers! It is not Paul's usual term for outsiders, appearing uniquely in 6.1 and 6.9. Gundry Volf *claims* that it is used in vice lists, but the example she cites of Lk. 18.11 is in fact the only

---

23. Gundry Volf 1990: 133.
24. Gundry Volf 1990: 134.
25. Gundry Volf 1990: 135.

time it appears in a vice list in the entire New Testament,[26] and here it appears to mean 'swindler or cheat' rather than unbeliever.[27] She may be right to criticize Barrett who suggests that ἄδικοι functions here in a 'strictly moral sense'.[28] It is most certainly a group designation as well (as in 6.1). But it is not clear that it functions any less as a moral designation than other vice labels that denote the outgroup (πόρνοι, πλεονέκται, εἰδωλολάτραι, λοίδοροι, μέθυσοι).

The problem is with reading 6.1 as merely a static theological designation (ungodly, unjustified) and failing to see that it is also an ethical behavioural designation. If 6.1 is read with an ethical inference, then there is no need to postulate a change in meaning at 6.9, in order to see a threat that those who ἀδικεῖτε may become ἄδικοι. The view that such a warning would mean that ἄδικοι would have to mean 'wrongdoers including believers' misses the point, for the point is precisely that, if one becomes an ἄδικος by sharing in their ethics and thus their fate, by definition one would not be a believer.[29]

Gundry Volf concedes that 6.9 may possibly be a warning. However, she argues that Paul would be threatening 'some Corinthians whose conduct makes him suspect false profession of faith'.[30] The problem with this is that if, on basis of their behaviour, Paul believes some in the community may not truly be πιστοί, why does he not either call them to faith, or for the community to expel them (as with the immoral man)? But rather, Paul threatens such individuals in order to ensure a change in *behaviour*. This suggests that Paul does not only see wrong behaviour as revealing 'false profession', but is warning that wrong behaviour endangers one's status as insider, and that a timely change in behaviour may avert this danger. If there is a warning here, it is to those believers who ἀδικεῖτε, calling them to desist lest they share the fate and status of the ἄδικοι.[31]

There is, if read as a warning, a certain parallelism between ch. 5 and ch. 6.[32] He who committed πορνεία was redefined as a πόρνος and thus

---

26. See n. 8 above.

27. I.H. Marshall 1978: 679.

28. Barrett 1971: 140.

29. Unless 'believer' is taken as one who holds a particular set of convictions, but then it would surely embrace the pseudo-ἀδελφός of ch. 5.

30. Gundry Volf 1990: 136.

31. Cf. Fee (1987: 242), who complains of arguments akin to Gundry Volf's that this 'fails to take seriously the genuine tension of texts like this one. The warning is real; the wicked will not inherit the kingdom... By persisting in the same behaviour as those already destined for judgment [the Corinthians] are placing themselves in the very real danger of that same judgment'.

32. Also the vices with which Paul is concerned throughout chs 5 and 6, sexual sin and property matters (πορνεία and ἀδικία), seem to control the 'vice' list of 6.9–10.

no true ἀδελφός. Now he who commits ἀδικία is in danger of being redefined as an ἄδικος and thus no true ἅγιος. There is however a significant difference. The man committing πορνεία is a πόρνος thus an outsider, not to be rebuked but excluded, while those committing ἀδικία are warned, as those who are at present still members of the community.

5.5. *Conclusions*

Whereas in 5.9–13 social interaction was tolerated by Paul, but was to proceed with believers fully conscious of the group dichotomy (and particularly its ethical foundation), now that same dichotomy prohibits a particular type of social relation with outsiders (their use as judges). If the Corinthians are to see the dichotomy as salient in this social situation then the 'cognitive, evaluative and emotive' aspects of Christian group belonging require to be raised. Paul's narrative here seeks to do just that. The Corinthians are made aware of their group belonging and the non-belonging of outside judges. The description of the eschatological role and fate of each group, and the claims made about their respective ethical attributes, serves to ensure that group belonging is highly valued. Emotional commitment to the group is stressed in the language of fictive kinship, and warnings of corporate shame. Importantly, the aspects of the dichotomy that are stressed are those relevant to the discussion of the legal process: the role in judgment and the property of being δίκαιος.

We can also begin to answer the questions we left open at the end of the last chapter. Does an ethical breach only reveal that a man is no true insider, or can it destroy a valid Christian identity? Does any ethical breach falsify/destroy Christian identity, or was incest/πορνεία somehow unique? 6.1–11 seems to support the contention that ethical breaches can potentially deconstruct Christian identity. Those who commit ἀδικία are warned of the fate of the ἄδικοι. Yet they are only warned. This particular ethical breach has not (yet) destroyed their claim to be insiders. Thus it differs from the case of the incestuous man. We shall explore further the question as to whether and why πορνεία constitutes a unique sin in the next chapter.

Chapter 6

THE πόρνη AND THE πορνεία (6.12–20)

6.1. *Introduction*

Thus far we have seen how sexual ethics both construct and potentially deconstruct Christian identity. To take on Christian identity is to be transformed from the identity of the outsider, which is stereotypically marked by vice (6.9–11). Conversely, for a man to engage in πορνεία renders him a πόρνος and thus deprives him of his status as an ἀδελφός (5.1–13). This contrasts with believers who commit ἀδικία – such are warned that they could forfeit Christian identity, but are still regarded as Christians (6.1–11). Why is πορνεία treated differently from ἀδικία? Is this simply a matter of the seriousness of the individual cases (habitual incest vs. minor fraud?) or is πορνεία a different kind of sin? This question will concern us as we consider 6.12–20. We shall examine how Paul relates sexual sin to his construction of the Christian body. What is it about the Christian body that makes union with the πόρνη problematic? How does the language of resurrection (6.13–14), membership of Christ (6.15), spirit-union with Christ (6.17–17) and the body-as-temple function (6.19)? What does Paul mean when he says that the sexual sinner sins uniquely εἰς τὸ ἴδιον σῶμα (6.18)?

We have also examined how ethical identity serves to control social behaviour. 5.9–13 permitted interaction with the πόρνοι τοῦ κόσμου, while not lessening the sense of the ethical difference between insider and outsider. 6.1–8 prohibited using outsiders as judges precisely on the basis that such were categorically unethical as ἄδικοι. Given that sexual relations are at the very least a form of social relations, what difference might the ethical identity of a sexual partner make to sexual interaction? 7.12–16 (cf. 7.39) evidences a discussion of the legitimacy of outsiders as marital partners. But can we learn anything from 6.12–20? Is it significant that Paul objects not only to πορνεία in general but specifically to sexual union with a πόρνη? What is the significance of designating the forbidden partner with this ethical label? Could the prohibition of intercourse with a πόρνη relate to her status as (a) an outsider and/or (b) one labelled immoral?

We are also concerned with how 6.12–20 relates to the rest of Paul's discourse. Traditionally it, along with 5.1–13, has been viewed as Paul's response to sexual libertinism among the Corinthians, and separated from 7.1–40 where Paul is seen to be responding to ascetic tendencies. But how certain is such a reconstruction? Does it hinder us exploring links between 6.12–20 and 7.1–40? Can 6.12–20 be used to illuminate Paul's concerns over sex and the body in 7.1–40 and *vice versa*? This particular possibility is one we shall explore in this and subsequent chapters.

We shall proceed as follows. First (6.2), we shall consider the context and function of 6.12–20 within the epistle. In 6.3, we shall investigate the opening discussion of ἐξουσία (1 Cor. 6.12). What does it reveal about the respective attitudes of Paul and the Corinthians to sexual behaviour? How does it relate to the rest of the discussion? Then in 6.4, we shall explore why and how Paul attempts to differentiate sex from food (1 Cor. 6.13–14). In 6.5, we shall consider Paul's presentation of intercourse with the πόρνη and union with the Lord as mutually exclusive options for the believer (1 Cor. 6.15–17). Why are these two possibilities viewed as mutually exclusive? What does the language of 'membership', 'union' and 'oneness' entail? 6.6 will consider 6.18–20. What does Paul mean by a sin εἰς τὸ ἴδιον σῶμα? How does the temple metaphor illuminate his understanding of the body? Finally we shall examine the identity of the πόρνη (6.7), before arriving at our final conclusions (6.8).

6.2. *The Background and Context of 6.12–20*

As was noted in the introduction, 5.1–13 and 6.12–20 on the one hand and 7.1–40 on the other have invariably been interpreted against their situational backgrounds, as responses to Corinthian libertinism and asceticism respectively. This reconstruction of such diverse backgrounds for the sections has discouraged attempts to read the whole as Pauline theology, and has often meant that key sentiments of the text have been attributed not to Paul but to his Corinthian opponents.

While the primary purpose of our study is not to reconstruct the ideology and practice of the Corinthian congregation, since convictions about the background have been so influential on interpretations of the text, it is necessary that we pay some attention to the context into which Paul writes. We began this process in section 4.2.4 when we questioned the likelihood of a principled libertine stance lying behind 5.1–13. We shall now (section 6.2.2) relate that finding to 6.12–20. In subsequent chapters we shall also examine and question the evidence for an ascetic background to 7.1–40. However, prior to this, the case for re-examining the reconstructions can be strengthened by asking one simple question: could libertinism and asceticism easily co-exist in the same congregation?

6.2.1. *A 'Dubious Schizophrenia'[1]*

Many, indeed perhaps most, modern commentators answer this question in the affirmative. Supposed parallels with reports of both asceticism and licentiousness in second-century Gnostic movements are taken as evidence (whatever the relevance of actual Gnosticism to Corinth[2]) that a theology that devalues the physical body could underpin both an anti-sex ethos and a denial of the moral relevance of physical acts.[3] The Corinthian Christians can then be said to share a common theological anthropology but practise two (contradictory) ethics.

Asceticism is undeniably found among Gnostic groups. The problem is that, as is now commonly admitted, the evidence for libertinism within Gnosticism (or indeed any other early Christian group) is suspect.[4] In truth, all we have are the allegations of the Gnostics' patristic opponents. Even after the extensive finds at Nag Hammadi there exists no internal Gnostic witness to libertinism. Perhaps the Fathers were not totally inventive, perhaps there were some notorious sex scandals among the Gnostics, but even if this were the case, it would not be evidence of an ideologically-based libertine 'movement' among them. Thus, no historical parallel can be established for what is postulated at Corinth – libertinism and asceticism coexisting in the same (small?) community.

Further, 1 Corinthians nowhere indicates that there exists such a fundamental division among the Corinthians with regard to sex. Paul appears to discuss sex and marriage with the whole church, and never attempts to point out such a basic inconsistency in the behaviour or arguments of the community. There is no talk of community divisions in 5–7. Goulder astutely observes that 'Paul himself would surely have exploited the difference. We might have expected him to say, "How can you condone whoredom and at the same time submit to demands for celibacy?" '[5]

If simultaneous libertinism and asceticism are unlikely, then there exists the possibility that the Corinthians were either libertine but not ascetic,[6]

---

1. The description is Deming's (1995: 29).

2. On which see 7.3.4 below.

3. For a recent proponent of this traditional hypothesis see Schrage who, although not so sure of a direct Gnostic influence, postulates the same ideological background. 'Eine entscheidende, überall und auch in Korinth zugrundeliegende Voraussetzung sowohl des Libertinismus wie auch der Askese ist eine negatives σῶμα-Verständnis, das denn auch gerade in 6,12ff frontal angegriffen und zürückgewiesen wird, wenn auch ohne den sonst meist erkennbar werdenden mythologischen Hintergrund' (1995: 15).

4. See Grant 1981: 161–70; 1983: 180; Deming 1996: 292–93 and esp. Broek 1983: 49–50.

5. Goulder 1999: 337.

6. As championed by Schmithals (1971), who argues for Jewish-Gnostics who stand 'against continence and for divorce when desired' (234). 1 Cor. 7 is then not a polemical attack on ascetics, but commending marriage to the libertines and prohibiting divorce.

or ascetic but not libertine.[7] It is thus necessary to examine the merits of both of these hypotheses independently. We begin in this chapter by scrutinizing the evidence for libertinism; we shall deal with the ascetic hypothesis in later chapters.

6.2.2. *Libertines?*

The usual structure of the libertine hypothesis is to present the offender's incest in 5.1–13 as just one of many cases of sexual immorality among the Corinthians, of which the resort to prostitutes of 6.12–20 proves to be another example, and then to postulate that these cases of πορνεία are being motivated or justified by theological argumentation.[8] Hence there is a libertine group whose slogan is πάντα μοι ἔξεστιν, and who probably base their arguments on the irrelevance of the acts of the transitory physical body for Christian existence. Paul's response, then, is first to order the expulsion of the most blatant example of libertine excess, before moving to tackle simultaneously the use of prostitutes and the ideology that formed the 'root of the trouble',[9] in 6.12–20.

Such theories do have some appeal. They explain a number of links – between πορνεία and boasting in 5.1–9; between 5.1–13 and 6.12–20; between 6.12 and 6.13–14; and between chs 5–6 and the mention of πορνεία in 7.2 – and ground the explanations in a reconstruction of the situation behind the entire letter. As we have seen, the reconstruction of a sexually libertine group is most often linked to the supposed asceticism that Paul encounters in 7.1–40, and both are held to be due either to some form of an over-realized eschatology or to a Gnostic or proto-Gnostic influence.

However, not only are there no secure historical parallels for a principled libertinism, these are various other problems with this hypothesis. First, aside from the incest of 5.1, there is no certain evidence of sexual misconduct at Corinth. Significantly Paul does not actually accuse the Corinthians of frequenting brothels in 6.12–20. It is at least possible that πόρνη-union is introduced as a *reductio ad absurdum* of a Corinthian assertion of ἐξουσία and/or of an anthropology that denied the significance of bodily acts (tackled by Paul in 6.12–13).[10] If Paul

---

7.   As argued by Kempthorne (1967), Deming (1996) and Goulder (1999). 6.12–20 is then not a response to a general libertine tendency, but to the one specific case of the immoral man.

8.   The syntax of 5.3–4 is often taken here so that τὸν οὕτως τοῦτο κατεργασάμενον has acted ἐν τῷ ὀνόματι τοῦ κυρίου Ἰησοῦ (5.3–4) indicating a theological justification for the offence (so A.Y. Collins 1980: 253). However, in context the invocation is better read as authority for either the community gathering, or the expulsion.

9.   Barrett 1971: 143.

10.   As Hurd 1965: 164, 277–78; Meeks 1983: 129; and Yarbrough 1984: 96–97.

thought that believers were having intercourse with πόρναι then it is difficult to understand why he does not react in a more forceful tone and demand the discipline/expulsion of the offenders as in 5.1–13.[11] Of course the existence of actual πόρνη-union among the Corinthians and the existence of a libertine movement do not stand or fall together. However, the uncertainty as to the existence of instances of union with πόρναι significantly weakens the evidence for an outbreak of licentiousness among the Corinthians, and thus justifies us in calling into question the veracity of the libertine hypothesis in its entirety.

More damaging, however, is that the structure of the text itself will not support the libertine hypothesis. That 5.1–11 precedes 6.12–20 is most significant, for if the Corinthians contended that 'all things were lawful' and revelled in their immorality, why does Paul believe that he can shame them by pointing to that immorality before he attacks their arguments for celebrating it? As we have seen (4.2.4), Paul appears to assume the sinfulness and shamefulness of the act that he cites in 5.1. He could not safely make this assumption were the Corinthians denying such.

Certainly there is a link being made in 5.1–8 between the offender and the Corinthians being πεφυσιωμένοι, but who is making the link, and why? Given that Paul can assume the sinfulness of πορνεία in 5.1–11, it would seem more reasonable to hold that it is Paul who links this offence with their unwarranted pride.[12] He seeks to deflate their spiritual pride by pointing out an unarguable incongruity between their claimed power and their failure to exercise power against the offender (cf. 4.17–21).[13]

This strategy is one used before in the letter. In 3.1–4 Paul falsified claims to spiritual status by pointing to the incontrovertible fact of factions (his evidence already cited in 1.11–12), which allowed him to compare them with the non-believing outgroup.[14] The same strategy is found in 4.19–5.2: a reference to Corinthian claims, and then a negative

---

11. It is also tempting to make something of the fact that Paul answers his own question 'shall I take the members of Christ and make them members of a πόρνη' with μὴ γένοιτο, using a negative response to a (outrageous) rhetorical question. However, to say that in 6.15 the question is rhetorical says little about the likelihood that Christians are resorting to prostitutes. It is the phrasing of the question, rather than the activity itself, which makes the answer so obvious.

12. That nothing in ch. 5 implies that libertarianism has caused the boasting is generally conceded (e.g. Barrett 1971: 122; Meeks 1983: 129; Fee 1987: 201–202; Clarke 1993: 87).

13. Thus we hold, with Yarbrough (1995: 90 n. 4) that the Corinthians are taking pride in their knowledge and spiritual ability (as 4.8) and simply do not see that their lack of action against the man serves to discredit their spiritual claims.

14. See above 3.3.3.

intergroup comparison based on evidence of incontrovertible failings. It occurred again in 6.1–8, where the lawsuits brought into question Corinthian pretensions: they are defeated and there is not even one σοφός among them.[15] In all three incidences Paul deflates Corinthian pride by pointing to obvious (and incontestable) weaknesses in the community's behaviour. Such a strategy would fail in 5.1 if the incident of πορνεία cited by Paul were held by the Corinthians to be the proof of, rather than evidence refuting, their spiritual claims.

The final piece of evidence given for the libertine hypothesis is the infamous maxim πάντα μοι ἔξεστιν (6.12), which has so often been seen as the slogan of the libertines. But, as we shall see (6.3), there are more satisfactory ways of understanding its function in 1 Corinthians 6.

6.2.3. *The Context of 6.12–20*

Thus, whereas the libertine hypothesis reads 5.1–13 in the light of 6.12–20, ignoring for the most part the significance of the order of the passages, it is better to read 6.12–20 in light of 5.1–13. What then was the issue in dispute in 5.1–13? It was not the sinfulness of πορνεία, but rather the effect that πορνεία has on the individual's Christian identity. The Corinthians continued to regard the sexual offender as an insider, failing to hold with Paul that his ethical practice repudiated his claimed status. They also failed to view the existence of a πόρνος within the community as a cause for concern. In short, while not viewing πορνεία as a positive or even a neutral activity, the Corinthians failed in Paul's eyes to take it seriously.

Paul has, in a sense, dealt first with the social and communal implications. In 5.1–8 he insisted on the expulsion of the offender on the grounds that a πόρνος had no place in the church. In 5.9–6.8 Paul deviated to deal with the social implications of the dichotomy between sanctified believers and unethical outsiders. 6.9, we have argued, was a transition point, where Paul, as well as underlining the group dichotomy and its social implications, hints at the effect of sin on the individual's identity. This is the issue that will continue to be discussed in 6.12–20: why sin, and specifically πορνεία, destroys Christian identity. We will thus argue that Paul is addressing an issue in 6.12–20, which we know from 5.1–9 exists between him and the Corinthians, the seriousness of sexual sin: not just why it is sinful – but why it is such a (uniquely?) serious infringement of Christian identity.[16] This reconstruction has the advan-

---

15. See above 5.2.2.

16. Thus we agree with D.B. Martin (1995: 175–76) that the Corinthians (or the 'strong') may not 'actually condone visiting prostitutes, but they certainly place such activities in the realm of misdemeanour'.

tage of allowing us to recognize that 6.9–11 is connected to 6.12–20, without making an unnatural textual and thematic division at 6.9.[17] It allows us to see a real dispute about the nature of πορνεία existing between Paul and his hearers in 6.12–20, which is in a sense 'the root of the trouble' of 5.1–9, without needing the libertine hypothesis, and without reading 5.1–13 in the light of the supposed conclusions of 6.12–20.

6.3. *The Question of* ἐξουσία *(6.12)*

6.3.1. Πάντα μοι ἔξεστιν

6.3.1.1. *Are all things lawful?* Whatever πάντα μοι ἔξεστιν may or may not have meant, it does not represent Paul's absolute position with regard to sexual ethics. For Paul all things are not permissible, as 5.1–8 and 6.9–11 clearly demonstrate. Certain activities define an identity incompatible with a Christian profession. Not even Augustine's 'love and do as you will' will suffice as a summary of Paul's ethics here.[18] As 6.12–20 will unambiguously reveal, πόρνη-union is first and foremost an offence against God and not against neighbour, or even self. To suggest that Paul's ethic is freedom tempered by love, or freedom constrained by the Spirit, rather than some form of normative rule against πορνεία, is to fall victim to reading Paul's anti-Torah rhetoric as opposition to law in general, and to miss the point that for Paul certain activities are simply innately wrong.[19]

The realization that Paul is unlikely to have found πάντα μοι ἔξεστιν an adequate summary of his position on πορνεία, or even a helpful starting point for the following discussion, leads naturally to the conclusion that this opening is forced upon Paul by his previous dialogue with the Corinthians. He has to deal with ἐξουσία because this particular concept is important to the Corinthians, and Paul believes that they have connected, or might connect, such to the discussion of πορνεία. However it is also probable that the Corinthian assertion of ἐξουσία takes as its starting point something that Paul has previously argued, which Paul now believes is being, or has the dangerous potential to be, misapplied to sex. If this is not the case, then, given Paul's absolute objection to πορνεία, it is difficult to see why Paul would not simply negate any claim to a universal

---

17. K. Bailey (1980) wishes to see 6.9–11 as part of the argument of 6.12–20 (so too Orr and Walther 1976: 198–204). Fee (1987: 240 n. 6), however, rightly observes that the grammar of 6.9 counts against this.

18. *Pace* the entire reading of Orr and Walther 1976: 202.

19. E.g. K. Bailey (1980: 30) states that Paul has the choice either of reverting to the rules of Torah, or of limiting the Corinthians by the notion of what is 'helpful'. With respect, he appears to have made the classic Lutheran *faux pas* of identifying 'the Law' with all law.

ἐξουσία (e.g. πάντα μοι ἔξεστιν; μὴ γένοιτο· ἄρας οὖν τὰ μέλη τοῦ Χροστοῦ ποιήσω πόρνης μέλη;).

There would seem good reasons to suppose that Paul had originally contended for the believer's ἐξουσία in the domain of foodstuffs and idols. ἐξουσία reappears at 8.9 (ἡ ἐξουσία ὑμῶν αὕτη) and in 10.23, in both occasions during the discussion of which foodstuffs are permissible and in what contexts. Here, although Paul places some limits on the use of the believer's freedom, he does maintain it in theory (unlike for sex in 6.12–20). Πάντα ἔξεστιν (10.23) really does mean one may eat πᾶν τὸ ἐν μακέλλῳ πωλούμενον (10.25) and πᾶν τὸ παρατιθέμενον ὑμῖν (10.27) at dinner as long as one eats πάντα εἰς δόξαν θεοῦ (10.31). (The repetition of πᾶς perhaps suggests that Paul is expounding and affirming the scope of the maxim in regard to food). Further, the discussion of ἐξουσία in 6.12 is followed by an attempt to differentiate sex from food and the body from the stomach (6.12–13). This is most readily understandable if the assertion of ἐξουσία was originally connected with a liberal attitude to questions of eating. Paul's choice in opening 6.12–20 with a discussion of ἐξουσία thus indicates that Paul is concerned lest a theology intended to underpin freedom in regard to foods be misapplied to sex. The danger is believed to be sufficiently present to require countering before the discussion of πορνεία can proceed.

However, if πάντα μοι ἔξεστιν, taken to its logical conclusion, cannot represent the Pauline position in regard to sex, then neither can it represent the Corinthians'. If *all* things were indeed lawful then by definition there could be *no* such thing as πορνεία. Yet, as we have noted, in 5.1–13 Paul assumed that the charge of πορνεία was one that served to shame the community, and that the label πόρνος would operate as a badge of deviance. Paul thus cannot believe that the Corinthians hold *all* things to be lawful.[20]

If not a countering an absolute Corinthian belief, then 6.12 is most probably opposing a Corinthian argument and most probably an argument that has taken Paul's assertion of ἐξουσία in regard to foodstuffs as its starting point (perhaps articulated by the maxim πάντα ἔξεστιν). As can be seen from the discussion at 5.9–11, the Corinthians were not averse to distorting or misinterpreting Paul's previous teaching. However, this does not necessarily mean that they accepted the misrepresented form of that teaching. In 5.9 there is no evidence that the Corinthians were avoiding the πόρνοι τοῦ κόσμου (understood as all outsiders), whom they appear to have claimed Paul was

---

20. Robertson and Plummer (1914: 121) rightly contend 'no sane person would maintain that it was meant to cover such things as πορνεία and justify πανουργίας'; but ironically this is precisely what they expect us to believe that the Corinthians maintained.

instructing them to avoid – indeed quite the contrary. Thus a Corinthian distortion of the meaning and scope of Pauline teaching on ἐξουσία (and perhaps a πάντα ἔξεστιν maxim) need not imply Corinthian libertinism, but could simply be an attempt to discredit Paul (by a similar *reductio ad absurdum* of his argument to that of 5.9–11), or to lessen the impact and gravity of his teaching on the subject of πορνεία. Paul thus strives to correct the interpretation and jurisdiction of his teaching before dealing with the issue in hand.

6.3.1.2. *Is Paul quoting the Corinthians?* Most commentators and translators have moved from reasoning similar to the above to the assumption that πάντα μοι ἔξεστιν should be placed in quotation marks.[21] It is held that Paul did not coin the expression for the purposes of argumentation in 1 Corinthians, but that it is a direct quotation from the Corinthian letter that Paul is addressing.[22] Paradoxically, however, these same commentators often attribute the formulation of the original maxim to Paul: Paul had used it, with a more restricted scope, in his previous teaching/correspondence on foods, and it is from this that the Corinthians have picked it up, applied it generally, and made it their own 'slogan' or 'catch-phrase'.[23]

While we can agree that Paul's rhetoric here grows out of his correspondence with the Corinthians, and the original concept of ἐξουσία is most probably the apostle's, the confidence with which commentators detect a quotation here does seem a little unmerited. Thus Omanson's complaint that 'interpreters usually do not state clearly how they have determined that Paul is quoting someone else's words' is most pertinent.[24]

Brian Dodd has usefully traced the history of interpretation of 6.12a through the commentaries of the last century or so, and shown how its attribution to the Corinthians has been a classic case of one scholar's suggestion becoming the next scholar's probability, and the final scholar's

---

21. For a demonstration of the almost total unanimity of commentators on this point see the table in Hurd (1965: 68). More recently, Fee (1987: 251) is 'almost' certain, while Thiselton (2000: 460) is certain of a citation (similarly Barrett 1971: 144; Schrage 1995: 17; R.F. Collins 1999: 243).

22. Goulder (1999: 345) will have it as the personal boast of the immoral man of 5.1–13. However, he can offer no convincing reason for his assertion.

23. Robertson and Plummer (1914: 121) will have it as Paul's own words current among the Corinthians as a 'trite maxim'. Conzelmann (1975: 109) sees it as derived from Paul's doctrine of freedom. Barrett (1971: 145 and similarly Schrage 1995: 17) holds out the possibility that these are Paul's own words now misused, while rejecting the notion, suggested by earlier commentators, that they were originally an anti-Jewish polemic (so Weiss 1910: 157).

24. Omanson 1992: 201.

fact.[25] In truth even the few reasons commentators have given for seeing a quotation here simply will not stand up to examination. *Contra* Weiss there is no grammatical reason to suppose such,[26] while Moffatt's fit between the sentiment of 6.12a and the moral laxity of ancient Corinth[27] evaporates with the reassessment of Strabo's evidence.[28] Commentators often point to the relationship between 6.12a's assertion of freedom and the ideology of the supposed libertines, as evidence that 6.12a must be a Corinthian quote. Thus 6.12a is 'the rallying cry of the libertines'[29] or the 'watchword of a gnostic party in Corinth'.[30] However, such an argument both assumes the existence of libertines, and neglects to note that since 6.12a, read as a citation, is key evidence for their existence, there is an inherent circularity in the logic.[31] Perhaps the strongest case for a citation can be made from the fact that the same phrase reappears at 10.23 – except that this is not exactly true. 10.23 simply asserts πάντα ἔξεστιν omitting 6.12a's μοι.

Of course the lack of evidence does not render the existence of a quotation impossible, merely unproven. If, as we have argued, Paul is countering a Corinthian ἐξουσία concept, we have no adequate reason to suppose that such has been articulated in the form πάντα μοι ἔξεστιν. However, given the repetition at 10.23 and the subsequent affirmation of the applicability of the word πᾶς to the food issue (10.25–32), we may have some reason to suspect that the truncated form πάντα ἔξεστιν has featured in previous Pauline-Corinthian dialogue. However, the μοι, if not the πάντα, would seem most probably a Pauline construct for the purpose of the present argument.

Thus, although we can agree with Meeks that the discourse is a 'corrective, second-order speech; that is, it takes up specific language or specific experiences known to the readers and reinterprets them' and that part of the language is probably Pauline, taken up by the Corinthians and 'interpreted in ways he finds unsatisfactory',[32] we can do so without requiring to postulate a verbatim citation. We may also, as Dodd has

---

25. Dodd 1999: 79–81.

26. Weiss (1910: 158) asserts that the lack of τοῦτο δέ indicates a citation, but this is without foundation. Indeed, as Dodd rightly observes (1999: 82), 32 known citations in 1 Cor. are marked by some introductory formula, against three unmarked (and these may not even be citations), so that the lack of an introductory formula speaks against rather than for a citation.

27. Moffatt 1938: 67.

28. See n. 118 below.

29. Héring 1962: 45.

30. Barrett 1971: 144; cf. Bruce 1971: 62.

31. Cf. Hurd (1965: 277) who dismisses the libertine thesis as an 'illusion' caused by taking 6.12 as an abstract Corinthian principle.

32. Meeks 1983: 122.

contended, regard the μοι as an indicator that 6.12 should be read as yet another example of Paul's use of the 'paradigmatic "I"' to enhance his teaching in the letter.[33]

Dodd himself totally rejects the notion of any citation at 6.12, seeing the whole as a Pauline construct, offering his self-example as a model to imitate. Thus Dodd follows those scholars who suggest that '6.12 has a formal place within the letter's strategy, taken as part of Paul's self-presentation of the free but self-restrained person with concern for community'.[34] The problem with this is, as we have already indicated, freedom tempered by community concern is neither an obvious starting point for, nor an adequate summary of, Paul's position on πορνεία. If Paul were free to construct his teaching without reference to a dialogical context it is difficult to see why he would begin with the sentiments of 6.12. Thus, while a healthy scepticism towards the existence of a Corinthian quotation should be maintained, more stress must be put on the attempt to mirror-read the dialogical context than Dodd allows.

We may thus surmise the following. Paul has previously contended, in the context of the food issues, for the ἐξουσία of the believer, perhaps (and we state it no stronger then this) using the formulation πάντα ἔξεστιν. Evidently the Corinthians have found this teaching agreeable, and have made much of their ἐξουσία (cf. Paul's reference to ἡ ἐξουσία ὑμῶν αὕτη in 8.9). Paul now sees the danger in a (perhaps mischievous) misapplication of such to the domain of sexual ethics (or perhaps this has actually occurred),[35] and so heads this off at the beginning of his teaching on πορνεία. He, Paul, has ἐξουσία over all things, but yet this freedom does not permit nor pertain to πορνεία. Indeed, as we know, the apostle is prone to offering the Corinthians his own self-controlled celibacy as a model for sexual abstinence (1 Cor. 7.7; 7.8; 7.40). If then the apostle's ἐξουσία is irrelevant to *his* sexual activity – how much more so that of his Corinthian children?[36] Thus πάντα μοι ἔξεστιν is both Paul presenting his

---

33. Dodd 1999: 78–90. Dodd points to uses at 1 Cor. 5.12; 6.12; 8.13; 10.28–11.2; 13.1–3; 14.15; 14.19.

34. Dodd 1999: 85.

35. By linking it to sexual ethics, the Corinthians could potentially turn Paul's ἐξουσία teaching against him in a number of ways. It could be used to undermine the seriousness of Paul's strenuous objection to πορνεία, which the Corinthians saw as more trivial. Alternatively it could perhaps be used to accuse Paul of antinomianism (a charge that he has frequently to rebut elsewhere, Rom. 3.8, 6.1). If the original Pauline assertion of ἐξουσία in regard to foods was offered in part as a justification for departing from the Torah's stipulations, then such a charge is both understandable and paralleled.

36. We might tentatively suggest paraphrasing 6.12 as follows:
'For me [too] "anything is permitted" – but not everything is beneficial
For me [too] "anything is permitted" – but I [unlike you?] will not be mastered by anyone.'

self-example, and simultaneously a thoroughly dialogical response to the Corinthians.

Who may be quoting whom is perhaps finally irrelevant. Wherever the truth may lie, the point is that, interpreted in the light of 5.1–6.20, πάντα μοι ἔξεστιν summarizes neither Paul's nor, taken at face value, the Corinthian position, to which he appears to be responding.[37] Neither holds *all* things to be lawful. We shall thus be safer limiting our interpretation of the exchange at 6.12 by the meaning of the entire passage, than falling into the error of interpreting the entire passage on the basis of the supposed logical conclusions of 6.12. The maxim seems forced into Paul's discussion by the situation, and since we do not know exactly what forces it upon him, it would seem more astute to concentrate on his response and rebuttal, rather than on speculative reconstructions of the details of the Corinthian arguments.

6.3.2. *Paul's Response to* πάντα μοι ἔξεστιν

Having argued that the maxim is peripheral to Paul's thought, introducing but not controlling this section, it is tempting to dismiss his immediate response to it as mere rhetoric, designed to refute a Corinthian assertion of ἐξουσία, and unlikely to reveal to us much of Paul's actual convictions. However, there are two strong reasons to suppose that such a move would be over hasty and that Paul's response may actually reveal to us much that is central to his convictions about sex. First, his response to the maxim here varies from that found in 10.23, indicating a crucial difference between Paul's attitude to food and to πορνεία, a difference that is expounded in 6.13–14. Secondly, the term ἐξουσία reappears in 7.4 in the context of marital sex and the believer's body, giving evidence that ἐξουσία, with which Paul here appears to play something of a word-game, actually reveals something about the apostle's attitude to the effects of sexual union on the believer's body. This is the first indication that there are connections between Paul's view of illicit sexual unions, and his understanding of marital unions. Granted, to make too much of a single, perhaps coincidental, verbal reoccurrence, would be dangerous. However, it will provide one piece of evidence, which we shall add to others, to produce a cumulative case for reappraising the apostle's central convictions on sexual union.

6.3.2.1. *The difference between sex and food (6.12 vs. 10.23).* In 10.23 Paul responds to the maxim in the following terms: Πάντα ἔξεστιν ἀλλ' οὐ πάντα συμφέρει· πάντα ἔξεστιν ἀλλ' οὐ πάντα οἰκοδομεῖ.

Here Paul limits ἐξουσία by concern for the good of the community. As

---

37. Thus Schrage's (1995) decision to discuss 6.12–20 under the heading of 'Freiheit und Sexualität' is wholly inappropriate (also Conzelmann 1975: 108).

Fee comments, the 'two qualifications in effect bring *exousia* to its knees'.[38] Συμφέρει is ambiguous in its reference but both οἰκοδομεῖ and the entire context of the discussion make it obvious that Paul is concerned with the benefit, not to the one asserting ἐξουσία, but to others and to the church. Individual assertion is limited by brotherly concern, as is shown in Paul's depreciation of his own apostolic 'right' to support (ἐξουσία again!) for the good of others and the church in 9.12 and 9.18.

This, however, is not Paul's line of argument against the maxim in 6.12:

Πάντα μοι ἔξεστιν ἀλλ' οὐ πάντα συμφέρει·

Πάντα μοι ἔξεστιν ἀλλ' οὐ ἐγὼ ἐξουσιασθήσομαι ὑπό τινος

The assertion of individual rights (μοι) is not here contradicted by concern for the other, but rather the concern with the individual continues throughout as Paul points to the destruction that the abuse of freedom can cause to a believer. *Contra* Fee,[39] there seems no good reason to define συμφέρει at 6.12 in the light of its parallel to οἰκοδομεῖ in 10.23, and every reason to define it exclusively in light of ἐξουσιασθήσομαι, and its context in 6.12–20: a context which unlike that of 10.23–30 concentrates on the danger of sin to the individual's relation to the Lord.

Despite the steady minority of scholars who wish to read 6.12–20 as Paul presenting πορνεία as an offence against the community[40] (as he does with πορνεία in 5.1–11 and ἀδικία in 6.1–6), there is no evidence of such. An attempt to shame the community (as 5.1, 6.5 etc.) is significant by its absence. To note the terms μέλος, σῶμα and ναός in 6.12–20, and to attempt to read into them the corporate metaphors, which they convey elsewhere, is to distort the passage and forget that here the physical σῶμα is in view, which is sufficient grounds to imply a different usage of the terms. Nor is there any concern here for other individuals. There is anxiety neither that another believer might be led into sin, nor for the πόρνη, and although Paul *can* make a moral argument on the basis of the duty owed to the spouse (7.3–4), here he chooses not to do so. Paul's response is both individualistic and Christocentric.[41] It is to do with the believer and his[42] relationship to Christ.

38. Fee 1987: 479, as also Robertson and Plummer 1914: 122.
39. Fee 1987: 252; cf. Thistelton 2000: 461–62, also Schrage 1995: 18–19: 'Das συμφέρον ist folglich die οἰκοδομή der Gemeinde bzw. die Agape'.
40. E.g. Kempthorne 1967.
41. Rosner (1994: 126) speaks of the 'decidedly theocentric orientation to the problem of πορνεία'.
42. In view of the fact that Paul goes on to speak specifically of πόρνη-union, he probably has the male solely in mind.

6.3.2.2. *The similarity between* πορνεία *and marriage (6.12 vs. 7.4)*. In Paul's response to the maxim ἀλλ' οὐ ἐγὼ ἐξουσιασθήσομαι ὑπό τινος we also find the first hints of his own convictions about the body of a believer and sex. The ἐξουσία, which the believer enjoys, can be lost or reversed if something or someone (τίνος) is allowed to exercise ἐξουσία over him. Freedom given, if misused, can lead to the end of that freedom in a new and undesirable slavery: slavery in this context caused by πορνεία (or perhaps by the πόρνη).

The notion of being mastered by τίνος obviously leads into the proceeding discussion of πορνεία and its effect on the believer, and it is possibly πορνεία that Paul has in view as the agent of mastery. However, even if this is so, as we shall see, πορνεία is a mastery for Paul, not by some notion of it being an addiction or an abstract denial of freedom, but because it sets up a new lordship over the body. That lordship compares and conflicts with the Lordship of Christ, and has to do not with vice so much as with the sexual partner who is given a claim on the body through sexual union. It is thus perfectly possible, both grammatically and contextually, that τίνος refers to 'someone', such as the πόρνη of 6.15–17, who gains power over the body of the believer through sexual union.[43]

In 1 Corinthians 7 we learn that the marital union places sexual obligations on a spouse and gives rights to their partner (7.3), but more interestingly that this is a result of an ἐξουσία exercised over the body of the believer: ἡ γυνὴ τοῦ ἰδίου σώματος οὐκ ἐξουσιάζει ἀλλὰ ὁ ἀνήρ, ὁμοίως δὲ καὶ ὁ ἀνὴρ τοῦ ἰδίου σώματος οὐκ ἐξουσιάει ἀλλὰ ἡ γυνή.

The partner is given an ἐξουσία over the body, which denies the ἐξουσία of the believer. He (or she) is, one might say, mastered (ἐξουσιάζεσθαι) by the spouse. It is also envisaged that only one person may hold ἐξουσία over the believer's body: if granted to a spouse, it is removed from the individual.

In 7.3–4 the mastery-by-spouse is, of course, not negatively evaluated. It is an inevitable consequence of marriage, and the spouse is not to resist its sexual implications. The assertion of the undesirability of mastery and corresponding loss of ἐξουσία mentioned in 6.12 thus (almost certainly) has πορνεία (or union with a πόρνη) in view and not marriage or sexual unions in general. But already we can see something which we will observe again throughout 6.12–20: *in the context of denouncing* πορνεία, *Paul gives*

---

43. As Kempthorne (1967: 569) and Goulder (1999: 344). Kempthorne and Goulder suggest that Paul is generalizing, from the fact that the immoral man of 5.1 has allowed the γύνη πατρος to have authority over him, to a general prohibition. They then suggest that the πόρνη of 6.15 is this same immoral woman. Such a precise identification seems unlikely (there is no reference to the case or solution of 5.1–11). However, as we shall argue later (6.7), it remains possible that the imperative to avoid πόρνη-union is broad enough to encompass the case of 5.1–11.

rationales, which if taken more generally, would serve also to prohibit marriage.

However negatively Paul's attitude to marriage is viewed, evidently he does not equate it to πορνεία. The spouse's mastery of their partner's body is not condemned (7.3–4) and he who marries does not sin (7.26). Yet, and we will return to this, there is a sense that the married believer has a second-class commitment to the Lord. His or her interests are divided (7.32–35). There is even a hint that being 'holy in body and spirit' is in some sense a status reserved for the single (Paul talks of ἡ γυνὴ ἡ ἄγαμος καὶ ἡ παρθένος as being ἁγία καὶ τῷ σώματι καὶ τῷ πνεύματι, 7.34). It is thus not much wonder that Paul has a clear preference for the singleness of those for whom it is possible (7.7–8; 7.25–27; 7.38). Thus there is a sense in which allowing a mastery of the body, even by a spouse, is undesirable for the believer: it conflicts with the highest notion of the 'body for the Lord'. If a mastery of the body is seen as the result of any sexual union, then we may well imagine Paul, both single and celibate, boasting οὐκ ἐγὼ ἐξουσιασθήσομαι ὑπό τινος, and commending such a self-example to the Corinthians, just as he will later suggest θέλω δὲ πάντας ἀνθρώπους εἶναι ὡς καὶ ἐμαυτόν (7.7) and λέγω ... καλόν αὐτοῖς ἐὰν μείνωσιν ὡς κἀγώ (7.8). Thus both Paul's μοι and his ἐγώ are paradigmatic, and it is perhaps possible to see 6.12 not only as an introduction to the discussion of πόρνη-union (6.12–20) but also as an introduction to the discussion of the desirability of marriage in 7.1–40.

We are inevitably running slightly ahead of ourselves here. These contentions will need both further evidence and further exploration. Moreover, 6.12 is certainly primarily presented as part of Paul's discourse on πορνεία, and not explicitly as an argument against believers marrying. But it does seem reasonable to postulate some connection in Paul's thought between his mention of ἐξουσία in 6.12 and that of 7.4. The nature of this relationship between πορνεία and marriage will be a major theme of the remainder of this study.

6.4. *Body vs. Stomach: Sex vs. Food (6.13–14)*

Paul moves on to consider the relation of sex and food to the body of the believer. Most commentators see Paul responding here to the anthropological convictions of the Corinthians – convictions that have underpinned the slogan of 6.12 and its libertine conclusion. The thesis is generally that the Corinthians hold the acts of the transitory material body to be irrelevant in ethical considerations and that Paul responds with an alternative anthropology based on the resurrection of the body.[44] Thus the debate in these verses foreshadows and relates to that of ch. 15.

---

44. So, with some variations, Barrett 1971: 147; Conzelmann 1975: 111; Fee 1987: 257.

However, our contention will be that central to Paul's intention here is not a desire to engage in anthropological controversy but to differentiate sexual ethics from food ethics. Whether σῶμα is taken as material body, personality, or whatever, Paul's point is that food is finally irrelevant but that πορνεία is not. The notion of the 'body for the Lord' excludes the notion that the body can ever be for πορνεία. These constitute mutually exclusive possibilities, just as πόρνος and ἅγοις constitute mutually exclusive identities in 5.1–13.

The logic of this passage is difficult, and it is easy to become bogged down in a plethora of reconstructions, slogans and counter slogans, dichotomies of stomach and body, destruction and resurrection. The key to understanding this passage lies in its structure. It can be seen as a series of four propositions.

A. τὰ βρώματα τῇ κοιλίᾳ (καὶ ἡ κοιλία τοῖς βρώμασιν),
B. ὁ δὲ θεὸς καὶ ταύτην καὶ ταῦτα καταργήσει.
C. τὸ δὲ σῶμα οὐ τῇ πορνείᾳ ἀλλὰ τῷ κυρίῳ (καὶ ὁ κύριος τῷ σώματι)[45]
D. ὁ δὲ θεὸς καὶ τὸν κύριον ἤγειρεν καὶ ἡμᾶς ἐξερεῖ διὰ τῆς δυνάμεως αὐτοῦ.

There is no logical necessity to view any of these statements as either contradicting, derivative from, or complementary to, any other. It is only as we begin to give meaning to the words and the concepts involved that we must come to a conclusion about the logic that lies between the several propositions.

The clue is probably in proposition C, which appears to be refuting another unspoken proposition:

X. τὸ σῶμα τῇ πορνείᾳ καὶ ἡ πορνεία τῷ σώματι

This statement would appear to be a deduction from A, and could also rest on a wider application of B hence:

Y. ὁ δὲ θεὸς καὶ τοῦτο καὶ ταύτην καταργήσει i.e. τὸ σῶμα καὶ ἡ πορνεία

If so, it may well be that D is designed to refute Y, just as C is to refute X.

Barrett's[46] reconstruction of these slogans is typical of many. He will have the Corinthians declare A on the basis of B. Digestion is a natural process of the transient body with no eternal significance. Some in the church, however, have applied the whole thesis to sexual activity (X and

---

45. We are probably safe in regarding καὶ ὁ κύριος τῷ σώματι as merely a formal balance for καὶ ἡ κοιλία τοῖς βρώμασιν (see Murphy-O'Connor 1978: 394–95, but otherwise Schrage 1995: 24).

46. Barrett 1971: 146–58.

Y). Paul for his part accepts AB, but directly refutes XY by drawing a distinction between κοιλία and σῶμα, destruction and resurrection, and thus sex and food.

> The belly is matter pure and simple, and has no permanence; but in Paul's usage body (σῶμα) means more than animal tissue. Even the 'natural body' is matter informed by the soul (ψυχή); and if there is a natural body there is also (xv.44) a spiritual body, matter informed by spirit (πνεῦμα). Body in fact is one of several terms used by Paul to denote not one part of man's nature but man as a whole.[47]

Barrett's reconstruction rests heavily on Bultmann's notion that 'man does not have a *soma*; he is a *soma*, for in not a few cases *soma* can be translated simply "I" (or whatever personal pronoun fits the context)'.[48]

For Bultmann this means that σῶμα is best encapsulated in our term 'personality', something that does not necessarily carry any physical connotation. σῶμα is to be viewed as 'more than material'. In the passage in question, those who have followed Bultmann have drawn strength from the fact that Paul uses σῶμα and ἡμᾶς interchangeably in 6.14.[49]

R.H. Gundry's reconstruction of 6.13–14 is given in the context of refuting precisely this Bultmannian notion of σῶμα.[50] Gundry accepts the notion that σῶμα refers to what man is, but contests the notion that this equals personality and excludes a reference to the physical aspect of human constitution. This leads Gundry to reject the contention that κοιλία and σῶμα form some sort of 'material versus more than material' contrast for Paul. Both then denote the physical aspect of a man. As a result, Gundry has to reject the notion that destruction is applied to κοιλία in contrast to the resurrection of the σῶμα.[51]

Gundry then offers two possibilities. The first is that B and D are parallel rather than contrasting statements, indicating that the κοιλία/σῶμα is transformed by destruction/resurrection at the Eschaton, and thus bodily appetites should not govern. His second, similar, offering is that AB constitutes the Corinthians' position. Paul then concedes the destruction of the κοιλία/σῶμα, but insists that, by means of resurrection, God counteracts this destruction so that the κοιλία/σῶμα is for the Lord.

The problem with both of these theses is that they require Paul to be rejecting the Corinthian assertion of A (at least as they understand it), and doing so by stating C. This is unlikely for two reasons. The one thing we

47.   Barrett 1971: 147; cf. Schrage 1995: 20 and Thiselton 2000: 462–63.
48.   Bultmann 1952: 194.
49.   Cf. Conzelmann 1975: 111.
50.   Gundry 1976: 51–83; cf. Käsemann 1969b: 19.
51.   As also Murphy-O'Connor 1978: 395, 'Paul must intend by *hēmas* what the Corinthians intended by *koilia*, namely, the human person viewed precisely as corporeal (*sōma*)'.

ca... certain of is that C negates not A, but its hypothetical extension to cover πορνεία (X). Paul limits rather than denies A. This means that Paul effectively concedes the point as far as the κοιλία is concerned, but forbids the extension of the rule to the σῶμα, thus differentiating between these two terms. Secondly, the concession of A would fit with Paul's known indifference to foodstuffs in themselves,[52] an area in which Paul, as we have seen, has most likely maintained πάντα ἔξεστιν.

The most likely reconstruction of events is this: A and B are statements which some in Corinth are using, possibly in connection with idol foods. Paul agrees with such, as he does with πάντα ἔξεστιν in regard to foods, but he is concerned lest, or because, some use such notions to trivialize the seriousness of πορνεία (as with 6.12). He can see where such arguments as A and B could lead (to X and Y), precisely because he can see that sex too is a desire, and it too involves the body of a man or woman.

This certainly means that Paul uses a κοιλία/σῶμα contrast (*contra* Gundry), but such should not be overplayed. Paul uses it to drive a wedge, not between two anthropological terms, but between πορνεία and the consumption of food. Indeed his argument implies his own conviction (6.18) – for it assumes that βρώματα are to do with the κοιλία and not the σῶμα, and likewise that πορνεία is not merely to do with the corresponding sexual organ.

The distinction however need not be seen as 'material versus more than material'. To interpret it as such is to assume a neo-Platonism in Paul that is not necessarily warranted.[53] The distinction is rather one of eschatological significance, for Paul does not infer that the 'immaterial' σῶμα survives the destruction of the 'material' κοιλία, but rather that the σῶμα will be raised in the manner of the Lord's raising. The effects of sex will transcend or affect this raising in a way that the effects of eating will not. To object that Paul says God will raise ἡμᾶς rather than σώματα ἡμῶν is futile, for the point is that 'God raised the Lord [bodily] and will raise us [bodily]'[54] (the link between σῶμα and resurrection is one Paul returns to in ch. 15). If this is not the point then statement D provides no type of proof of statement C, nor does it interact with B.

---

52. 1 Cor. 10.26; Rom. 14.14.

53. On which see D.B. Martin 1995 and Adams 2000.

54. As Schrage 1995: 25 (cf. Rom. 8.11). It is possible that Paul hesitates to use 'body' in the discussion of resurrection, as he is aware of the Corinthians' difficulty with this issue, which he will later address. Certainly this provides a better explanation than Gundry's suggestion that since Paul has used the word twice in 6.13 and will use it again in 6.15, 'stylistically he hesitates to use the word again so quickly and unnecessarily'. However, Gundry seems justified in contending that 'the three appearances of *soma* before and after verse 14 should determine the nuance of the pronoun "us" and not vice versa' (1976: 60). Note also 6.19 where σῶμα and ἑαυτός are used together.

It cannot be overstated that the issue here is the distinction ⸢ ⸣ ᴉ food and sex, and that this governs all else. Food is trivial, a natura. urge to be followed, lacking in any eternal consequences, irrelevant to the identity of the believer (8.8).[55] Sex, however, goes to the root of who the believer is. His devotion to the Lord is incompatible with πορνεία. The Lordship of Christ here and now places a demand on how one physically lives and acts that excludes the physical acts that constitute πορνεία. The eschatological fate of the believer also places demands on his physical existence that are incompatible with πορνεία. To lose sight of the physical reference implied in σῶμα is to lose sight of the fact that it is a physical activity that Paul has in view. Being in Christ brings no obligations into the realm of eating; indeed it frees the believer in this regard. But if one is in Christ then τὸ σῶμα τῷ κυρίῳ by necessity means it is οὐ τῇ πορνείᾳ.

The discussion began with the πάντα μοι ἔξεστιν of 6.12 – a food ethic that must not be brought into the arena of sex – and it continues in this vein of separating food and sex. Indeed, it is almost tempting to think that 6.13–14 might not be Paul steering further Corinthian food slogans away from the rocks of πορνεία, but might be Paul attempting to rationalize a difference between food and sex, which he requires as a corrective to the implications of a universal ἐξουσία ethos such as is represented in 6.12.

In summary then, Paul contends that sex is in a different ethical category from food. The 'body for the Lord' and its resultant role in eschatology precludes πορνεία, which contradicts both the present purpose and the future fate of the body. Even if eating in some contexts is deemed undesirable for the believer (when it is to the detriment of another believer), the impropriety of πορνεία and its contradiction to the devotion of the believer to the Lord exists on a different level.

6.5. *Union with the* πόρνη *or Union with the Lord (6.15–17)*

6.5.1. *Exclusive Limbship:* ὁ Χριστός *or* ἡ πόρνη *(6.15)*

Thus far Paul has asserted, rather than argued for, the incompatibility of Christian identity with the use of the body for πορνεία. The argument will follow in 6.16–20, where Paul will argue for the somatic and pneumatic implications of identity in Christ, and their conflict with the somatic results of illicit sexual union. 6.15 is something of a transition point. Like the previous verses, 6.15 proves also to be an assertion rather than an argument. The shocking suggestion that someone should be taken from Christ and given to one such as a πόρνη precludes anything but a negative response. Thus we have an almost rhetorical question producing an

---

55. See Jaquette 1995: 137–53.

effectively unnecessary answer (μὴ γένοιτο). However, the verse serves two distinct purposes. First, its very language prepares us for the discussion of the body, in which Paul is about to engage, setting up the terms and categories that will become key to Paul's explanation in the following verses. Secondly, the sharpness in which the incompatibility of πορνεία and identity in Christ are set, reveals that Paul has in mind not only the incongruity of membership of Christ and that of a πόρνη, but the total impossibility of such.[56]

6.5.1.1. *The nature of limbship.* τὰ σώματα ὑμῶν μέλη Χριστοῦ ἐστιν alerts us to the fact that it is the status of the believers' bodies and their relation to Christ that will be under discussion in the proceeding verses. In light of what follows, the physical nature of the statement should not be evaded: the subject of the clause is not ὑμεῖς but τὰ σώματα ὑμῶν; the body is not the property of Christ, but is said to be the μέλη Χριστοῦ – the 'limbs' of Christ. Obviously the latter is metaphoric. However, in view of the direction the argument will soon take, the intimacy of the identification of the body and the Lord should not be missed. We must beware of simply decoding the statement to say – 'you are Christ's'. This becomes more obvious when we consider the question that immediately follows: ἄρας οὖν τὰ μέλη τοῦ Χριστοῦ ποιήσω πόρνης μέλη; Here membership of a πόρνη quite clearly refers to a sexual union of bodies. Thus already the body's membership of Christ is being described in the same language as a sexual union. At this point no distinction is made between the nature of these two relationships (to Christ and to the πόρνη), only between the respective partners. This comparison of the connection to Christ and sexual connection to a πόρνη will prove critical to our understanding of Paul's thinking in the remainder of the chapter.

But what does it mean to say that 'your bodies are members of Christ'? Many commentators read this statement in conjunction with the body language of 12.12–26, which conceives of the church collectively as the body of Christ.[57] Thus individual believers are to exhibit mutual interdependence, as would the various components of a physical human body. However, there seems little contextual warrant for making such a connection. 12.12–26 is concerned with the relationship of believers to one another, whereas the present passage exhibits a concern solely with the relationship of the individual believer to the Lord. Further, 6.12–20 conceives of the implications of that relationship for the use of the actual physical body of the believer whereas the actual physical body of the believer is not referred to in 12.12–26.

---

56. What Schrage (1995: 28) refers to as 'eine unmögliche Möglichkeit'.
57. So Kempthorne (1967: 570–72) and K.E. Bailey (1980: 35–36).

Others have, more plausibly, read 6.15 as a conclusion to 6.14. Thus the believer's body's membership of Christ is conceived of as a membership of the risen body of the Lord (Jesus).[58] There are, however, various problems with this suggestion. First, although implied, neither the body of the believer, nor that of Christ, are actually referred to in 6.14. The object of 6.14 is ἡμᾶς whereas the subject of 6.15 is τὰ σώματα ὑμῶν so there is no direct linguistic connection. Secondly, 6.14 does not actually contain the notion that the believer's body will be/has been raised with, or in union with Christ (cf. Rom. 8.11 and 2 Cor. 4.10). Rather two separate, although parallel, acts of resurrection are portrayed: one past, the other future (καὶ ... καὶ). The linkage of the two is not in the identification of the objects of resurrection, but that both are accomplished by the same δύναμις of God, which will reverse the divine action of destruction (6.13b). Thirdly, to link 6.14 and 15 requires us to impute some form of participatory resurrection into 6.14.[59] This inevitably struggles, not only with the temporal sequence of the verse (*raised ... will be* raised), but to avoid the inference of realized eschatology (we *have been* raised with Christ; cf. Eph. 2.5; Col. 2.12), which that temporal sequence forbids. It is better, then, to take 6.14 as being constructed as a response to the notion of the future destruction and thus present irrelevance of the sexual body (our hypothetical Y). (Paul thus argues that, since the destruction of the body will be counteracted, its transitory nature is no grounds for ethics.) This leaves us to view 6.15 as being the beginning of Paul's exposition of his other statement about the body in 6.13–14: that is, 'the body not for πορνεία, but for the Lord', an exposition that will continue throughout 6.15–20.[60]

The rejection of the participatory resurrection interpretation of 'membership of Christ' may also go some way to explaining why Paul states that 'your bodies are members of Christ' and not 'your bodies are members of Christ's *body*'. This is because the status of the body as 'for the Lord' has not primarily to do with the eschatological purpose of the body, but with the current presence of the Holy Spirit in the body of the believer (6.19–20). The notion of what it means for the body to be a 'member of Christ' is to be understood not in terms of a mystical participation in Christ's exalted body, but in terms of the spirit-union of

---

58.   So Fee 1987: 258 (similarly Conzelmann 1975: 111) who, rejecting the parallel with 12.12–26, contends that 'the body of the believer is *for* the Lord because through Christ's resurrection God has set in motion the reality of our resurrection. This means that the believer's physical body is to be understood as "joined" to Christ's own "body" that was raised from the dead'. (However, Fee's practice of placing terms in quotation marks shows his resistance to taking such participatory language seriously.)

59.   As Conzelmann 1975: 111: 'the eschatological hope is actualized'.

60.   With Robertson and Plummer 1914: 125.

the believer with the Lord, a union that, as we shall see, is effected through the Spirit's presence in the body. Thus membership of Christ is not an innate property of the believer's body, but rather indicates that Christ possesses his or her body through the Spirit.

6.5.1.2. *An alternative limbship.* Notice also that the unspecific πορνεία of 6.12–15 has now given way to the specific act of sex with a πόρνη. This again will prove critical. The effect of the sexual act that is envisaged is not simply that the believer commits a sin, but that the believer joins his body to the body of another, in a manner that endangers (or destroys) the relationship between his body and Christ. Two questions follow from this. What is it about the body's relationship to the Lord and the relationship actualized with a πόρνη, through sex, which renders the two incompatible? Further, how much of the objection to πόρνη-union flows from the notion that sex creates an alternative membership to that of Christ, and how much flows from the fact that the alternative envisaged is that with a πόρνη? We shall return to these questions.

The final thing that we can take from 6.15 is that sex with a πόρνη is not deemed to be simply detrimental to Christian identity, but destructive of it. The body is envisaged as a limb of Christ: a limb that cannot become the πόρνη's unless first removed from the Lord. Fisk argues: 'it is not clear from this text that Paul believed that using a prostitute immediately severed all ties to Christ'.[61] On the contrary, it would seem that Paul's choice of the verb αἴρω (take up, take away, remove) rather than the simpler λαμβάνω would indicate precisely such a severance.[62] As Kempthorne[63] correctly points out, αἴρω is used only here and at 1 Cor. 5.2 in the assured Pauline letters,[64] and 5.2 (as we have argued) clearly indicates a terminating transaction. Remembering that the same metaphor of membership (limb-ship) is used of both relationships (to Christ and to the πόρνη) in which the body may be involved, the picture appears to be one of amputation: the body-as-limb severed from an attachment to the Lord. Thus 6.15 should be read as a straight choice; the removal of members of Christ makes them into something else – the members of a πόρνη.

It is perhaps worth considering Dale Martin's thesis at this juncture. For Martin, the σῶμα's membership of Christ relates to the believer's participation both in the community (= body of Christ) and in Christ

61. Fisk 1996: 554.
62. As Robertson and Plummer 1914: 125.
63. Kempthorne 1967: 568–74.
64. The two incidences in the disputed letters Eph. 4.31 and Col. 2.14 strengthen, rather than weaken, the case. Both carry the notion of movement that puts an end to the prior state (although these, as with 1 Cor. 5.2, do carry the prepositions ἀπο and ἐκ respectively).

himself.[65] 'The man's body and Christ's body share the same pneuma; the man's body is therefore an appendage of Christ's body, totally dependent on the pneumatic life-force of the larger body for its existence.'

Martin then suggests that

> the man who has sex with a prostitute is, in Paul's construction, Christ's 'member' entering the body of the prostitute. Since her body is also only part of a larger whole, the cosmos, the simple action of copulation between a man and a woman becomes for Paul copulation between Christ and the cosmos... The Christian man penetrating a prostitute constitutes coitus between two beings of such different ontological status that Paul can hardly contemplate the consequences.[66]

We shall examine Martin's understanding of the relationship between the believer and the Spirit later,[67] but for the moment the question is: does Christ's member (and thus Christ himself) enter the body of the πόρνη? Is the body of Christ, however conceived, really as permeable as Martin suggests? Or rather is Paul's point not that in entering the πόρνη the believer ceases to be the member of Christ and becomes that of the πόρνη? Or, to put it another way, either Christ or πόρνη may have ἐξουσία over the believer's body, but not both. It is not that Paul is *trying* to maintain a radical separation between Christ and the cosmos, but rather his imperative proceeds on the assumption that these two things *are* distinct, and one can only be in one domain or the other (just as one is either an ἀδελφός or a πόρνος, a ἅγιος or ἄδικος).

---

65.   D.B. Martin's use of the term 'body of Christ' is slippery. He desires to connect Paul's anxiety about the boundaries of the body (1995: 174) to pollution fears both in 5.1–13 and 6.12–20. However, in a characteristic weakness of his thesis, he neglects to articulate the difference between the concern of 6.12–20 for the *physical* body of the believer, and the concern for the *corporate* body in the preceding sections (particularly 5.1–13). Both are telescoped into the term 'the body of Christ'. Indeed Martin is perhaps guilty here of sleight of hand. He correctly notes Paul's concern with community purity in 5.1–11, but then expresses that concern using the metaphoric language of the 'body of Christ', a language that Paul notably does not use in this chapter (preferring the leaven analogy). Thus 'Paul's primary concern in this passage is the purity of the church, *the body of Christ*, his anxieties center on the man as a potentially polluting agent *within Christ's body*, an agent whose presence threatens to pollute *the entire body*' (168, emphasis added). Having thus put the metaphor into Paul's mouth, Martin then insists that it is not a metaphor but a metaphysic, thus 'Paul's primary worry is that the pneuma of Christ's body will become polluted by the corrupting presence of the sinful sarx represented by the body of the immoral man' (169). The assertion is unjustified. The controlling corporate metaphor is leaven throughout, and although one could substitute the sense of this by a body image, one can only do so on the basis that both are interchangeable *metaphors*.

66.   D.B. Martin 1995: 176–77.

67.   See 6.6.2.2 below.

6.5.2. *Exclusive Unions:* ὁ κύριος *or* ἡ πόρνη *(6.16–17)*

6.5.2.1. *Comparable unions.* Here Paul begins to offer an explanation (not complete until 6.18–20) for why Christian identity and sex with a πόρνη are mutually exclusive options. The limbship metaphor of 6.15 has already suggested that it is the body's relationship to Christ and the relationship between the body and the πόρνη, effected by sex, that stands at the heart of the objection. The description of *both* relationships as 'memberships' indicates that the incompatibility proceeds from the contention that these relationships make similar claims (or have similar effects) on the believer's body.

Our contention is that 6.16–17 continues by comparing, rather than contrasting, union to the Lord and union to a πόρνη. Consider first the grammar of the verses:

v. 16a ὁ κολλώμενος   τῇ πόρνῃ   ἓν σῶμά ἐστιν

v. 17   ὁ δὲ κολλώμενος   τῷ κυρίῳ   ἓν πνεῦμά ἐστιν

Subject, verb, and word order are identical. Certainly the difference between σῶμα and πνεῦμα is not without significance, but the similarities are certainly more striking. Thus we should not use the single difference to mask the parallel and see Paul's argument as contrastive rather than comparative, as many translators seem prone to do. The RSV, for instance, rather outrageously renders these verses:

6.16a   He who *joins himself* to a prostitute becomes one body with her

6.17   he who *is united* to the Lord becomes one Spirit with him.

Thus changing not only the verb used for κολλώμενος but also the voice.[68]

But what is the nature of the comparison? The key must lie in the application of the Genesis text (2.24), normally related to marital consummation, to sexual union with a πόρνη. This serves to stress the significant effects of πόρνη-union upon the believer's body, and to do so in such a way as to infer a comparison with the effects of Christ-union.

Paul's application of the Genesis motif begins even in his description of union with a πόρνη. He speaks of ὁ κολλώμενος τῇ πόρνῃ. In itself, this may seem like a neutral description of sexual union. But the choice of the participle κολλώμενος already begins to turn description into evaluation, for it is obviously drawn from its usage in Gen. 2.24 (LXX), the second

---

68. The Jerusalem Bible is even more culpable: 'a man who goes with a prostitute ... but anyone who is joined to the Lord'. AV, NEB, NIV and NRSV correctly maintain the parallel.

half of which Paul proceeds to cite.[69] Similarly, being ἓν σῶμα with the πόρνη could simply be a sexual euphemism describing the joining of bodies during intercourse. However, it too begins an evaluation of the significance of the sex by preparing for the contention that it creates the partners μία σάρξ. Although μία σάρξ could again be a mere sexual euphemism (and is arguably so in the Genesis text itself), it makes an explicit inter-textual connection that serves to indicate that sex with the πόρνη is in some way, in its effects on the body of the believer, comparable to marital union.

Thus, if the Corinthians have seen sex with a πόρνη as merely physical activity, Paul is already suggesting that it is something more. Paul's description (ὁ κολλώμενος τῇ πόρνῃ ἓν σῶμά ἐστιν) may at first appear to describe the sex in a manner consistent with the Corinthian understanding, but the description prepares for an evaluation that points in a different direction. As the term σῶμα has already been transformed by notions of resurrection and participation in Christ, so the seemingly innocuous description of the sexual liaison (κολλώμενος) is transformed by use of the marital imagery into an evaluation of permanency and seriousness that the term itself does not obviously possess. This is even before the same term is applied to union with the Lord.

The description (6.17) of union with the Lord (κολλώμενος) and the resulting contention (ἓν πνεῦμά ἐστιν), verbally and grammatically echo those of the πόρνη-union, and the Genesis proof text. Despite the fact that the comparison is incomplete (Paul does not say Christ and the believer become ἓν σῶμά), 6.17 must relate to what is said about the body. The pneumatic union of believer and Lord must include some notion of somatic union. We can give good reason for this contention. 6.16–17 is best understood as a development and explanation for 6.15. Thus pneumatic union with Christ explains the contention that the σῶμα is the member of Christ, just as the somatic union with the πόρνη explains the description of sex with the πόρνη as becoming her limb. If 6.17 *contrasts* pneumatic union with somatic union, stressing the difference of the two (as the δέ might suggest if taken as adversative) then it is difficult to see how it relates to the rest of the argument. Indeed it would then serve to relativize πόρνη-union (undercutting 6.16's high evaluation) and stand against the 'either Christ or πόρνη membership' dichotomy of 6.15. Thus

---

69. Although the LXX uses προκολλᾶσθαι, nothing should be implied from Paul's failure to use this compound form (*pace* Miguens 1975: 44–45, who argues that Paul wished to avoid the sexual overtones of the verb in the LXX). Mt. 19.5 also uses κολλάω in citing Gen. 2.24. Philo (*Spec.* 2.29) discusses Gen. 2 using both forms of the verb, without attaching significance to the variance (cf. Rosner 1994: 131 n. 31).

the use of κολλώμενος and the notion of oneness relate Christ-union both to πόρνη-union and to the application of the Genesis text.

Our suggestion is that, although Paul does not speak of Christ-union as rendering the believer ἓν σῶμα with the Lord (perhaps avoiding such language as it has just been used of sexual union), yet spirit-union subsumes and includes the participation of the believer's body in Christ. This is indicated in 6.19 where the Spirit is said to dwell in the believer's body, having consequences for that body.

However, some commentators appear reluctant to accept that Christ-union and πόρνη-union are being compared in 6.17. For instance, R.H. Gundry has simply used rationalism to say that the unions *must* be contrasted.

> Nor can we bridge the logical gap by asserting that he who joins his soma to a harlot has more than a superficial relationship with her. Is it more than superficial? To be sure, the union produces one body, or one flesh (vv. 15–16). But to what extent? Coitus with a prostitute is casual, occasional, momentary, and non-indicative of any other union. On the other hand union with Christ is fundamental, constant, and all embracing – as also is marriage. Therein lies the reason that sexual union within marriage does not take away virtue and consequently does not contradict union with Christ. The very superficiality of fornication with a harlot makes that relationship spurious and interruptive of both Christian life and marriage.[70]

This may be laudable theology, but it is most inadequate exegesis. Is there anything in this text that suggests that Paul's problem with πόρνη-union is that it is a 'superficial relationship'? Does Paul really compare Christ-union and marriage, and then contrast the two to πόρνη-union? On the contrary, Paul dares to apply to πόρνη-union a Scriptural text associated with marriage, precisely to bolster his more daring comparison of such union to union with the Lord – unions that are incompatible due to their *similar* claims on the body.

---

70. Gundry 1976: 5 (see also Miguens 1975). This might work if Paul were diminishing the importance of the σῶμα/σάρξ in comparison to the πνεῦμα in this passage. But the opposite is true. The presence of the πνεῦμα serves to raise the importance of the activity of the σῶμα throughout (esp. 6.19–20). Thus the σῶμα-union is being presented as a significant and not an ephemeral union.

Remarkably, other commentators have read Paul as saying the opposite and commended him for this. D.S. Bailey 1959: 9–10 writes: '[Paul] displays a psychological insight into human sexuality, which is altogether exceptional by first-century standards. The apostle denies that coitus is, as the Corinthians would have it, merely a detached and (as it were) peripheral function ... of the genital organs. On the contrary, he insists that it is an act which, by reason of its very nature, engages and expresses the whole personality, in such a way as to constitute a unique mode of self-disclosure and self-commitment.'

6.5.2.2. *Christ, the* πόρνη *and marriage*. Thus we have three things that are being compared: πόρνη-union, marital union (implicitly), and Christ-union. The first two are identified in that they both constitute the believer one flesh/body with the partner. There is nothing here that serves to differentiate marital from πόρνη-union except perhaps the status of the partner. The second two (bodily union with a πόρνη and spirit-union with the Lord) are identified in the manner in which they are described, and the fact that one precludes the other.

Significantly, the comparison evidences similarities to our discussion of ἐξουσία above (6.3.2.2). As we observed, marriage (7.4) and πορνεία (6.12) both gave to another an ἐξουσία over the body. This mastery was used as an objection to πορνεία (οὐκ ἐγὼ ἐξουσιασθήσομαι ὑπό τινος) to insist on its incompatibility with Christian identity. However, since marriage and πορνεία appear to share the property of giving ἐξουσία over another, logically the same argument should preclude marital union as well: but that logic is not drawn out. Thus the comparison of marital and πόρνη-union, and the propensity to present πόρνη-union as incompatible with Christ-union precisely due to a property that it shares with marital union, is found in both instances.

Of course this is not to say Paul totally identifies the nature of Christ-union with that of πόρνη-union; πνεῦμα and σῶμα are not confused in 6.16. But it is to say that Paul's stress is on the similarity and thus incompatibility of the two admittedly differing unions. Both unions make contradictory claims on the σῶμα. We contend that this is because spirit-union includes and subsumes body union. The believer becoming ἕν πνεῦμά with the Lord precludes him becoming ἕν σῶμα with the πόρνη because as a result of the spirit-union his *body* is also united to the Lord, is a member of Christ, is 'for the Lord', and is a temple of the Holy Spirit.

As for marriage, Paul doubtless sees marital union as differing from πόρνη-union, but for reasons very different from those Gundry supposes. Indeed, many of the properties of, and concerns about, the πόρνη-union expressed in 6.12–20 will be seen to correspond to those attributed to marriage in 7.1–40. There is nothing in 6.12–20 that serves to differentiate the two unions. Differentiation does occur in 7.1–40 (marriage is not a sin, unbelieving spouses do not threaten the sanctity of the believer), but, we shall argue, *the differentiation is required precisely because of the possible implications of the similarities between the two in Paul's thought*. This is not because marriage is viewed as πορνεία, but because marriage, like πόρνη-union, effects a bodily union that conflicts with (bodily consequences of) the union with the Lord.

Boyarin notes the logic of Paul's argument, and concludes, 'Paul is truly revealing his hand here. For him sexuality per se is tainted with immorality... Here, however, Paul makes the point not openly but indirectly'.[71] We might almost agree. Certainly something is indirectly revealed here about the conflict between Christ-union and human sexual unions, something that both illuminates Paul's anxiety over marriage in ch. 7, and perhaps explains his denials of its illegitimacy.[72] However, in view of ch. 7, to suggest that Paul views sexuality as being immoral is to overstep a little. Marriage will be seen as a conflict of allegiances precluding true holiness (7.32–34), as a θλῖψις τῇ σαρκί (7.28) and Paul will require to deny that it is sin (7.36), but the suggestion that marriage is πορνεία will never be made, not even to be denied. Having said this, Boyarin's thought would certainly be a valid conclusion from 6.12–20 read in isolation.[73]

6.5.3. *Metaphors and Meanings*

The logic of Paul's argument relies on the conviction that sex with a πόρνη has significance for the body beyond the sex act itself and that this is incompatible with the significance for the body of Christian identity. The question is, how much can we take from the metaphoric way Paul describes this incompatibility? (And we are dealing here with metaphors, since *literal* limbship of Christ can hardly be contemplated!) Are the metaphors (of membership, union and oneness) simply designed to convey that Christian identity is incompatible with πορνεία, that πορνεία is a serious breach of Christian ethics? We might call this an ethical reading. Or, ought we to read more into Paul's metaphors? Do they speak beyond this to Paul's actual understanding of both sexual union and the believer's relationship to Christ? Do they speak specifically to what Paul believes to be the particular problem with πόρνη-union? We might call this a realistic interpretation.[74]

6.5.3.1. *An ethical reading.* If we take the ethical option, we might reconstruct the logic of these verses in the following manner. Paul who, as we have argued throughout this study, believes that identity in Christ is partly constituted by distinctive Christian living, is concerned that identity in Christ governs the whole person, including physical actions of the body (the body for the Lord). Πορνεία, precisely because it is sinful, and because it is an identity marker of life outwith Christ (6.9–11), endangers identity in Christ (as indeed would any vice). Πορνεία, it so happens, is

---

71. Boyarin 1994: 171.

72. As Boyarin rightly comments, if we note the logic of 6: 12–20, 'the connection between chapters 6 and 7 of Corinthians is now much clearer' (1994: 172).

73. A point made well by Burkill (1971: 116) when he asks of 1 Cor. 6.15–20: 'if becoming "one flesh" with a harlot nullifies the presence of Christ in the man concerned, why does not sexual intercourse within marriage have a similar effect? The apostle offers no clear answer.'

74. A realistic reading is not precluded by insisting that the language must be metaphoric (cf. Caird 1980: 131–32).

committed through illicit bodily union with another person (a euphemism
for intercourse). Thus illicit physical union with another person violates
identity in Christ. Since identity in Christ may be expressed metaphorically as union with, or membership of, Christ, it may be *said* that union
with a πόρνη conflicts with union with Christ, and indeed that the two are
mutually exclusive.

If we adopt this interpretation, we could agree with Gundry that
'becoming one flesh' 'needs to refer quite simply to physical union through
sexual intercourse and nothing more ... an unsophisticatedly physical
meaning'.[75] It is only larger in that it is destructive of a spiritual 'union'
with Christ. Further, we might agree with Fee, that the suggestion that
union with Christ is 'physical' is simply a metaphor for the Lord's claims
on the body, which exclude πορνεία. Thus 'since sexual immorality
involves bodily union, he [Paul] gets at the prohibition of the one (sexual
immorality) through metaphorical implications from the other (the
"parts" of the body)'.[76] Indeed, Paul might only refer to union with a
πόρνη as it was a manifestation of πορνεία that linguistically could be
conveniently contrasted to union with the Lord. The πόρνη herself would
be irrelevant – not really a rival to the Christ for Lordship over the body.

6.5.3.2. *A 'realistic' reading.* There are, however, a number of factors in
the context that cumulatively serve to undermine such an ethical
interpretation and suggest that Paul sees real physical effects stemming
from sexual unions. First, as we shall see, the mention of the sin εἰς τὸ
ἴδιον σῶμα in 6.18 suggests the uniqueness of sexual sin, on the basis of
either its unique locus in, or unique damage to, the body. This strengthens
the contention that Paul is suggesting that πορνεία uniquely 'does'
something to bodies, which is the cause of its danger. Secondly, marriage
deprives a person of ἐξουσία over his or her own *body* and transfers such
to their spouse (7.4). This could merely indicate that marriage implies
rights and duties with regard to sex. However, as was noted, the fact that
Paul begins the discussion of πορνεία in 6.12–20 with the refusal to let τὶς
have ἐξουσία him (6.12) may suggest that all sexual unions have to do
with an ἐξουσία over the body, which might partly explain Paul's
ambivalent attitude towards marriage. Even when licit, sexual unions give
to another an unwelcome ἐξουσία over the believer's body. Further, when
Paul argues for singleness in 7.32–35, he not only states that the married
person's interests are divided and his/her devotion to the Lord incomplete,
but also implies that only the unmarried person may truly be holy καὶ τῷ
σώματι καὶ τῷ πνεύματι (7.34). Again, sexual unions conflict with
identity in Christ, and do so precisely through their effect on the body.

75. Gundry 1976: 62.
76. Fee 1987: 258.

Thus it does seem that Paul envisages sexual union to have 'realistic' effects on the body beyond the sex act and its moral consequences. It also appears that Paul envisages identity in Christ to have a 'realistic' effect on the body beyond an obligation to behave in a particular manner. Thus the prohibition of sexual union with a πόρνη, as well as the concern over sexual union with a spouse, proceed on the basis of the conflict between these two unions. But how might this operate?

We might see 'union with the Lord' as some type of marriage demanding the sexual fidelity of the human partner to the divine, which additional sexual union would then 'adulterate'. The idea of Christian identity as being marriage to the Lord is explicitly found in 2 Cor. 11.2–3, which utilizes the OT motif of Yahweh as sole husband of Israel and the danger of Israel 'playing the harlot' with other gods.[77] However, both the OT and 2 Cor. 11.2–3 use marriage and adultery as a metaphor for obedience – neither envisages any conflict with literal marriages. Further, the use is corporate – the people collectively are God's partner – whereas if 1 Corinthians 6 envisaged spiritual marriage to the Lord, then the thinking uniquely would concern the individual believer. So the 'realistic' participation of the believer in the Lord of 6.16–17 need not be interpreted sexually. As we noted, Paul does not actually say that the believer is 'one body' with the Lord as with the πόρνη. Further, he can equally express the believer's participation in Christ using a non-sexual metaphor. The believer's body is the Temple of the Holy Spirit (6.19). How then is realistic participation to be understood?

Eduard Schweizer makes the suggestion that Paul thinks of 'a spiritual body of the exalted κύριος' (the σῶμα Χριστοῦ), in which the believer participates through baptism. Thus 'Paul is contending that the resurrection (or exaltation) sets Christ in the sphere of the Spirit, and that union with Him ensures believers of spiritual life, which is life in the community'.[78] However, Gundry[79] argues against such a suggestion, and indeed against the whole notion of realistic participation. He does so on three grounds: (1) Such a spiritualizing of σῶμα would play into the hands of those who deny the importance of the present body. (2) It fuses together the present body and the future body, which Paul separates in 15.35–36. (3) 'Realistic union' lacks parallels in Paul's thought. (He rejects notions of parallels in Eucharistic participation (11.27–32), baptism for the dead (15.29), and the 'realistic' sanctification of the unbeliever through

---

77. Hos. 1–3; Ezek. 16; Isa. 50.1–2; 54.1–8; 62.5. As Rosner (1994: 128) points out, the theme is easily connected to a man committing adultery with prostitutes, since prostitution was used as a metaphor for Israel's apostasy, and actual prostitution is connected by the Hebrew Bible to the cults of the ancient East, involvement in which was apostasy.

78. Schweizer 1969: 418–20 (cf. Proudfoot 1963: 146).

79. Gundry 1976: 66–68.

the believer's body (7.12–16) – such is not a salvific participation in
Christ.)

However, although Gundry is correct to reject a participation in the
exalted body of Christ, his objections to realistic participation can be
overcome. The first falls if we postulate (as we argued above[80]) that it is
the believer's *present* body (rather than the σῶμα πνευματικον), which is
united to the Lord. The second objection then similarly vanishes. The
current body participates in Christ through the indwelling of the Holy
Spirit (6.19).[81] Thus spiritual union with the Lord involves bodily union,
and Paul's point in placing the believer's union with Christ beside the
impossible union with a πόρνη is found precisely in the notion that the
body is a member of Christ (6.15). As for Gundry's demand for
corroborating evidence for 'realistic union', such *is* found in 7.12–16. It is
not in the notion of the believer's body sanctifying the unbeliever's, but
in the fact that there is a legitimate concern that the unbeliever's body
might pollute the believer through the sexual relationship. This concern
requires the declaration of the unbeliever's sanctity through their
marriage to a believer. The declaration would logically not extend to
extra-marital unions with outsiders – leaving them as a source of
pollution. However, the question remains as to why marriage sanctifies
the outsider.

6.6. *The Temple of the Spirit (6.18–20)*

6.6.1. *Sinning* ἐκτός *and* εἰς τὸ σῶμα *(6.18)*

At first glance, that Paul in 6.18 commands the believer not to flee the
πόρνη but to φεύγετε τὴν πορνείαν, and that his target is not ὁ
κολλώμενος τῇ πόρνῃ but more generally (ἄνθρωπος and) ὁ πορνεύων,
might suggest that he has moved from a concern with the bodily effects of
πόρνη-union to more general observations about πορνεία as an ethical
infringement.[82] However, we are still dealing here with the σῶμα, and
with the relationship between sex and the σῶμα (as ἐκτός or εἰς). This is
not explicable by the contention that πορνεία is committed bodily, and
thus may damage the body, for this is equally true of many other ethical
infringements (gluttony, drunkenness, suicide). Yet Paul appears to be

---

80. See 6.5.1.1 above.

81. The anticipated resurrection gives the present body additional validity, as it will not
simply be replaced and rendered redundant by the σῶμα πνευματικον, for indeed the present
σῶμα is the kernel (κόκκος, 15.37) from which the σῶμα πνευματικον will rise.

82. If those who have seen here an allusion to the story of Joseph fleeing Potiphar's wife
are correct, then the injunction may be slightly less abstract, and a fleeing of the person of the
πόρνη may still be in view (see Godet 1886: 311; Bruce 1971: 65; and esp. Rosner 1994: 137–
40).

claiming that πορνεία is a unique offence.[83] Therefore Paul is not merely arguing that πορνεία is an act incompatible with Christian ethics.

6.6.1.1. *Is Paul again quoting the Corinthians?* At the outset we must reject the temptation to postulate at 6.18c yet another Corinthian slogan,[84] whereby 'a notorious Pauline crux becomes a mere Corinthian quirk'.[85] Such a notion does have something to commend it. Slogan and qualifications are usually seen as the style of 6.12–7.1 (although various conclusions of this study dispute the point).[86] Further the full sense of πᾶν ἁμάρτημα can be preserved. (The exception of πορνεία becomes the Pauline contradiction of a sweeping Corinthian claim rather than an inconsistency in his argument).[87]

So, taken on its own, the first part of 6.18 *could* constitute a Corinthian slogan. However, the burden of proof, as always, must rest on those who would contend for this, and such a burden has not been discharged. There is no internal evidence of a quotation and no particular reason why Paul might not have wished to stress the unique nature of sexual sin to bolster his imperative to flee it. More damaging, however, is the failure of those who have contended for a Corinthian slogan to explain Paul's response. As Byrne notes, if the Corinthians deny the moral relevance of the body, then Paul's refutation must rest on the 'his own' element of the reply (the fact the πορνεία unlike other sins affects one's own body in a particularly damaging way). 'But the person holding the position expressed in the slogan might just as well retort: "Whether it is my body or not does not

---

83. The attempt to retain the solely ethical concern leads many commentators into implying artificial divisions between πορνεία and other physical sins, which are extraneous to the text. Take for example, Alford's notion of other physical sins being abuses of the body (gluttony, drunkenness), whereas sexual sins contradict the truth of the body from within (cited in Robertson and Plummer 1914: 127), or the notion that the act of eating is sinful only in the excess, whereas the act of πορνεία is innately sinful (Bruce 1971: 65), or additionally that sins of excess stem from conviviality, whereas πορνεία comes from internal desires.

84. *Contra* Moule 1953: 196; Kempthorne 1967: 571–72; Miguens 1975: 39; Murphy-O'Connor 1978: 395; Morris 1985: 99 and Omanson 1992. The reconstruction of the Corinthian position offered by each is markedly different. Kempthorne will have the Corinthians argue that the act of the incestuous man (5.1) cannot affect the church, as the father's wife is 'outside the body' (i.e. not a member of the church). Murphy-O'Connor and Omanson will have the body morally irrelevant for Christians. Miguens goes further in arguing that no sin affects one's real 'personality'.

85. Fisk 1996: 541.

86. See 6.3.1.2 above on 6.12; 9.4.1 on 7.1 and 9.7.4 on 7.34.

87. Cf. Fee 1987: 261–62. Gundry's objection to finding a Corinthian slogan here is not well founded. He argues that the Corinthian libertines would not have divorced all sins from the physical body, but rather would have associated sin with the body and disassociated both from the true self/spirit (1976: 74). But, as Murphy-O'Connor points out, such a slogan would merely be asserting that the body has nothing to do with sin, its acts cannot be sinful, and that true sin exists only on another level (1978: 393).

alter the case. Sin has nothing to do with the body, mine or anyone else's".[88]

6.6.1.2. *Against (into) the body*. Thus it is more likely that the whole verse is a Pauline construct: the δέ indicating an exception to the rule that all (other) sins are committed ἐκτός the σῶμα.[89] But what does this mean? How is the reference to the body to be understood? How does the locative language serve to differentiate πορνεία from other sins, which may also involve the body?[90]

Barrett[91] denies that Paul treats πορνεία as a different *kind* of sin. The difference is rather one of degree. 'Comparatively speaking' all other sins are outside the body. He approvingly cites Calvin's contention that Paul 'does not completely deny that there are other sins, which also bring dishonour and disgrace upon our bodies, but that he [Paul] is simply saying that those other sins do not leave anything like the same filthy stain on our bodies as fornication does.'[92] Under such reconstructions, πορνεία is then simply a particularly serious ethical breach, which happens to be committed bodily. It is not a peculiar offence against the Christian's bodily participation in Christ.

Such is a possible interpretation of 6.17 taken alone. But its context in 6.12–20 suggests that more attention should be paid to the contention that πορνεία is unique, and unique in its effects upon the believer's body. Paul has consistently stressed the central role that the body plays in the believer's relationship to Christ, and (as we have seen) he was at pains in 6.16 to stress the significance of sexual union for the body. This all suggests that the locative language of 6.17 should be taken seriously: πορνεία has a particular effect upon the body, in light of the body's relationship to the Lord. The locative language also continues in 6.19–20, where the body is the temple of the Holy Spirit ἐν ὑμῖν, and believers are to glorify God ἐν τῷ σώματι.

Fisk[93] has taken seriously Paul's notion of the effects of πορνεία upon the body. However, he does not wish to interpret the body in the light of Paul's references to it as the member of Christ or the temple of the Spirit. Paul, for Fisk, is making observations on the danger of πορνεία to bodies

88. Byrne 1983: 609–10.
89. A parallel to the notion of the 'every sin…but' is found in Mt. 12.31 πᾶσα ἁμαρτία καὶ βλασφημία ἀφεθήσεται τοῖς ἀνθρώποις, ἡ δὲ τοῦ πνεύματος βλασφημία οὐκ ἀφεθήσεται. See also Mk 12.44 and 14.29 for evidence of superficial contradictions that must be read in English as 'all other/but' (as Gundry 1976: 73–74; Fisk 1996: 544).
90. For a useful chart of all the positions that have been taken on this issue see Fisk 1996: 542–43.
91. Barrett 1971: 150–51.
92. Calvin 1960: 131.
93. Fisk 1996: 540–58.

in general, rather than to the Christian body as a participant in Christ. He thus suggests that Paul uses three *separate* arguments against πορνεία in 6.15–20: as a violation of Christ (6.15), as a violation of the body (6.16–18), and as a violation of the Spirit (6.19–20).

He contends that the violation of the body should be understood in the light of the Jewish wisdom tradition, which considered sexual sin as 'profoundly (and even uniquely) self destructive'.[94] He submits that 1 Cor. 6.16a is parallel to, if not reliant upon, Sir. 19.2b:

> Wine and women will mislead the wise, and the man who unites with prostitutes is shameless (ὁ κολλώμενος πόρναις πολμηρότερος ἔσται). Decay and worms will possess him, and the shameless person will be removed.

He then argues that 6.18 should be interpreted in the light of the union of 6.16a, hence: 'The body against which one sins sexually (18c) is the body which has been joined illicitly to another (16a). Sexual sin is uniquely body-defiling because it is uniquely body joining'.[95]

Fisk's argument is intriguing, but ultimately unconvincing. The parallel with Sirach is not close enough to be suggestive of anything much. Besides which, that passage read in context (Sir. 18.30–19.3) seems more concerned with prostitution as one example of a number of ruinous financial indulgences than πορνεία as a unique body violation.[96] Fisk's supposed examples of sins against the self are also suspect parallels. The inference of many of the passages he quotes, again when read in their context, is that ignoring wisdom's advice brings grievous consequences on oneself;[97] only a few speak of sins against the self (ψυχή), and none of them speak of sins against the σῶμα.[98] Further, for Fisk's contention that 'sexual sin is uniquely body-defiling because it is uniquely body joining' to work, he would require to show that physical consequences flow from the unique body joining that happens in intercourse. He offers scant evidence

94. Fisk 1996: 557.

95. Fisk 1996: 556.

96. Πολμηρότερος can be translated 'more rash' or 'more reckless', which gives a slightly different meaning to the passage Fisk quotes.

97. E.g. Prov. 20.2 'he who provokes the king's anger, sins against his own life', but the inference is that he takes his life into his own hands (the king may well kill him). Many of Fisk's examples appear to be suggesting that folly brings its own inevitable reward, and that by acting foolishly a man shows his disrespect for his own person.

98. In referring to various passages from Prov. 5–7 as evidence of the views of the 'destructive capacity of sexual sin' and the physical danger it brings, Fisk ignores the fact that the author's concern appears to be that prostitution is a threat to reputation bringing financial ruin (5.9–11) and adultery risks a husband's vengeance (6.34). These certainly are physical dangers, but not unique to sexual offences, and hardly evidence that sexual sin automatically damages the body.

that such is the case. Where 'joining' is used in his examples in connection with sex it seems to be simply a euphemism.

However, still more difficult to accept is Fisk's notion that 6.16–18 should be read, as an objection to πορνεία as a sin against one's own body, separately from the christological rationales of 6.15 and 6.19–20. The three οὐκ οἴδατε ὅτι all appear to move us towards justifications for the preceding statements, rather than to new arguments in the thesis. Even within the 'block' (6.16–18) that Fisk would carve out, he seems to ignore 6.17.

Fee's suggestion seems preferable. For Fee, 6.18's 'sin against the body' is governed, as is the whole of 6.13–20, by the notion of 'the body for the Lord'. Thus Paul's

> concern is not with what affects and does not affect the body per se, but with the special character of sexual immorality and how that sin is directed specially against the body as 'for the Lord'. In fornicating with a prostitute a man removes his body (which is a temple of the Spirit, purchased by God and destined for resurrection) from union with Christ and makes it a member of her body, thereby putting it under her 'mastery' (v.23b; cf. 7.4). Every other sin is apart from (i.e., not 'in') the body in this singular sense.[99]

This has the advantage of being able to pull together the disparate threads of 6.12–20. It allows the interpretation of 6.18 on the basis of the preceding two verses, without losing the Christocentric emphasis of 6.14, 6.17 and particularly 6.15.

Fisk offers three criticisms of Fee's reading. First, Paul speaks of a sin against the σῶμα, not σῶμα ὡς τῷ κυρίῳ. Secondly, it gives insufficient weight to the words τὸ ἴδιον σῶμα. Thirdly, Fee does not recognize the 'general, non-restrictive character of v.18 which suggests it would apply even to those whose bodies do not belong to Christ'.[100] However, such objections can be overcome. The first evaporates if we read 6.18 in the context of 6.15–20. Thus the sin against the σῶμα develops the notion of the infringement of the body's membership of and union with Christ (6.15–17), the same body that is the temple of the Holy Spirit and belongs to the Lord (6.19). Secondly, the phrase τὸ ἴδιον σῶμα may simply mean that the believer jeopardizes his *own* 'body for the Lord', as opposed to that of another believer, or of the community.[101] Fisk's third objection is simply invalid. There is not a 'general non-restrictive character' to this

---

99. Fee 1987: 262.

100. Fisk 1996: 550.

101. Such an interpretation may seem to render ἴδιον redundant, but a parallel can be drawn with Eph. 5.22 where wives, seemingly superfluously, are commanded to submit τοῖς ἰδίοις ἀνδράσιν.

warning – not unless the verse is again taken out of context of the entire passage.[102]

Here we are going further than Fee. We are reading εἰς τὸ ἴδιον σῶμα not only in conjunction with 'the body for the Lord' (6.13), but with the full force of the realistic implications of metaphorical articulation of the body as Christ's member (6.15), united to the Lord (through the pneumatic union) (6.17) and as the temple of the indwelling Holy Spirit (6.19). Unlike other sins which (merely) involve the body, the sexual sinner uniquely sins 'into' (εἰς) this body, directly terminating the body's participation in Christ.

To sin against (ἁμαρτάνειν εἰς) is invariably used of offending against another person.[103] To use it of an object is unparalleled. Thus it is almost as if Paul has personified the body – perhaps because of its close association with Christ (as his member). Further, to place ἁμαρτάνειν εἰς in juxtaposition with ἐκτός is, as far as one can see, also without parallel. This contrast would seem to imply a locative meaning for εἰς (sinning 'into' rather than 'against' the body). The body becomes a location, rather than a victim. The πόρνη unites with and enters the body, defiling the location in which the Spirit dwells, ending the body's spiritual participation in Christ.

Thus sexual immorality is a unique sin. It is uniquely against the body conceived of 'realistically' as a member of Christ.[104] Of course, other sins can exclude a man, even a believer, from his inheritance in Christ (6.9–11), but this need not mean that our verse should be read other than absolutely.[105] For Paul does not say that sexual immorality is unique in its damning consequences, but in its locus and effect: in the *manner* in which it disrupts union with Christ. Sexual immorality is unique precisely because it is no mere ethical breach, but because it is a direct transfer of the body out of union with Christ and into that with a πόρνη.

6.6.2. *The Abode of the Holy Spirit (6.19–20)*
In this verse we perhaps find some clues as to how Paul perceives of this realistic participation in Christ, how the Spirit relates to the body, and why this makes πόρνη-union quite so objectionable.

---

102. The use of ἄνθρωπος is no indication of a proof against πορνεία for all humanity. 1 Cor. 7.1b and 7.7 use ἄνθρωπος, while obviously offering advice only to believers.

103. 1 Cor. 8.12 and 12.2 speak of sinning against Christ. 1 Cor. 8.12 speaks of sinning against a brother. Mt. 18.15, 21 and Lk. 17.4 speak of the sins of another against a believer. Lk. 15.18 and 21 speak of sinning against heaven and Acts 25.8 of sinning against Caesar.

104. As Schrage 1995: 31: 'Πορνεία zerbricht *eo ipso* die Kommunikation mit dem Herrn und ist insofern eine Sünde wider das eigene Soma, den Ort dieser Korrelation zum Herrn.'

105. *Contra* Robertson and Plummer 1914: 128.

6.6.2.1. *The body as a location.* As we have noted, the locative language of
6.17 (ἐκτός, εἰς) serves to portray the body as a place that can be entered.
The same continues in 6.19–20. Once more Paul speaks specifically of the
σῶμα, rather than simply of the believer. In comparing the body to a
temple, Paul utilizes the image of a building familiar in antiquity. Paul's
Gentile readers would certainly have been familiar with entering temples
for the purposes of worshipping a particular divinity, but also with the
notion that these buildings housed the paraphernalia of the cult of a
particular divinity, if not (on occasion) the divinity itself. Jewish readers
might think similarly of the Jerusalem temple.

Paul explicitly alludes to these locative images. The body is not only a
temple of the Holy Spirit, but that Spirit is precisely said to be ἐν ὑμῖν,
dwelling in the body of the believer. Further, the believers are instructed
to glorify God ἐν τῷ σώματι ὑμῶν; that is, to use the temple for its
appropriate purpose, as a place in which God is glorified.

6.6.2.2. *A sacred space.* Paul reminds the Corinthians that the body is the
location of the Holy Spirit in the believer.[106] This would seem to be a
clarification of the contention that the believer was a member of (6.15) or
ἓν πνεῦμα with Christ (6.17) and it explicitly claims somatic implication
for that pneumatic relationship.[107] The pneumatic union occurs in the
somatic location. This is stressed in the word order of the passage: literally
'your bodies are temples of the in you, Holy Spirit.'

The Spirit is an important theme of the epistle as a whole (2.10–26; 3.16;
12.1–13), and its possession was doubtless at the root of Corinthian self-
assurance. Paul's connection of the Spirit to the body thus protects
against any tendency to devalue that body in light of spiritual experience
(cf. its connection to the resurrection in 6.13–14). It also (as 3.1) connects
the possession of the Spirit to the discussion of ethics. Implicitly those
who fail to conform jeopardize their possession of the Spirit. The Spirit is
not an intrinsic property or quality of the believer, but is ἀπὸ θεοῦ: a
conditional gift.

Significantly Paul names the Spirit as the ἁγίου πνεῦμα. To designate
the Spirit as holy is not as typical of Paul as one might suppose,[108] and,
despite the repeated discussion of the Spirit in 1 Corinthians, he does so
only here and at 12.13. Here the holiness of the Spirit connects obviously

---

106. As Schrage (1995: 29) will have it, 'Gerade die Leiblichkeit ist vielmehr der Ort der
Präsenz des πνεῦμα'.

107. As the ἥ, which most translators unfortunately neglect, shows that the οὐκ οἴδατε
ὅτι indicates not a new theme in the argument but a continuation of it.

108. Although Paul refers to the Spirit as holy on six occasions in Rom., surprisingly he
never does so in Gal., Phil., 2 Thess. or Phlm. and only twice in 2 Cor. and thrice in 1 Thess.

to the image of a sacred temple. Thus the holiness of the Spirit implies the holiness of the body in which it dwells.

The theme of holiness and the body also emerges in 1 Corinthians 7. Paul refers to the anxiety of the ἄγαμος and the παρθένος to be ἁγία τῷ σώματι καὶ τῷ πνεύματι, in contradistinction to the married believer. We shall explore this later. But might it hint that sexual union with another compromises the holiness of the body: the temple is not fully devoted to God? At 7.12–14 Paul discusses the legitimacy of continuing in marital union with an ἄπιστος. He defends this legitimacy by asserting that, by virtue of the marriage, the unbeliever is somehow sanctified (ἡγίασται). We shall return to this later. But implicitly the sanctity of a sexual partner is thus significant. Unbelievers require sanctification. If the spouse (or any partner) remains unholy, they would be unfit sexual partners for believers.

6.19–20 then provides the closing rationale for Paul's argument against a believer having sex with a πόρνη. An unholy union cannot occur in a sacred location. But the unholiness in view need not be only the unholiness of the act (as πορνεία) but also the unholiness of the partner (as a πόρνη). A πόρνη is by definition both an outsider, and unholy. She is certainly not a spouse and thus is not sanctified by marriage. She is thus an unholy person who should not enter the sacred space, which is the believer's body. But what happens if she does?

In 3.16–17 Paul has already made mention of the temple. Here he spoke not of the individual believer, but of the community. Although the context is different,[109] we are justified in thinking that the warnings issued there find an echo in this second temple metaphor. The first metaphor also began with the οὐκ οἴδατε ὅτι formula. It also spoke of the τὸ πνεῦμα τοῦ θεοῦ οἰκεῖ ἐν ὑμῖν. Paul also asserted that the ναὸς τοῦ θεοῦ ἅγιός ἐστιν. But here there was also a dire warning about the sacrilegious possibility of a believer destroying the temple and thus causing God to destroy him.

Can the body-as-temple also be destroyed? If the holy temple is polluted by the entry of the unclean, might it not cease to be sacred space, thus ceasing to be a place in which the Holy Spirit can dwell?[110] God cannot be glorified in a polluted temple. Thus again, Paul implies that physical relationship with the πόρνη destroys the spiritual relationship to the Lord, and that it does so precisely because the spiritual relationship involves the body. The pneumatic union includes, or is located in, the somatic. At any rate it would appear that Paul again implies that the body may either be

---

109. *Pace* Kempthorne 1967: 572–73 (followed by Newton 1985: 56–58) who argues that the temple motif in 6.19 is also corporate.

110. Cf. Josephus, who suggests that the offences of the Jewish revolutionaries pollute the Jerusalem Temple (*BJ* 5.412), so that it is no longer the place of God (*BJ* 5.19–20), and indeed that God leaves it (*BJ* 6.300).

for the Lord or for πορνεία; a member of Christ or of a πόρνη; spiritually united to him, or physically to her.[111]

Again our reading here stands in contrast to that of Martin.[112] Like him we accept that Paul uses a logic of invasion to object to πόρνη-union. The πόρνη is a polluting agent that cannot enter the holy place. However, unlike Martin, we do not suggest that Christ or his Spirit (or the 'body of Christ') are permeable. Rather, it is the believer's body that it permeable and vulnerable to pollution from the πόρνη. Her contact with his body through sexual union causes not the pollution of Christ or his Spirit, but the pollution of that body, which necessitates the withdrawal of the Holy Spirit and thus the destruction of the believer's spiritual union with Christ.

6.6.2.3. *Divine property*. Fee notes that grammatically οὐκ ἐστὲ ἑαυτῶν is better read as part of the question of 6.19 rather than of 6.20.[113] If this is correct, then Paul indicates something else with the temple metaphor: the temple is the property of the resident divinity. This thought moves Paul from the temple metaphor into the slavery metaphor of 6.20.

Here the image is of a slave market and not manumission from slavery.[114] Unlike a redemption metaphor[115] it does not presuppose an end to bondage but the transfer of ownership from one form of bondage to another. The believer's body has become the property of God. The freedom to use the body contrary to God's glory is thus denied. So too is the freedom to submit to any alternative mastery (such as that from which the believer has previously been purchased).

It is interesting that in this concluding metaphor Paul has moved from the language of participation to the language of ownership and mastery. However, just as in the case of the participation language, the implication is that the believer's body may have only one master, and thus that Christ's mastery of the body precludes sexual intercourse with the πόρνη. In a sense this echoes the initial discussion of ἐξουσία. Only one person may have ἐξουσία over the believer's body – and intercourse gives this to the sexual partner. However, there is also an element of contradiction. The opening implied that the believer has freedom, and the danger was that its abuse might lead to a new enslavement. Such theology is more in keeping with Galatians. In 6.20, however, the choice is not between

---

111. As Schrage 1995: 33: 'Als solche Sünde gegen den Ort der Herrschaft des Kyrios ist die ungebundene sexuelle Gier zugleich Frevel an der Stätte des Pneuma'.

112. D.B. Martin 1995: 174–79.

113. Fee 1987: 263; also Barrett 1971: 151.

114. As Fee 1987: 265, otherwise Deissman 1927: 318–30; Barrett 1971: 152 and K. Bailey 1980: 33–34.

115. Cf. Gal. 3.13; 4.5.

freedom and mastery, but between masters: who owns the body? These two diverse ideas come together only as they support the contention that sex with the πόρνη is a mastery incompatible with identity in Christ (conceived of either as slavery to, or freedom in, the Lord).

6.7. *Who is the* πόρνη?

Without evident exception, major commentators translate πόρνη simply as 'prostitute'. They assume that Paul is referring to a professional class of prostitutes, whose services are most probably engaged in the context of a brothel.[116] Where there is discussion of the identity of the prostitute, it is limited to the decision as to whether she should be classed as a 'cultic' or 'secular' prostitute, with the cultic option rightly being dismissed by most recent commentators.[117] But is this all there is to be said?

6.7.1. *How 'Professional' was Prostitution?*
The notion that prostitution was conducted by a definable class of women (operating mainly from brothels) for whom it was the main economic activity is distinctly anachronistic. A closer investigation of the evidence of ancient prostitution reveals a much more varied and flexible situation.

Kirchhoff[118] demonstrates that ancient prostitution was not limited to a 'professional' group, but was endemic among a whole class of women. There was, for instance, no strict differentiation between the brothel, the guesthouse and the tavern.[119] The assumption was that female personnel in any such establishment were sexually available for a financial consideration.[120] The same was true of those working at bathhouses.

As regards slavery, female (and male) slaves are generally sexually available, both to their owners and, at their owners' discretion, to others. Slaves engaged in tasks outside the home were often sexually available for

---

116. As implied by Fee when he discusses this passage under the heading 'Going to the Prostitutes' (1987: 249–66).

117. The cultic option rests primarily on an uncritical reading of Strabo's testimony (Strabo, *Geog.* 8.6.20) that there were a thousand prostitutes in the Temple of Aphrodite. Not only is the evidence itself suspect, but in any case it relates not to the Roman Colony but to its Hellenistic predecessor destroyed in 146 BC (see Murphy-O'Connor 1983: 55–57). However, some still argue for cultic prostitution (e.g. Miguens 1975: 47).

118. Kirchhoff 1994: 40–68.

119. For example, at Herculaneum the structure generally taken as a brothel seems also to have offered dining facilities.

120. It is interesting that Rahab, who the LXX clearly labels a πόρνη (Josh 2.1; 6.17–25), is described by Josephus as keeping an inn (τῷ τῆς ʽΡαάβης καταγωγίῳ, *Ant.* 5.8). This may be an attempt to alter an uncomfortable biblical text, but if Kirchhoff (1994: 23) is correct about the sexual availability of the staff of inns, the term could represent a euphemism rather than a direct amendment.

a financial consideration: such employment supplementing the income otherwise earned for their master or mistress, and many of those engaged in the entertainment industry (guesthouses, taverns and baths) would be slaves.[121] In addition, many slaves would work as artisans or traders outside the home, and these too could often be engaged in supplemental prostitution. Among the freed, while enforced prostitution was technically illegal, the freedwoman (or man) lacking a trade might well find it difficult to avoid, and the freedwoman remaining in the patron's home would find any sexual demands impossible to resist. Even among the freeborn poor, it appears that those engaged in many forms of trade often resorted to supplemental prostitution.[122]

Thus one should beware of equating modern prostitution with that of ancient Corinth. While the brothel and the 'professional' prostitute doubtless existed, prostitution appears to be more endemic. In Corinth itself there were large numbers of bathhouses, taverns and other places where prostitution might occur. Thus large groups of women were at times potentially involved in the provision of sexual services, and large numbers of venues and social interactions potentially served as locations for such transactions.

Further, there are varying types of relationship with women, not perhaps obviously classed as prostitution, in which a man could engage (with his slave, or in the taking of a freed or enslaved concubine). In most of these cases the woman would have little control and be financially dependent on the man. Thus, as Kirchhoff contends, 'the boundaries between professional prostitutions and other forms of extra-marital sexual intercourse were ... fluid'.[123] It may well be, however, that Paul from a Jewish perspective would have made little attempt to differentiate between a concubine, for instance, and a conventional prostitute.

6.7.2. Does πόρνη mean Prostitute?
However, even if we qualify our understanding of prostitution with the above considerations, it is legitimate to examine whether ἡ πόρνη simply designates a prostitute in the first place.

New Testament usage would seem to support such a translation,[124] as

---

121. Kirchhoff 1994: 48–49.

122. Juvenal (*Sat.* 11.162–70) implies that singers, dancers and mimes were generally viewed as sexually available (see also Tacitus, *Ann.* 1.72). Kirchhoff suggests that, for many traders, 'Prostitution ein Gewerbe war, das sich geschäftsfördernd auswirkte' (1994: 46). Interestingly the *Lex Iulia de Maritendis ordinibus*, which proscribes freeborn citizens from marrying prostitutes and their daughters, also prohibits the daughters of innkeepers, bakers and butchers, professions that have direct contact with their customers, and according to Kirchhoff are thus similarly tainted with prostitution (1994: 50–51).

123. Kirchhoff 1994: 37, author's translation.

124. Mt. 21.31–32; Lk. 15.30 and Jn 8.41.

would the etymological root of the πορν- word group, which apparently derives from the Greek πέρνημι denoting a foreign woman sold as a slave – an obvious source of prostitutes.[125] In fact, in Greek literature, apart from Jewish or Christian texts, the entire πορν- word group, although actually quite rare, invariably relates to prostitution.[126] Thus here the πόρνη is certainly a prostitute, but πορνεία must also be restricted to prostitution. Hellenistic-Jewish and Christian writers, however, use the πορν- group more frequently, and with wider application.[127]

As for Paul, πορνεία quite obviously means more than prostitution. In view of 1 Cor. 5.1 it evidently includes incest. 1 Thess. 4.3–6 indicates that adultery is also included. 1 Cor. 7.2 may well imply Paul has in view any extra-marital sexual relations.[128] When we turn to the personal labels πόρνος and πόρνοι, such can evidently be applied both to the incestuous man (5.11), and more generally to the pre-conversion identities of 'some' Corinthians (6.9–11) which presumably indicates more than simply involvement with prostitution.

What then of the πόρνη? Must this be a specific designator for the prostitute, or might it simply be the female πόρνος – any woman involved in extra-marital sexual relations? Would a Corinthian woman (aside from a former prostitute) who identified herself among the 'some' who were πόρνοι in 6.9–11 perhaps accept the ascription of πόρνη for her previous

125. Hauck and Schultz 1968: 580; Kirchhoff 1994: 21.
126. See Hauck and Schultz 1968: 580–81; Kirchhoff 1994: 22.
127. See Hauck and Schultz 1968: 587–90. As for the term πόρνη itself, in the LXX 1 Kgs 3.16–28 the women who appear before Solomon are πόρναι but they may be prostitutes or the concubines of a Jew. So too the women a priest is forbidden to marry in Lev. 21.7. Further, in Gen. 34 the raped Dinah is described as being treated like a πόρνη although no money changes hands. The only unambiguous factor is that all have sexual relations outside of regular marriage, and that this is assessed negatively. In the wisdom literature, although πόρνη can simply denote the prostitute (e.g. Prov. 6.26; 29.3; Sir. 9.6) at other times she is simply contrasted with a monogamous wife (e.g. Sir. 23.23). The other major uses are metaphorical, where Israel for her lawbreaking idolatry is described as a πόρνη: Yahweh's unfaithful and sullied bride. However, the metaphor does not necessarily imply prostitution, merely unfaithfulness to the true lover (Kirchhoff 1994: 23–25). As Kirchhoff concludes (35), 'πόρνη/זונה ist eine Frau, mit der die Adresseten nicht verkehren dürfen, Prostituierte gehören zu lediglich dazu'.
128. Malina (1972) denied that the term πορνεία was wide enough to encompass fornication. He argued that it was limited to sexual sins condemned by the Hebrew Scripture, where (he argued) non-commercial extra-marital intercourse was not rejected. Malina, however, has been criticized for wrongly assuming an ethical continuity between the Testaments, and failing to consider that if the Rabbis could read the Scriptures as condemning fornication, then there is no reason to believe that first-century Christians (or Jews) could not (see Jensen 1978: 174–75). Malina attempts to argue that πορνεία 'refers to incest throughout' 1 Cor. 5–6. However, Paul implies that many or all outsiders are πόρνοι, yet that incest is 'not among the Gentiles' (5.1).

identity? If πόρνος designates a man who commits incest or adultery, how else might such a female be designated?[129]

Perhaps, given that usually πόρνη specifically designates the prostitute in Greek literature (although the term is rare), it is impossible to escape the conclusion that the Corinthians would *primarily* find a reference to such in the term and that Paul would expect this. But perhaps Paul's wider use of the πορν- root in the context (a use foreign to readers of non-Jewish Greek texts) might serve to defamiliarize the term, and create in it a certain ambiguity. Thus πόρνη is a pejorative term that includes primarily the prostitute, but also implicitly any women who can be stereotypically denoted by sexual vice.

6.7.3. *The* πόρνη *as an Outsider*

Whether πόρνη specifically relates to prostitution, or includes other sexual offences, a πόρνη is by definition an outsider. πόρνοι cannot inherit the kingdom of God (6.9), and are to be excluded from the church (5.1–13). Those believers who once could be identified as πόρνοι have been transformed by baptism from that unethical identity (6.9–11).

But, as we have already submitted in relation to the πόρνοι τοῦ κόσμου of 5.10 (see section 4.5.1), there is the suggestion that, for Paul, not only are πόρνοι numerous among outsiders, but all outsiders *might* be considered to be πόρνοι as a class. 5.9–13 seemed to be moving in the direction of equating πόρνοι with κόσμος so that a call to avoid the former (when understood to relate to all πόρνοι and not simply pseudo-ἀδελφοί) was a call to avoid the latter. Thus perhaps when Paul rejects sex with a πόρνη in 6.15–16, although he *primarily* designates any woman who is personally guilty of πορνεία, his reference may also imply a rejection of sexual relations with any woman who could be identified as a πόρνη simply by membership of the unethical outgroup.

If so, this would resonate with 6.1–8. There, as we saw, Paul rejected believers appearing before judges. He rejected this on the basis that the judges were ἄδικοι. The label in itself makes the argument – those who are not δίκαιος are never suitable to judge lawsuits. But Paul applies the label to outsiders as a class, regardless of the morality of the individual judge. The use of any outsider as an arbiter between insiders is forbidden.

If πόρνη can be applied to any outside woman, then Paul is (at least implicitly) rejecting believers having sex with any outsider. His description in itself makes the argument – even one who wishes to have sex with a πόρνη would not wish to become one flesh (= be as if married) with her. But Paul rejects sexual relations with outsiders as a class, regardless of the morality of the individual woman. The use of an outsider as a sexual

---

129. Kirchhoff (1994: 18) complains of the male bias of exegetes who relate only the female form to prostitution.

partner is forbidden. This evidently would prevent not only extra-marital relations, but also the contraction of marriages with outsiders (believers are to marry μόνον ἐν κυρίῳ, 7.39).

Logically, this would also render existing marriages with unbelievers illicit. This is an implication which, significantly, Paul denies in 7.12–16, but the reasoning of that denial is revealing. The suggestion seems to have been made that believers should divorce unbelieving spouses (ἄπιστοι). The rationale seems to have been that such were in some way 'polluted' and thus unfit to be married to a believer. Although Paul rejects the conclusion (that divorce should occur), he does not reject the rationale offhand. He does not simply deny that unbelievers are unfit sexual partners due to their polluting effects. Instead, he implicitly admits this in accepting the need to argue that they have been sanctified through marriage to the believer. It is only by this special pleading that he can keep pre-existing mixed marriages intact. Thus μόνον ἐν κυρίῳ rule of 7.39 is not simply pragmatism, but it would appear that there is something about the 'unsanctified' state of unbelievers as a class that makes them unfit sexual partners. This parallels the rejection of unions with πόρναι, as a class, in 6.12–20.

Once again we find connections between Paul's thought in 1 Cor. 6.12–20 and 1 Corinthians 7, which require exploration. We saw that facets of Paul's argument against πόρνη-union (that the body is a member of and united to, Christ) logically forbade all sexual unions including marriages. We have seen that these concerns are echoed in 7.1–40. Paul denies marriage is sin, but expresses concern over a conflict of loyalties between spouse and Lord. Now we have seen that if the stress is placed on the object of union (the πόρνη), and if this is interpreted broadly, logically this would forbid sexual unions with all outsiders. This again resonates with the discussion in 7.1–40, where Paul insists marriages should be contracted only with believers, and while denying that existing mixed marriages should terminate, he exhibits concern for the status and sanctity of the unbelieving spouse.

6.8. *Implications*

6.8.1. *The Body, the Lord, and the Spirit*

We have observed how Paul uses two categories to describe the somatic implications of Christian identity. His basic category is that of the body's participation in Christ – metaphorically described as the body being a 'member' of Christ, 'united to' and 'one spirit with' the Lord, and the temple of the indwelling Spirit. However, he also uses the notion of the Christ's ownership of the body – metaphorically described as the Lord's temple and the Lord's slave. Both categories denote the 'body for the Lord' and exclude πορνεία. It is the first category that is of particular interest. It is the more prevalent of the two, (is perhaps the basis for the second) and informs us, not only that the believer's relation to Christ has implications for his use of his body, but also that that relation to Christ is somehow conceived of in somatic terms.

The function of the language is clear: to preclude those who claim Christian identity from involvement in certain sexual activities (classed as πορνεία) and particularly from sexual union with women classed as πόρναι. Indeed, as we have seen, the language chosen to denote participation in Christ (μέλη Χριστοῦ, ὁ κολλώμενος τῷ κυρίῳ) is shaped and selected for the rhetorical purposes of the ethical argument. However, this is not to say that the ethical purpose exhausts the meaning of the terminology and argument deployed. We must explore the concepts in their own right, not only for what they reveal about Paul's ethical convictions, but for what they reveal about Paul's underlying anthropological and christological convictions. To reduce the discourse immediately to its ethical function represents a failure to attempt to understand the fullness of Paul's meaning. Further, since there are connections between Paul's concerns about sex and the believer's body in 6.12–20 and his discussion of marriage in ch. 7, we need to explore the concepts in these chapters as a whole. An immediate reduction of the language to its ethical function is unable to do this, and will tend to view each passage as a separate ethical discourse rather than an inter-connected discussion about the believer's sexual body. Thus, prior to considering the ethical function, and certainly prior to any attempt to seek an interpretation of Paul's meaning in categories (we may view as) more comprehensible to the modern reader, we must focus further on the descriptive task. What exactly is Paul saying? What does the language of Christ-union and πόρνη-union actually signify for Paul? What have we observed so far?

To begin with the negative: the somatic language of the Christ-union is for Paul no 'mere metaphor'. It does not simply denote participation in the Christian community (= body of Christ), as much as this may be a tempting theological solution to the problem of Paul's meaning. Neither does it denote some type of participation in the cosmic body of the risen Christ. The language is anthropological rather than christological, the interest lying in the body of the believer and not that of Christ (of which, save perhaps for the implications of 6.14a, nothing is said). The believer is not said to *have* risen with Christ, and neither the risen body of the believer nor that of Christ is discussed. Rather the focus is on the present body of the believer, and the participation of the believer in Christ through that body.

What then can be said of the participatory language as it pertains to the body of the believer? It appears that Paul envisages the relation of the believer's body to Christ in terms of the Spirit. Christ-union results in the believer becoming 'one Spirit' (ἕν πνεῦμα) with the Lord. It is this that links the body to Christ, and renders πόρνη-union an impossibility. It is envisaged as the Holy Spirit indwelling the body of the believer as it would a temple, rendering the body as holy ground. Thus believers are instructed to glorify God ἐν τῷ σώματι ὑμῶν, as worshippers would in the consecrated temple of the divinity.

The articulation in this passage of participation in Christ in terms of the indwelling of the Holy Spirit in the body of the believer, although not the only way Paul can portray the believer's relationship with Christ, is certainly not without parallel. In Rom. 8.11 the Spirit τοῦ ἐγείραντος τὸν Ἰησοῦν ἐκ νεκρῶν (i.e. of God) is said to dwell in the believer (οἰκεῖ ἐν ὑμῖν), and through the indwelling of the Spirit (διὰ τοῦ ἐνοικοῦντος αὐτοῦ πνεύματος), God gives life to the mortal body (τὰ θνητὰ σώματα ὑμῶν).

We can again make mention of Martin at this point. Martin has taken seriously the participatory nature of Paul's language and its physical implications. He articulates the participatory language in the contention that 'the man's body and Christ's body share the same pneuma'.[130] There are, however, problems with this. First, Paul makes no mention of the 'body of Christ' in 1 Corinthians 5–6. This is rather a category that Martin imposes on Paul's several metaphors in 6.12–20 and on his discussion of the church in 5.1–13.[131] Secondly, although frustratingly Martin does not engage in close exegesis of 6.12–20, it appears that he has placed stress on Paul's contention that Lord and the believer are ἕν πνεῦμα (6.17). But is he correct to build so much on this? This is not Paul's usual articulation of the believer's relationship to the Spirit, and although we should take it seriously, the suspicion may be that this formula is contextually shaped for its parallel with ἕν σῶμα. Paul more usually speaks of the indwelling of the Holy Spirit, or of the believer's possession of the Spirit, concepts that maintain a separation between the believer and the Spirit (which is of God or Christ).[132] In 1 Cor. 6.19–20, which may explain the ἕν πνεῦμα reference, the believer has received the Spirit into his body, but it remains the Holy Spirit, from God, and thus both separate and separable from that body.

To bring into focus Paul's conception of participation in Christ as the presence of the Spirit in the body of the believer, forming the believer's link to Christ, may not appear to explain what such language might *mean*. It may well be that such talk of the presence of the Spirit is no more comprehensible to us than other aspects of the language of union with

130. D.B. Martin 1995: 176.
131. See n. 66 above.
132. In 1 Cor. Paul repeatedly speaks of the πνεῦμα as being τοῦ θεοῦ (2.11, 2.14, 3.16, 6.11, 7.40), ἐκ τοῦ θεοῦ (2.12) as well as ἀπὸ θεου (6.19).

Christ. However, as much as some re-articulation of the Pauline language
might be thought desirable, for the moment we must remain with what
Paul actually says. At this point at any rate, Sanders may be thought
correct when he contends that it is 'best to understand Paul as saying
what he meant, and meaning what he said: Christians really are one body
and one Spirit with Christ'[133] (although we would wish to nuance this last
assertion). If Paul has a conception of the Spirit as indwelling the
believer's body, and of this having implications for the use of such a
body, and being endangered by inappropriate bodily union, then,
however comprehensible or otherwise we may find such an idea, we are
obliged to take it seriously in any attempt to understand the apostle's
thought. We must certainly explore it fully (something this study may
contribute to) prior to any reduction of it to its ethical function, or any
rearticulation of it in alternative categories (which lies beyond the scope
of this study).

6.8.2. The body, Sex and the πόρνη

Sexual union (even casually with a πόρνη) effects a physical union, which
has effects on the body. Paul argues that sexual union makes the believer
'one flesh/body' with the sexual partner – in a sense that would normally
be restricted to the marital union. Paul implies that sexual union gives the
sexual partner an ἐξουσία over the body. This ἐξουσία appears to be
envisaged as an extraneous power (it is not just a conjugal right, although
within marriage it is the basis of such). In making the body become one
flesh/body with the other, some sort of authority/sovereignty over the
believer's body is transferred to the partner, an authority that the believer
should ideally reserve to himself (6.12a) or, better, invest in the Lord
(6.20).

Again, we could quickly reduce such talk to its ethical function,
working back from the fact that Paul's contentions on sex and the body
rule out πόρνη-union for the believer (6.12–20) while permitting union
with a spouse (7.1–40), even a spouse who is an outsider. The obvious
ethical function could be taken as a guide to interpret Paul, and to decode
what Paul *must* have meant by his apparently enigmatic statements on the
issue. He *must* simply be targeting extra-marital unions (πορνεία). But
such a temptation must be resisted. It represents a failure to analyse what
Paul *actually* says about sexual union, what the possible implications of
these convictions might be, how ch. 7 (as we shall see) shows Paul's
awareness of those implications, and how that chapter serves to qualify
those implications.

---

133.   Sanders 1977: 522 in the context of criticizing Bultmann for reinterpreting Paul in
existentialist categories, and then contending that this is what Paul *meant* (see further the
discussion in Riches 1993: 139–42 and Engberg-Pedersen 2000: 16–22).

We can clearly see that sex with a πόρνη affects the 'body for the Lord'. It does something to the body (making one flesh), and grants something to the partner (an ἐξουσία) that is incompatible with the Lord's claim and effect on the body. What happens in the sexual union is presented as incompatible with the Christ-union. However, nothing is said in this chapter about the status of the sexual union or the sexual partner, which would serve to differentiate between πόρνη-union and any other sexual union.[134]

Paul draws an analogy between Christ-union and sexual union that has the effect of undermining the legitimacy of the sexual union. The basis of that analogy is in the common properties of the two unions. Both involve the body of the believer. Both create a form of 'oneness' with an external other. Both give some form of ownership and authority over the body to that other. Πόρνη-union gives to another what by right, and by Spiritual union, belongs to the Lord. Thus linking the body to the other (the πόρνη) destroys the believer's union with the Lord (through the Spirit dwelling in the body). Thus, as union with the Lord marks an entry into Christian existence, so union with the πόρνη (as disunion with the Lord) marks an exit. Logically all sexual activity would have the same effect, since all would 'take' from the Lord, 'make' with another, and thus 'break' the Spiritual union in the body. As such the sex act is not outside, but inside, the body-as-temple.

Further, as we have seen, although the logic of Paul's argument could prohibit all sexual unions, the specific objection to a πόρνη could particularly undermine sex with outsiders. The πόρνη as a source of pollution, defiling the temple of the Spirit, echoes Paul's implicit admission of the pollution of the ἄπιστοι in 7.12–14. Here pollution is not based upon the sexual ethics of the individual outsider, but on all outsiders as a class. To preserve marital unions with outsiders Paul requires awkwardly annexing them into the category of the holy (normally reserved for believers).

What Paul appears to have done in 6.12–20 is bring together two ideas to argue against πόρνη-union: a logic that sees sexual union per se as a conflict with the concept of the body's participation in Christ and a logic that sees outsiders as unfit sexual partners due to their unholiness and the body's participation in Christ. Onto the marital/extra-marital distinction, Paul has superimposed the dichotomies of the body as participant in Christ/participant in another and endogamous/exogamous sexual relations. These come together in the case of the πόρνη: sex with whom is a bodily participation in someone other than Christ, is by definition extra-marital, and is by definition with an unholy outsider. Aspects of Paul's

---

134. As noted by Héring 1962: 45; Burkill 1971: 116; Boyarin 1994: 170–72.

argument in 7.1–40 thus illuminate the complexities of 6.12–20, just as 6.12–20 in turn illuminates the argument of 7.1–40, a notion we shall develop in subsequent chapters of this study.

6.8.3. *Sex, the Body and the Perseverance of the* ἅγιοι

6.8.3.1. πόρνη-*union as a different kind of sin*. In 4.3.1 we noted that the incestuous man's commission of πορνεία defined him as a πόρνος, denying his Christian identity. However, we left open the question as to whether πορνεία was identity-changing or merely identity-revealing. Did the man, by his sin, forfeit Christian identity or merely reveal he lacked it? We also left open whether all sins, only πορνεία, or indeed only this acute type of πορνεία, would have such an effect.

In Chapter 5 we noted that Paul reminded the litigating believers that the ἄδικοι would not inherit the kingdom. We argued (section 5.4.2) that this was an implied warning to those believers that those who commit ἀδικία endangered their identity in Christ. Thus believers *can* forfeit identity by unethical conduct other than πορνεία. However, this left open the question as to whether sexual sin was in any sense uniquely destructive of identity in Christ? Why was the one committing πορνεία labelled πόρνος and excluded (5.1–9), when those committing ἀδικία were merely warned, rather than being labelled ἄδικοι and excluded (6.7–11)? Is there a distinction between πορνεία and other types of sin?

We can now answer this question. It appears that πορνεία *is* to be considered a unique sin. It may not perhaps be unique in its *ability* to destroy, but it is unique in the *manner* in which it destroys, Christian identity. Christian identity is conceived of in somatic terms: the body participates in Christ and is the locus of the Holy Spirit in the believer. Thus taking the body and joining it to another in the sexual union of πορνεία breaks the pneumatic union and destroys Christian identity. This destruction occurs not simply because of ethical behaviour incompatible with Christian identity, but because the behaviour, by its very nature, destroys the believer's relationship to Christ. Such is not true of other sins.[135]

6.8.3.2. *A comparison with idolatry*.
It is worth briefly comparing our contentions here with Paul's treatment of idolatry in 1 Cor. 10.1–22. In this passage a direct parallel is drawn between Christian believers and the experiences of the Israelite community in the wilderness at the time of Moses. The parallel serves as a warning to the believers against the commission of idolatry, and implies that idolatry brings with it a severe penalty.

---

135. However, πορνεία is not among the *peccata irremissiblia*. 1 Cor. 5.5 implies that the offender can still be saved by reconversion (see above 4.4.2).

Paul begins by stressing the parallels between the Israelites and the Christian community. The Israelites are οἱ πατέρες ἡμῶν (10.1), who in passing through the sea underwent a type of baptism (10.2); who in eating the spiritual manna and drinking from the 'Rock' engaged in a type of Lord's Supper. Yet the Israelites, for all their spiritual benefits, displeased God and were 'overthrown in the wilderness', all because some of them were idolaters, engaging in πορνεία and putting God to the test (10.6–10). The warnings to the Corinthians are clear – their belonging, their baptism, their participation in Christ and in the Lord's Supper, will not protect them from the loss of their Christian status should they engage in idolatrous practices.[136] Even although they think that by such things they will stand, the possibility of falling remains (10.12).[137]

There is a real warning in this passage that idolatry is potentially destructive of Christian identity. The stressing of the parallels between the experience and destruction of the Israelites and the current situation of believers makes this clear. Even those who have participated in the divine benefits are not immune from danger. The Israelites had parallel benefits

136. It has been argued that Paul does not threaten the believers with a loss of salvation, but with physical death. Drawing from the fact that the idolatrous Israelites are said to be κατεστρώθησαν ἐν τῇ ἐρήμῳ (10.5) ὑπὸ τῶν ὄφεων ἀπώλλυντο (10.9) and ἀπώλοντο ὑπὸ τοῦ ὀλοθρευτô (10.10), Sanders concludes that 'the force of the typological argument is that those who commit idolatry will be killed' (1983: 110). The case for a physical punishment is strengthened if one takes 1 Cor. 5.5 to refer to the physical suffering/death of the immoral man, and when one considers that Paul sees illness and death as the result of the profaning of the Lord's supper (11.30–32). However, be that as it may, it seems most probable that Paul is also warning the Corinthians about the possible loss of salvation (with Fee 1987: 459 and Gundry Volf 1990: 123–24). Some of the Israelites became πόρνοι and εἰδωλολάτραι (10.7) whom we know Paul deems excluded from the kingdom (6.9).

137. Gundry Volf (1990: 120–30) argues that although Paul warns against 'falling away' he does not imply that Corinthians who sin like the Israelites will forfeit salvation, but rather that they will prove that their Christian profession is, and always was, false. Thus Paul's meaning may be paraphrased 'let the one who appears to be saved (by virtue of being a partaker of the Lord's supper) beware that she does not behave like a non-Christian (in committing idolatry) and fall under judgment, thereby disproving her Christian profession!' (127) Gundry Volf's work begins, however, with an exegesis of Rom. 8.29–39 that reaches typically Reformed conclusions concerning the election and perseverance of believers. This has a tendency to control her exegesis of 1 Cor. 10. Unfortunately her reading makes little sense of the text. She views 10.11–12 as a warning to pseudo-Christians. But Paul declares (10.11) that these things are written 'for our instruction' (πρὸς νουθεσίαν ἡμῶν) (cf. 10.6). If intended for pseudo-Christians, why not either call for their expulsion from the community (as 5.1–9) or for their true conversion? Further, Gundry Volf surely requires to separate the 'warning' of 10.11–12 from the promise of 10.13 that God will give the ability to endure temptation. This promise cannot be addressed to the one who only 'appears to be saved'. (For further criticism of Gundry Volf see Oropeza 1999 and 2000: 28–33, 193–96.)

and yet still failed.[138] Christian identity may thus be lost through idolatry as well as πορνεία.

However, we must note that, unlike 5.1–9, we are dealing here with a warning about idolatry as an end to Christian identity, and not a claim that any believer has already lost that identity.[139] There are two possible explanations of this. On one hand, we might view idolatry as being on a par with the ἀδικία of 6.7–8: an activity, which is viewed incompatible with Christian identity, but nevertheless does not automatically lead to a loss of identity. Those committing idolatry are thus warned but not yet expelled as apostates. However, the explicit nature of the warning (10.12) and the forceful presentation of the incompatibility of idolatry and participation in Christ (10.21), seems to count against this. On the other hand, it is more likely that Paul warns rather than excludes as he does not consider that the Corinthians are at present committing idolatry, although they are dangerously exposed to it. Thus, unlike 6.7–8, no warning *would* be possible for those *actually* committing idolatry; offenders would be expelled like the immoral man of 5.1–9, severed from Christ like any who engage in πόρνη-union. As with 6.12–20, a warning is issued to those not actually committing this offence, but viewed as being in imminent danger. But as with πορνεία there is no call to repent, or to desist, but simply a call to avoid (φεύγετε, 10.14; cf. 6.18) the behaviour in question.

So it may well be that idolatry, like πορνεία, is considered immediately destructive of Christian identity. Certainly 10.14–22 seems to set up many of the same categories as 6.12–20. Believers participate in Christ, yet idolatry presents the believer with an alternative and incompatible κοινωνία this time with δαιμόνια. A simultaneous participation is

138. There has been a stream of exegesis that has seen Paul as combating the Corinthians' false confidence in the ability of the sacraments to render them immune from the dangers of participating in pagan rites (e.g. Barrett 1971: 220). Thus, against such sacramentalism or 'magical view of the sacraments' (Fee 1987: 443), Paul contends that, even although the Israelites had equivalent outward symbols, still they perished.

However, such an interpretation is suspiciously 'Protestant'. It views baptism and the Lord's Supper as 'external signs' (Gundry Volf 1990: 125–27), which in the end prove to be no substitute for true discipleship. Does Paul really make such a distinction? Rather, his point would seem to be that the Israelites, like the Corinthian believers, were truly the people of God. (They were '*our* fathers'. Not only baptized, and receiving the spiritual food, but also drinking from the supernatural Rock that is Christ; cf. M.M. Mitchell 1991: 252.) The point is not that they had false confidence in symbols, but that despite their full participation in God's benefits as God's people, they still fell through idolatry. They all ran the race, but some did not receive the prize (9.24–27). So too the Corinthians, despite their *genuine* participation in Christ, still must guard against the real and mortal danger of idolatry.

139. As Gundry Volf (1990: 121): 'Paul does not yet pronounce judgment on the Corinthians as idolaters. In contrast to the discussion on the incestuous man in chap. 5 and the profaners of the Lord's supper in chap. 11, they are not so far judged guilty, therefore, punishment is still a possibility to be avoided'.

impossible. The logic here could be the same as 6.12–20, implying that idolatry too is a sin εἰς τὸ σῶμα, bringing the believer's body into contact with that which is incompatible with the Holy Spirit. However, this possibility is no certainty. Paul's use of body language here is unequivocally communal. There is a choice between two allegiances, two identities, but whether there is the same concern for somatic conflict as we have found in 6.12–20 must remain an open question. Perhaps πορνεία truly is unique.

Chapter 7

READING 1 CORINTHIANS 7

7.1. *Introduction*

7.1.1. *Setting the Questions*

Precisely because it concerns marriage, 1 Corinthians 7 is key to understanding the sexual and social implication of Christian identity. Marriage is not only a means of structuring individual sexuality, but also a means of structuring society itself. It not only regulates relationships between individuals, but it is a building block for wider social relations. Thus understanding the relationship between Christian identity and marriage in Paul's thought is crucial in understanding his attitude to Christian social existence as a whole. What difference does Christian identity make, in Paul's view, to the believer's attitude to marriage? Obviously Paul permits both marriage and celibacy – so we look to the nuances of his discussion to understand his views. Where does the emphasis fall? How does Paul's attitude differ from that of the wider Graeco-Roman society?

In 1 Corinthians 7 Paul appears to be facing simultaneously in two directions. On the one hand, the text clearly indicates his preference for celibacy: he explicitly states it (7.7; 7.8; 7.26; 7.38), and also points out the difficulties and conflicts faced by the married believer (7.26–27; 7.32–35). Yet, on the other hand, the apostle protests that marriage is not sin (7.36–37), even declaring it to be καλόν (7.38), advisable as an antidote for πορνεία (7.2; 7.9) or if a man feels himself to be acting improperly towards his παρθένος (7.36). These opposite motions require explanation – not because they are necessarily inconsistent – but because they raise the question as to why anyone, in a treatise which so evidently urges celibacy, requires to deny that marriage is sinful. Who suggested that it was, and for what reason?

7.1.2. *Constructing the Dialogical Context*

Almost unanimously, modern exegetes answer by contending that 1 Corinthians 7 is to be understood as Paul's response to Corinthian ascetics.[1] These ascetics advocate celibacy (for variously explained reasons), putting it forward as normative for believers, and perhaps even (in view of Paul's rejection of the ideas) suggesting that believers already married should either permanently abstain from intercourse, or terminate their marriages by divorce.[2] This 'ascetic hypothesis' provides an explanation for the tension in the text. Paul sympathizes with the ascetics (and wishes to demonstrate such to them): hence his pro-celibacy sentiments. However, he rejects their insistence that celibacy be compulsory for all believers (such leaves weaker Christians vulnerable to πορνεία), and particularly their idea that those presently married should remain chaste or divorce: hence the contrary sentiment, and protestation of the moral acceptability of marriage.

The text is thus viewed as a highly rhetorical response to these ascetics, rather than primarily as Paul's own considered ideas on marriage and celibacy. They, and not he, set the agenda for the discussion. We are thus not to view Paul, as the patristic writers invariably did, as the primary proponent of asceticism: such a contention represents a failure to take account of the true *Sitz im Leben* of the text which modern exegesis has now uncovered.[3]

Having decided that the text is responsive, the focus then moves to reconstructing the arguments and motivations of the supposed ascetics, and much effort (see section 7.3 below) has been spent on this quest. Not only does this mean that the text is not read of itself as Pauline parenesis, but more significantly, many of the sentiments and even expressions of the chapter are attributed to the Corinthians rather than to Paul. They, and *not* he, contend that 'it is good for a man not to touch a woman';[4] sexual abstinence for prayer becomes their practice;[5] and the attribution to the unmarried woman of some type of holiness 'in body and spirit' denied to the married (7.34) is held to be their language and not Paul's.[6] The result of the exercise is often that the Pauline text is held to reveal more about

---

1. Gundry Volf (1994a: 105) can go as far as to state that '1 Corinthians 7 presupposes (*sic*) sexual asceticism in the Corinthian church and that Paul is responding to this development' (see also Gundry Volf 1996: 519).

2. See e.g. Maxwell 1992: 260.

3. So e.g. Scroggs 1972: 295–96.

4. Dunn (1995: 54) is correct to observe that 'the recognition that 7.1b is probably a quotation from the Corinthians' letter ... is old and well established'; the concept goes back as far as Origen. In a list of 24 scholars from the 1880s to the 1960s, Hurd (1965: 68) notes that 10 affirm 7.1b as a quotation. Since then the trend for seeing a quotation is impressive (e.g. Hurd 1965: 163; Barrett 1971: 154; Scroggs 1972: 296; Murphy-O'Connor 1981: 603; Meeks 1983: 102; Yarbrough 1995: 94; Fee 1987: 275–76; and Gundry Volf 1996) although not quite unanimous (cf. Bultmann 1952: 202; Conzelmann 1975: 114; Fiorenza 1984: 223).

5. So e.g. Maxwell 1992: 260 and Gundry Volf 1996: 531.

6. E.g. Barrett 1971: 181–82.

the practice and doctrine of the hypothetical ascetics than of its own author: the clamour of their voices drowns out his.

This study will question this scholarly consensus, not for its own sake, but because we wish to read 1 Corinthians 7 as Paul's own consideration of sex and marriage. Negatively, we shall ask whether the ascetic hypothesis is tenable – is it able to provide an adequate explanation of either the text or context of 1 Corinthians 7? We shall examine this below (and the pervasiveness of the hypothesis stands as our justification for the space that we devote to assessing it). Positively, we shall examine whether the tension in Paul's approach to the issue of celibacy and marriage can be explained (and is better explained) with reference to Paul's own convictions about Christian sexuality and identity in the world, as we have found them in 1 Cor. 5.1–6.20, and as they are confirmed in 1 Corinthians as a whole.

1. On the desirability of marrying per se, we have noted in Chapter 6 how the objections that Paul offered to sex with a πόρνη rendered marriage itself problematic. We shall explore, when we turn our attention to the text of 1 Corinthians 7 (Chapter 9 below), whether this might not provide adequate explanation of Paul's nervousness about marriage. Could the logic of Paul's argument in 1 Cor. 6.12–20 explain why it might occur to Paul, or to anyone reading him, that marriage itself might be sinful? Could it account for Paul's desire to pre-empt, or to respond so emphatically to, such a notion?

    However, 6.12–20 also revealed Paul's concern about πορνεία, a unique sacrilege against the body's participation in Christ, and destructive of Christian identity. This perhaps begins to explain the other side of Paul's discourse, an advocacy of marriage as a safeguard against such a destruction, and the rejection of practices (marital abstinence) which might leave the married unnecessarily vulnerable.

2. On the question of mixed marriages and divorce (7.12–16; 7.39), given our previous findings, Paul's concern for the status of mixed marriages is perhaps not surprising. We have observed the clarity of Paul's distinction between believer and unbeliever. We have observed his desire that identity in Christ be the salient identity of believers in an increasing number of social situations (prohibiting certain interactions with outsiders). Thus the contentions that *new* mixed marriages (which are at the very least a social encounter between individuals, which potentially form a strong social unit) are not contracted is perhaps explicable. Further in 6.12–20 we observed that πόρναι as a class were deemed unfit for sexual relations with a believer, and we suggested that the label πόρνη might not simply denote a prostitute but cover any woman stereotyped with a sullied sexual identity (6.7) – including all outsiders.

However, we have also noted Paul's desire that believers 'remain in the world' (5.10), not withdrawing from social existence and its inevitable social interactions, but rather transforming their inter-individual relationships to intergroup encounters (see section 4.5). Believers are to engage in social transactions on the basis and in the knowledge of their new Christian identity. Thus Paul's encouragement of the persistence of *existing* mixed marriages, but his simultaneous insistence that the status of the sexual partner as insider/outsider matters, is perhaps likewise explicable.

Certainly mirror-reading the text cannot entirely be avoided. If nothing else, the opening περὶ δὲ ὧν ἐγράψατε (7.1a) indicates that 1 Corinthians 7 is constructed, at least in part, as a response to Corinthian questions or objections (perhaps to Paul's previous teaching). There is a prior discourse. But it is to Paul's thoughts that 1 Corinthians 7 gives us primary access, and it is to these we shall primarily turn our attention. As far as the Corinthians are concerned, any attempt to uncover their attitudes to sex and marriage (attitudes which presumably provoke Paul's response) must be reconstructed not only from the text of 1 Corinthians 7 but (given the uncertainties of mirror-reading and the dangers in claiming certain results)[7] from all available evidence. This means using both what we can glean about their attitudes to sexuality from 5.1–6.20, and, given that marriage is not just a response to sexuality but part and parcel of social existence, what we can glean from their attitude to their social world from the entire epistle. (This will be our focus in Chapter 8.) The wider data must be used to correct and control the possible results of any mirror-reading experiment taken from a mere 40 verses. It shall be one of our criticisms of the ascetic hypothesis that its recent proponents have generally failed to utilize such a wider textual control.

We shall proceed to consider 1 Corinthians 7 as follows. (1) In 7.2 we shall offer a number of general objections to the ascetic hypothesis, serving to justify the call to rethink the context of the chapter. (2) In 7.3–4 we shall consider and critique the various motives attributed to the supposed ascetics, showing the weaknesses with each, but in the awareness that refuting any of the supposed motivations for Corinthian asceticism will not invalidate the ascetic hypothesis as a whole. (3) In Chapter 8 we shall explore the social implications of the renunciation of marriage, namely, how marriage is integral to the social world of the ancient city. We shall examine what type of attitude to the social world would be likely to accompany the renunciation of marriage, and what sort of response the renunciation is likely to provoke from that world. We

7. On the problems of mirror-reading see Barclay 1987.

shall then compare this picture to the social ethos and social experience of the Corinthian church distilled from the epistle as a whole. What was the attitude of the congregation to its social environment – its response to the world? What type of response did it provoke from its social environment? We shall then ask whether these findings support the ascetic hypothesis as it stands, or whether they suggest another background for 1 Corinthians 7. In Chapter 9, we shall re-examine the text as Pauline theology. Here we shall be searching for the apostle's own convictions on marriage and sexuality and demonstrating how these fit with what we have discovered in 5.1–6.12. Further, we shall attempt to show how these convictions, and the Corinthians' likely response to them, might provide a better explanation of the text of 1 Corinthians 7 than does the ascetic hypothesis.

7.2. Objections to the 'Ascetic Hypothesis'

7.2.1. The failure to reconstruct Corinthian attitudes to marriage with regard for the social ethos of the whole letter

We have already alluded to this important consideration, and we shall return to it in Chapter 8. Any renunciation of marriage is a renunciation of a social institution key to the self-conception of ancient society. It is not merely an ethical decision on the exercising of sexuality but also a response to the world.[8] We have a fair amount of evidence of the Corinthian church's response to the world from the remainder of the epistle – evidence that has in recent years produced a great number of studies of the social ethos of the church.[9] It is beholden on those who would postulate asceticism as lying behind 1 Corinthians 7 to explain such a 'response to the world' with reference to the wider evidence of the social ethos, either to show that such evidence can support their contention, or, if it does not, to account for, and provide evidence of, two disparate social ethics operating within the one congregation.

We shall be questioning later whether either of these options is plausible. Does the evidence indicate that the social ethos of the Corinthian congregation could support such a radical response to the world as the renunciation of marriage, or the opposite? Will the evidence support a fundamental split in social ethos within the Corinthian church? However, for now, the important thing is to note that few of the recent proponents of the ascetic hypothesis have attempted to explain, or even noted, the disparity between their reconstructions of 1 Corinthians 7 and current scholarly thinking on the social ethos of the church based on the

8. A point made repeatedly by P. Brown 1988.
9. E.g. Theissen 1982; Barclay 1992; Chow 1992; Clarke 1993; D.B. Martin 1995; Horrell 1996a; De Vos 1999; and Adams 2000.

rest of the epistle.[10] This chapter often seems to be studied on its own, ripped out of context, and explained without reference to the wider social situation. We shall insist, when we return to this issue, that any particular explanation of 1 Corinthians 7 must be tested by, and be coherent with, the general reconstruction of the situation behind the entire epistle.[11]

7.2.2. *The Failure to Account for the Balance of the Argument*
Despite the stream of thought in 1 Corinthians 7 that insists on the legitimacy of marriage, and rejects both divorce and all but temporary abstinence within marriage, the greater part of 1 Corinthians 7 appears to be arguing *against* the desirability of marrying (7.1, 7.7–8, 7.17–35, 7.37–40). (In addition, our consideration of the text in Chapter 9 shall show that many sections that have been read as relativizing both marriage and celibacy in fact serve to undermine the reasons for marrying.) This is difficult to explain if Paul's main dialogue partners are ascetics, and his main purpose to temper their enthusiasm. While Paul, under such a reconstruction, might possibly wish to mark points of agreement, the amount of space devoted to the benefits of celibacy, and the fact Paul appears to be *arguing* for such, would seem better explained by the contention that his audience were *less* enthusiastic for celibacy than was Paul.

7.2.3. *The Failure to Read 1 Corinthians 7 in the Context of 5.1–7.40 as Pauline Sexual Ethics*
1 Corinthians 7 is often wrenched out of its immediate context within Paul's discussion of sex in 5.1–7.40. This is achieved by two means. First the περὶ δέ of 7.1 is taken unproblematically as the start of a new part of the epistle. In 1.1–6.20 Paul is presented as responding to oral reports, and then in 7.1–16.12 to the issues raised by the Corinthian letter.

While it may well be the case that Paul begins at 1 Cor. 7.1 to deal with issues raised by a Corinthian letter, the continuing theme of πορνεία should encourage us to read chs 5–7 as a whole. There are also a number

---

10. Earlier commentators, who constructed the ethos of the entire epistle with regard to pneumatism, realized eschatology and Gnostic comparisons, are perhaps less culpable. Our complaint is primarily against those who are aware of recent work on the social ethos of the Corinthian church, and/or of criticisms of reconstructions of the epistle purely on the basis of spiritual/eschatological opposition to Paul, and yet who do not consider this when reconstructing 1 Cor. 7 (e.g. Fee 1987: 269; M.Y. MacDonald 1990; and Gundry Volf 1994a, 1996).

11. It is here that Deming's (1995) methodology fails for, at the end of his reconstruction of Paul's thought in 1 Cor. 7 in terms of the Stoic/Cynic debate, he lays down the challenge to other scholars 'to clarify other sections of 1 and 2 Corinthians from this perspective' (214). This seemingly begs the question as to *whether* such a reconstruction of Paul's dialogue with his converts in 1 Cor. 7 can be reconciled with the rest of the Corinthian correspondence.

of other links between the passages: the concern with ἐξουσία (7.4; cf. 6.12); the concern with relations between believers and unbelievers (7.12–16; cf. 5.9–13, 6.1–11 and 6.12–20); the connection between sexual unions and slavery and freedom (7.15 and 7.17–24; cf. 6.12 and 6.20); and the concern with sex and the believer's body (7.4 and 7.34; cf. 6.12–20). If Paul is dealing with an issue raised by the Corinthian letter from 7.1, he is choosing to do so immediately after dealing with the sexual issues raised by the oral report. If Paul connects 5.1–6.20 with 7.1–40, we do well to heed that connection.[12]

Secondly, the division of Paul's target audience in 1 Corinthians 5–7 into libertines and ascetics also serves to hamper an appreciation of Paul's thematic treatment of sex.[13] Instead of reading Paul's discussion of sex and marriage as a whole, and interpreting 7.1–40 in light of 5.1–6.20 and *vice versa*, scholars postulate two separate situational backgrounds for the two parts, two separate audiences, and read each part of the text individually against that background.

The danger is that, in stressing the situational nature of Paul's letter, we end up by contending that the text tells us more about the Corinthians' views on sex than about its author's own concerns. We have already rejected the existence of a 'libertine' faction (see sections 4.2.4, 6.2.2), and we now question the existence of an 'ascetic' faction, but, be that as it may, we must assume that Paul counters whatever Corinthian notions he views as erroneous by asserting his own position, largely in his own words.[14]

7.2.4. The Weakness in Methodology
As we have noted, at the centre of the ascetic hypothesis has been the confidence of its advocates in attributing certain sentiments and phrases of the text of 1 Corinthians 7 to the Corinthian opponents rather than to Paul, and from these to reconstruct not only their practice but also its

---

12. Remarkably Wimbush (1993: 422), having indicated that 1 Cor. 7 seeks to answer Corinthian questions, draws attention to 'the otherwise fortuitous juxtaposition of the issue of *porneia* in chapters 5–6, followed by the issue of marriage and celibacy in chapter 7'!

13. Following Weiss 1910: 169 and Chadwick 1955: 264–65, this division appears to be accepted by all major commentators (with some exceptions, e.g. Schmithals 1971 and Goulder 1999).

14. Aside from the difficulty of 'mirror reading' Paul for the attitudes of his opponents, there is also, in the concentration on such, a failure to recognize that the Corinthians are dealing with issues of sexuality precisely as a Pauline community. They are for the most part probably reacting to, or against, the apostle's teachings. As Wimbush puts it, 1 Cor. 7 'supplies us with neither the undiluted language nor the pure sentiment of the Corinthians. And it is very plausible that in this chapter we have to do *as much* with radical interpretations – literalist or spiritualized – of Paul's teaching *as* with any external influences or "backgrounds". Thus, it is Paul's sentiments and teaching that should *first* be the subject of interest' (1987: 6).

underlying ideology. This immediately raises the question of exegetical method. How far may we use the Pauline text to uncover his opponents' position?

There is a tendency among proponents of the hypothesis to assume that they are able to distil allusions to Corinthian assertions from what Paul directly refutes, and allusions to otherwise unrecorded assertions from what he appears to concede or rework. Gundry Volf, for example, believing that 7.1b and 7.34 cannot really reveal Paul's theology, is confident they must reveal that of the Corinthians. 7.1b, she suggests, 'reveals the ascetics' view of continence as morally good, or contributing to salvation'.[15] (But even if we could be sure this was a citation, could we be so sure what the Corinthians meant by καλόν?) She is also confident that what Paul denies in 7.4 (a spouse has authority over his/her own body) and in 7.36 (marriage is sin) must certainly be what the Corinthians affirm. She contends that Paul's seeming concession in 7.5 of limited abstinence for prayer reveals the heart of the Corinthians' motivation for asceticism, despite the fact that prayer is not mentioned anywhere else in the chapter. Mirror-reading is simply never that clear cut;[16] other alternatives do exist (as we hope to show when we turn shortly to the text), and Paul's arguments may well be more complex than they first appear.[17]

7.2.5. *The Lack of Consensus on the Nature of the Corinthian Asceticism*

Despite the almost universal conviction that Corinthian ascetics lie behind Paul's writing, scholarship has been unable to reach any consensus on the motivations of this opposing movement. The tendency has been to reconstruct the ideology of the ascetics, and to support such reconstructions by appealing to other (often-reconstructed) phenomena of celibate

15. Gundry Volf 1996: 522. For an even more uncritical example of mirror-reading see Maxwell 1992: 257–61.

16. See Barclay 1987.

17. One of the few to address the question of method in reading the text has been A.C. Wire (1990). Wire's aim is set out in the title of her book *The Corinthian Women Prophets: A Reconstruction through Paul's Rhetoric*. Assuming the existence of such a group, she aims to reconstruct its behaviour and theology. Her method is to insist on reading the Pauline text not as objective description but as persuasive rhetoric. She insists that all speech is shaped with its audience in mind, for 'to argue is to gauge your audience as accurately as you can at every point, to use their language, to work from where they are to move them to where you want them to be'. So far so good, but then she insists that 'because everything spoken must be shaped for them, the measure of the audience as the speaker knows it can be read in the arguments that are chosen' (1990: 3). This is surely a logical jump. For all that can be assumed is that if rhetoric is reasonable effective (and that is always an 'if') the audience will be able to recognize their own position and their problems with, and objections to, that of the persuader. There can be no assurance that we, as a removed third party, will be able to read the measure of the audience even as the speaker knows it.

ideologies in the history of religions.[18] These other ideologies may be seen either as direct influences upon, or merely as parallels to, the Corinthian ascetics' theology. Thus Hurd suggests that the Corinthians believed that marriage would cease with the imminently expected Parousia (as Mk 12.25 and Lk. 17.26);[19] Balch suggests that they sought to be θεῖοι ἄνδρες attaining revelations by asceticism (as Philo's Moses);[20] Horsley suggests a divine marriage to Sophia (as Philo's Therapeutae);[21] various scholars have looked to Gnostic texts, and so we might go on. More recently, attempts have been made to reject the 'religious' explanations and seek an answer in Graeco-Roman philosophy, the Stoic-Cynic marriage debate (Deming)[22] or the common philosophical/medical understanding of the Graeco-Roman elite (Martin).[23]

We shall review some of these suggestions in the next section. However, the plethora of mostly incompatible explanations raises important questions. First, if the text of 1 Corinthians 7 can be made to fit such a large number of possible reconstructions, does it contain enough fixed evidence for either the defence or the falsification of any possible suggestion? This consideration again supports the insistence that the entire letter, and not just this one chapter, must be considered when the veracity of any theory is being tested. Even if we were to accept the ascetic hypothesis, the fact that so many motivational theories have been offered should perhaps encourage some agnosticism towards such. Alternatively, we may question the underlying hypothesis and seek a new way forward.

7.2.6. The Suspicion of Apologetic Intent

It is, of course, a genetic fallacy to dismiss any theory simply on the grounds of its apologetic value. Nevertheless, we are entitled to be cautious of the fact that many proponents of the ascetic hypothesis are able and willing to make use of it to support theological agendas. We may have much sympathy with Nejsum in his criticism of conservative exegetes when he complains that 'the apologetically coloured reading of these texts is characterised by the effort to explain away, tone down or reinterpret the elements of sexual asceticism in Paul's sexual ethics'.[24] Instead of reading Paul as an ascetic, by virtue of the ascetic hypothesis, some of the apparently ascetic elements in the letter can be attributed to the

---

18.   Since the ascetic movements that are offered as parallels to that supposed in Corinth are often also hypothetical reconstructions from other texts, this raises the evidential question as to whether a supposition can ever corroborate a parallel supposition.

19.   Hurd 1965: 276–78.

20.   Balch 1971: 351–64.

21.   Horsley 1979: 46–51.

22.   Deming 1995; see also Balch 1983.

23.   D.B. Martin 1995: 205–208.

24.   Nejsum 1994: 48.

Corinthians and Paul pictured as less radical, indeed advocating marriage and marital sexual relations in the face of an ascetic onslaught. As Nejsum points out, 'in this fashion it is possible not only to ensure that one of the texts expressing the most pronounced sexually abstemious attitudes [7.1b] is no longer assigned to Paul, but also to prepare the way for reading the rest of the chapter as an exhortation to ascetic Corinthians, so that the "sign" of the chapter becomes reversed, and Paul ends up *defending* sexuality'.[25]

Further, there have been apologetic agendas not only in seeing Paul responding to ascetics, but also often in the identification of the Corinthian ascetics themselves. It has suited many commentators to equate Paul's supposed 'ascetic opponents' with their own. Calvin drew parallels between them and both his 'papist' opponents and the pro-celibacy Fathers with whom he was in disagreement,[26] and many Lutherans, following Lütgert, have painted them as 'enthusiasts' akin to Luther's Anabaptist disputants.[27] Some scholars, however, have recently moved in the opposite direction, finding in Paul's anti-marriage opponents a group of radical women, whose theology and practice can be constructed as an alternative model of early Christianity to the patriarchal version represented by Paul. Wire (1990) will have them as misunderstood heroines: a radical liberal female group, demolishing social divisions and standing opposed to patriarchy in the name of Christ. The theological convenience to their interpreters of all such reconstructions should give us some cause for caution.

7.2.7. *The Lack of Patristic Support*
Despite the fact that the Fathers generally valued singleness and asceticism, for the most part we find them dealing with 1 Corinthians 7 in response to Encratic and Gnostic groups who (at least in Patristic opinion) all too enthusiastically rejected marriage and viewed sexuality as evil. However, unlike later interpreters, these early exegetes (with the single exception of Origen) do not read 1 Corinthians 7 as a response to hyper-ascetics, but as the apostle's own considered views on marriage and sexuality. That, despite the possible apologetic advantages of such a move,

25. Nejsum 1994: 49. For examples of obvious apologetics see Cartlidge 1975; Phipps 1981; or Fee 1987: 270. Fee ends up saying of Paul's response to the 'eschatological women' 'he finally stands over against them with the strongest kinds of affirmations of marriage'. However, Fee's apologetic utilization of the 'eschatological women' thesis is perhaps not surprising when one considers that Scroggs's seminal article (1972: 283–303), which largely initiated it, had an unashamed apologetic motivation (also Scroggs 1974).

26. Calvin 1960: 134, 140.

27. Deming (1995: 21 n. 61) notes that Lütgert took the term 'enthusiast' from the Reformation debates. Lütgert explicitly suggests that Paul stands in relation to his opponents as Luther did to his (1908: 86).

those temporally closest to Paul see no need or reason to view him as responding to ascetic extremists should give us pause for thought. A brief consideration of several exegetes, from the mid-second through to the fifth centuries, who deal extensively with 1 Corinthians 7, will demonstrate this fact.[28]

Clement of Alexandria (c. 150–215 AD), the first to make extensive use of 1 Corinthians 7, does so in his attack on Marcion and his followers who disparaged marriage and reproduction.[29] Despite the fact that he wishes to present Paul as a defender of marriage[30] and to interpret 1 Corinthians 7 as positive towards marriage (Paul's concern is to limit *second* marriages rather than marriage per se),[31] he does not attempt to attribute any of the sentiments of 1 Corinthians 7 to Paul's opponents.

If Clement saw Paul as praising marriage, then his near contemporary Tertullian (160–220 AD) gave a differing interpretation. He too contended against the outright renunciation of marriage, but insisted both on Paul's preference for celibacy and on the total rejection of second marriages. Tertullian's interpretation of 1 Corinthians 7 is that Paul,[32] while upholding the freedom to marry, partially abrogates it. 'It is good, he says, for a man not to touch a woman. Therefore it is bad to touch one. For nothing is opposed to the "good" except the "bad"'.[33] Marriage is thus a lesser evil rather than a good. Tertullian, unlike Clement, fully exegetes 7.31–35, showing how the apostle, although allowing marriage, does not desire that any should marry, but again, 1 Corinthians 7 is in its entirety Paul's own unapologetic view of marriage.

Origen's (c. 185–254 AD) exegesis of 1 Corinthians 7 is apparently the first to take note of the contextual background against which Paul wrote.[34] He is certainly the only Father to postulate extreme asceticism among the Corinthians: suggesting there was dissension in the congregation with some men and women trying to practise too much continence in marriage. He is again the first to view the opening maxim of 7.1b as written by the Corinthians to Paul, advocating marital abstinence, to

28. Few early commentators actually discuss 1 Cor. 7. Massingberd Ford (1964), in her survey of early patristic exegesis, has shown there is a surprising silence on 1 Cor. 7 in the first and early second century. Neither 1 Clement, nor Ignatius, nor Polycarp, nor the *Didache*, nor Diognetus, nor Justin Martyr, nor Athenagorus, nor Theophilus, nor, with one exception, Hermas, make any reference to it. This stands in blatant contrast to the writings of the later second and early third-century Church Fathers who make extensive use of the text.

29. *Strom.* 3.12, 3.5–10.

30. *Strom.* 3.53 suggests that Paul is married to his 'yokefellow' of Phil. 4.3, and cites 1 Cor. 9.5 as further evidence.

31. *Strom.* 3.82.4.

32. Paul and all the apostles are unmarried; 1 Cor. 9.5 relates to 'ministering women' rather than wives (Tertullian, *Mon.* 8).

33. Tertullian, *Mon.* 3; translation Le Saint (1951).

34. *Origen on 1 Corinthians* edited by C. Jenkins 1907.

which Paul replies that mutual consent is required lest one partner be led into sin. Paul in his response is concerned with two things: first πορνεία, but also excessive zeal. In this light, neither marriage nor virginity is to be disparaged. Paul's wish is to modify excessive abstinence and to stress equality and fairness in marriage. Origen's exegesis is, however, followed neither by the commentators of late antiquity nor by those of the medieval church.

A fuller exegesis of 1 Corinthians 7, although lacking in the subtlety of Origen, is found in the work of Jerome (*Adversus-Jovinianum* 393 AD). Jerome is responding on the one hand to Jovinian's equating of marriage and virginity,[35] and on the other to Marcionite and Manichean disparaging of marriage. Jerome responds with an exposition of 1 Corinthians 7, which he sees as Paul's response to the Corinthians' neutral question as to whether 'they ought to be unmarried and for the sake of continence put away their wives, and whether believing virgins were at liberty to marry'.[36] Gone, however, is Origen's notion that the Corinthians' asceticism was overblown, or that 7.1b represents a citation of the Corinthian letter. Rather, we find a return to a reading of Paul identical to that of Tertullian: 'If it is good for a man not to touch a woman it is bad to touch one: for there is no opposite to goodness but badness'.[37]

Even Augustine (354–430 AD), who sets out to strike a *via media* between Jerome and Jovinian, makes no recourse to Origen's suggestions on the background to Paul's discourse. 1 Cor. 7.1b, 7.28b and 7.32–33 are regarded as no less than the voice of God from the clouds, which Augustine should have heeded.[38]

These Patristic commentators then differ on their views of marriage and celibacy, but the notion that Paul upholds celibacy, and even praises abstinence within marriage, is not particularly problematic. Nor do they find it necessary to attribute the phrases or sentiments of the text to other than Paul. However ingenious their exegesis may be, no one attempts to relativize Paul's asceticism by suggesting he is making concessions to ascetic enthusiasts, or that he is quoting an 'ascetic Corinthian' letter at

---

35.   Jovinian (according to Jerome) had taught that marriage and virginity were on a par. Jerome rejects the teaching of this 'Epicurus of Christianity' as the 'hissing of the old serpent' (Jerome, *Jov.* 1.1–5).

36.   Jerome, *Jov.* 1.7.

37.   Jerome, *Jov.* 1.7. Jerome sees 1 Cor. 7.5 not as a concession to the Corinthians, but as evidence of the apostle's own view that even marital sex is not good. For how can it be good if it hinders prayer?

38.   Augustine, *Conf.* 2.2.3. In *Bon. Conj.* 6.6, Augustine offers what appears to be a direct rebuttal of the views of Tertullian. He comments: 'we do not call marriage a good in this sense, that in comparison with fornication it is a good: otherwise there will be two evils, one of which is worse'. Yet there is still no attempt to distance Paul from the sentiment of the verse.

any given point. Origen alone considers the background to the letter in depth. He alone postulates that the Corinthians were doing more than asking neutral questions, but may have been, in Paul's opinion, over fond of celibacy. As for the other patristic exegetes, it occurs to them neither to follow, nor even refute, Origen's exegesis.

Until relatively recent times, commentators differed little from the Patristic outlook, either showing no real interest in what activity of the Corinthian church might have provoked Paul to write at such length on marriage, or contenting themselves with the notion that the Corinthians wrote a somewhat neutral letter to Paul asking for advice on the subject.[39] Few proposed a background in Corinthian asceticism – and even then only tentatively.[40] Indeed it is only with the twentieth century that the ascetic hypothesis becomes the dominant explanation of the text.[41] While, of course, it is possible that modern commentators are correct and earlier exegetes wrong, the fact that almost none closer to Paul in time, or through most of the long centuries since, have seen the need for such an hypothesis to explain the text should at very least give us cause for thought.

7.3. Consideration of the Proposed Motivations for Corinthian Asceticism

7.3.1. Hellenistic Jewish Motivations
Two scholars have offered Jewish explanations of the Corinthian phenomena. Balch[42] suggests that the Corinthians were influenced by a presentation of Moses as an ascetic prophet, such as is offered by Philo in

---

39. See the discussion in Hurd 1965: 155–56. Hurd notes the number of commentators who viewed the Corinthians asking the rather neutral question: 'Is marriage desirable?' Some commentators even reconstructed the Corinthians' question as inferring that marriage should be compulsory (e.g. Godet 1886: 320–21 and Ramsay 1900: 287).

40. Interestingly, Calvin shows an unusual interest in the background to the epistle, setting the Corinthians' questions on marriage against the environment of the 'great cleavages in the Church at Corinth'. He then obliquely comments that 'as soon as the church was founded, a wrong belief crept into it by the trickery of Satan. What it meant was that a large proportion, holding a silly admiration for the unmarried state, looked down their noses at the sacred state of marriage' (Calvin 1960: 134). However, Calvin appears to be speaking of the early church as a whole (perhaps thinking of Paul's opponents in the Pastorals – or Paul's early patristic exegetes) for he comments 'perhaps this infection had attacked the Corinthians also' (Calvin 1960: 134). He certainly does not follow Origen in attributing 7.1b to the Corinthians.

41. The modern origins of the thesis may well lie with Weiss, who comments of 1 Cor. 7 'steht P. hier einer hyperasketischen Stimmung gegenüber' (1910: 169). (Weiss is the earliest of the long list of advocates cited by Gundry Volf 1994a: 119 n. 1.) However, the notion that some in Corinth saw celibacy as a duty was suggested earlier (e.g. Massie 1901: 527–38).

42. Balch 1971: 351–64.

his exegesis of Exodus 34,[43] which Balch contends was common in that era. According to Philo, Moses withdrew from sexual activity in order to receive divine revelations. Thus the Corinthians, also wishing to receive divine revelations, are seen to be modelling themselves on the 'divine man' figure of Moses.

Balch's reading has had few followers,[44] principally because his sole evidence of the relevance of Philo's description of Moses to the Corinthians is that Paul exegetes Exodus 34 in 2 Corinthians 3. This is not convincing. There is no evidence that Paul exegetes Exodus 34 in response to his opponents, and in any case we cannot safely identify opponents in 2 Corinthians with those in 1 Corinthians (there is, for example, no evidence of ascetic concerns in 2 Corinthians).[45] However, as we shall see, the more general notion that the Corinthians pursued celibacy for the sake of prophetic inspiration has been more resilient.

Horsley[46] postulated that the Corinthians had renounced physical marriage, in order to take on a spiritual marriage with Sophia, the personification of wisdom. He detected 'extensive and comprehensive' language parallels for the notion of such marriage in Wisdom, Philo, and Apuleius' *Golden Ass*. However, only in Philo's account of the Therapeutae does actual asceticism stem from such ideology. Even more fatally, Horsley cannot show a more general trend for the concept of marriage to Sophia beyond a metaphoric use in the Jewish wisdom tradition. Apuleius does have Lucius in temporary abstinence to prepare for a vision of Isis, but there is no mention of marriage to the goddess replacing actual intercourse. Further, there is no textual evidence that the Corinthians personified wisdom. Indeed there is no mention of Sophia at all in 1 Corinthians 5–7 (except in the irony of 6.5). The notion of spiritual union with Christ precluding actual physical union is, as we have seen, found in 1 Cor. 6.15–20, but here it is clearly deployed by Paul. This is hardly the tactic we would expect from a man about to combat Corinthian ascetics denouncing marriage for the sake of a similar spiritual union.

We can push this a little further, and insist that if Hellenistic Jewish explanations are to be offered as explanations for 1 Corinthians 7, they must also be related to the rest of the epistle. It is highly unlikely that the Corinthians would develop an ideology of sexuality from any form of Judaism, unless such were influential in other areas of their life and thought. But to postulate a Hellenistic-Jewish influence at Corinth is highly problematic. Certain issues that have apparently arisen in Corinth (i.e. the question of eating food sacrificed to idols, or attending meals in a

---

43. Philo, *Vit. Mos.* 2.66–70.
44. One exception would be Bartchy 1973: 145.
45. See the criticism in Deming 1995: 11–12.
46. Horsley 1979: 20–54.

pagan temple) seem difficult to envisage arising in a community heavily influenced by Judaism.[47] There are few themes in this letter that are suggestive of a Jewish influence, and the one epistolic theme to which proponents of Hellenistic-Jewish reconstructions make most reference – that of wisdom[48] – is specifically cited by Paul as something sought not by Jews, but by Greeks (1.22).[49] If there is such scant evidence of a Hellenistic-Jewish influence in the epistle as a whole, it is difficult to set much store on the contention that such might explain 1 Corinthians 7.

7.3.2. Motivations from Graeco-Roman Philosophy
The notion that Paul's opponents were under the influence of some philosophical tendency to reject marriage is no novelty. Grotius in the seventeenth century pointed to the discussion of marriage among the Stoics and concluded that the Corinthians were 'really philosophers under the name of Christians (although nonetheless Christians)'.[50]

More recently Deming[51] has examined the Stoic/Cynic discussion of marriage and suggested that 1 Corinthians 7 be read against this background.[52] Rather than reading Paul or the Corinthians in the light of the Middle Platonism of the Patristic age, as ascetics disparaging the body or sexuality, we are to read the chapter in the light of far older philosophical debates, where it was the wisdom and not the morality of marriage that was under discussion. As Deming rightly insists, 'not all forms of celibacy stem from a theology of sexual asceticism'.[53] One may forgo marriage for other reasons than a moral suspicion of the body and its pleasures.

According to Deming, Paul's correspondents (whose position is still encapsulated in 7.1b) hold to a Cynic notion that sexual relations are time consuming, robbing the wise man of his time for philosophy (or, in the Christian's case, prayer). Paul responds with a familiar Stoic notion that there is a καιρός for each activity, for sex and for prayer. The Corinthians' advocacy of divorcing unbelieving spouses is based on the Stoic notion of

47. With Fee 1987: 13–14 and Adams 2000: 94–95.
48. Cf. Goulder 1991 for a recent articulation.
49. As Munck 1959: 148–59.
50. Grotius as cited by Deming 1995: 6.
51. Deming 1995.
52. There is a longer tradition of *comparing* the Pauline dialogue to the Stoic/Cynic material on marriage or suggesting connections between them (starting with Clement of Alexandria [so Deming 1995: 6] and more recently Weiss [1910: 169, 205 n. 2], Balch [1983], Yarbrough [1995: 31–65] and Wimbush [1987: 37–38]). The unique contention (and weakness) of Deming is to seek to explain the entire discourse and context of 1 Cor. 7 in terms of the Stoic Cynic materials. Wimbush and Balch merely looked at Stoic influences on Paul's thought and Yarbrough (1995: 117–22) in the end looks to the realized eschatology and elitism of the strong to explain the dialogue.
53. Deming 1995: 2.

the desirability of the marriage of the like-minded. Marriage to an outsider is a form of slavery, and proverbially the king and the wise man are free (the Corinthians view themselves as kings, 4.8), and so marriage to an outsider is a threat to their ἐξουσία. Paul responds by insisting that outward circumstances do not enslave. 1 Cor. 7 is to be seen then, according to Deming, as a typical περὶ γαμοῦ discussion paralleled in the writings of Diogenes, Philo or Epictetus; although Deming does leave some room for the 'Judeo-Christian' (*sic*) tradition to have entered the debate.

The problems with this are manifold. How widespread were such philosophical concerns?[54] Was the περὶ γαμοῦ topos really such a Graeco-Roman commonplace given that Deming is pointing to a limited number of texts produced by a scholarly elite? Is the time one has for σχολή (or prayer) a general concern, or the privileged indulgence of the wealthy few?[55] In any case, even if it is plausible, given the existence of the Stoic-Cynic marriage debate, that in any discussion on the subject of marriage, either Paul or the Corinthians should appeal to Stoic or Cynic thought to support their position, to postulate, as Deming does, that the Stoic-Cynic debate *explains* the discussion of 1 Cor. 7, is most improbable. He fails to explain *why* a Cynic-style opposition to marriage might appear among the Corinthians.

Additionally, once again this reconstruction of 1 Cor. 7 falls foul of our insistence that 1 Cor. 7 be read as an integral part of 1 Corinthians. Deming offers justification of his reading of 1 Cor. 7 neither from the epistle as a whole,[56] nor from the chapter's immediate context. He reads 7.1–40 purely as a marriage discussion, ignoring the fact that the chapter is part of a section (5.1–7.40) whose focus is more widely on sexual ethics (incest, πόρνη-union, etc.). Neither does Deming consider the social context and implications of the ideas on marriage, which he considers the Corinthians to have adopted, for the church's existence in its urban context.[57] Nor (and we shall return to this in the next chapter)[58] do the Stoic-Cynic dialogues themselves provide a plausible social parallel for Corinthian asceticism: they represent a debate between philosophers on how the individual philosopher should behave, and not a community's discussion about how to structure their common life. The Cynic was always a lone individual.

---

54. D.B. Martin (1995: 6) comments that 'ancient philosophers – who represent a tiny fraction of the population – cannot be used to reconstruct views of the broader population'.

55. Deming does not discuss the social level of the Corinthians. However, his insistence on the relevance of the philosophical debates to them would seem to require a fairly high degree of education.

56. See n. 11 above.

57. See Esler's (1996a) criticism in his review of Deming.

58. See section 8.2.2.

Dale Martin[59] has made slightly more plausible suggestions. He sees the issues between Paul and the Corinthians in 1 Corinthians 7 as being part and parcel of that which divides them throughout the letter, namely, their respective ideologies of the body. (Thus he places 1 Corinthians 7 in the context of the epistle as a whole.) Examining the writings of the philosophers and the medics, the views of whom he would have us accept were common among the educated classes of the Graeco-Roman world,[60] he suggests that the Corinthian elite[61] have a view that the body requires balance, and a concern that sexual intercourse threatens its continued strength. Paul meanwhile is more concerned with the vulnerability of the body to invasion, here in the form of illicit joining to a polluted world through πορνεία.

But there are problems here too. First, such elite anxieties might lead a doctor to counsel moderation or a philosopher to praise singleness (although these more often also counsel moderation), but would they recommend abstinence, divorce, or denounce marriage as a 'sin'? Secondly, why is it that such concerns have manifested themselves in this Christian community? What is the connection with Paul's teaching, or indeed the message of Christ at all? Although it is possible that such anti-sex views developed in the church not for specifically Christian reasons, Martin fails to show any historical parallel for a non-Christian *community*, or a significant part of a community, sharing such a degree of concern about sex. Thirdly, how representative are the fears of the doctors? As Fox contends, 'the views of the doctors were not widely known. Nor were they unanimous'.[62]

7.3.3. *Hellenistic Dualism and Corinthian Pneumatism*
While seeking explanations in Hellenistic Judaism or Graeco-Roman philosophy has a long and venerable history in the interpretation of 1 Corinthians 7, the mainstream of scholarship has flowed in another direction. Rightly, most scholars have sought to place the dynamic of 1 Corinthians 7 into the framework of explanation of the theological conflicts of the letter as a whole. Here the Tübingen theses, which

---

59.   D.B. Martin 1995.

60.   Although, as D.B. Martin perhaps damagingly concedes (1995: 204), 'the devaluing of sexual intercourse by some medical writers and Epictetus was, of course, not the only attitude current in the first century. If we take into account others besides the upper classes, and perhaps even if we do not, it was probably no more than a minority opinion'.

61.   His reconstruction assumes that the Corinthians, with whom Paul is in dialogue, are entirely or predominantly from the small, educated, elite of the Roman Empire. Thus it is particularly dependent on the Meeks-Theissen reconstruction of the social composition of the Corinthian congregation, and particularly vulnerable if the thesis of Meggitt (1998) is even partially correct.

62.   Fox 1986: 361.

dominated the nineteenth and early twentieth centuries, caused not a few problems. F.C. Baur had viewed all New Testament conflicts as essentially a struggle between the thesis and antithesis of Jewish and Hellenistic Christianity. He thus contracted the four parties of 1 Cor. 1.12 into two: a pro-Pauline (Hellenistic Christian) and a pro-Petrine (Jewish Christian) faction.[63] This macro-reconstruction of the letter gained little ground, however, in the interpretation of 1 Corinthians 7. There was (is) an accepted understanding that Judaism held to a strong affirmation of married life, which it viewed as a duty, whereas asceticism was perceived as a tendency within Hellenism. This, plus the obvious fact that Peter was married and Paul is normally considered single, counted heavily against an ascetic faction identifying themselves with Peter against Paul.[64] The only solution was to see the ascetic movement as an extremist interpretation of Paul's own views: a faction more Pauline than Paul.[65]

This landscape significantly altered with Lütgert.[66] Totally rejecting Baur's hypothesis of a Jewish-Christian influence, he attributed the Corinthian resistance to Paul, in the *entire* letter, to hyper-Pauline 'enthusiasts'. This group placed undue stress on various elements of Paul's own theology: namely, possession of the Spirit, which they believed gave them a special access to γνῶμις, and a freedom of action in Christ (ἐξουσία) beyond what Paul had himself advocated. These factors led to their emphasis on ecstatic gifts, and to the social disruption that Paul addresses in the letter. Lütgert saw this emphasis on spirit and freedom as also leading to a devaluation of the physical body. This devaluation resulted in the licentiousness, which Lütgert assumed was implicit in the text. The ascetic corollary resulted from that same deprecation of the body, but also in reaction to the libertinism of other believers and the immorality of surrounding pagan society. His theory served to pull all of the disparate issues of the Corinthian epistle together, including those of both ch. 6 and ch. 7, and it was to become widely influential down to the present day, being followed in some form or other by almost all commentators.[67]

The elevation of the spirit and the spiritual, the deprecation of the body

---

63. Baur 1831: 61–206.

64. Both Meyer and Moffatt trouble themselves to deny that the ascetics can be followers of Peter, while Ramsay (1900: 288) states, of the consensus c. 1900, that 'it is commonly said that the section of the Church in Corinth which "was of Cephas" upheld marriage because Cephas was married, while the section which "was of Paul" argued that the single life was better, because Paul was either unmarried or a widower' (see further the discussion in Hurd 1965: 155–56).

65. Cf. Meyer (1881: 192), 'the apostle's sentiments upon this point were in themselves, as we see from the chapter before us, quite of a kind to be readily misunderstood or misinterpreted by many of his disciples as being unfavourable to marriage'.

66. Lütgert 1908.

67. The thesis of Fee's commentary is basically a variation on this theme.

and the material, and the resulting move to asceticism, were not generally seen as any type of unique Corinthian phenomenon. Rather the supposed Corinthian ideology was seen as part of a larger move towards dualist cosmology and asceticism. It was viewed as lying on a trajectory of cosmological thought which could be traced from pre-Christian Hellenism (originating with Plato) through on into the Gnostic philosophies, and indeed then into the middle-Platonism of the Fathers.[68]

7.3.4. *Gnosticism*

Some scholars labelled the Corinthian opponents as outright Gnostics or some form of proto-Gnostics.[69] Others (e.g. Lütgert and Schrage)[70] simply appealed to Gnosticism as a parallel movement to that in Corinth, exhibiting both a material dualism and the phenomena of sexual libertinism and asceticism. However, to label the Corinthians as Gnostics is simply an anachronism: all our evidence of Gnosticism comes from the second century at the earliest.[71] Those who have spoken of the Corinthians as proto-Gnostics have made much of mainly linguistic links with later Gnosticism (πνευματικοί, σοφία, γνῶσις), and the supposed parallel in simultaneous tendencies towards libertinism and asceticism.[72] However, the differences from later Gnosticism are certainly as notable as any similarities.[73] There is in Corinth no sign of the spiritual elitism (all are said to possess γνῶσις, 8.1) and while there may be some evidence of a deprecation or trivialization of the physical body (regarding body as inferior to soul is hardly unique to Gnosticism), there is no sign that the Corinthians regarded it as evil. Thus, while it is possible to argue that there are some parallels between Gnosticism and Paul's Corinthian opponents, the pertinent differences make it impossible to use these to fill in the blanks in our knowledge of the Corinthian church.[74]

Despite the dubiousness of Gnostic parallels, the conviction that

68. This is the general trajectory that Murray summarized as a 'change in the whole relation of the writer to the world around him ... a rise of asceticism, of mysticism, in a sense of pessimism; a loss of confidence, of hope in this life and of faith in the normal human effort; a despair of patient inquiry, a cry for infallible revelation; an indifference to the welfare of the state, a conversion of the soul to God ... an intensifying of certain emotions; an increase of sensitiveness, a failure of nerve' (Murray 1925: 155). (Wimbush [1993] presents a modified version of this thesis.)

69. E.g. Schmithals 1971.

70. Lütgert 1908; Schrage 1995: 55.

71. See Yamauchi 1973: 36–43, 173–86.

72. It was argued in sections 6.2.1 and 6.2.2 that the libertine parallels are untenable. In any case, using the supposed ascetic/libertine parallels to justify comparisons with Gnosticism begs the question as to whether there are libertines and ascetics in the Corinthian church.

73. See Wilson 1972–73 and 1983: 102–14

74. See further D.B. Martin 1995: 70–71; Deming 1995: 35–40; and Adams 2000: 94.

material dualism and sexual asceticism constitute a basic 'enthusiastic' tendency within early Hellenistic Christianity has meant that the challenge has made little difference to such interpretations of 1 Corinthians. The same assumption that a concern with the 'spiritual' leads to material dualism, contempt for the flesh, and logically either sexual asceticism or libertinism or both, survives even without Gnostic parallels. 'Gnostic dualism' is often simply replaced with 'Hellenistic dualism' in the lingo of the interpreters, with little more ado.

7.3.5. *Realized Eschatology*
The notion that the Corinthians believed that they had already experienced resurrection has a long pedigree in the explanation of 1 Corinthians 15, going back at least as far as Chrysostom. It was, however, Käsemann who first used it to supplement Lütgert's 'enthusiast' reading, and to provide an explanation for the Corinthian ideology seen capable of encompassing all the various issues in the epistle. Käsemann suggested that when Jewish Christian apocalyptic theology took root on 'Greek soil' it evolved into an eschatological enthusiasm, against which Paul was reacting. The enthusiasts stressed the present possession of the Spirit to such a degree that the future elements ceased to be of any relevance, believing the baptized believer participated immanently in resurrection and exaltation, being liberated from the old aeon. It was:

> a sacramental realism which sees the complete redemption to have already been effected, in that by baptism a heavenly spiritual body has been conferred and the earthly body has been degraded to an insubstantial, transitory veil. This is the root of all that has gone wrong in Corinth; the contempt for discipline and decency, the want of consideration for the weaker brother at the Lord's Supper and in daily life; the rise of women ecstatically gifted and the over-valuing of glossolalia and sexual asceticism, which are being regarded as the outward expressions of angelic status. Those who are endowed with pneuma are exempt from the laws of those who have nothing but psyche.[75]

Various parts of the text of 1 Corinthians have been used to support the 'realized eschatology' thesis. First, scholars refer to the discussion in ch. 15. Here the Corinthians' rejection of the resurrection of the dead (15.12) is explained by the contention that, as the Corinthians believed they had already experienced a spiritualized resurrection, they have no room or reason to expect the resurrection of Paul's future eschatology. Secondly, this is related to Paul's ironic taunt in 4.8: '*already* you are filled! Already you have become rich!' which is taken as a reference to a Corinthian

---

75. Käsemann 1969a: 126.

insistence that they have already received all the benefits of the Eschaton.[76]

7.3.5.1. *The life of angels.* When we turn to 1 Corinthians 7, more specific explanations have been offered of how this realized eschatology has resulted in the renunciation of marriage. It has been postulated that the Corinthians believed themselves, post-resurrection, to be living 'like the angels', and that they connected this with an early tradition of Jesus' sayings which are recorded at Mk 12.25 ('for when they rise from the dead, they neither marry nor are given in marriage, but are like the angels in heaven') and Lk. 20.34–36 ('The sons of this age marry and are given in marriage; but those who are counted worthy to attain to that age and to the resurrection from the dead, neither marry nor are given in marriage, for they cannot die any more, because they are equal to angels and are sons of God, being sons of the resurrection').[77] The notion of angelic existence is then connected with 1 Corinthians in two ways. First, the Corinthians' obsession with the gift of tongues, described by Paul in 13.1 as 'the tongues of men and angels' is noted. Secondly, it is noted that the rare verb γαμίζω (to give in marriage) is used in both gospel passages and in 1 Cor. 7.28. Thus it is suggested that a version of Jesus' statement was known in Corinth and used by the ascetics.[78]

7.3.5.2. *Galatians 3.28.* Another suggestion, often offered as complimentary, is that the Corinthians believed that at baptism a new creation was brought into being where there really was (taking Gal. 3.28 as evidence of an early baptismal creed) 'no male *and* female'. The creation order of the sexes ('male *and* female he created them', Gen. 1.27) was reversed.[79] In this new creation, which the Corinthians believed themselves to be presently experiencing, sexual distinction and sexual roles have been abolished and marriage is at an end. This idea of asexual new creation has been linked by some commentators to the myth of primal androgyny, a belief in antiquity, and evidenced in some Gnostic texts, that the original created form of human was without gender distinction.[80]

The fact that in 1 Cor. 7.17–24 and 12.13 Paul appears to reformulate the baptismal formula cited in Gal. 3.28 is produced as evidence that it was known and important to the Corinthians, and also viewed as problematic by Paul. In 1 Cor. 7.17–24, Paul appears to deviate from the

76. Hence Barrett (1971: 109), 'for them there was no "not yet" to qualify the "already" of realized eschatology' (cf. Käsemann 1969a: 125–26 but also Thiselton 1977).
77. Balch 1971: 354; Bartchy 1973: 149–51; Meeks 1974: 202.
78. Balch 1971: 357; Cartlidge 1975: 227, 229–30.
79. Meeks 1974: 185.
80. Meeks cites evidence from Philo, Plato, the Rabbis and Gnostic sources (1974: 185–89).

issue in hand (marriage) to deal with the seemingly unconnected issues of circumcision and uncircumcision, slavery and freedom, which could be explained if Paul saw the baptismal formula and particularly its third assertion (no male and female) as lying at the root of Corinthian asceticism. Further, in 1 Cor. 12.13, Paul appears to restate the baptismal formula, but this time omitting the offending 'male and female' pair. This is used to suggest that Paul is encountering, in the Corinthian church, an influential group who have made much of an abrogation of sexuality implicit in the formula.[81]

7.3.5.3. *Eschatological women.* Most of those who have seen the baptismal formula's assertion 'not male and female', or the Dominical logia on the eschatological cessation of marriage, lying behind the Corinthian renunciation of marriage, have proposed that it is primarily women who are promoting and seeking to practise such asceticism. Such women are seen to be applying the community's realized eschatology to gender issues: arguing that the gender roles of the old creation have ceased with the 'new creation' realized in baptism, and doing so, at least partly, to underpin their social emancipation within the community. Evidence for this is also taken from Paul's discussion of dress in worship (1 Cor. 11.3–16). This passage is read as Paul's response to the practice of some of the Corinthian women, who, during charismatic worship, took the culturally abnormal step of either removing their head covering, or letting down their hair, in order to symbolize their new status in Christ.

7.3.6. *Various Concoctions*
In truth, just as Käsemann built on Lütgert, most recent explanations of 1 Corinthians 7 have combined these various possibilities in their explanation of the motivations of the ascetics. Whether, of course, when the possibilities are combined they are mutually strengthened, or whether commentators are simply hedging bets, is an open question. We shall look at three recent, and not untypical, offerings.

Gordon Fee believes Paul's opponents to be elite members of the Corinthian church who are 'modifying the gospel towards Hellenism'.[82] These insurgents believe themselves to be *pneumatikoi* – experiencing the Spirit through ecstatic gifts, and having privileged access to gnosis and sophia – but they are less sure of their apostle's spiritual credentials. Thus far Fee basically follows Lütgert, suggesting that 'their worldview has been "tainted" (ingrained by a lifetime) by Hellenistic dualism. Because

81. Scroggs 1972: 291.
82. Fee 1987: 10.

they were "spiritual" they took a dim view of continuing existence in the material world, including the body.'[83]

Fee then dismisses as anachronistic the notion that the Corinthians are Gnostics. The only Gnostic phenomenon evidenced in Corinth is dualism, which can be explained on other grounds: namely, the Corinthian conviction that they are spiritual and their realized eschatology (they believe that in the Spirit they are now experiencing the Eschaton).

His explanation of 1 Corinthians 7 is in a similar vein.

> What would seem to lie behind this position is once again their present pneumatic existence, which has Hellenistic dualism at its roots and their own brand of 'spiritualized eschatology' as its repeated expression. As those who are 'spiritual' they are above the merely earthly existence of others; marriage belongs to this age that is passing away.[84]

Fee makes the suggestion that we may be dealing in this chapter with 'eschatological women' who view themselves as already having achieved the resurrection and thus being, like the angels, beyond marriage. He also suggests that these women may have taken Paul's notion that Christ breaks down gender distinctions (Gal. 3.28) in the 'wrong direction' and thus rejected marriage. However, neither of these points is developed at length.

Margaret Y. MacDonald rehearses the traditional assumption that the libertines and ascetics were demonstrating their transcendence of the world in both freedom and abstinence, respectively. However, it is the notion of ascetic women and their motivations on which she concentrates. From 11.2–16 and 14.33–36 she infers that women in the church were a problem for Paul. From Paul's seeming reuse of the Gal. 3.28 pairs in 7.17–28, and his omission of the male/female pair at 12.13 she suggests that 'nor male and female' may lie at the root of the problem.[85] D.R. MacDonald[86] has suggested that Gal. 3.28 originated in a Dominical Saying recorded in the Gospel of the Egyptians: 'When you tread upon the garment of shame and when the two are one and the male with the female neither male nor female',[87] which D.R. MacDonald suggests refers to the 'trampling' of the body to achieve the reunification of the sexes in baptism and a return to the perfection of androgyny, by the renunciation of sexual relations. M.Y. MacDonald then suggests that a similar theology inspired Paul's pneumatic opponents at Corinth. 11.2–16, she suggests, evidences women who during ecstatic worship believed they had

---

83. Fee 1987: 11.
84. Fee 1987: 269.
85. M.Y. MacDonald 1990: 164–65.
86. D.R. MacDonald 1987: 17–21.
87. Clement, *Strom.* 3.13.92; similar expressions are found in *2 Clem.* 12.2 and *Gos. Thom.* 27, 21a, 22b. D.R. MacDonald argues that these evidence an oral tradition more primitive than Gal. 3.28.

transcended sexual differences, becoming symbolically like men in dress. These women may also be the primary concern in ch. 7. Paul's opponents believe they have 'transcended the material world' rising with Christ at baptism to a 'primordial perfection ... which included a new sexless state'. In worship, they symbolically removed their veils, but 'with the ritual ended, the fact that the male was with the female meant that they should avoid sex altogether'.[88]

Judith Gundry Volf's reconstruction of the motivations of the ascetics is even more eclectic than Fee's. She argues that the Corinthian asceticism is based on, 'Corinthian pneumatism, a theology of ἐξουσία, a view of the physical body as consecrated to the Lord and of sexual unions as therefore sin, and the view that the new creation in Christ excluded marriage and sexual union' and goes on to state that: '1 Corinthians 7 may well suggest other aspects of a theological basis for sexual asceticism not mentioned here, but I do not claim to deliver an exhaustive analysis'.[89]

In an exercise of mirror-reading Paul's response, she suggests that the ascetics are appealing to their ἐξουσία as a right to abstain from sexual relations in marriage, or, in some instances, the right to divorce. The ascetics insist on such in order to facilitate their 'devotion to prayer'. Gundry Volf then sets out to show that to devote oneself to something (and particularly prayer) often carries with it, in the literature of antiquity, a notion of forgoing other pursuits. She argues that 'sexual (as well as other types of) asceticism was in fact widely associated with religious activities in antiquity'.[90] She then connects the Corinthians' sexual asceticism to their ecstatic experience of the spirit (the prophecy and ecstatic speaking) and compares this to what she sees as a type of celibate prophet in Graeco-Roman antiquity. She suggests a general ancient view that sexual abstinence facilitated 'divine inspiration and insight'.[91] The Corinthians are thus engaging in inspirational asceticism.

She, however, rejects Lütgert's basic notion that the ascetics' theology of freedom points to a Gnostic or even Hellenistic dualism. She does this on the basis that 7.34 suggests that the ascetics, rather than despising the body, were insisting on its importance for the Lord. She infers that the ascetics saw this *physical* devotion to Christ as inconsistent with physical union with a spouse. Whereas Paul had concluded that union with Christ was incompatible with union with one outside Christ, the Corinthians had 'drawn more far-reaching conclusions' and saw union with Christ as precluding all sexual union.[92] Gundry Volf also suggests that the

88. M.Y. MacDonald 1990: 169–70.
89. Gundry Volf 1996: 519–20.
90. Gundry Volf 1996: 532.
91. Gundry Volf 1994a: 105.
92. Gundry Volf 1996: 536.

Corinthians used the baptismal tradition of Gal. 3.28 as a 'theological rationale' for their asceticism. This 'eschatological slogan' was seen as abolishing the sexual distinctions of Gen. 1.27, so that 'instead of male and female, in Christ there are ... ascetics'.[93]

Gundry Volf's offering is perhaps a more pronounced example of the eclecticism of the answers to the question of the Corinthians' motivations, but she is not alone in casting a wide net. Pneumatic 'enthusiasm', realized eschatology, material dualism, theologies of freedom, living like angels, and baptismal recreation of primordial androgyny have become something of a pick-and-mix available to those intent on seeing Corinthian ascetics. Thesis has been piled upon thesis, until such point that one can forget that the original assertions require proof. Where earlier commentators assumed opponents and then offered evidence for a suggestion as to their identity, now there is a tendency to assume that the opponents are ascetic pneumatics with a realized eschatology, and almost certainly women, and to proceed from that point.

7.4. Problems with Eschatological/Enthusiastic Explanations

7.4.1. Dualism and Pneumatism

As we saw, despite the dragon of the Gnostic Corinthian thesis having been slain (to most people's satisfaction), its ghost still lives on in appeals to 'Hellenistic dualism' which is presented as encapsulating the same style of material dualism (disdain for the physical world, suspicion of the physical body, and thus a tendency towards asceticism).[94] Martin has perceptively exposed the problems with much of scholarship's presuppositions about such dualism.[95] He rejects the notion that a material/immaterial dualism existed in Greek thought (such is a Cartesian re-reading) and insists rather in a hierarchy of essence. Even Plato does not disparage the world or the body for being 'physical',[96] and in any case Stoicism rather than Platonism was the dominant philosophy of the first century. Adams has gone further; insisting that first-century Graeco-Roman thought did not in general devalue the 'world'. Indeed Stoicism took a positive view of the cosmos and supported an ethic of living in accordance with the ordered universe.[97] Hence generalizations about 'Hellenistic dualism' and its automatic connection with world-denying asceticism become most doubtful.

---

93. Gundry Volf 1996: 537.

94. See Fee 1987: 11, 269; M.Y. MacDonald 1990: 169.

95. D.B. Martin 1995.

96. Interestingly Clement (*Strom.* 3.18–19) sought to block Marcion's appeal to Plato. Plato, Clement insisted, while rejecting sex and birth, recognized the excellence of the world.

97. Adams 2000.

However, even were we to accept that some form of material dualism was current in the Corinthian church, what is the evidence that such would be relevant to any consideration in 1 Corinthians 7? In fact there is scant evidence that it can be thought of, even in part, as a motivation of the supposed ascetics. Indeed if, as most of the proponents of the hypothesis assume, the concern that the virgin be 'holy in body and in spirit' is an echo of Corinthian thoughts, then, as Gundry Volf rightly argues,[98] it would appear that, as an instrument of devotion, the ascetics value, rather than deprecate, the material body.

Even the notion that Corinthian pneumatism lies at the heart of the ascetic theology is difficult to demonstrate from the text. There is no reference to the Holy Spirit in 1 Corinthians 7 (except in the last verse), and there is no reference to spiritual gifts (aside from the gift of celibacy). Yet Gundry Volf can confidently assert, concerning 7.40 (Paul's claim to have the Spirit of God), that it means he claims the Spirit for his opinion concerning the remarriage of widows, and that this implies that the ascetics 'claimed the Spirit in support of their views' and 'sexual asceticism is thus linked here to Corinthian pneumatism'.[99] This is hardly convincing.

His assertion that he '*too*' (κάγω) has the Spirit, *could* perhaps be mirror-read to suppose that the Corinthians claimed a spiritual high ground. However, Paul uses his assertion of the Spirit to commend singleness to widows: a view hardly likely to be contested by ascetics. So why does he appeal to the Spirit here? It makes more sense if Paul expects his commendation of celibacy for widows to be controversial. Thus he asserts his charismatic authority for unpopular advice. Further, perhaps we have here another of Paul's paradigmatic 'I's. Perhaps he too is a widow, and thus asserts that the Spirit is for him adequate compensation. At any rate, 7.40 is poor evidence for pneumatic asceticism among the Corinthians.

7.4.2. *Over-Realized Eschatology*
The thesis that the Corinthians exhibit a realized eschatology is also too quickly taken for granted by most scholars.[100] It is based upon several assumptions that are at least questionable.[101] There is, for one, little definite evidence of such in the text of 1 Corinthians itself. The much-cited passage of 4.8, 'Already you are filled! Already you have become rich! Without us you have become kings' does not actually suggest that the Corinthians believed themselves to have experienced the resurrection. (Paul could have said 'already you have been raised'.) It certainly suggests

---

98. Gundry Volf 1996: 519–20

99. Gundry Volf 1994a: 106.

100. Even Thiselton (1978: 510), in defending realized eschatology, concedes this point.

101. For criticisms, see Ellis 1974: 69–74 and Wedderburn 1987; note also Thiselton's defence and restatement (1978).

that the Corinthians, in Paul's view, had an over-inflated opinion of their present blessings and achievements in Christ. But, as Martin states:

> In Paul's eyes, those of an apocalyptic Jew, this might appear to be a premature claim of blessings that are supposed to be experienced only in the salvation of the Eschaton; but that does not mean that the beliefs of the strong came from Jewish eschatology.[102]

Apocalyptic theology, with its concentration on the not-yet, comes to the fore when suffering is experienced, and such suffering reinforces a belief in a world of present crisis and future vindication. Paul evidently was experiencing physical hardships which the Corinthians were not (4.9–13), so it is little wonder that his emphasis was more focused upon the future aspects of the Christian hope than was the Corinthians'. As to the precise language of Paul's ironic description of the Corinthian claims, it may well be that it owes much to the popular Cynic-Stoic contention that the wise man lacks no good thing, no true wealth, and alone is worthy to be called a king.[103] This notion could have been cited by an over-confident group within the Corinthian church without them either being Stoics themselves or believers in a present resurrection. At any rate there is no evidence that Corinthian complacency emanated from an eschatological belief.

Nor is it indisputable that 1 Corinthians 15 demands that the Corinthians believed in a realized resurrection.[104] Such seems to be a reading of the chapter in the light of 2 Tim. 2.18 (where Hymenaeus and Philetus are said to claim that 'the resurrection has already taken place'). Nothing in the text of the chapter *demands* such an interpretation.[105] Martin, for instance, argues that ch. 15 indicates that the Corinthians object to the notion of a physical resurrection per se, and not to its future aspect. This would certainly seem a better reading of 1 Cor. 15.12.[106]

---

102. D.B. Martin 1995: 106; cf. also Wedderburn 1987: 27 and Barclay 1992: 64.

103. Diogenes Laertius, *Lives* 7.122; see Conzelmann 1975: 87 and Wedderburn 1987: 25.

104. Even if the Corinthians had believed such, how they would maintain it in the face of the death of some of their number (11.30) is most uncertain.

105. Ellis (1974: 73–74) rejects the notion that the Corinthians believed they had already risen. Wedderburn (1987: 37) more cautiously concludes, 'the view that the Corinthians held the belief rejected in 2 Tim. 2.18 . . . is not the only possibility, and indeed is not even the best possibility, for solving the problems'.

106. Thiselton (1978), however, in defending realized eschatology, more or less abandons the notion of a belief in past resurrection. Arguing that 'the case for a realized eschatology at Corinth is usually lost by sheer overstatement' (523), he states that 'the question is not whether the Corinthians believed that their resurrection was past, but whether they placed such weight on the experience of transformation is the past and present that when they thought about the resurrection the centre of gravity of their thinking was no longer in the future' (524). Thiselton's contentions on 1 Cor. 15 may be thought persuasive. However, one might ask whether he has not lost the case for realized eschatology by sheer *understatement*. For if, as Thiselton contends, the Corinthians were over-confident in and over-focused upon,

However, even if we were to accept the over-realized eschatology thesis, one must again question its relevance to 1 Corinthians 7. 1 Corinthians 7 does not appear to be directed against a realized eschatology. If such an eschatological error lay at the heart of the denial of marriage then we would expect Paul to counter it in the strongest terms. But as Deming shows, although Paul certainly stresses apocalyptic themes in his teaching in 1 Corinthians 7, they are related to the present aspects of the apocalyptic and not the future. 'Paul says that the frame of this world *is* passing away, the time *has* been shortened, and he speaks of the *present* distress ... certainly not the tack one would expect from Paul if chapter seven represents his efforts to fight an enthusiastic asceticism stemming from a realized eschatology.'[107] Indeed it appears that Paul is using the present (eschatological) crisis (7.26) to promote celibacy rather than to combat asceticism. Not only does the present crisis lead to one holding loose to the social world (living ὡς μή, 7.29–30), but in its light, anxiety for the things of the world (which is the lot of the married) is particularly undesirable (7.32–34).

7.4.3. *On Living the Life of the Angels*
If realized eschatology in general lacks support from 1 Corinthians as a whole and 1 Corinthians 7 in particular, the notion that the Corinthians renounced marriage as they saw themselves presently living as the angels, connected this with their ecstatic speech, and took from this that sexual relations were inappropriate, is even more difficult to defend.

Of the four references to angels in the epistle,[108] only one can easily be connected to the Corinthians' spiritual experience: 'if I speak in the tongues of men and of angels' (13.1). Although 'tongues' almost certainly refers to the Corinthians' experience of ecstatic speech, it is possible that the 'tongues of angels' is simply a Pauline hyperbole.[109] At any rate, even if the Corinthians believed themselves to speaking angelic languages, this is not proof that they believed themselves actually to be enjoying a new angelic existence.[110] When we turn to 1 Corinthians 7 we find no mention

---

their present ability in the Spirit, so that they 'made too little of the future of their Christian outlook' (524) but (most of them) did not actually deny a future resurrection, we may certainly speak of them as spiritual enthusiasts who underplay eschatology – but how appropriate is it then to speak of them as having a *realized eschatology*?

107. Deming 1995: 30. See 1 Cor. 7.26–31; also Fee 1987: 336.

108. 1 Cor. 4.9; 6.3; 11.10 and 13.1.

109. So Conzelmann 1975: 221 n. 27.

110. Job's daughters are said to speak in angelic languages, but they are not considered angels (*T. Job* 48–50).

of angels at all. Nor is there any reference to ecstatic speech, which we might connect with such celibacy.[111]

The attempt to connect 1 Corinthians 7 to the Dominical logia (Mk 12.25 and Lk. 20.34–36) is likewise problematic. The Synoptic passages contain no reference to ecstatic speech; thus the only real connection that they share with 1 Cor. 7.28 is the verb γαμίζω. However, although γαμίζω may be rare, it is not unique, appearing also at Mt. 24.38 and Lk. 17.27 where there are references to neither angels nor asceticism.[112] In any case, given that the Synoptic sayings both refer to the cessation of marriage *after* the resurrection of the dead, their application in Corinth would depend on a particularly crude type of realized eschatology, which explicitly affirmed that the resurrection had already occurred. This incurs all the difficulties, which we have already outlined above.[113] Further, since Luke explains the redundancy of marriage beyond the resurrection by the fact that those raised 'cannot die any more' (and thus implicitly do not need to replenish their numbers by procreation), the thesis would appear to require the Corinthians to be confident that they had been raised immortal. How would they reconcile this with the death and illness of believers recorded at 11.30?

7.4.4. *Galatians 3.28 and the Eschatological Women*
The relevance of Gal. 3.28[114] to the understanding of 1 Corinthians 7 is also questionable. The prevailing thesis has been that the Corinthians have used a baptismal liturgy (similar to that found in Gal. 3.28), and particularly the declaration that in Christ 'there is no male and female' as

---

111. Except perhaps the reference to abstinence for prayer in 7.5. But it is difficult to connect this to a notion of angelic existence, not least because if the Corinthians did believe that they were living the life of angels, they would not argue for abstinence (temporary or permanently) *for prayer*, but because sex was totally inappropriate to their new existence.

112. Deming (1995: 27–28) notes that, since Mt. 24.38 and Lk. 17.27 originate from the 'Q' source, whereas Mk 12.25 does not, this is evidence that the verb has wide enough use for us to view Paul as using it independently in 1 Cor. 7.28.

113. Thiselton's (1978) defence and restatement of the realized eschatology thesis would appear incapable of saving the angelic asceticism theory (he makes no mention of it when discussing 1 Cor. 7) – since he doubts a Corinthian belief in a past resurrection, which it requires. Nor is it clear from Thiselton what alternative motivations he attributes to the ascetics. He speaks of them as spiritual theorists advocating an idealized state, as opposed to Paul who practically wishes them to take account of the realities of human nature. But why does their spiritual theory include asceticism?

114. Of course, since Gal. 3.28 is not as it stands an eschatological statement, its use to argue for an end to gender roles and thus marriage would not necessarily require one to believe that the Eschaton had already occurred. However, the belief in such a radical transformation in the present would sit comfortably with a realized eschatology, and most commentators who connect Gal. 3.28 to Corinthian asceticism so view it.

a 'theological basis for sexual asceticism'.[115] If there are presently no male and female, then there should be no sexual relations either. 1 Corinthians 7 is then seen as Paul's response to the Corinthians taking the baptismal affirmation in an ascetic direction, and 1 Cor. 7.17–24 as Paul's redirection of the implications of the liturgy itself. Scroggs has gone so far as to call these verses Paul's 'explicit commentary on Gal. 3.28'.[116]

In 7.17–24 Paul is seen to be arguing against change in social status, using the other two pairs from Gal. 3.28 as examples of how baptismal identity does not, indeed should not, have implications for the present social position of believers. If, despite their baptism, slaves are to remain as slaves, freemen as free, Jews as Jews, and Gentiles as Gentiles, then it follows that men and women should also continue in their present social places. The old social roles may be relativized by the new allegiance to Christ (7.19) but they are not presently eradicated. Additional evidence that the 'male and female' pair has become an issue in Corinth, and is seen as problematic by Paul, is taken from Paul's omission of it when he refers to the baptismal formula in 12.13.[117]

But there are questions that require to be answered. Do we know for certain that the Galatians formula was known at Corinth and that, if it was, it contained the reference to 'neither male and female'? Betz argued that Gal. 3.28 represented a pre-Pauline formulation as 'Paul's use of the saying in his letter is secondary in function'.[118] He then argued that the 'parallels in other literature suggest that we have before us a form of a saying … which must have had its place and function in early Christian baptismal liturgy'.[119] However, the parallels of which Betz was speaking are 1 Cor. 12.13 and Col. 3.11, both of which exhibit not only major similarities, but also *major differences*, in grammar, vocabulary and content, from the text of Galatians.[120] Most obviously both omit the male/female pairing (28c). Betz noted this, and also that the Gal. 3.28 form of the male *and* female pairing differed from the style of the other two pairings, and from this he concluded that 28c 'appears to be a

---

115. Gundry Volf 1994b: 95; also suggested by Meeks 1974: 202; Fee 1987: 270; Wire 1990: 126; and M.Y. MacDonald 1990.

116. Scroggs 1972: 293.

117. Balch 1971; Bartchy 1973: 129–30.

118. Betz 1979: 181–84.

119. Betz 1979: 181; also Meeks 1974: 180–81.

120. Despite the similarities noted by the commentators (Scroggs 1972: 292; Meeks 1974: 180 n. 74), the differences are, in fact, quite considerable. 1 Cor. 12.13 has a repeated εἴτε in the place of the οὐκ ἔνι…οὐδὲ formula of Gal. 3.28, whereas Col. 3.11 uses a repeated καὶ throughout. The Ἰουδαῖος οὐδὲ Ἕλλην of Gal. becomes plural in 1 Cor., and in Col. the order is reversed and the parallelism of περιτομὴ καὶ ἀκροβυστία added. The δοῦλος οὐδὲ ἐλεύθερος contrast in Gal. is likewise plural in 1 Cor., and in Col. it is replaced by the list βάρβαρος, Σκύθης, δοῦλος, ἐλεύθερος. Indeed, apart from the notion of pairings, there is little in the way of linguistic or grammatical connection between the formulae.

secondary addition to an earlier version'.[121] Thus, according to Betz, the
original formula, the one echoed in 1 Corinthians and Colossians, did not
contain the male/female pairing. This would obviously present major
problems for the insistence that it is known and utilized at Corinth.

Whether or not we accept Betz's conclusion about Gal. 3.28c being a
secondary addition, the indications are that if Gal. 3.28 evidences a
baptismal liturgical tradition of the early church, the form of that
baptismal tradition was very fluid: its language, and vocabulary differ
greatly in every instance in which it is recorded.[122] Thus we cannot use
Gal. 3.28 as a demonstration that a certain form and content must have
been known in Corinth. We cannot assume that Gal. 3.28 is the basic
structure, and other renditions represent alterations of it. Thus, while it
may be the case that the clause 'male and female' drops out of Colossians
and 1 Corinthians for situational reasons, it may also be the case that the
pairing was not automatically associated with the liturgy, or variants are
being referred to which never contained such a reference at all.[123] Thus, as
1 Cor. 12.13 and Colossians 3 may simply reflect a different form of a
variable tradition, we should perhaps be wary enough to speak of Paul's
possible reinterpretations of a baptismal tradition *akin* to that of Gal. 3.28
in 1 Corinthians, rather than stridently assuming that Paul is wrestling
with Gal. 3.28 verbatim.[124] The omissions might then be without
significance.

Indeed, the 'situation reasons' for deliberate omissions in Colossians 3
and 1 Corinthians 12 do not stand examination. The argument that the
pairing is deliberately omitted from Col. 3.11, as it runs against the
author's conservative attitude to wives and husband (Col. 3.18–19),[125] has
always been somewhat unlikely. The author also has a conservative
attitude to masters and slaves (Col. 3.22–25) and yet that coupling
remains in 3.11. So why drop the reference to 'male and female'? It is more
probable that the 'male/female' pairing is simply not in the tradition as the
author has received it.

121.   Betz 1979: 182.
122.   If D.R. MacDonald (1987: 17–21) is correct in seeing in other parallels from early
Christian literature evidence of an earlier oral baptismal reunification tradition (Clement,
Strom 3.13.92; *2 Clem.* 12.2; *Thom* 21a, 22b, 37), then comparing these to the recorded
canonical versions indicates that the tradition is remarkably fluid.
123.   When Scroggs (1972: 291) comments on the absence of the male/female pair in 1
Cor. 12.13 that 'it is easier to imagine Paul eliminating it here than irrelevantly adding it in
Galatians', he makes the assumption that there is a fixed form from which the apostle adds or
subtracts, and also that the pairing is irrelevant to the context of Galatians (cf. Kahl 2000).
124.   When Fiorenza (1983: 218) asserts, 'Paul explicitly refers to Gal. 3.28 in 1 Cor. 12.13
and 1 Cor. 7.17–24' she is simply wrong. The Corinthians do not share with us the benefit of
having the Galatian epistle to which Paul can refer.
125.   As Gundry Volf 1994b: 99.

When we turn to 1 Cor. 12.13, there are strong reasons to reject the notion that Paul is consciously omitting a male/female pairing. In 1 Corinthians 12 Paul is insisting on the interdependence of the members of the church/body: differences in gifts do not negate an essential unity of the church, since the gifts are given by the one Spirit for the corporate, and not the individual, good. Paul then uses the baptismal formula to stress that all, no matter what their background, have received this one Spirit and are part of this one body. To use, at this juncture, a formula favoured by the Corinthians, omitting what they saw as its climax, would totally undermine Paul's argument and play into the Corinthians' hands. For its omission would be glaringly obvious to them. Paul offers no justification for it – and this in the context of expounding on the unity and equality, which the remainder of the formula implies. Is Paul really so rhetorically inept? Would he really draw attention to the anti-hierarchical and egalitarian potential of the formula, and at the same time arbitrarily omit the one facet from which he does not want the Corinthians to draw such principles (and in which they, or some of them, take such delight)? Is it not easier to postulate that Paul's use of the baptismal tradition in this context is evidence, not of a battle over its gender implications, but of Paul's obliviousness to any such problem surrounding it?

Turning to the rhetorical context of 1 Corinthians 7, if the social implications of a baptismal formula[126] were the basis on which the Corinthians stressed a new asexual existence in Christ, and thus were a major ground of the dispute between Paul and the Corinthians, then we would expect to see evidence of this in the text. However, 1 Corinthians 7 does not mention baptism at all, nor does it use the 'in Christ', or 'we are one' language of Gal. 3.28 and 1 Cor. 12.13. Indeed, baptism is mentioned in only two instances in the entire letter: 1.10–17 and 12.13. In the first occurrence (1.10–17) Paul complains of the *disunity* that baptism is causing among the Corinthians, not for any doctrinal reasons, but because of an interest in the baptizer.[127] There is here a total absence of any theological battle over the nature of baptism. There is no suggestion that the Corinthians are proclaiming an egalitarian sociology alien to Paul; indeed quite the contrary. In the second occurrence (12.13) it is Paul

---

126. However, we should take care in speaking of the 'social implications' of the formula. If there is no one form of the formula then there is certainly no objective ground from which to observe its inherent meaning. But, in any case, implications depend upon the reader. For Paul the formula, whatever it meant, did not have the same 'social implications' that some later interpreters were to apply to it. Thus when Fiorenza (1983: 211–13) discusses at length what the formula 'asserts' and how it is 'best understood' it is not at all clear what she is getting at.

127. *Contra* Meeks (1974: 202) who refers to a 'peculiar understanding of baptismal initiation into heavenly wisdom, which Paul is at pains in chs 1–4 to correct' there is no real evidence that the Corinthians connected wisdom with their baptism.

who stresses the social implications of baptism. There is nothing to suggest that the Corinthians had already drawn overly enthusiastic social implications from baptism; indeed Paul strives to *remind* them of the implications of their baptism for their equal value before God.[128]

We are left then with 1 Cor. 7.17–24, which is supposed to be evidence beyond doubt that Paul is combating a radical interpretation of Gal. 3.28. This thesis is constructed by pointing out that Paul introduces what are the otherwise unconnected pairings of circumcision/uncircumcision and slavery/freedom into the debate on sexuality.[129] But is a reference to a baptismal tradition the only possible link between these pairings and marriage? We shall suggest, when we turn to the text, that circumcision and slavery are perhaps not that irrelevant to the discussion in hand, and thus a hypothesis of a redirection of the Galatians formulation is not required. Slavery and circumcision can be connected to marriage as parallel social states that the believer may be in when called, which are, on the one hand, irrelevant to his status in Christ (those in them should live ὡς μή) but, on the other, states that the believer is being encouraged not to seek, as they are in some way detrimental to full service of Christ. (The believer is commanded not to sell himself into slavery, and Paul is hardly likely to approve the uncircumcised entering into a circumcised state.) But this will require longer discussion, and we will return to it later.

The 'eschatological women' thesis has largely been built on the foundation that Gal. 3.28 has become a contentious point in Corinth – a foundation that now looks rather uncertain. However, as we have seen, this is not the only basis on which it is promoted. Its proponents also point to the structure of 1 Corinthians 7, where Paul for the most part carefully balances instructions to men and to women (7.2–4; 7.10–16; 7.28; 7.32–34), and argue that the parallelism 'conceals a major concern with women'.[130] Thus, in 7.10–11, the fact that the women are addressed first and given a longer instruction is taken to indicate that women were the main instigators of the separations and doing so in order to rid themselves

128.   In all of this we are being asked to believe that Paul's strategy for combating the interpretation of Gal. 3.28c is total silence, never once mentioning the male/female pairing. But where is the evidence that Paul ever adopts the strategy of shying from referring to problematic phrases? Most scholars see in 6.12; 7.1; 7.34 (?); and 8.1–4 Paul quoting and then reinterpreting phrases that perhaps originated from himself but have become problematic. Are we to believe that Paul in this one instance remains silent on an all-important phrase? Or is the silence better seen as more evidence of the irrelevance of the 'not male and female' part of the baptismal tradition to his dispute with the Corinthians?

129.   '[I]t is obvious that vss. 17ff break into the context' (Scroggs 1972: 293 n. 31). Scroggs goes on to suggest that 7.17–25 and 7.26–31 were originally a homily on the baptismal liturgy interrupted by 7.25. This goes to demonstrate the obsession with, and confidence in, identifying pre-formed material by his generation of scholars.

130.   M.Y. MacDonald 1990: 170; cf. 1996: 133–34.

of husbands less enthusiastic about celibacy.[131] Similarly, the fact that female widows alone are addressed in 7.39 (cf. 7.8) is taken to indicate the existence of financially independent women, able to contribute to the leadership of the church, who have a determination to remain unmarried.[132] Further, the continual use of the term παρθένος, which on three of the four occasions it is used certainly refers to a female (7.28; 7.34; 7.36), has been taken to indicate a Corinthian concern with the virginity of women.[133]

Not only is such a reconstruction a rather self-assured use of mirror-reading, where the ability to read accurately between the lines is assumed, it also can be contested from the text itself. Perhaps 7.10–11 does have in view a particular woman divorcing her husband – but why should this be taken as being for ascetic reasons? Indeed the point of Paul's stipulation that she does not remarry seems hard to explain if her motivations are ascetic. The concern with widows rather than widowers (7.39) could simply reflect the demographics of the congregation. Beyond this, much of the text appears to reflect male concerns. καλὸν ἀνθρώπῳ γυναικὸς μὴ ἅπτεσθαι does *not* look like the slogan of an ascetic *women's* movement! Similarly 7.26–27 (καλὸν ἀνθρώπῳ τὸ οὕτως εἶναι. δέδεσαι γυναικί ...) reflects concern with whether *men* should marry (the characteristic even-handedness is lacking). So also 7.36–38 (whether a *man* should marry/marry off his παρθένος). To argue, as many have, that these verses betray a male interest in *female* celibacy,[134] would seem like an attempt to simultaneously retain and consume the proverbial cake. Where the focus is more on the female this provides evidence that women are the instigators and focus of the celibacy, but where the male is the focus (or even exclusively mentioned) this can be explained as a male concern with female purity. While such a reconstruction is not impossible, it can only operate on the assumption that celibate women are the focus of the passage. It certainly cannot provide proof or even evidence of such.

As for taking 1 Cor. 11.2–16 as corroboration for the notion that there were in the Corinthian church eschatological women who claimed freedom from traditional gender roles, there are also a number of problems. First, the tone of 11.2–16 is notably less impassioned than other parts of the letter. The passage is introduced by the commendation of 11.2 before the dramatic change in tone at 11.17 where Paul moves on to consider the disparities at the Lord's supper. His dealing with the subject of the head in worship is thus introduced, not by a declamation of

---

131. M.Y. MacDonald 1990: 170.
132. M.Y. MacDonald 1990: 171.
133. M.Y. MacDonald 1990: 171.
134. M.Y. MacDonald 1990: 171–72.

dangerous practice (as in 11.17), but first with commendation of the
congregation's obedience to his traditions (11.2) and then a gentle
correction to Corinthian practice and understanding (θέλω δὲ ὑμᾶς
εἰδέναι, 11.3). Is this really the manner in which we would expect Paul to
deal with these women, if they were the source of concern (and of the
asceticism) that the proponents of the 'eschatological women' thesis
assume?[135] Does this really suggest a Pauline response to a group that
promotes, articulates, and is presumably obstinate in, such a radical and
disruptive theology?

Secondly, even assuming that those engaging in the practices of which
Paul disapproves are exclusively women,[136] it is less than clear how they
themselves interpreted the significance of their actions. There are three
possible ways in which the passage has been reconstructed: women
unveiling or uncovering in worship; women letting their hair down in
worship; or women cutting their hair short.[137] Of these three, the first
would seem to make best sense of the text.[138] However, against the notion
of uncovering or unveiling it has been objected that there is no evidence
that such would have been considered culturally improper in first-century
Corinth.[139] But can we assume that, whatever the practice is to which Paul
objects, it was culturally shocking? Certainly Paul claims an analogy
between the practice and a woman being 'shorn or shaved' (11.6) which he
appears to suggest would be considered self-evidently shameful (cf. 11.14–

135.   It is significant that there is no sign of an attempt to correct eschatology in this
passage whatsoever.

136.   Meeks (1974: 201) asserts that 'if the passage places most emphasis on the female,
that must be because in Corinth it is the charismatic women who are donning the attire of the
opposite sex'. But must it? Could it simply be that it is the change in female attire that most
concerns Paul? In any case there are many comments in the passage (11.4; 11.7; 11.14) that
concern male attire (cf. Murphy-O'Connor's [1980] suggestion that part of Paul's problem is
that men are wearing hair in a manner associated with homosexuality).

137.   The traditional view is that some sort of external covering (perhaps veil) is being
removed. That hair was being cut in a masculine fashion is suggested by W.J. Martin (1970)
and accepted by the NIV. More recently, loosing of the hair (letting it down in public) has
been suggested by several scholars (e.g. Hurley 1972: 190–220; Murphy-O'Connor 1980: 488–
89 and Fiorenza 1983: 227).

138.   None of the options are without difficulties (see the discussion in Fee 1987: 496–97).
Fee rightly rejects the 'short hair' option as it cannot make sense of the *analogy* taken from
hair or the grammar of 11.5–6. The 'loosed hair' option must also probably be rejected since
it would make little sense of Paul's insistence that long hair is a woman's 'glory' (so F.
Watson 2000b: 534).

139.   Arguing for the loosed hair view, Hays (1997: 186) contends, 'It was not the normal
custom for women in Greek and Roman customs to be veiled; thus, it is hard to see how their
being unveiled in worship could be regarded as controversial or shameful.' Interestingly, Fee
deploys exactly the same argument against loosed hair. He rejects the option as 'there is no
sure first-century evidence that long hair in public would have been a disgrace of some kind'
(Fee 1987: 496).

15), but this would operate even if the Corinthian practice itself was not. Similarly, when Paul seems to assert the social impropriety of uncovering in 11.13, he in fact has to *argue* for it from the analogy with hair in 11.14–15.[140] Nothing in this passage requires that the Corinthian action was culturally improper – merely that Paul finds it objectionable.[141] Thus it is quite possible that the Corinthians did not see themselves as rejecting a cultural norm or even engaging in an innovative practice. It is possible then that their actions did not symbolize to them a rejection or rewriting of traditional gender roles.[142] The connection of head covering with the order of the sexes could well be one made only on Paul's mind. The argument from the christological and natural order of the sexes might have been deployed to deal with a Corinthian practice, rather than a Corinthian theology, objectionable to Paul.

7.5. *Conclusion*

In section 7.2 we provided a number of reasons for questioning the ascetic hypothesis, and demonstrated the general weaknesses of the thesis. Then in 7.3–4 we have examined and assessed the various ideas that scholars have postulated as the motive for Corinthian asceticism – and shown the weaknesses of each in turn. However, our endeavours so far do not serve to destroy the thesis: for perhaps stronger argument could yet show some of these reconstructions to be *possible*, and almost certainly further reconstructions will be offered. Thus if our case against the ascetic hypothesis is to prevail we will require further evidence. It is that we proceed to offer as we demonstrate that both context (Chapter 8) and the text itself (Chapter 9) render the ascetic hypothesis untenable.

---

140. With F. Watson 2000a: 54: 'Paul cannot rely on his readers to agree that woman's unveiled face is an occasion for shame, and he therefore attempts an argument by analogy'.

141. It has often been suggested that female 'covering' represents a Jewish or Eastern practice, culturally normal for Paul but perhaps alien to his Gentile converts, and possibly rejected by them precisely for that reason.

142. Even if the Corinthians did see some symbolism in the woman adopting male attire in worship, it is not necessary to postulate that this involved the eradication of gender difference, or even a new social equality. The Corinthians may have viewed the change in attire as merely symbolizing, or being consistent with, a woman's permission to exercise the ministries of prayer and prophecy, ministries with which, assuming 14.34–36 is an interpolation, Paul would have had no problem. If so, then the view that the lack of a covering poses some greater threat to gender roles may again be solely in Paul's mind. (For other possible theological reasons for the Corinthians rejection of a veil see F. Watson 2000a: 53–54.)

Chapter 8

MARRIAGE, RENUNCIATION AND SOCIAL CONTEXT

It is now our intention to explore the social dynamics of 1 Corinthians as a whole, and to ask how an understanding of these might better inform our attempt to understand the seventh chapter. Specifically, we wish to explore whether the ascetic hypothesis is compatible with everything else that the epistle tells us about the Corinthian community's social attitudes. We shall proceed in a number of steps. First, (section 8.1) we shall explore the relationship between marriage and first-century Graeco-Roman society. What are the prevailing assumptions about marriage, and what obligations and pressures to marry are put upon individuals? In section 8.2 we shall explore some groups and individuals that seem to renounce marriage, or refrain from marrying. What is the attitude of such groups towards society in general? Is it possible to renounce marriage, without renouncing ancient society as a whole? In section 8.3 we shall consider what attitude Graeco-Roman society might be expected to adopt towards a social group who renounced marriage. What opposition might such a movement experience? Further, given that many have postulated that those renouncing marriage at Corinth were (mainly?) women, we shall consider the particular response urban society might adopt to such a phenomenon. Then, in section 8.4 we shall consider the social ethos of the Corinthian congregation, as revealed in the letter as a whole. What is the church's attitude to its social environment? In general, does it affirm or deny the social assumptions and institutions of Graeco-Roman Corinth? What can we say of society's attitude to the church? What is the nature of the relationship between church and society in Corinth? In section 8.5, we shall draw our observations together, and ask how far the social ethos and experience of the Corinthian church matches that which we would expect of a group that fostered the renunciation of marriage. Then, last, we shall consider, from the text of 1 Corinthians, the possible relationships there could be between any ascetics and the rest of the congregation. Need the social ethos and experience of any ascetics be identical to that of the church in general? What possibilities might the text either suggest or preclude?

8.1. *Marriage and Society*

> Thus whoever destroys human marriage destroys the home, the city, and the whole human race.[1]

Marriage is, in most societies, not merely a response to notions of ethics and sexuality but a social institution with a key role in propagation, socialization, economics and social control. It follows that the individual's or social group's attitude to marriage is part and parcel of their reaction to the wider society.

The sheer demographic facts of life in antiquity were always going to encourage the larger community's concern for the household unit. Infant mortality was extremely high by modern standards: perhaps 25 per cent in the first year of life, and 50 per cent in the first ten years. Life expectancy was low: perhaps 25 years from birth, with war, famine or plague always threatening to cut it further. Thus there was always going to be pressure on those in the short years of fertility to couple and reproduce.[2] It has been estimated that women living into adulthood would need to bear an average of five or six children, simply to keep the population stable. Given the stigma attached to illegitimacy, such a need for procreation would result in a pressure to marry.[3]

Ancient philosophy reflected and reinforced this concern with the reproduction of the population, presenting marriage as the building block of the πόλις, and thus it and procreation as civic duties. Deming has traced the philosophical discourse on marriage from Aristotle to the Stoics and has shown how it was not primarily viewed as an outlet for sexuality but as an assumed part of the social and cosmic order.[4] Marriage is the public marker that the male citizen has adopted his civic responsibilities as husband, father and citizen, for by it he establishes a household (οἶκός).[5] For Plato the household is a microcosm of the city-state.[6] For Aristotle the cosmos consists of the plurality of cities, which are composed of citizens organized in households: this is the natural order.[7] Stoicism adopted the same assumptions as Plato and Aristotle about the cosmos and the place of marriage within it. In the divine plan, the

---

1. Musonius Rufus, *Fragments* 14.11–13.

2. The statistics are from Garnsey and Saller (1987: 138). Garnsey's figures are based on averages for pre-industrial societies; inscriptional evidence from antiquity is reckoned incapable of providing significant indicators for the population as a whole (on which see Brunt 1971: 132–33).

3. As Treggiari puts it, 'women owed the state children, young men had the additional duty of maintaining the male line and the family name, *nomen*' (1991: 84).

4. Deming 1995: 50–107.

5. Foucault 1986: 150–51; Deming 1995: 52.

6. Plato, *Resp.* 5.8.

7. Aristotle, *Pol.* 1.1.1–12.

cosmos consisted of cities, and cities of households, and households were constituted by marriages. Thus, by linking the natural order to the divine, nature becomes a divine principle (and the gods favour and patronize marriage). Stoicism also added ethical principle to the natural: virtue was to be found in living κατὰ φύσιν and thus marrying was viewed as fitting (καθῆκον).[8] Certainly there are some changes. The Stoics placed more emphasis on duty to the wider κόσμος than the immediate πόλις, reflecting the political reality of the demise of the autonomous city-state and the rise of empire.[9]

   Civic order and the strength of the marital bond were also closely connected in ancient thought. As the duty to society was discharged in the duty to marry and beget heirs, so marital *concordia* was connected to the *concordia* of city and state. Marriage was a 'reassuring microcosm of the social order'.[10] Edwards's study, *The Politics of Immorality in Ancient Rome* (1993), suggests a symbiotic and symbolic relationship between the marital microcosm and the civic macrocosm.[11] The authority of the *paterfamilias* within the household parallels State authority: the Senate are the *patres* of the nation.

   Marriage is thus an affair of State, and not merely a private matter.[12] The greatness of Rome is seen as dependent on maintaining the *mos maiorum* of early Rome, an idealized golden age where, through the rose-tinted glasses of the moralists, household structure was preserved and adultery rare. The Republican Censor embodied this concern of the political elite for the general state of morals and family among their own members and the wider citizen body.[13]

   Even as the Empire eclipsed the Republic, the link between social structure and marriage remained. The Empire too embodied the notion of the household in macrocosm: Augustus taking the title *pater patriae*. (On various occasions the emperors also take on the office and role of censor.)[14] In a similar vein the *Lex Iulia* of the Principate indicates the

---

8.   Long 1986: 179, 189–205.

9.   Deming 1995: 56 (cf. Foucault 1986: 81–95).

10.   P. Brown 1988: 16.

11.   Edwards 1993: 29–62.

12.   Veyne (1987: 34) notes that paradoxically the contracting of Roman marriages was a private act, requiring no formal ceremony, celebrant, document or procedure, yet it had most definite legal and public consequences.

13.   Plutarch, writing in the early second century AD, says of the Republican censor, 'it carried a wide range of powers, including that of examining the lives and morals of the citizens. The Romans believed that no one should be left to his own ways and desires without being subject to inspection and review, either in choosing a wife, or in begetting children' (*Cat. Mai.* 16.1–2).

14.   The Emperors used the precedent of the Republican censor as a basis for their concern for domestic propriety (although Claudius was the first Emperor actually to assume the office of censor).

Imperial State's concern with public morals and domestic life, particularly in light of the proverbial decadence and immorality of the late Republic. The *lex Iulia de adulteriis* (the Julian law on punishing adulteries, 18 BC) was concerned with penalizing adultery and, passed in the same year, the *lex Iulia de maritandis ordinibus* (the Julian law to promote marriage in the senatorial and equestrian orders) which encouraged, by rewards and penalties, appropriate marriages and child-rearing.[15]

In this all too brief survey of marriage and society we can see that family order is firmly within the public sphere in Graeco-Roman thought. Marriage and childbearing are at the heart of the concept of civic society. Practically, society is concerned for its survival, a survival that requires a continual supply of new citizens. But, perhaps more importantly, ideas of authority and order in society are modelled on those of the family. Socio-political and domestic order are then taken together as part of a greater cosmic given. Disorder in the family symbolizes, and is seen to cause, disorder in the state, and indeed cosmic upheaval. As Mitchell rightly puts it, 'good marriages contribute to the concord of the political body, and bad marriages lead it into discord, so the marriages within a community must be of concern to the statesman'.[16]

8.2. *Exceptions that Prove the Rule*

There are, of course, some exceptions to this anticipated order of family life. But these, as we shall see, are not examples of, and thus cannot be models for, an alternative celibate social existence within a wider all-embracing society. There are, when they exist, examples of individuals who stand outside society, rejecting it, and often being rejected by it. Scholars have been at times too quick to offer these as social parallels to the supposed Corinthian ascetics, without considering the social context of such examples.

---

15.   Edwards suggests that these measures should not be read as practical responses to practical problems, but as a 'symbolic discourse, bearing as much or as little relationship to patterns of behaviour in ancient Rome as the effusions of the Roman moralists, and in dialogue with, indeed part of, moralistic discourse' (1993: 35). Hence we should be wary of taking the descriptions of immorality in the late Republic at face value. They are 'metaphors for social and political disorder'. (Veyne 1987: 38 also speaks of the 'illusion' of the late republican marriage crisis – although he attributes it to the preponderance of theoretical discourses on whether to marry.) Similarly, according to Edwards, we should view the Augustan legislation as part of the propaganda of the restoration of the *res publica* with its idealized social norms. Marriage is thus symbolically connected to the political order.

16.   M.M. Mitchell 1991: 121.

8.2.1. *Graeco-Roman Religion*

Sexual abstinence within Graeco-Roman religion, made much of by certain commentators on 1 Corinthians 7,[17] is almost without fail only a temporary phenomenon.[18] While it might provide parallels for Paul's mention of limited abstinence for prayer (1 Cor. 7.5), it does not do so for the renunciation of marriage. As Gillian Clark puts it, religious duties were 'not an alternative but an addition to a woman's normal duties, imposing only temporary disruption ... there was almost no possibility of a religious commitment which replaced marriage ... life virgins are almost unattested'.[19]

Of course that 'almost' could be significant. Gundry Volf[20] has attempted to trace the phenomenon of the 'inspirational ascetic' in Graeco-Roman antiquity and connect such to the Corinthian ascetics. She points to various examples of virgin priestesses serving as oracles: the Pythia at Delphi;[21] Cassandra the prophetess of Apollo; another prophetess of Apollo at Patara in Lydia; and some of the Sibyls who are called *virgo* and παρθένοι.[22] But these are relatively small numbers of women over very large periods of time. They are individuals existing on the margins of society (and, the anthropologists would assure us, it is precisely that marginality and social ambiguity which gives them their power).[23] They are exceptional individuals, existing on the social borders and reinforcing those borders, and are in no way 'types' for a group's social existence.[24]

Perhaps the Vestal virgins appear closer to the social mainstream.

---

17. E.g. Gundry Volf 1994a.

18. See the inscriptions cited by R. Parker (1983: 74 n. 4). Parker (1983: 75) also notes that washing after intercourse is equally used as a barrier between the sacred and the secular. He thus states of such Greek religious rules, 'they are not the products of asceticism ... nor is it easy to see them as expressions of a strong internalized feeling that the sexual act is degrading or disgusting'.

19. G. Clark 1989: 34. (See also Treggiari (1991: 83) and R. Parker (1983: 86) who states, 'sacred requirements of purity that imposed long periods of abstinence were exceptional. In the classical period, most priests and priestesses throughout the Greek world were either married people or people conducting normal family lives, who may at the most be bound to temporary periods of chastity, or married people past the age of frequent sexual activity'.)

20. Gundry Volf 1994a: 110–15.

21. However, Parker (1983: 93) notes that although 'in theory a maiden ... in practice the post was normally filled by an old woman' who would certainly previously have been married.

22. See Gundry Volf 1994a: 10–11 for references.

23. E.g. Douglas 1966: 94–113.

24. Gundry Volf also points to Philo's portrayal of Moses, John the Baptist and the prophetess Anna (Lk. 2.36). However, both Philo's Moses and John fit into the lone prophet mould. John's 'living in the wilderness' may, as Gundry Volf asserts, show his sexual abstinence, but it also shows that he (like many prophets) is an anti-societal figure living

However, again they are not a model of celibacy to which young women may aspire, but quite the contrary. As Peter Brown puts it:

> [T]he message conveyed by such women ... was that their state was of crucial importance for the community precisely because it was anomalous. They fitted into a clearly demarked state in civic society. Though eminent and admired, they were not thought to stand for human nature at its peak ... The vestal Virgins stood out as glaring anomalies. They were the exceptions that reinforced the rule ... [they] heightened the awareness of contemporaries that marriage and childbirth were the unquestioned destiny of all other women.[25]

Suetonius records the extreme reluctance of the populace to have their daughters chosen for such a role.[26]

8.2.2. *Celibate Philosophers*

As we have seen, the thrust of the reasoning of the Academy and the Stoics favoured marriage as a necessary and desirable part of the social order. But what of that philosophy that did question marriage or at least its wisdom for the philosopher? Can we find here models or parallels for unmarried existence within society? Two examples stand out, the Cynic and the Epicurean.

Two phases of the Cynic movement are relevant to our consideration here: the original Cynics of the third and fourth centuries BC, whose exploits and teaching are recorded in Diogenes Laertius' *Lives of the Eminent Philosophers*, and the attempt to appropriate that Cynic tradition by the Roman Stoics of the first century AD, for example Epictetus.

According to Diogenes Laertius, Diogenes of Sinope (c. 400–325 BC) certainly rejected marriage. He suggested that men adopt communal responsibilities towards women and children, defining marriage as simply intercourse between 'the man who persuades' and the 'woman who is persuaded'.[27] He also apparently advocated masturbation for the satisfaction of the sexual urge, in place of conventional conjugal relations.[28]

---

alone, eating odd foods, and standing outside and against normal society. As for Anna she had 'lived with her husband seven years from her virginity, and as a widow till she was eighty-four', but she is also a social misfit – living in the Temple and fasting continually.

25. P. Brown 1988: 8–9.

26. Suetonius, *Aug.* 31. The very fact that they were *chosen* for, rather than *choosing*, such a lifestyle means that they cannot be considered as examples of the 'heroic freedom of the individual will': they are not ascetics (with P. Brown 1988: 8).

27. Diogenes Laertius, *Lives* 6.16 (see Deming 1995: 64).

28. Diogenes Laertius, *Lives* 6.46.

However, Diogenes' rejection of conventional marriage patterns forms part of a wider rejection of the normal assumptions of social existence. His radical individualism sought αὐταρκεία (self-sufficiency) in living according to nature rather than social custom. Whereas others had seen family life and civic duty as part of the natural order, Diogenes' Cynicism viewed them as unnatural and thus to be set aside by the wise man. Thus not only was Diogenes said to 'praise those who were about to marry and refrained', but he also praised 'those who intending to go on a voyage never set sail, those who thinking to engage in politics do no such thing, those also who proposing to rear a family do not do so, and those who make ready to live with potentates, yet never come near them after all'.[29] He rejects not only marriage but also all the duties of the citizen: property, civic pride, indeed self-respect as it was defined by contemporary society. Social existence is subverted in the name of the Cynic lifestyle. Thus, such Cynicism does not challenge our view that marriage is an integral part of the social order; rather it tends to confirm it, since it rejects both marriage and that social order. [30]

The Stoic philosophical tradition later sought to present such Cynic figures as Diogenes as heroes of philosophical devotion. On the face of it, then, the Stoic incorporation of the Cynic tradition would seem to point to an admiration of celibacy within a movement that otherwise upheld social and political existence. Appearances, however, can be deceptive.

If we take, for example, Epictetus' discussion of the Cynic lifestyle in his third Discourse,[31] we quickly discover that although the Cynic figure is idealized, the adoption of the lifestyle is discouraged, and the significance of the Cynic's refusal to marry significantly altered from that presented by the *Lives*. First, the purpose of the discourse itself is to dissuade Epictetus' correspondent from adopting a Cynic lifestyle: his contemporary Cynics are contemptible,[32] and the idealized figures from the past are not patterns that a man should seek to follow, but representatives of an extraordinary divine vocation, to which few are called.[33] The Cynic again has become the peculiar exception to the otherwise universal social rules.

Moreover, despite the fact that the idealized Cynic exempts himself

29. Diogenes Laertius, *Lives* 6.29.
30. Meeks (1974: 171) deals with such Cynicism under the heading 'models of alienation'. Much the same ethos can be found in the Cynic Epistles (see Deming 1995: 71–72).
31. Epictetus, *Diatr*. 3.22.
32. Epictetus, *Diatr*. 3.22.50. Branham (1996: 15–16) refers to the 'habitual contrast between the contemporary and the classical, the real and the ideal'.
33. Epictetus, *Diatr*. 3.22.2–13.

from the normal household and political duties in order to follow his higher calling, that calling is *not* antithetical to the political and domestic existence of humanity.[34] Epictetus' Cynic, unlike that of the *Lives*, has no natural philosophy that derides social existence. As Billerbeck puts it:

> The rejection of friendship, marriage, begetting of children, and engagement in politics called for positive reinterpretation, if Cynicism, especially among the Romans, was not to become suspect as a subversive movement. The ideal Cynic, therefore, will not withdraw from his duties as citizen because he rejects them; on the contrary, he renounces them in order to put himself in the service of the whole of mankind.[35]

The Cynics then have a particular role to play in the domestic and political structure. They are to be those:

> whose duty is to oversee the rest of men; those who have married; those who have children; who is treating his wife well, and who is ill; who quarrels; what household is stable, and what is not; making his rounds like a physician, and feeling pulses.[36]

We are a long way from the subversion of the Cynics of the *Lives*. Epictetus' Cynic has been reintegrated into respectable society. He is not a threat, nor challenge, to the social order, but has become, like the Vestal virgin, the exception that proves, indeed reinforces, the rule.

When we turn to the Epicurean philosopher, we find that he is more akin to the Cynic of the *Lives*, renouncing marriage and political participation in the same breath. The political order is held to exist by coercion incompatible with *eudaimonia*, and the cosmic order of gods, cities and households is held to be a dangerous illusion.[37] Unlike with Cynicism, Epictetus does not trouble himself to reinterpret Epicurean views in a less subversive direction. Instead he simply ridicules their anti-social implications. Of Epicurus' vision of a city-state without marriage,

---

34. Indeed, in the ideal world, the Cynic (if such were necessary) would marry (*Diatr.* 3.22.69) and even now may do so in extraordinary circumstances (*Diatr.* 3.22.67–68). Lucian recounts Epictetus' haranguing of the Demonax, calling him to marry and have children, as, 'this also is fitting for a man who pursues philosophy, namely, to leave behind for nature another in his place' (*Dem.* 55).

35. Billerbeck 1996: 208.

36. Epictetus, *Diatr.* 3.22.72.

37. Diogenes Laertius, *Lives* 10.118–19. Epicurus also notoriously rejects Graeco-Roman religious assumptions about the intervention of the gods, earning his followers the label 'atheists', evidence again of how anti-social his teaching was perceived to be.

Epictetus derisively asks, 'where are the citizens to come from?' before proceeding to denounce his teaching as 'subversive of the city-state (πόλις), destructive to the family (οἶκός)'.[38]

8.2.3. Judaism and Celibacy

The proverbial assumption that Judaism affirmed marriage and procreation as God-given and universally incumbent obligations is, generally speaking, sound (although, as we have seen, it differed little here from most Graeco-Roman thought up to the first century AD). But what of those groups that reportedly did countenance an abstention from marriage: the Therapeutae, and the Essenes?

Since our evidence for the Therapeutae comes solely from Philo of Alexandria, let us begin by considering Philo's own view of marriage. Philo accepts basic Stoic premises. The κόσμος consists of city-states made up of households based on marriages. Without a wife a man is imperfect and homeless, but the married man has time for politics while his wife manages the household.[39] Breach of the Mosaic Law on marriage undermines the household and the city alike.[40] The wise man fulfils his God-given duties as statesman and householder. It is the bad man (ὁ φαῦλος) who is without home or city-state.[41]

This should all be remembered when Philo's idealized accounts of the Essenes and Therapeutae are given as evidence for his approval of celibacy. Like Epictetus, Philo can praise an ideal, and offer it as an object lesson in philosophical/religious devotion,[42] without offering it as a model of social existence to be followed. The Therapeutae are a Platonizing allegory of the superiority of the immaterial, and if the example of their abandonment of marriage is meant to encourage anything, it is the pursuit of piety through contemplation rather than a renunciation of family life.

In any case, if there was historically a group of Therapeutae, such as Philo describes, it would not offer a model of celibate existence within society. It would have been a deeply anti-social group, constituting an

---

38. Epictetus, *Diatr.* 3.7.19–21. Interestingly in this passage Epictetus also impresses on the Epicurean the civic duties of piety, marriage and children as he lives 'in an imperial state' (ζῆς ἐν ἡγεμονούσῃ πόλει).

39. Philo, *Ios.* 29, 38–39; *Quaest. in Gen.* 1.26; 4.165.

40. Philo, *Spec. Leg.* 3.31; *Abr.* 135–41.

41. Philo, *Gig.* 67.

42. See Deming 1995: 91–92.

alternative society.[43] Not only do they renounce marriage;[44] they also abandon their property,[45] disown slavery,[46] leave their family and fatherland,[47] and adopt a life of fasting and abstinence.[48] They constitute a new society, which becomes their new fatherland,[49] and their new family.[50] Like the Cynics of the *Lives*, they have renounced all elements of the present social order.

When we turn to the Essenes we find accounts in Philo and Josephus, in addition to the evidence that we have from the Dead Sea Scrolls and the Qumran excavations. Philo states that the Essenes 'eschew marriage' and that 'no Essene takes a wife',[51] but again we find he presents them as those who have also rejected property, home and wider social relations.[52] Thus once again they are an anti-social group, who provide a philosophical object lesson.[53] When we turn to Josephus' account,[54] we find that although Josephus notes positively the Essenes' repudiation of marriage, it is the underlying motive rather than the practice he salutes. Celibacy demonstrates that they 'shun pleasures as a vice and regard temperance and control of the passions as a virtue' and also shows their wariness of 'women's wantonness'. Further, Josephus also shows his sensitivity to the charge that the Essenes are anti-social when, first, he affirms that they adopt and educate the children of others (a practice familiar to Romans

---

43.   *Pace* Barton 1997: 84 who argues that 'their philosophy is not anti-social' since they constitute an 'alternative society'. This is hardly the point; they reject society as it stands, make no critique of or attempt to reform such, but withdraw to form a new order. Indeed their setting up of a new fatherland, new households and fictive kinship units serves to underline their break with their previous social existence. Under Barton's definition an anarchist group could not be considered 'anti-social', providing they had regard for their fellow anarchists!

44.   Philo, *Vit. Cont.* 32–33, 38.

45.   Philo, *Vit. Cont.* 13–18. They leave this prematurely to their heirs, and thus are in effect socially dead.

46.   Philo, *Vit. Cont.* 70–71.

47.   Philo, *Vit. Cont.* 18.

48.   Philo, *Vit. Cont.* 34–35; 73–74.

49.   Philo, *Vit. Cont.* 22.

50.   Philo, *Vit. Cont.* 72.

51.   Philo, *Hypoth.* 2.3.

52.   Philo, *Omn. Prob. Lib.* 77–78.

53.   *Pace* Barton's insistence that Philo's repeated presentation of the Essenes 'shows the extent to which he views the Essene way as an alternative to the normal house-hold based community' (1994: 30). Barton fails to consider Philo's assumptions about marriage as a part of the God-given natural order, and his disparagement of those who despise it. In a characteristic failure of Barton's thesis he neglects to differentiate between a principled rejection of family ties, and the use of such a motif to stress the comparative importance of other loyalties by those who would not wish to encourage the rejection of marriage.

54.   Josephus, *BJ* 2.120–25.

without heirs) and, secondly, that they 'do not, indeed, on principle, condemn wedlock and the propagation thereby of the race'.

In the Dead Sea documents themselves there is nothing to indicate the renunciation of marriage by the sect. Despite this, however, the sectarians living at Qumran appear to have been a community of celibate males,[55] while those sectarians living outwith Qumran 'in the camps' did marry and beget children.[56] But again, even among the celibate, we do not have an example of an alternative mode of being-in-society. Those at Qumran renounced not only marriage but also civic life (obviously) and private property (which they held in common).[57] The renunciation of marriage is thus part of a renunciation of society as a whole.

8.2.4. *Conclusion*

Marriage is thus, as we said at the outset, an accepted part of the social structure. It is universally seen as part of the cosmic order: a given, and even a moral, imperative. Certain individuals could perhaps be permitted to stand as honourable exceptions: a priestess here, and an idealized Cynic there, but none offer a serious model for existence within society apart from the responsibilities of marriage and citizenship. The only place where we approach figures with an ability to challenge these assumptions is with Diogenes of Sinope and his ilk (as portrayed in the *Lives*), Epicureanism and perhaps some of the Qumran sectarians. However, all of these reject more than simply marriage. The radical Cynic is anti-societal, in the strongest sense of the word. He does not challenge the linkage between society and marriage but rejects both together. Indeed, the Cynic rejects the basic prevailing cosmological assumptions: that the social order derives from what is natural. Epicureans have certain similarities; they too break the sacred chain of divine, cosmic, political and domestic givens. They radically reject surrounding society, and are in turn rejected by it. The Qumran community again withdraws from normal society, which is viewed as corrupt. We might thus suggest a rule: to reject marriage is to reject society as it was generally conceived, and thus to reject the moral and cosmological assumptions of the Graeco-Roman (including the Jewish) world. To renounce marriage is to renounce the world.[58] We may summarize with the words of Wimbush:

---

55.   In addition to the testimony to celibacy of Philo, Josephus and Pliny (*Nat.* 5.73), the fact that the Community Rule makes no reference to female members would appear to indicate that there were none. This is an argument from silence, but archaeological evidence seems to speak in its support. The main graveyard contained few female and infant remains and these were on the periphery (see Vermes 1987: 8–9, 18).

56.   CD 7.7–9; Messianic Rule 1.8–10.

57.   1QS 1.12; 5.2.

58.   As Fiorenza (1983: 225) observes, 'Paul's advice to remain free from the marriage bond was a frontal assault on the intention of existing law and the general cultural ethos'.

> This response represented a clear critique of the world, since family life, sexual relations, and the laws and traditions governing them were perhaps the most important socializing forces in Greek and Roman antiquity. Renunciation of marriage ... would have been seen as an unambiguous declaration of independence from the world.[59]

Furthermore, the few examples that we have of individuals who renounce marriage are actually renouncing *marrying* rather than *marriage*. There are no examples here of married people rejecting either their own marital state, or sexual activity within marriage. We might postulate then that it would require an extraordinary rejection of society for the renunciation of *existing* marriages to occur.

8.3. *The Response of the World*

8.3.1. *Disrupting the City*

If the ancients could not conceive of social existence without marriage then two things follow. First, we would expect that groups or individuals that renounce marriage would, to some degree, also renounce the wider social structure and the cosmology that underpins it. Secondly, we can expect Graeco-Roman society to interpret any threat to the marital order as a threat to that wider social order. Thus, the reticence to marry will be perceived as an attack upon the household, the city and the political order, and as such both anti-social and seditious (we may recall Epictetus' charges against Epicurius). Further, since marriage is perceived as part of the natural rational order, renunciation will be viewed as both perverse and irrational.

The second-century tale of *Paul and Thecla* serves as an excellent illustration.[60] The tale presents a drama of social opposition, first in Iconium and then at Antioch. It centres on Thecla's decision to renounce her engagement to Thamyris and to follow the teaching of an ascetic Paul. Although perhaps consciously unhistorical,[61] and certainly overstated, we can assume that the tale would strike a familiar note with its readers in its portrayal of the opposition which they would expect should they follow Thecla's example and renounce marriage.

Here Paul rides into the city of Iconium proclaiming 'the word of

---

59. Wimbush 1993: 423.

60. Perhaps attested as early as Tertullian (*Bapt.* 17.5) if the *Acts of Paul and Thecla* was originally part of the larger *Acts of Paul* (see Rordorf 1986: 43–44).

61. On historicity see Rordorf (1986). For our purposes the historicity is of limited importance, since even if an historical Thecla narrative lies at the core we cannot know if it placed any stress on the question of her marriage, and even if the tale is entirely unhistorical, it still attests to social attitudes to renunciation in the first century, in such a way as to be credible to its original audience at some time before the end of the second century AD.

God about continence and the resurrection' (περὶ ἐγκρατείας καὶ ἀναστάστεως), and blessing 'those who have kept the flesh chaste', 'the self-controlled', 'those who have wives as not having them' (ἔχοντες ὡς μὴ ἔχοντες) and 'the bodies of virgins'.[62] Thecla, transfixed by Paul and his teaching, responds by refusing marriage to her betrothed Thamyris.

The theme of the narrative is the struggle between the civic authorities and citizenry of Antioch and Iconium on the one hand and Paul and his protégée Thecla on the other. The dramatic tension is caused by Paul arriving into an otherwise peaceful city with his disruptive message, a message that dislocates Thecla from her social environment and provokes violent opposition to both her and her mentor. That opposition comes from her family and compatriots in equal measure. Her mother complains to her fiancé that Paul 'disrupts (ἀνασείω) the city of the Iconions, and your Thecla as well; for all the women and young men are taught by him that "One must fear the one and only God and live in chastity".'[63]

Despite the double grounds of the above complaint, throughout the story it is the Pauline stance on marriage and not monotheism that provokes opposition. No charge of atheism or sacrilege is levelled against Paul and Thecla,[64] but rather Thecla is brought first before the magistrate at Iconium for her refusal to marry Thamyris (a capital crime!) and then before the governor of Antioch for her rejection of a certain Alexander's rough wooing. On the first of these occasions it is her own mother who denounces her with the words, 'burn the lawless one (τὴν ἄνομον), burn her who refuses to be a bride (τὴν ἄνυμφον) in the midst of the theatre, that all the women that have been taught by this man might be afraid'.[65]

Thecla rejects marriage and in doing so repudiates the norms, assumptions and social ties of city and family. In response both institutions reject her. The tale echoes the real outrage of society against the renunciation of marriage, and particularly among the daughters of its elite citizenry. There is no place in which one may adopt a celibate lifestyle within the existing social world. The dramatic tension, which the story creates, remains unresolved even at the end. Only Thecla's exit from the

---

62. *Acts of Paul and Thecla* 5–6, author's translation.

63. *Acts of Paul and Thecla* 9. Elliot translates 'will overturn the city'. Interestingly Luke uses ἀνασείω (23.5) in the charges brought against Jesus before Pilate: that by his teaching he 'stirs up the people' (ἀνασείει τὸν λαόν). There the charge was connected with instilling rebellion against Caesar (23.1–2).

64. The text anachronistically suggests that simply to be denounced as a 'Christian' invites death (16). It is the threat to marriage and the πόλις, which the apostle represents, that invites such a denunciation. This may well reflect the experiences of the later church (it is certainly reflected in the other apocryphal Acts – see below).

65. *Acts of Paul and Thecla* 20.

world of the city, and entry into an itinerant lifestyle represented by Paul, allows her to remain celibate.

Additional examples of such opposition can be found in the other apocryphal Acts, where the persecution (and often martyrdom) of the apostle and his converts almost formulaically proceeds from the renunciation of marriage.

In the *Acts of Thomas*, Judas Thomas, en route for India, comes upon a wedding. The apostle prays for the couple, and as a result the Lord appears to them in the bridal chamber and instructs them to 'refrain from this filthy intercourse' that they might 'become temples holy and pure, being released from afflictions and troubles, known and unknown' and 'not be involved in the cares of life and of children, whose end is destruction'.[66] The result is perhaps predictable. The young couple 'refrained from filthy lust', and the bride acknowledges the Lord as her 'true husband' as opposed to her 'temporary husband'. Her father then flies into a rage and orders the arrest of the apostle as a sorcerer.[67]

A second episode concerns Mygdonia, the wife of the Indian courtier Charisius. She receives the teaching of the apostle on the dangers of carnal sin and she too expresses the desire to become 'a holy temple'.[68] When she refuses intercourse with her husband he denounces the apostle: 'I heard this sorcerer and deceiver teaches that no man should cohabit with his wife, and he reverses what nature demands (ὁ ἡ φύσις ἀπαιτεῖν), and the deity has ordered (καὶ ἡ θεότης ἐνομοθέτησεν).'[69]

Marital celibacy is thus viewed as sacrilegious and perverse. When the matter is reported, the King promises to avenge Charisius (and all other husbands) against the apostle, who is then flogged and imprisoned.[70]

A similar pattern can be found in *Acts of Peter*. Here Peter persuades four concubines of Agrippa, and then Xanthippe, wife of Albinus, to renounce intercourse. Matters, however, go further:

> And many other women delighted in the preaching concerning chastity and separated from their husbands, and men too ceased to sleep with their wives, because they wished to serve God in chastity and purity. And there was a great commotion in Rome (θορύβου οὖν μεγίστου ὄντος ἐν τῇ Ῥώμη).[71]

Civil unrest, and the desire of Agrippa and Albinus for personal revenge, lead to action against Peter, causing his eventual arrest and martyrdom. In all these cases, the renunciation of marriage, or the marital bed is seen

---

66. *Acts Thom.* 12.
67. *Acts Thom.* 13–15.
68. *Acts Thom.* 84, 87.
69. *Acts Thom.* 96.
70. *Acts Thom.* 102–106.
71. *Acts Pet.* 34.

as anti-social, unnatural and irreligious. Is it any wonder that such teaching is so closely connected with the ethos of martyrdom?

8.3.2. *Wild Women*

If the ancient city was sure to react negatively to a renunciation of marriage, then, if such a renunciation were made by women who were engaged in a foreign and innovative religion, we would expect that reaction to be all the more profound. Social and political order are tied up in Roman thought with conformity to traditional patterns of religious and social adherence. Disorder in the city or state is often symbolized by the moral and social dislocation of women. Women are seen as the Achilles heel of civic society. Extraneous forces that would disrupt the commonwealth prey on the gullibility of women, who are particularly vulnerable to disruptive religious innovations.

At least from the time of Euripides (c. 400 BC), the Bacchanalian myth of wild ecstatic religions seducing women and turning them against husbands and natural civic subordination seems to have influenced the ancient psyche. Writing only two generations before Paul, Livy records the introduction of the Bacchic cult to Italy where women initiate a nocturnal rite, unbraiding their hair, engaging in ecstatic worship and purportedly various types of immoralities.[72]

Men as though out of their minds prophesied with frantic jerking of their bodies; married women dressed as Bacchants with hair flowing freely would run down to the Tiber.[73]

> A high proportion of them are women, the source from which this evil has sprung; then too there are males almost indistinguishable from the women, rabid debauchers and debauchees stupefied with sleeplessness, wine and the noises and shoutings of the night.[74]

The Senate is immediately concerned for the interests of both the State (*cum publico nomine*) and the relatives of the families concerned.[75]

A speech, which Livy attributes to the Consul Postumus, reveals the deep-seated and connected fears that such an incident provokes: a departure from ancestral religion, alien rites, (the perception of) immorality, and the confusion of gender roles combine to constitute 'an evil in the body politic', which although not yet having 'sufficient strength to overthrow the state'[76] requires immediate official action. The end of the

---

72. Livy, *Epon.* 39.8–19. The episode is set in 187 BC and Livy appears to offer it as an example of the moral decline at the beginning of the second century.

73. Livy, *Epon.* 39.13.12, translation by Walsh.

74. Livy, *Epon.* 39.15.9.

75. Livy, *Epon.* 38.14.

76. Livy, *Epon.* 38.16.3.

episode is the execution of a great number of initiates, both male and female.[77]

The fear of the propensity of foreign religions (particularly ecstatic ones) to mislead women, and by so doing upset civic and domestic harmony, remains a powerful topos in antiquity[78] and is a device that is readily used to discredit foreign religions (including Jews and later Christians) and justify suppression. Josephus narrates Tiberius' violent proscription of the Isis cult, when the charlatan Mundus used it to seduce the *matrona* Paulina.[79] Josephus also blames Tiberius' expulsion of the Jews from Rome on the conversion of Fulvia to Judaism and her subsequent defrauding by a renegade Jew who takes advantage of her religious devotion.[80]

From the above we can see how any religious innovation which was (or had the appearance of) unsettling women in regard to their social position within society (i.e. πόλις or οἶκός) was likely to be viewed as highly dangerous. The Thecla narrative, which we have just examined, bears this out. For a man to refuse marriage is a breach of his social responsibilities, but for a woman it is a direct challenge to the male-oriented social and political order. As the Stoic Hierocles commented, 'it is impossible to conceive of a governed without a governor'.[81] To renounce marriage, for a woman, would be a treacherous declaration of independence, and that which motivated the renunciation would be regarded with the utmost suspicion.

8.3.3. *New Testament Evidence*
Further evidence of the Graeco-Roman attitude to any religious movements which were perceived to threaten marriages by leading women astray can be found in 1 Peter and the Pastoral Epistles. These authors are well aware that the reputation of their churches may be damaged if they are seen as socially disruptive.

77. The story (or at least the fears it suggests) has perhaps some basis in historic fact. An inscription containing the decree of the Senate proscribing the Bacchic cult was found as Vindobona in Calabria. (See the Appendix to Walsh 1994: 180.) Cicero also narrates an ancient legal tradition banning women from sacrificing nocturnally (*Leg.* 2.35 and 37).

78. See Balch 1981.

79. Josephus, *Ant.* 18.65.

80. Josephus, *Ant.* 18.81–84. Although not solely concerned with women, we can see the Roman concern with the social danger of conversion to foreign religions in Tacitus. 'Proselytes to Jewry adopt the same [sexually immoral] practices, and the first lesson they learn is to despise the gods, shed all feelings of patriotism, and consider parents, children and brothers as readily expendable' (*Hist.* 5.5). We can note how Tacitus puts together the rejection of ancestral religion, fatherland and family. The same three all-important aspects of the Graeco-Roman social order are brought out in Livy's account of Postumus' speech against the Bacchanalias.

81. Hierocles, *On Marriage* 4.502, 21–22.

Present-day controversies over the teaching of the author of 1 Timothy obscure the fact that the last thing this author wanted was for the church to appear socially controversial. He urges, if not submission, then an attitude of respect to state authority, 'that we may live a quiet and peaceable life, godly and respectable in every way' (2.2). Slaves are to respect masters 'so that the name of God and the teaching may not be defamed' (5.24). Church leaders are to be respectable (3.2) and respected (3.7) members of society, married (3.2; 3.12) and able to keep control over well-ordered households (3.4–12). Everywhere there is a concern lest there be any hint of social impropriety, a concern linked to a desire not to attract any avoidable social disapproval.

The Pastor is particularly nervous about women, painfully aware of the danger that any accusation of social impropriety might cause for the church. Women too are to be respectable (2.9–10), 'managed' by their husbands (3.12) and knowledgeable of their place in the hierarchy of the household and the church (2.11–12). The one socially anomalous class, the 'widows', is treated with special caution. Younger widows are to marry, bear children and manage households so that they 'give the enemy no occasion to revile us' (5.14). Only older widows, who are 'beyond reproach' and have previously discharged their social duties in service and child-rearing (5.10), may be given the financial support necessary to remain unmarried. The Pastor knows that 'unmanned' women endanger the social perception of the church.

Moreover, not only is the Pastor aware of the presuppositions of the Graeco-Roman society concerning the potential disruption of women: he also shares them. He views unmarried women as a danger to the social harmony of the church, with a potential to commit every form of destructive anti-social vice which endangers the body politic (5.11–13). The author of 2 Timothy goes even further, reiterating the Graeco-Roman fear of the susceptibility of women to religious innovation, warning against those who 'make their way into households and capture weak women, burdened with sins and swayed by various impulses, who will listen to anybody and never arrive at a knowledge of the truth' (2 Tim. 3.6–7).

Given that the Pastor is so keen to uphold the social order, and given the close connection between that order and the institution of marriage, it should not surprise us when he pronounces anathema on the 'liars whose consciences are seared, who forbid marriage and enjoin abstinence from foods' (1 Tim. 4.2–3). As Pagels has noted, in his rejection of these teachers the Pastor aligns himself with the social conservatism of the citizens of Iconium, and against the apocryphal Paul of the Thecla narrative.[82]

82. Pagels 1988: 24.

The author of 1 Peter is also concerned for the social reputation and thus the social order of his congregation. In addition to respect for state authority (2.13–14; 2.17) he demands that slaves submit to masters (2.18) and wives to husbands (especially non-believing husbands), while exercising the wifely values of chastity and modesty (3.1–6). Balch suggests that what has occurred is that 'certain slaves and wives converted to Christianity; therefore persons in Roman society reacted by accusing them of being immoral, perhaps seditious, and certainly insubordinate'[83] (i.e. the proverbial vices of an eastern cult). The Pastor views the church as vulnerable to such charges, and despite the fact that he admits (indeed celebrates) a certain level of alienation from society, he is at pains to prevent the church appearing socially radical. To rock the social boat will bring down the slander and opposition of society.

8.3.4. *Conclusion*
Marriage is part of the accepted social, natural and religious pattern of antiquity. To renounce it is to take a deeply anti-societal stance: it is to 'break the discrete discipline of the ancient city'.[84] The radical nature of such a stance will be reinforced by an equal and opposite reaction of rejection by the surrounding culture. Too many people have too much invested in the status quo for it to be otherwise.[85]

8.4. *The Social Ethos of 1 Corinthians*

8.4.1. *The Church's Relation to its Social Environment*
As we have seen, the renunciation of marriage is a deeply anti-societal stance, possible only for those who reject the social order and its underpinning cosmological assumptions, and invariably provoking a negative reaction from surrounding society. If this were to be accompanied by a perception that women were engaging in an ecstatic foreign religion, questioning social roles and endangering domestic order, we could expect that negative reaction to be all the more pronounced. So is this the social experience of the Corinthian church?

Previous generations of Corinthian scholars would have had less hesitation in answering this question in the affirmative. The stress on the theology of the Corinthians (invariably seen as influenced by some form of Gnosticism or at least a Hellenistic disparagement of both the material

---

83. Balch 1981: 95.

84. P. Brown 1988: 3. Brown goes on to speak (rather poetically) of the vision of Christian ascetics that, 'with marrying at an end, the huge fabric of organised society would crumble like a sandcastle touched by the "ocean flood of the messiah"'.

85. It should hardly surprise us that second and third century Christian asceticism is so heavily connected to the world-denial inherent both in the theologies and experience of martyrdom and in the neo-Platonic and Gnostic suspicions of the material world.

world and the body) seemed to support reconstructions of the Corinthians as alienated from their surrounding world.[86] However, not only have recent scholars been questioning the existence of these anti-material theologies in the Corinthian church (Gnosticism, spirit/matter dualism, and even 'realized eschatology' have, as we have seen, come under sustained attack) but the move to sociological investigations of the church has generated quite different conclusions. We have moved from postulating a socially radical church to envisaging one whose dominant ethos is more in tune with the social assumptions of urban life.

The question of the social *level* of the Corinthian Christians must remain a somewhat open one (the growing consensus led by Meeks and Theissen having been recently challenged by Meggitt).[87] However, the question of the social *ethos* and social experience of the church (its 'response to the world') stands somewhat independently. Barclay rightly comments that there is 'no necessary correlation between economic deprivation and apocalyptic world-view', warning against the assumption that high-status believers will automatically adopt a 'non-sectarian perspective'.[88] But the corollary is also true: the observation that the Corinthian church is not highly sectarian does not depend on (albeit it is strengthened by) the thesis that the congregation includes members of high status.[89]

The first thing to note from the epistle is an apparent absence of conflict between believers and outsiders. 'Believers in Corinth appear neither to feel hostility towards, nor experience hostility from, non-Christians.'[90] When Paul lists the *apostolic* catalogue of sufferings (4.9–13) he emphasizes elements of social ostracism and opposition (the apostles have become a θέατρον κόσμῳ, 4.9; are ἄτιμοι, 4.10; are λοιδορούμενοι, διωκόμενοι and δυσφημούμενοι, 4.12–13) and he does so, at least in part,

---

86. It is significant that both Gnosticism with its rejection of the material world as evil, and Marcion with his rejection of the Creator God as evil, evidence profound hostility to sexual activity.

87. That the Corinthian Christians were drawn predominantly from the lower social strata was first alleged by Celsus (cf. Origen's *Contra Celsum* 3.48) and accepted by Deissmann (1927). The 'new consensus' that the early church (and Corinth in particular) incorporated individuals from a cross-section of society, including some from the elite, was led by the work of Theissen (1982) and Meeks (1983), and has been followed by many recent studies (e.g. P. Marshall 1987; Chow 1992; Clarke 1993; Witherington 1995; D.B. Martin 1995). The challenge has come from Meggitt (1998).

88. Barclay 1992: 68. Meggitt (1998: 153–54 n. 417) accepts the point.

89. As Barclay (1992: 68) comments, 'The social status of the dominant minority in the Corinthian church is certainly a factor of some significance. But it would be a mistake to build everything on this foundation alone ... wealth and its associated social status are not necessarily wedded to a non-apocalyptic and non-sectarian perspective'.

90. Barclay 1992: 57.

in contrast to the public reputation which the Corinthians enjoy (as ἔνδοξοι, 4.10).

We can also note the relationship of the Corinthians to a number of social practices and institutions. Some, for example, are happy to instigate proceedings in the law-courts (6.1–6). This has seemed to many scholars to be clear evidence of the social position of some believers on the basis that only the elite were able to afford and succeed in such actions.[91] However, be that as it may, the instigation of actions is clear evidence that at least some in Corinth had confidence that the legal system could operate in their favour, thus not expecting any official hostility to believers. Neither could they see any problem in responding to disputes in accordance with the expected social pattern of the city: utilizing the services of the court. Identity in Christ has not altered the relationship of the Corinthian Christians to this one key social institution.

If Theissen is correct that the divisions at the Lord's supper (11.17–34) stem from the, perhaps common,[92] practice of wealthy hosts holding banquets and allocating food and drink in accordance with social position (hence 'one is hungry another drunk'), then we can again see how the Corinthians assumed Graeco-Roman social values were unaffected by Christian identity.[93] The existence of the church in itself was no challenge to such social norms.

The social integration of the Corinthian church can also be seen in the fact that some of its members are invited to the homes of unbelievers rich enough to host meals (10.27), and that Paul expects outsiders to 'drop in' to the community meetings (14.24). It is also at least possible that the desire of the Corinthian 'strong' to stress their freedom in regard to foodstuffs reflects a desire to minimize, or eliminate, any call for social withdrawal from cult-saturated public life. Again, this thought has been used as evidence of a social elite among the Corinthians, who have most to lose in terms of influence and wealth, by social withdrawal.[94] Yet even

91. E.g. Theissen 1982: 97; Winter 1991; 1994: 106–21; D.B. Martin 1995: 76–79; Chow 1992: 75–80 and esp. Clarke 1993. However, see the critique of Meggitt (1998: 123–25) who argues that while a bias towards those of higher status may have discouraged the poor from taking their social superiors to court, there is no reason to believe, and indeed evidence to suggest, that court cases occurred between 'social equals from the lower echelons of Corinthian society'.

92. The practice is well attested in the literature (cf. Pliny, *Ep* 2.6; Juvenal, *Sat.* 5; Martial, *Epigrams* 3.60).

93. Theissen 1982: 145–68; also Witherington 1995: 243–47.

94. As Horrell (1996a: 105) states, 'the wealthy, however, would have been more accustomed to accepting dinner invitations and eating meat in a variety of settings, and would have risked losing their position within a social circle if they had rejected all invitations where "consecrated meat" might have been expected'. See also Theissen (1982: 121–40) who identifies division of the Corinthian 'strong' and 'weak' as being socio-economic, but note also the criticism of Gooch (1993).

without such a postulation, the very fact that eating with outsiders, whether at private meals or pubic events, is of concern to the Corinthians, evidences their social integration and expectation of normal insider/outsider social relations.

The seeming tendency to place value on rhetoric (2.1–5)[95] and the possible disdain for Paul's refusal to accept financial support and his insistence in earning his own living (4.12; 9.1–23),[96] have again been offered as evidence for high status attitudes among the Corinthians. However, whatever the strengths of these arguments, we can be more certain in taking these features as evidence that the Corinthians are accepting the common values of Graeco-Roman society. Even a social underclass may have cultural assumptions and expectations about the conduct and quality of those who would lead them. Further, the seeming Corinthian tendency to identify with certain individual leaders (1.10–17; 3.3–5), and the resulting σχίσματα and ἔριδες in the congregation has also been plausibly explained with reference to the Graeco-Roman practice of aligning oneself with a higher status patron to advance one's standing in the community.[97] Even if none of the Corinthian Christians were of high status, lower status Christians may have carried a practice learned in society into the church, seeking to identify with Paul or Apollos (or other perhaps local leaders) as those having status within their new community.

Thus, whatever the social level of the Corinthian Christians, their social ethos seems clear. They continued to engage with their social environment without, for the greater part, viewing its institutions and values as incompatible with their new Christian identity. Indeed, in their behaviour as a new community, it appears they largely adopted the assumptions and practices of contemporary society.[98] The tendency of the Corinthians to accept, rather than to reject or confront, the values and practices of their surroundings would go a long way towards explaining why they might experience little in the way of hostility from that society.

8.4.2. Paul's Own Attitude
If, then, the Corinthians evidence little sectarianism, having a positive relationship with outsiders, feeling neither alienated nor estranged from

95. Pogoloff 1992; Witherington 1995: 124.
96. Theissen 1982: 44–46; P. Marshall 1987: 245–47; Witherington 1995: 209.
97. Clarke 1993: 93–94.
98. As Adams (2000: 102), 'The Corinthians would have viewed their new religious club, or *collegium*, as a microcosm of the larger society and of the whole κόσμος. They would have sought to mirror in their group norms and intra-group relations the norms and values of the dominant culture.'

urban Corinth and its social practices and institutions, where does Paul stand? On the one hand Paul seems to agree with their choice to remain integrated into civic society. Social withdrawal is neither possible nor desirable (5.9). Believers should continue to purchase meat from the market (10.25), dine with outsiders (10.27), and even remain in mixed marriages (7.12–24). On the other hand, Paul appears critical of the community's lack of distinctiveness at a number of key points. As we have seen, he stresses the social opposition that the gospel has brought to him (4.9–13; 15.20–32), inferring that it is to the Corinthians' shame that they have not experienced similar opposition. He condemns their participation in lawcourts, their dining practice, and the celebration of rhetoric. He views their σχίσματα and ἔριδες as worldly, human (σαρκικός, κατὰ ἄνθρωπον) behaviour (3.3). As we have seen, his notion of Christian identity demands a more rigorous attitude to sexual morality (and to group boundaries) than the Corinthians have adopted.

His message of the cross stands opposed to the values and priorities of the world. It nullifies those things on which Graeco-Roman society placed most stress: social position, birth and wealth (1.26–29). It antagonizes the rulers of this world (2.6–9). It is proclaimed in the perversity of divine weakness rather than with rhetorical skill or philosophical knowledge. Paul stands before the Corinthian church and its social assumptions with a deeply unsettling, apocalyptic vision of reality. Humanity is divided into two separate castes: the saved and the perishing (1.18); the saints and the unrighteous (6.1–2); the morally corrupt mass, and those 'washed, justified and sanctified' (6.9–11). The outside world is for Paul a dangerous place and even if identity in Christ does not preclude the believer existing in it, it is to transform every aspect of social life.

Paul, according to most contemporary scholars, is no social conformist confronted by the radical anti-structural views of his opponents. Rather they are the social conformists following accepted social norms, and he stands in uneasy relationship to them, with his unsettling apocalyptic dualism, and at least the germs of a notion of a radically new social order existing through the subversion of the cross.

8.5. *The Corinthian Church, Society and Asceticism*

8.5.1. *The Social Situation of 1 Corinthians 7 according to the Ascetic Hypothesis*

This picture of a socially conformist church and a more radical Paul does not fit the social picture required by proponents of the ascetic hypothesis, who still insist in portraying Paul as the social conservative, worried about outside opinions, and the Corinthian ascetics as the social radicals.[99] The reconstruction is still too closely tied to the old Gnostic models, and has taken little or no account of the emerging consensus on the degree of the social integration of the Corinthian church.

M.Y. MacDonald serves as a good example. She reconstructs pneumatic women transcending sexual differences in baptism. These women are instigating separations, with the widows among them remaining unmarried. She then labels Paul's response as 'a concern for propriety and social respectability',[100] going on to argue that

> Paul was striving to curtail social disruption in Corinth. Such disruption, no matter how sincere the intentions that inspired it, could distract the community from its focus on the Lord. Secondly, disorderly behaviour could bring unnecessary suspicion on a group which sought to embrace the whole world.[101]

Paul's purpose, then, in defending marriage is due to his concern 'to promote order within the community and to stabilize the place of the group within the wider context of Graeco-Roman society'.[102] MacDonald is well aware of the disruptive implications of the renunciation of marriage and of women asserting a new social role, but she insists on this picture, taking no account of the scholarly views on the social dynamics of the rest of the epistle.

The only scholar who seems to address this paradox is Wire. She again reconstructs the 'Corinthian woman prophets' as an extremely anti-authority group, celebrating liberty (in their openness to 'alternative patterns of sexuality', e.g. welcoming the irregular couple of 5.1!) and united in 'common opposition to family patriarchs and those who force others into traditional patterns'.[103] They are not a marginal grouping within the church, but a wide movement in which 'women in the community from every age group and marriage status are choosing to withdraw from sexual relations and enter a less sexually defined state'.[104] They experience rising status in the church, but (and here is the difference) they also experience a rising social position in the wider society. 'We may tend to picture a decision for asceticism as a withdrawal from the social scene, but here the women were moving out of relative seclusion into

---

99.   Fiorenza (1983: 216), drawing out the social consequences of Gal. 3.28, proposes that the church provided an experience of '...an alternative community in the midst of the Graeco-Roman city for those who had come into contact with it. As an alternative association which accorded woman – and slave-initiates equal status and roles, the Christian missionary movement was a conflict movement which stood in tension with the institutions of slavery and the patriarchal family.'

100.   M.Y. MacDonald 1990: 175.

101.   M.Y. MacDonald 1990: 175–76.

102.   M.Y. MacDonald 1990: 179.

103.   Wire 1990: 92.

104.   Wire 1990: 65.

wider and more direct participation in public life.'[105] How does she justify the anomaly of an anti-patriarchal anti-marriage group being acceptable in Graeco-Roman society? She does it by turning all received wisdom about first-century Graeco-Roman society on its head, portraying it as an increasingly liberal and liberated society. Perhaps taking the complaints of the moralists over the collapse of traditional society too much at face value,[106] she suggests that post-Republican society should be seen as low-grid/low-group: a free market society where freedmen, new money and women were on the rise at the expense of the rank and privilege of the old Patrician and patriarchal orders (which the socially conservative Paul represents). Hence the women prophets are not rebelling against the spirit of the age, but are very much in tune with it.

Wire neglects to note that the decline of traditional power, values and authority is a traditional theme of Roman literature, and should not be taken too literally. Some new social groups undoubtedly rise and old ones fall (such was always the case), but to suggest that either patriarchy or the 'class' system, as the average citizen would have experienced it, were under threat is simply wrong. Wire's reconstruction of a liberated woman's movement in an increasingly liberated society looks suspiciously like the experience of, for example, certain elements of the woman's movement of the 1960s, rather than the Corinthian church in the first century.

8.5.2. *The Relation of the Ascetics to the Congregation as a Whole*
Of course the ascetic hypothesis might be defended by arguing that the Corinthian ascetics are a small group, out of step with the dominant social ethos of the church. Thus while the majority of the Corinthians may take a more conformist attitude to society than Paul, there might exist a group that differs from Paul in the opposite direction: a group that is more socially radical.

As a matter of fact, few proponents of the ascetic hypothesis propose this. Wire has every Corinthian woman as an ascetic prophet. MacDonald and Gundry Volf see them in key positions in the church and very much respected.[107] But could such a reconstruction allow both the consensus on the social ethos of the Corinthian church, and the consensus on the existence of ascetics in its midst to be affirmed? Two factors would suggest not.

First, if the renunciation of marriage is so deeply anti-social, we would expect the majority of the congregation (those who keenly affirm society) to react strongly against such an anti-social minority, either objecting to their anti-social ethos itself, or concerned (like the authors of 1 Peter and the Pastorals) lest the socially disruptive few damage the reputation of the

105. Wire 1990: 93.
106. See the comments at n. 15 above.
107. Wire 1990: 65 (quoted above); M.Y. MacDonald 1990: 173; Gundry Volf 1994a: 116.

entire congregation.[108] However, there is no evidence of this in the epistle. There is no evidence to suggest that marriage or its renunciation had become a divisive issue among the Corinthians.[109] Evidence of division is absent from chs 5–7 (except in the lawsuits of 6.1–11). Indeed, although the rest of the epistle does evidence divisions among the Corinthians, most commentators have given up the attempt to view these as theological fault lines within the group – preferring to find explanation in Graeco-Roman status competition. The notion that the church could be so fundamentally split over its attitude to marriage sits uneasily with this contention.

Secondly, if there was such a fundamental split in the congregation then it is puzzling why Paul makes no mention of it. There is no attempt to deflate the pride of either group by pointing to division in the community (as we find at 1.12–13; 3.3–4; 11.18), or to moderate the ethos of the ascetics by pointing out the divisive nature of their insistence that marriage is 'sin'. There is not even an attempt to suggest that the enthusiastic celibacy of a few might place weaker believers in danger of sinning (as we find in 8.7–13).

8.5.3. Conclusion

Where then does this leave us? It leaves us at an impasse. The general consensus of scholarship, that Paul writes to a church that enjoys a high level of social integration, does not match the radical anti-societal ethos that we would expect from a group that renounces marriage. Neither can the evidence, that the church experiences little in the way of persecution from wider society, be reconciled with the reaction of social hostility, which we would anticipate society exhibiting towards a group who renounced marriage. These seldom-noted contradictions require resolution.

The next stage is to re-examine closely the text of 1 Corinthians 7. We must ask whether, despite the contextual difficulties with the hypothesis, the text requires us to postulate Corinthian ascetics, or alternatively whether the text might be better explained by alternative means.

---

108.   Particularly if we envisage that the ascetic group not only renounces marriage for themselves, but contend that marriage is 'sin' and married Christians lack a holiness attributable only to the single.

It has been suggested to me that perhaps the ascetic group were not so radical, possibly merely refraining from marrying, while being neither imperialistic nor provocative about their preference. Such a reconstruction is however to be rejected for two reasons. First, what would Paul's problem be with such a mild preference for celibacy? Secondly, one of the key pieces of evidence for the existence of ascetics is 'mirror-reading' Paul's denial that marriage is sin to evidence a group who contended just that. Thus, if such evidence is removed, while the coherence of the hypothesis may increase, the reasons for advancing it are severely weakened. Do such 'mild ascetics' still propose that the married should divorce? If so, then is this not likely to be socially disruptive? If not, then just what parts of the 'mirror-read' evidence remain to support the hypothesis at all?

109.   This is true even in 5.1–9. There is no evidence that some had less tolerance of the immoral man than the rest.

Chapter 9

REREADING 1 CORINTHIANS 7

9.1. *Introduction*

Our exploration of Paul's discussion of πόρνη-union (Chapter 6) caused us to rethink our view of his attitude to the compatibility of sexual unions and Christian identity. We saw that the implications that he draws from the body being 'for the Lord' have at least the potential to undercut all sexual unions, including marriage. We observed in passing that Paul's denial in 7.1–40 that marriage is sin might well relate to this. We noted additionally that other themes in 6.12–20 have echoes in the text of 1 Corinthians 7 (sexual union as giving an ἐξουσία over the body, the question of the holiness of the body). We thus contended that any reading of 1 Corinthians 7 required keeping 1 Cor. 6.12–20 in view.

In the past, the 'ascetic hypothesis' has principally prevented such a reading. It has demanded that 1 Corinthians 7 be viewed as a highly situational response crafted for a background starkly differing from that of 1 Corinthians 6, rather than as a continuation of Paul's thought. The previous two chapters have (hopefully) served to undermine this hypothesis. We have demanded that any reading of 1 Corinthians 7 must take into account both 6.12–20 and the social dynamics of the epistle as a whole. In the previous chapter, noting the degree to which marriage was an assumed part of ancient social order and the respective attitudes of Paul and the Corinthians to that social order, we concluded that a renunciation of marriage among the Corinthians must be considered *prima facie* improbable.

The task now is to engage in a close reading of 1 Corinthians 7, with two related objectives in mind. First, although the social context of the epistle counts heavily against the ascetic hypothesis, we must consider whether the text of 1 Corinthians 7 compels such a reading. Secondly, if the ascetic hypothesis is not required, we must consider how the text might (better) be read. Here we are seeking a reading that considers, and is consistent with, the text itself, the text primarily as an articulation of Paul's ideology of sexuality (with 6.12–20), and the text as a part of the dialogical context of the entire epistle.

Evidently 1 Corinthians 7 is, at least to some degree, situational. (It begins, after all, περὶ δὲ ὧν ἐγράψατε, 7.1.) However, it is still *Paul's* articulation of his opinion on marriage, and part of his wider discussion of sex and Christian identity in 5.1–7.40. Thus we should look in the first instance to Pauline rather than Corinthian convictions for an understanding of the text. Evidently, as a direct response to Corinthian writings, the chapter carries its own particular background: the textual unit has its own dialogical pre-history. However, any reconstruction of that pre-history must not consider 1 Corinthians 7 other than as part of the wider dialogical context of the epistle as a whole.

We shall proceed as follows. In 9.2 we shall consider the possible context for Paul's dialogue on marriage with the Corinthians. In 9.3 we shall consider how Paul's thoughts in 6.12–20 might be developed in 7.1–40. Then in 9.4–9 we shall turn to the text itself, examining the plausibility of the ascetic hypothesis and whether our reading of the dialogical context might better explain Paul's remarks. Simultaneously, we shall consider what we might learn from the text about Paul's attitude to Christian identity, if we discard the ascetic hypothesis.

9.2. Reconstructing the Dialogical Context

The previous chapter alerted us to the respective views of Paul and the Corinthians in regard to the difference that Christian identity makes to the believer's behaviour and attitude toward the social institutions and values of antiquity. The Corinthians appear, while celebrating their spiritual achievements, on the whole, to construct their new Christian identity socially in conformity to these values and assumptions, while Paul has a vision of Christian identity defined, to a greater degree, as antithetical to them. We saw the same in our consideration of 1 Cor. 5.1–6.12: Paul has a clear vision that identity in Christ brings in a new social order, dividing humanity between stereotypically immoral outsiders and morally transformed insiders. For Paul, this dichotomy of identities changes social relations transforming social encounters into intergroup encounters and even preventing certain (previously accepted) social interactions between parties of differing identities. On the other hand the Corinthians are less keen to link Christian identity to moral status, or to view this as transforming social behaviour and disrupting previous social assumptions.

If this pattern were followed with regard to marriage patterns, what would we expect? Surely that the Corinthians would be more likely to affirm the normal assumptions and practices of ancient society, and less likely to view Christian identity as making conflicting claims on the sexual body than would Paul. We could perhaps expect a Pauline critique of Corinthian attitudes as being too 'worldly', such as we find from him in regard to their tolerance of division (1.10), evaluation of wisdom (3.1–4), attitude to the incestuous man (5.1) and engagement in lawsuits (6.5). On the other hand we might expect a Corinthian resistance to the full social (or anti-social) implications of Paul's view that identity in Christ transforms attitudes to this key social institution. However, before we engage in reconstructing the form that such a dialogue might take, let us examine another dialogue, for which we have better evidence in the text of 1 Corinthians, for a possible parallel dynamic.

9.2.1. 1 Corinthians 5.9–13 as Textual Evidence for the Form of a Dialogue
In 5.9–13 we are given an insight into the various stages of a dialogue between Paul and the Corinthians. Not only do we have Paul's present contentions on the relevance of Christian identity to social interaction (with whom a believer may or may not eat), but we also have both a record of what Paul has previously written (ἔγραψα ὑμῖν ἐν τῇ ἐπιστολῇ ... 5.9) and some hints as to what the Corinthian response to that statement was, which now provokes Paul's rejoinder.

Paul had previously instructed the Corinthians μὴ συναναμίγνυσθαι πόρνοις. But what was meant by the injunction? Evidently there were two possible interpretations, depending upon whom πόρνοι was taken to designate. One interpretation (the one for which Paul contends in 5.9–13) takes πόρνοι to designate purported believers who engage in πορνεία (such as the incestuous man of 5.1–9). It calls for an alteration in social behaviour towards a limited group of individuals. The other interpretation (the one that Paul denies in 5.9–13) takes πόρνοι as a designator of outsiders. It calls for the termination of social contact either with *all* outsiders (as stereotypically πόρνοι) or with outsiders who commit πορνεία.[1] Since the notion that Paul has changed tack between letters[2] seems somewhat implausible (Paul's contradictory back-pedalling would be obvious to the Corinthians) it seems better to take Paul at face value and assume that he called for social withdrawal from a limited group of moral apostates.

What is certain is that the Corinthians have put into practice neither interpretation of the dictum. They have not disassociated themselves from the immoral man of 5.1–9 – the prime example of an internal πόρνος – but neither have they disengaged from social interaction with outsiders in general. Whatever the Corinthians' response to the world has been, it has been less sectarian even than that actually envisaged by Paul.

The Corinthians have received Paul's enjoinder μὴ συναναμίγνυσθαι πόρνοις, and have 'read' him as advocating a profound withdrawal from outsiders, which in fact he never intended. Given that the Corinthians presumably know something of Paul's attitude to outsiders and social existence, it would seem likely that their misinterpretation of his command

---

1. See above sections 4.5.21 and 6.7.3.
2. As suggested by Hurd 1965: 222.

is wilful, taken for its ability to make the otherwise comprehensible (but still unacceptable) command to disassociate from internal πόρνοι appear ridiculous. The Corinthians thus circumvent a socially disruptive Pauline instruction by engaging in a *reductio ad absurdum*, and portraying both the command and its author as more anti-social than either was in reality.[3]

In responding, Paul has two objectives. He must reject the allegation that he commended such an anti-social stance towards outsiders, while restating and clarifying his call for disengagement from apostates. He achieves the first merely by denial, and then by stating fully the implications of their *reductio* (5.10): they should know better than to think he could have commanded such! With the misapprehension dismissed, Paul then restates his imperative (5.11), but this time clearly specifying both the objects and extent of the intended withdrawal.

We can observe the structure of Paul's retort:

5.9   He quotes his previous ambiguous instruction.

5.10   He names and refutes the Corinthian misinterpretation.

5.11   He unambiguously clarifies and restates the instruction.

The statements of 5.12–13, however, merit further examination. These are presented in an AB/AB structure: the 'A' statements forbid the judging of outsiders and the 'B' command the internal judging and expelling of offenders.[4]

5.12A	τί γάρ μοι τοὺς ἔξω κρίνετε;	For what have I to do with judging those outside [the church]?[5]
5.12B	οὐχὶ τοὺς ἔσω ὑμεῖς κρίνετε;	Are you not to judge those inside?
5.13A	τοὺς δὲ ἔξω ὁ θεὸς κρινεῖ.	God will judge[6] those outside [the church].
5.13B	ἐξάθατε τὸν πονηρὸν ἐξ ὑμῶν αὐτῶν	Drive out the evil person from among you.

The 'B' sequence is unproblematic. It is Paul's restatement of the imperative that he has been arguing for throughout 5.1–13: that the

---

3. Rom. 3.8, where Paul's notion of a law-free gospel appears to have been (maliciously) interpreted as an invitation to licentiousness, represents a parallel wilful over-interpretation of Paul.

4. As Fee 1987: 226.

5. οἱ ἔξω simply designates the outgroup. Jews applied it to Gentiles; Mk 4.11 applies it to those who are not disciples; and Paul uses it in 1 Thess. 4.12 to denote unbelievers (cf. Col. 4.5).

6. Or 'God judges'; the tense of κρινεῖ (or κρίνει) is, as ever, uncertain, but is probably future in light of 6.2–3.

community is to exercise internal discipline. In that this discipline is effected through the removal of the incestuous man from the church, this imperative is identical to the misunderstood imperative μὴ συναναμίγνυσθαι πόρνοις. What is less clear is how the 'A' sequence should be understood. Some commentators, spurred on by the connecting κρίνω word group, appear to take the sequence as a transition to the subject of judicial judgments in 6.1–8. Hence, Fee argues that the Corinthians 'may not be about the kind of litigious "judging" that is about to be addressed'.[7] But the awkwardness of Fee's language betrays the problematic nature of his assertion. For the problem in 6.1–8 is *not* the Corinthians' tendency to judge outsiders, but again their failure to judge insiders and settle internal disputes 'in-house'. Thus we should reject the direct relation of 5.12A and 5.13A to 6.1–8 and look for its meaning in the preceding discussion.[8]

Who then is judging outsiders, that Paul needs to deny the propriety of such action? It hardly appears that the Corinthians are – they seem all too reluctant to exercise any type of judgment. Remembering that what Paul denies in 5.12A is *his* desire to judge outsiders (hence the μοι), it seems probable that the verse is a defence against a Corinthian attack on Paul: an accusation that *he* demands (or engages in) the judging of outsiders. It also seems likely that both the accusation and the denial form part of the discussion of Paul's μὴ συναναμίγνυσθαι πόρνοις command.

Thus Paul is again defending himself against the Corinthians' propensity to over-interpret him as making anti-social demands. The 'A' sequence is the refutation of this interpretation that has accompanied the positive restatement of the imperative throughout 5.9–13 (the 'B' sequence). Examine the following:

B	5.9	Restatement of original imperative	ἔγραψα ὑμῖν ἐν τῇ ἐπιστολῇ μὴ συναναμίγνυσθαι πόρνοις
A	5.10	Rebuttal	οὐ πάντως τοῖς πόρνοις τοῦ κόσμου τούτου ...
B	5.11	Imperative	νῦν δὲ ἔγραψα ὑμῖν μὴ συναναμίγνυσθαι ...
A	5.12a	Rebuttal	τί γάρ μοι τοὺς ἔξω κρίνειν;
B	5.12b	Imperative	οὐχὶ τοὺς ἔσω ὑμεῖς κρίνετε;

---

7. Fee 1987: 226.

8. 5.13 appears to suggest that any attempt by believers to judge outsiders is to usurp a Divine prerogative. This appears to contradict 6.2–3 where the believers' participation in the eschatological judging of outsiders (whether it be ὁ κόσμος or οἱ ἄγγελοι) is presented in a positive light, indicating a competency to judge presently between believers.

A 5.13a Rebuttal   τοὺς δὲ ἔξω ὁ θεὸς κρινεῖ.

B 5.13b Imperative   ἐξάρατε τὸν πονηρὸν ἐξ ὑμῶν αὐτῶν

We can observe that Paul enforces the application of the correct interpretation of 5.9, while striving to prevent its mishandling. This also helps to explain the emphatic μοι of 5.12b. We can also observe that, despite the fact that it has proved a hostage to fortune, Paul has not withdrawn his command μὴ συναναμίγνυσθαι πόρνοις, but rather has repeated and clarified it shorn of its ambiguities. The Corinthians may comply with or disregard it, but they can no longer exploit its imprecision.

9.2.2. 7.1–40 as a Parallel Dialogue: A Hypothesis to be Tested

In 5.9–13, without straying too far into the hypothetical, we have eavesdropped on the conversation between Paul and the Corinthians. We have heard how the Corinthians attempt to circumvent Paul's unpopular social injunction by engaging in a *reductio*, making Paul's call sound more socially radical than it is in reality. We have seen Paul's response, denying the implications of the *reductio* and restating and clarifying the command. Might such a conversation have occurred in the case of marriage?

That Paul had a preference for singleness is made clear in 7.1–40, where a string of arguments are offered for it. Of course (as we saw in Chapter 8) contemporary attitudes to marriage would mean that any call for the single to remain so would be viewed as anti-social, if not downright disruptive. Thus the Corinthians' more positive attitude to social values and institutions (seen also in Chapter 8) make it likely that Paul's preference would be poorly received. What then if Paul had called for unmarried believers to remain single, giving his injunction in the form καλὸν ἀνθρώπῳ γυναικὸς μὴ ἅπτεσθαι? (We assume for the moment that this is a Pauline construction.) If this had initiated a conversation parallel to that revealed in 5.9–13, what form would we expect it to take?

The statement καλὸν ἀνθρώπῳ γυναικὸς μὴ ἅπτεσθαι is in various regards similar to the command μὴ συναναμίγνυσθαι πόρνοις. Both, as Paul intends them, call for an alteration to normal social practice, but both are also capable of being read as demanding a higher level of social disengagement. With one Paul calls for withdrawal from the apostate; with the other (we shall argue) he advocates a preference from singleness. However, just as the first may be heard as (or reduced to) a command to withdraw from all outsiders, so the second may be heard as (or reduced to) a command to renounce all sexual relations (taking καλόν as a moral absolute and ἅπτεσθαι as a reference to all sexual contact). With both, it is possible that the Corinthians, in order to defeat Paul's lesser (although still anti-social) call, could engage in a *reductio ad absurdum* and hear a call more disruptive than Paul intended.

Our suggestion will be that the sequence in the case of the marriage discussion is as follows. Paul (possibly also in the 'previous letter' of 5.9) has written καλὸν ἀνθρώπῳ γυναικὸς μὴ ἅπτεσθαι. He has not intended such as a moral absolute (this seems impossible in view of his protestations in 7.1–40), but as strong advice to those contemplating marriage to follow his own example, earnestly to consider full devotion to the Lord, and remain single. Such advice has been uncomfortable for the socially integrated Corinthian church. Is the married householder, with his concern for family honour and social duty, to be considered a second-class believer? Is the single believer to depart from social expectation, family and perhaps even legal obligation? Is pressure to be put on the Christian *paterfamilias* to allow or encourage his son or daughter to forgo marriage? Such notions would be anathema to any that share Graeco-Roman attitudes to marriage and value their acceptance within that social world.

Such thoughts have encouraged the Corinthians to push Paul's dictum to its extreme interpretation, in order to defeat it. As with the injunction of 5.9, its inherent (although unintended) ambiguities are exploited. Where would such a *reductio ad absurdum* lead? To the conclusion that Paul viewed marriage as sinful and sexual relations in marriage as forbidden, that he wished betrothals broken off, and all existing marriages dissolved by divorce. This is obviously an impossible notion for the Christian community and thus, Paul's advice, like that of 5.9, can be dismissed as ridiculous and unworkable.

If the Corinthians have reacted in much the same manner to Paul's remark καλὸν ἀνθρώπῳ γυναικὸς μὴ ἅπτεσθαι as to his instruction μὴ συναναμίγνυσθαι πόρνοις, then we would expect the same type of apostolic response: a combination of restating, clarifying and commending the original statement and, simultaneously, refuting its misinterpretation. Paul rejects the notion that καλὸν ἀνθρώπῳ γυναικὸς μὴ ἅπτεσθαι means that marriage is sin, or sexual intercourse prohibited. He must refute the inference that he is laying down impossible and anti-social commands for his converts. But, at the same time, it is not marriage that his opponents are attacking, but rather Paul's preference for singleness. If he wishes this advice to be considered he must restate it and its basis in such a way as leaves no ambiguities to be exploited.

Such is of course a situational hypothesis based upon mirror-reading, and will require testing when we move to consider the text. However, it has a number of advantages over the ascetic hypothesis. First, unlike the ascetic hypothesis, it is consistent with what the rest of the epistle reveals about the respective attitudes of Paul and the Corinthians to social values and institutions. Secondly, unlike the ascetic hypothesis, we can see a parallel dynamic in 5.9–13. Thirdly, unlike the ascetic hypothesis it provides an easy explanation for the fact that although 7.1–40 protests the propriety of marriage, Paul's major interest is to provide reasons why one should not seek to marry.

Why else, in a passage supposedly arguing against asceticism, does Paul offer so little grounds for the legitimacy of marriage?[9] (After the reasoning of 7.2 he never again offers any argument for marriage, simply stating it is *not* sin.) Why, in a supposed attempt to quell over-enthusiastic asceticism, does Paul give so many arguments for singleness (7.26; 7.28b; 7.32–35;[10] 7.38; 7.40 and, we shall argue, implicitly in 7.23–24)? Why, in a church that is supposedly rejecting marriage, does Paul use eschatology to relativize marriage? One can suggest that Paul argues in such ways to win the Corinthian ascetics over, or because he has some sympathy with them. However, the text of 7.1–40 reads more like an argument against marriage, which is being careful not to prohibit it absolutely, than an argument against an absolutizing of asceticism, exhibiting some sympathy and concessions to ascetics.

9.3. *Reading the Text as Pauline Theology*

In 1 Corinthians 7 Paul may well be responding to a Corinthian letter, but given that this letter is almost certainly provoked by his previous teaching, and that his response is articulated as part of his wider discussion of sexual behaviour (5.1–7.40), we are justified in reading 7.1–40 as an articulation of Paul's thought, and part of that discourse. We shall argue that 7.1–40 serves to explain, develop and qualify Paul's argument in the previous passages and that the concerns of 6.12–20 in particular help to explain Paul's argument in 7.1–40.

Even a cursory reading of 7.1–40 reveals that Paul not only protests the legitimacy of marriage, but that he repeatedly advises against marriage as somehow interfering with full devotion to the Lord (7.1, 7–9, 25–40). At the same time, the discussion shows a concern with πορνεία (7.2, 5, 9, 37–37?) and the legitimacy of mixed marriages (7.12–16, 39). Of course, reasons are given for these instructions in 7.1–40 itself, but what we have learned of Paul's attitude to sex from 5.1–6.12 and especially 6.12–20 already begins to provide us with some understanding of Paul's rationales.

---

9.   The notion that Paul is trying to be 'all things to all men' and keep, as far as possible, the ascetics on side is the usual explanation. Chadwick (1955: 265) observes: 'It is a curious passage. On the one hand, Paul is evidently trying to safeguard the permanence and even to assert the positive value and obligations of the married state; on the other hand, he is equally anxious to assure the Corinthian ascetics that at heart he stands with them and deprecates marriage.' But *does* Paul assert anything positive about marriage? He certainly gives no positive reason for entering into it. It seems that the passage is only 'curious' if one insists in seeing Paul as contending against asceticism.

10.   Despite attempts by commentators to argue that this passage points out the dangers in over-anxiety about celibacy as well (see section 9.7.4).

9.3.1. *Paul's Problem with Sexual Union for those United with Christ*

In Chapter 6 we observed that, although the subject of 6.12–20 was the incompatibility of Christ-union with πόρνη-union, the logic of the argument presented all sexual union as incompatible with Christ-union. Christ-union and 'becoming one flesh' with a sexual partner constituted two comparable and mutually exclusive unions, representing two mutually exclusive possibilities for the body. Although sex with the πόρνη is specifically in view, the argument is that it, *like marriage*, creates the believer 'one flesh' with the sexual partner, a 'oneness' incompatible with being 'one spirit' with the Lord (6.15–17). Other arguments against πόρνη-union also seemed to undermine all sexual unions. The believer is not 'his own' and thus cannot give his body to another (6.20). None should have mastery (ἐξουσία) over the believer (6.12), but this is precisely what occurs in marriage (7.4).[11]

Our suggestion is that this view of sexual unions explains Paul's ambivalence about marriage in 7.1–40, which to some degree, develops, explains and qualifies 6.12–20. Marriage itself will be declared to be no sin for the believer, but yet it remains problematic and even undesirable.[12] Only the single (ἄγαμος καὶ παρθένος) can be fully 'holy in *body* and spirit' (7.34). Marriage is a form of slavery, undesirable for those 'bought at a price' (7.23). It creates anxiety (μεριμνάω) and tribulation (θλῖψις) dividing the married man's interests between τὰ τοῦ κυρίου and τὰ τοῦ κόσμου (7.32–35).

Thus there is a direct flow from 6.12–20 into 7.1–40. Themes and key words reappear, and some loose ends appear to be tied down.[13] Marriage is presented as an ambiguous institution for some of the same reasons that πόρνη-union was excluded in 6.12–20. Given these concerns, it would seem perfectly reasonable for Paul to conclude καλὸν ἀνθρώπῳ

---

11. As Schrage 1995: 64, 'die Ehe entzieht dem Verheirateten das Verfügungsrecht über sich selbst und seinen Leib, so daß er den anderen über sich verfügen läßt und seiner und seines Leibes nicht mehr "mächtig" ist'.

12. P. Brown (1988: 56) well summarized Paul's view, '*Kai memeristai*: for Paul, a man to whom the highest ideal of life was to be "united to the Lord," to "become one spirit with him," this [marriage] was a crushing disqualification. The married person, whose heart [we might better say body] was inevitably divided, was almost of necessity a "half-Christian"…. He left the world of the married householder a long way behind, bobbing in the stormy wake of his own urgent call to live a life of "undistracted" service before the coming of the Lord.'

13. Gundry Volf (1996: 536) suggests that the ascetics have taken Pauline teaching on bodily consecration, such as 6.13b-17, but drawn 'more far reaching conclusions' than Paul, and that this partly motivates their asceticism. However, it would seem far easier to take Paul at face value. If 7.32–35 reveals the far-reaching conclusions possible from a certain interpretation of 6.13b-17, why not conclude that such conclusions are Paul's? And why, if Paul knew the Corinthians were drawing extreme ascetic conclusions from such as 6.13b-17, would he restate such a hostage to fortune, prior to contesting such conclusions?

γυναικὸς μὴ ἅπτεσθαι. Indeed, the implication of 6.12–20 could have been that the marital union is as sinful as any other sexual union, and thus it ought to be avoided by the single and either marriage, or sex within marriage, put aside by the married. Certainly, if Paul contended for such an understanding of sex as we have observed in 6.12–20, then someone *might* easily draw these conclusions from it, or alternatively such may occur to Paul. When the discussion of whether sex and marriage are καλὸν or sinful is seen to flow logically from Paul's own concerns, much of the necessity to posit ascetic opponents lying behind 7.1–40 simply evaporates. Gundry Volf's contention that, 'he would not have to deny that marriage was a sin apart from the Corinthians holding such a view'[14] may be dismissed as palpably false. Can it really be a coincidence that the question of the renunciation of marriage (7.1–40) is raised immediately after the apostle has implicitly equated πόρνη-union with marriage, and hinted at the incompatibility of both with Christ-union?

9.3.2. *Paul's Problem with Exogamous Unions*
If the logic of 6.12–20 implicitly precludes all sexual union, then the immediate focus is to preclude sexual union with any women labelled πόρνη. As we have seen, a πόρνη is by definition an outsider, but it also appears Paul can stereotype all outsiders as πόρνοι (see above, section 6.7.3). Thus, just as 6.12–20 brings into question sexual unions in general, in another sense it questions sexual union specifically with outsiders. Participants in Christ cannot participate sexually with outsiders (πόρνοι). If pushed to its logical conclusion such an argument would not only render the contracting of exogamous marriages impossible: it could also demand the termination of any existing exogamous unions.

7.1–40 indicates that Paul's thinking moves in this direction. First, he differentiates between exogamous and endogamous marriages. Despite his views on sexual union, he will deny, without further explanation, that marriage is a sin, but marriage to an outsider is explicitly forbidden (the widow may marry μόνον ἐν κυρίῳ, 7.39). Secondly, in the case of existing marriages, the same differentiation applies. The Dominical dictum of 7.10 forbids believers divorcing fellow believers, but significantly marriage to an outsider is treated differently. Although the believer is still not to dissolve the union (7.12–13), the fact that the Dominical instruction is not considered applicable, and Paul's own instruction is required, indicates that there is a categorical distinction between cases. Further, the argument of 7.14 exhibits a unique concern for ἁγιασμός and the possible ἀκαθαρσία of the unbeliever. The logic of the discussion is that if the

---

14. Gundry Volf 1996: 523.

ἄπιστος spouse was not sanctified by virtue of marriage to the believer, then he/she would be an illegitimate sexual partner as one who was ἀκάθαρτος/η.

We shall return to this passage below (section 9.5.2). But again we find connections between 6.12–20 and 7.1–40, which support our contention that the chapters should be read as a piece.

9.3.3. *Paul's Concern with* πορνεία

Paul's concern with πορνεία is clear throughout 5.1–6.20. Πορνεία is the vice of the outsider, and those who engage in it forfeit their identity in Christ. As far as 6.12–20 is concerned, the prohibition of πορνεία simply as an ethical breach is not the sum of Paul's concern: the effects of sexual union, and the identity of the partner, clearly hold significance. However, finally, πορνεία must be the reason that sex with the πόρνη is unacceptable and other unions are not. It is the only rationale with the power to discriminate between πόρνη-union and marital unions (whether endogamous or exogamous), which Paul finally declares to be legitimate.

Again, πορνεία plays a key role in the discussion of 7.1–40. As much as marriage may be problematic for Paul, it is always preferable to πορνεία (7.2) or even the temptation to such (7.9; 7.36–37). The former may impede existence in Christ, but the latter is destructive of it. So once again 7.1–40 with its reticence towards marriage, yet its acceptance of marriage to avoid πορνεία, makes sense when read against the background of 6.12–20.

9.3.4. *Implications*

When interpreters do recognize Paul's preference for celibacy in 1 Corinthians 7 it is often suggested that Paul counsels such for practical reasons in view of his eschatological convictions. Either the impending end of the world renders marriage merely pointless, or else the cosmic upheavals or tribulations associated with the last days make marriage inexpedient.[15] However, the above considerations indicate that Paul's preference for celibacy and his consideration of mixed marriages should be seen not merely as eschatological expediency, but as part of a deeper ambivalence towards sexual unions and their compatibility with identity in Christ. We thus need to examine the evident eschatological concerns of the chapter, and how these interface with Paul's basic anthropological/christological concerns. This will be an important question as we re-examine the text.

---

15. See e.g. Cartlidge 1975: 225.

9.4. *Denials and Affirmations (7.1–9)*

9.4.1. *The Maxim of 7.1b*

περὶ δὲ ὧν ἐγράψατε, καλὸν ἀνθρώπῳ γυναικὸς μὴ ἅπτεσθαι·

As we noted, the second part of this statement is inherently ambiguous. Commentators invariably move to settle that ambiguity by discussion of what the terms mean. καλόν is either the claim of a comparative good, or a moral absolute. ἅπτεσθαι is either a sexual euphemism, or a designation of marriage. Thus the statement as a whole is either a denigration of sexual intercourse, or a repudiation of marriage. Only having settled this point is the question of whether the maxim is a quote from the Corinthians' letter or a Pauline formulation in response to that letter settled.

The suggestion of this study is that the statement's ambiguity is precisely the point. 7.1–40 is, to a degree, a response to that ambiguity, and a Pauline attempt to redirect the interpretation of the statement, just as we have seen Paul redirecting statements at 5.9 and 6.12 (+13?). We should thus avoid attempting to settle an inherent meaning on 7.1b. It means different things to different people. We may observe how Paul returns to the word καλόν throughout this section:

7.1b καλὸν ἀνθρώπῳ γυναικὸς μὴ ἅπτεσθαι

7.8b καλὸν αὐτοῖς ἐὰν μείνωσιν ὡς κἀγω.

7.26 καλὸν ἀνθρώπῳ τὸ οὕτως εἶναι.

7.38 ὁ γαμίζων τὴν ἑαυτοῦ παρθένος καλῶς ποιεῖ καὶ ὁ μὴ γαμίζων κρεῖσσον ποιήσει

Three times he affirms that to remain single is καλόν, but in each case concedes that such cannot be a moral absolute, until he concludes in 7.38 that to marry is also καλόν, although the person who remains single does better (κρεῖσσον ποιήσει). By the end it is clear what Paul would have the Corinthians take from the statement of 7.1b – the comparative good of singleness as opposed to marriage. Paul's interpretation of the dictum is not really in doubt. But other possible interpretations do exist, and Paul's argument would seem to show awareness of such. The maxim is compatible with the notion that marriage is sinful, a notion that Paul denies in 7.28 (and his application of the terms καλόν to marriage in 7.38 is best seen as a direct counter to that interpretation).

Fee has presented considerable precedents for interpreting ἅπτεσθαι as a sexual euphemism,[16] and thus he argues that the object of the phrase is

---

16. Fee 1987: 275 n. 31 cites Plato, *Leg.* 8.840a; Aristotle, *Pol.* 7.14.12; Plutarch, *Alex. M.* 21.4; Josephus, *Ant.* 1.163; Marcus Aurelius, *Med.* 1.17.6 and also the LXX at Gen. 20.6; Ruth 2.9; Prov. 6.29 (cf. BAGD 102–103).

to promote asceticism within marriage. Caragounis has objected that the maxim cannot have sexual relations within marriage in view, or we would expect ἀνήρ rather than ἄνθρωπος, and γυνή would have been qualified with the possessive adjective 'his'.[17] Against both solutions, it cannot be assumed that we are presented with an either/or choice. Caragounis is correct that the dictum is unlikely to have been specifically framed to support asceticism within marriage, yet it could certainly be taken to argue for such. Fee is correct to emphasize the precedents for ἅπτεσθαι as a sexual metaphor, yet such does not exclude the fact that to suggest that existence without sexual intercourse is (comparatively) good could easily have been used as an argument for singleness over marriage (where singleness is assumed to entail a celibate existence, and marriage sexual intercourse). The maxim *is* then compatible with the notion that sexual union, even within marriage, is either illegitimate or inadvisable, a notion that Paul denies in 7.3–5.

Our suggestion here is precisely this: Paul has (previously) coined the statement as a commendation of the single (thus celibate) life.[18] The Corinthians, unsympathetic to Paul's promotion of singleness, have taken his maxim (like that of 5.9) to extremes, interpreting him as showing animosity to all sexual union. This then is the matter about which they wrote – an objection to Paul's teaching on marriage and sex.[19]

Thus, whereas περὶ δὲ may well introduce a topic from the Corinthian letter,[20] it does not indicate that a citation from that letter follows. There is no unambiguous introduction of a citation, or even of a statement which summarizes a Corinthian position (such as we find in 15.12 or 2 Cor. 10.10). Indeed there is no grammatical reason to suppose that 7.1b should be read as other than part of Paul's discussion of the topic.

καλὸν ἀνθρώπῳ γυναικὸς μὴ ἅπτεσθαι is thus a topic sentence. However, it almost certainly repeats a maxim that Paul has previously

17. Caragounis 1996: 547. (Caragounis thus argues that ἅπτεσθαι simply means marriage; as Robertson and Plummer 1914: 130.)

18. Paul elsewhere uses καλόν to indicate a preferred course of action (1 Cor. 9.15, Rom. 14.21).

19. The Corinthians may have objected to other aspects of Paul's teaching in their letter. 1 Cor. 9 may evidence an objection to Paul's claim to apostolic authority. 1 Cor. 15 perhaps indicates objections to Paul's teaching of bodily resurrection. 5.9–13 would seem to indicate that Paul knows in detail Corinthian objections to his instruction. Although it is possible that his knowledge of these comes from the same oral source as his information on the incest, the apparent precision of Paul's knowledge may indicate that these objections have also been written.

20. Hurd (1965: 63–64) first made the suggestion that the περὶ δὲ statements of 1 Cor. refer to topics raised by the Corinthians' letter. M.M. Mitchell (1989) objects that περὶ δὲ only refers to a new topic known to both reader and writer, and not necessarily to a letter. However, given that 7.1 makes explicit reference to a letter, Hurd's suggestion seems reasonable (see Horrell 1996a: 90).

communicated to the Corinthians. By referring to it, Paul reaffirms his confidence in it, and begins the battle for its correct interpretation.[21] Thus he sets about excluding possible misinterpretations of his meaning. It does not involve the renunciation of marriage as sinful. It does not involve abstinence within marriage or the termination of existing marriages. But Paul will counter the Corinthian objections to that maxim not by retraction, but by explanation and redirection of meaning. There is an interpretative battle for the meaning of καλὸν ἀνθρώπῳ γυναικὸς μὴ ἅπτεσθαι about to be waged.

On the basis of how καλόν is redeployed to commend singleness, one strongly suspects that the real issue between Paul and the Corinthians is neither sexual abstinence, nor divorce, but whether the unmarried should marry. It is marriage he wishes to advise against, and this advice our socially integrated Corinthians wish to defeat by their misinterpretations. Thus, it is the relation of the description καλόν to the decision whether to marry to which Paul continually returns. Further, the only use of the περὶ δὲ in this passage, aside from 7.1, is in 7.25. Thus, if it is correct to see the περὶ δὲ phrases of 7.1–16.12 as references to the Corinthians' letter, this would suggest that the state of the unmarried (παρθένοι) is the issue particularly raised by the Corinthian letter.

9.4.2. Paul's Affirmation of Marriage and Marital Intercourse (7.2–5)

Paul begins by referring to their letter, most likely aware that he is bringing to notice the criticism and ridicule of his position that this letter probably contained. He then reaffirms his contentious advice: καλὸν ἀνθρώπῳ γυναικὸς μὴ ἅπτεσθαι. Nothing they have said has caused him to retract. He is giving no ground. However, he immediately proceeds with a limited affirmation of marriage (7.2),[22] and an almost absolute denial of the 'right' of abstinence within marriage (7.3–5).[23]

---

21. Deming attempts to solve the awkward grammar of 7.26 by suggesting it be translated, 'I think that it is good because of the present necessity, that "it is good for a man" to be thus'. He then offers this additional citation as additional evidence that Paul is quoting the Corinthians at 7.1b (1995: 110–12). However, even if his translation is correct, the inference he draws goes too far. For, if Paul quotes from 7.1b at 7.26, this shows only that the form of 7.1b is fixed and important as it stands. This does not show that it is a slogan, or that it originated with the Corinthians. If Paul is contending for the interpretation of his own maxim, to quote from it, in the process of clarifying what he meant and why he said it, would make perfect sense.

22. Taking ἔχειν as a referent to marriage rather than a sexual euphemism. The same verb is used for the marital relationship at 7.12–13 and 29 (with Caragounis 1996: 547 and Yarbrough 1995: 97 against Fee 1987: 278 and Hurd 1965: 162).

23. There seems no good reason to hold the abstinence for prayer to be a Corinthian invention, rather than Paul's own thought. There are good Jewish parallels for abstinence for study of Torah or prayer (e.g. *T. Naph.* 8.8; cf. Str-B 3.371; Barrett 1971: 156; and Conzelmann 1975: 117 n. 26). Gundry Volf (1996: 531) objects that it is improbable that Paul

Thus Paul has given notice that καλὸν ἀνθρώπῳ γυναικὸς μὴ ἅπτεσθαι neither by necessity, nor by intent, prohibits marriage or sexual relations. Paul's affirmation that marriage is an option διὰ τὰς πορνείας is, of course, hardly a ringing endorsement;[24] but then it is not intended to be. Paul has just affirmed the statement καλὸν ἀνθρώπῳ γυναικὸς μὴ ἅπτεσθαι, and he is not about to relativize it to the level of presenting marriage as *equally* καλόν. His intention throughout this section is to commend singleness and not marriage. However his statement in 7.2 suffices for two purposes: it denies that his affirmed dictum totally forbids marriage, and it serves to differentiate marriage from πορνεία: marriage is not to be equated with sinful sex (clearing the way for Paul to describe marriage as a lesser καλόν at 7.38). Limits are thus put on the possible implications of the dictum, without in any way encouraging marriage. Paul introduces a practical hierarchy: celibacy-marriage-πορνεία.

His reaffirmation of marital sex in 7.3–5 should be read in much the same light. Paul is affirming that καλὸν ἀνθρώπῳ γυναικὸς μὴ ἅπτεσθαι does not serve to reduce sex to sin. Indeed to abstain from marital relations may be a quicker route to sin, both because it is depriving the other and because it may lead to πορνεία through the wiles of Satan. It is no accident that Paul gives the command prohibiting unilateral withdrawal of sexual relations μὴ ἀποστερεῖτε ἀλλήλους using the same verb as he used to castigate lawsuits among believers in 6.8. The denial of marital sex is a serious sin against a fellow believer.[25] Thus, as in 7.3, Paul has denied another possible misinterpretation of his dictum, but in doing so he has given no solace to those who would seek to undermine his strong preference for singleness.[26]

---

would have given the Corinthian ascetics an excuse of which they might take advantage, and thus he must be making a minimal concession to their concerns. But she does not make clear why Paul would make such a concession unless he was sympathetic to its rationale. It seems more likely that Paul mentions the possibility of abstinence from prayer as an indication that this is the only reason that he might permit abstinence (and even then only under certain conditions), in contradiction to the Corinthian portrayal of him as opposing all marital intercourse.

24. Jewish parallels are found at *T. Levi* 9.9–10, Tob. 4.12 and esp. *Gen. Rab.* 9.7.

25. Indeed 'deprive' may be a weak interpretation of the verb. Other NT uses suggest a theft or defrauding (1 Cor. 6.7–8; Mk 10.19; 1 Tim. 6.5; cf. LXX Mal. 3.5; Sir. 4.1; 34.21 esp. Exod. 21.20).

26. A possible objection to this reading is that μὴ ἀποστερεῖτε ἀλλήλους (7.5) is best read as an imperative (as Robertson and Plummer 1914: 134 and Fee 1987: 281), and that this suggests a prohibition of an action which is either occurring or in danger of occurring. However, as we have seen, a precedent for a Pauline statement which is aimed not at countering behaviour, but countering a possible misreading of Paul's desires is found in 5.9–13. We noted that when Paul counters the misconstrual of his command of 5.9, he proceeds by way of rebuttal with an implied imperative against judging outsiders. As Paul's imperative

9.4.3. *The Concession (7.6)*

Identifying what Paul means when he says τοῦτο δὲ λέγω κατὰ συγγνώμην οὐ κατ' συγγνώμην οὐ κατα' επιταγήν (7.6) is notoriously problematic. Paul wishes to stress that something (τοῦτο) is not a command (ἐπιταγή) but a concession/permission/indulgence (συγγνώμη). Commentators have made various identifications of the τοῦτο: (1) marriage, as a concession from the single ideal because of the danger of immorality (taking the ἐχέτω of 7.2 as an instruction to marry);[27] (2) sexual relations within marriage, as a concession to immorality;[28] (3) the abstention for prayer, as a concession to the Corinthians' asceticism;[29] (4) the coming together after abstention, as a concession to the danger of temptation;[30] (5) what Paul proceeds to say in 7.7, concerning his desire for singleness.[31]

Fee argues for the third option, pointing out (quite correctly) that, despite argument to the contrary,[32] 7.2–4 definitely contains imperatives, and that thus only 7.5's permission for abstinence can possibly be a συγγνώμη.[33] The problem for Fee is that although 7.5 is certainly a concession, it is not clear how it might ever have been construed as anything else: the εἰ μήτι ἄν ἐκ συμφώνου is far too hesitant for it to be in danger of sounding like a command.[34] Thus Paul's statement appears superfluous. Further, it is difficult to make sense of 7.7 in the light of such an interpretation. 7.7 is related grammatically to 7.6[35] and it is not clear what relevance Paul's desire that all men be as he (presumably single in the light of 7.8) could have to whether marital abstinence is a concession or a command. Fee offers no explanation.

Winter makes a strong, almost convincing, case that 7.7 itself is the focus of the τοῦτο. He suggests that, 'the neuter demonstrative pronoun, "this", when used with the verbs of saying as in 7.6, refers to the subordinate clause introduced by an implied "that" (ὅτι) in 7.7a, and its place in the sentence emphasises the importance of the forward referent'.[36]

---

there served as a rebuttal of one interpretation of his purpose, that he intended the judging of outsiders, we should read 7.4–5 in the same light, as a move by Paul to block the Corinthian accusation that he commends, or requires, the renunciation of sex within marriage.

27. The traditional interpretation (Godet 1886: 326; Moffatt 1938: 76; Morris 1985: 104).

28. Murphy-O'Connor 1983: 61; Deming 1995: 116 (Conzelmann 1975: 118 and Robertson and Plummer 1914: 135 combine this with the above).

29. Barrett 1971: 157; Yarbrough 1995: 98–100; Fee 1987: 283–84; Schrage 1995: 71.

30. Meyer 1877: 229; and recently Poirier 1996: 2.

31. Orr and Walther 1976: 207; Winter 1997 (mooted by Yarbrough 1995: 98).

32. I.e. Conzelmann's assertion (1975: 118) that 'the imperatives must not be pressed'.

33. Fee 1987: 283.

34. So Hurd 1965: 161–62.

35. This is true whether we accept the δέ of apposition or take the less likely textual variant, the logical γάρ as the connecting particle in 7.7.

36. Winter 1997: 58; cf. Orr and Walther 1976: 207.

Thus 'I say this ... that I wish ...'. Winter then offers evidence that τοῦτο is 'used as preparation for a subordinate clause with ὅτι understood in twenty-five cases'. However, a close investigation reveals that only three of Winter's supposed 25 cases resemble his reading of 7.6–7, with an implied and *omitted* ὅτι.[37]

Despite this, Winter's thesis is attractive. His reading fits with other statements in our passage where Paul is at pains to stress that his preference for celibacy is not binding on the Corinthians. 7.25 will protest that Paul has no ἐπιταγή κυρίου but only his γνώμη. 7.35 will assert that he does not intend to lay constraints on the Corinthians, but merely advises to their benefit. To read 7.6–7 in line with these statements makes good exegetical sense. The fatal problem is with the meaning of συγγνώμη. Under the ascetic hypothesis the 'concession' would be to the Corinthians' desire for asceticism. But even were we to grant this, what would Paul be conceding, if what he goes on to say is what he desires (θέλω)? And if we reject the ascetic hypothesis the statement makes even less sense. If we could translate συγγνώμη in the direction of γνώμη (either as advice, or lenient judgment, or something said for one's good) then the whole would make sense, and the statement would be at one with 7.25 and 7.35. However, there appear to be no parallels to support such a translation.[38]

So we are left with the imperatives of 7.2–5. Or better, since the singular τοῦτο refers to a single saying, the command of 7.2 (with ἐχέτω taken as marry). 7.2 is certainly framed as a command, but it is evidently (unlike the imperatives of 7.3–5) not supposed to be taken as such: Paul's counsel for the single to remain so contradicts it. Thus it makes sense to see Paul wishing to stress that he did not mean to command marriage, but to concede it, either to the Corinthian desire to marry, or because of the dangers of immorality. Further, 7.7 makes sense as a follow-up statement. Having stressed that marriage is simply a concession and not an all-embracing command, Paul proceeds in contradistinction to give his real desire, that which he will argue for in the subsequent sections, that those who are able (by virtue of not being married, and not requiring to marry to avoid immorality) follow his example of singleness.

9.4.4. *Paul's Real Desire (7.7–9)*

Verse 7 is crucial to the understanding of the rhetorical dynamic. Θέλω δὲ πάντας ἀνθρώπους εἶναι ὡς καὶ ἐμαυτόν expresses Paul's central desire, in contrast to what he appeared to command. It can only be his singleness

---

37. These are 1 Cor. 7.29, Gal. 3.17, Eph. 4.17; of the others, 17 contain an explicit ὅτι, two obviously are backwards references (1 Cor. 7.35; Phil. 1.7), one has no 'verb of saying' (2 Cor. 9.6), one is a wrong reference, and one is missing (Winter 1997: 59 n. 7).

38. Bultmann is explicitly forbidding, 'Though the context might support "personal opinion" there is no example of this: γνώμη is the word used in such cases' (1964: 716).

that is in view here.[39] Note also the re-emergence of the term ἄνθρωπος which relates back to the opening assertion of 7.1b. The qualification of Paul's desire, which follows (ἀλλὰ ἕκαστος ἴδιον ἔχει χάρισμα ...), serves as the rationale for the concession of 7.6 and is paralleled by 7.9. Paul offers marriage as a concession because not all share the χάρισμα, which enables singleness. Implicitly the only reason one should marry is the lack of such a χάρισμα. There is no accommodation of those who marry simply because they do not share the apostle's desire for singleness.

When Paul says ἕκαστος ἴδιον ἔχει χάρισμα ἐκ θεοῦ, ὁ μὲν οὕτως, ὁ δὲ οὕτως, does he envisage alternate gifts of singleness and marriage? It is hardly to be thought so.[40] At 7.9, singleness requires the exercise of ἐγκράτεια. This is not a 'gift of celibacy', but a virtue universally praised in antiquity as a possession of the free man: it is 'the dominion one has over oneself or something' and is expressed in self-restraint.[41] If ἐγκράτεια is here portrayed as a χάρισμα, then it is one that we might imagine the Corinthians would highly value (cf. 1.7 and 12.14), and one consistent with the self-example Paul offers of himself as a free man, having authority over all things, but mastered by no one (2.15; 3.22–23; 4.3; 6.12; 9.1; esp. 9.24–27). Thus although the Corinthians may not value singleness, they are hardly likely to wish to see themselves as lacking this particular χάρισμα. When we turn to marriage, there is no notion in 1 Corinthians 7 that marriage is the legitimate exercise of an alternative gift, but a consistent presentation of marriage as an option where there is a lack of ἐγκράτεια. Marriage is for the avoidance of πορνεία, and exercised where otherwise the individual is powerless to resist its temptation (7.2, 7.9 and 7.36–37), not where he possesses a relevant χάρισμα. When Paul suggests in 7.7 that he understands that some may marry, as (whatever other gifts they possess) they lack the essential ἐγκράτεια, in a sense he sets a trap. For if any Corinthian wishes to take advantage of this seeming concession to marriage, he need not only confess that his gifts are different to Paul's, but also that he lacks ἐγκράτεια. In regard to this important virtue, he must accept himself less virtuous, and less spiritually endowed.

What Paul has done is to claim that he, and the person choosing singleness, demonstrate a propensity for ἐγκράτεια, which those who choose marriage obviously lack. He has again, as so often in this letter, claimed the spiritual high ground for himself and his position. Further, his rhetoric has allowed him to diminish the worthiness of marriage for the believer, while at the same time explicitly denying the charges which have been levelled against him of declaring marriage a sin.

---

39. See Thiselton 2000: 512–13 for a discussion of Paul's marital status.
40. With Conzelmann 1975: 118; against Fee 1987: 285.
41. Grundmann 1964: 340; cf. e.g. Philo, *Spec. Leg.* 2.195; Josephus, *BJ* 2.120.

The argument reveals Paul's strong preference for singleness, a preference that he will do all but command the Corinthians to follow. However, we may also see that there is no real place in Paul's thought for the married celibate. Even with mutual agreement, periods of celibacy are to be limited. Paul could have commended prolonged or even permanent abstinence as an option for couples who possess a mutual ἐγκράτεια; such would be the logical corollary to the notion that those who possess ἐγκράτεια should remain single (is the married celibate more prone to adultery than the single to fornication?). But he does not. Such reveals to us that Paul's concern is that the ἀγάμοι and χῆραι heed his counsel for singleness, rather than a concern with sexual union as such. With the dismissal of the notion that his teaching implies marital sex to be wrong (7.3–5), the subject drops out of Paul's paraenesis, never to return.

9.5. *The Denial of Divorce (7.10–16)*

Having by implication rejected the inference that καλὸν ἀνθρώπῳ γυναικὸς μὴ ἅπτεσθαι either directly prohibits marriage or makes all sex sin, Paul now rejects a third possible conclusion: that existing marriages should be dissolved by divorce. The Lord's word on the matter is clear, and, as if that were not enough, Paul goes further in explicitly extending the prohibition to mixed marriages.

However, the issue of divorce is different from the two other aspects of the *reductio*. Whereas the renunciation of marriage, or the concept of sexless marriage, would be anathema to the Corinthians, divorce per se would certainly not. The option of divorce is likely to have been as socially important to many Corinthians as the institution of marriage itself. To forbid divorce is as counter cultural as to commend singleness.[42] Thus if we are correct in seeing the Corinthian church as loathe to depart from societal norms, we can expect them to have had difficulty with Paul's prohibition of divorce.

9.5.1. *Divorce and Remarriage of Believers (7.10–11)*
7.10 has long been interpreted as a Pauline move to counter Corinthian women who wished to divorce their husbands in order to live a life of sexual continence.[43] Paul prohibits such divorce, citing the authority of Jesus, then in 7.11 gives instructions against remarriage in cases where the

---

42. See Thiselton 2000: 540.

43. Robertson and Plummer 1914: 140; Moffatt 1938: 78 'some wives of an ultra-spiritual temper, may have gone or wished to go further than to suspend marital relations (vss. 3–4) ... The feminist party in the local church evidently claimed freedom to desert or divorce a husband'; also Fee 1987: 295 and Wire 1990: 82–97. Murphy-O'Connor (1981) argues the opposite case: that we have a non-ascetic woman that is being divorced by her ascetic husband.

command is broken and divorce occurs.[44] However, objections have been raised to such a reading. First, 7.11 appears to many scholars to be Paul permitting divorce, contrary to the command of the Lord given in 7.10.[45] Secondly, why tell women, who want to divorce in order to be celibate that, if they divorce, they must remain single or else be reconciled to their husbands?[46] Single is precisely what they want to be. Drastic solutions have been proposed to solve these seeming incongruities, even the most desperate: Weiss sees 7.11a as a probable interpolation.[47]

The first objection is easily overcome. Paul prohibits divorce, then prohibits divorcees remarrying. Such a move may be accepting that divorces, although illegitimate, may occur, but also may be designed as an additional attack upon divorce. The structure of the Lord's teaching as recorded in Mk 10.2–11[48] (which may well approximate to the tradition to which Paul is referring) contains something of the same logic. In response to the Pharisees' question, Jesus prohibits divorce on the grounds of the permanence of the 'one flesh' (quoting Gen. 2.24), what 'God has joined together, let not man put asunder'. However, when subsequently questioned by his disciples, Jesus responds: 'Whoever divorces his wife and marries another, commits adultery against her, and if she divorces her husband and marries another, she commits adultery' (Mk 10.11–12). Thus Mark explains the prohibition of divorce in terms of the prohibition of remarriage. Why? Possibly because it is envisaged that one divorces in order to remarry, or in the expectation that one will. Removing this possibility then destroys one motive for divorce, and also makes divorcing less socially attractive. But more plausibly, the prohibition of remarriage as a breach of the seventh commandment presupposes that the prior marriage still persists despite the divorce. Divorce is powerless to dissolve marriage, being devoid of theological and moral significance: that which God has joined together man *cannot* put asunder.[49] The same connection

44. Some commentators, believing Paul to have in mind a specific instance, see 7.11a (ἐὰν δὲ καὶ χωρισθῇ) as providing an instruction if this particular divorce has occurred before his prohibition (7.10) reaches Corinth. (Weiss [1910: 178] thinks this possible, Allo [1934: 164] is undecided, but Dungan [1971: 90 n. 1] and Murphy-O'Connor [1981] have been less hesitant.) However, the grammar does not require this (see Fee 1987: 294 n. 22), and further, it is to assume that Paul had never before prohibited divorce at Corinth: a presupposition that is at best unprovable (cf. Neirynck 1996: 163).

45. Cf. Dungan 1971: 91.

46. As Fee (1987: 295) sees Paul doing.

47. Weiss 1910: 178.

48. Also Mt. 19.3–9.

49. Cf. Hooker 1991: 236. Catchpole's (1974) suggestion, that Mark records and reconciles two unrelated primary traditions about Jesus, seems unnecessary. Hooker's suggestion, that Mark (or his source) draws out the implications of Jesus' teaching on divorce for his community, seems more plausible. If so, we can see Paul either following the same expanded tradition, or engaging in the same logic.

between divorce, and remarriage as adultery, is not explicit in 7.10–11, but may well underlie it. Thus Paul, in 7.11a, does not contradict, but fully reflects the word of the Lord in 7.10.[50]

The second problem remains even still. Why does Paul frame a prohibition of divorce in such a way as to command the divorcing ascetic to do exactly what she wants: remain single? The answer, that the prohibition is in case she becomes dissatisfied with the celibate life and wishes to remarry, hardly seems satisfactory.[51] Dungan seems correct to suggest both that, 'we should look elsewhere [than to ascetic women] for an explanation', and that the answer is to be found in 'normal divorce'.[52] If we are dealing with 'normal divorce' according to normal social patterns, then the problem evaporates. 7.11a both reflects the teaching of Jesus on the indissoluble nature of marriage, and serves to undercut one social motivation for divorce. This solution is also supported by the notion that the wife might be reconciled (καταλλάσσω) to her husband, which suggests that a 'normal' process of domestic estrangement has been the reason for the divorce.[53]

Thus 7.10–11 is best understood not by postulating Corinthian ascetics who wish to divorce, but Corinthians who engage in the normal social practice of divorce, and whom Paul confronts with what must be a less than socially agreeable prohibition.

9.5.2. *The Rest: Unbelievers and Holiness (7.12–16)*
The crux of this passage lies at 7.14. What does Paul mean when he states that the unbelieving spouse is sanctified in (ἡγίασται ἐν) his or her partner? In what sense are their children ἅγιος? Who raised the question that family members might be ἀκάθαρτος, and why? Any investigator into these matters may quickly grow to share Conzelmann's sense of frustration when he complains that 'the explanations that have so far been suggested are almost without exception unsatisfactory'.[54] Indeed 'almost' may be a little too optimistic! However, like Conzelmann himself, we shall hazard our own observations.

From the beginning, it is necessary to accept that Paul's use of the language of holiness and cleanliness here is unprecedented,[55] and to seek not to reconcile his language but to account for its variance. Elsewhere ἁγιασμός is a predicate only of believers and of the Christian community

---

50. Given that the 'Q' tradition appears to record the divorce-adultery link independently of Mark (Mt. 5.31–32; cf. 19.1–9), it seems quite safe to say we have an early, and well-attested Jesus tradition, which may well be known by Paul.
51. As Fee 1987: 296.
52. Dungan 1971: 91–92.
53. Also suggested by Thiselton 2000: 523.
54. Conzelmann 1975: 122.
55. With Barrett 1971: 164.

– a predicate that serves to differentiate from the outside world.[56] As the LXX uses the term to denote cultic objects set aside from the common for the worship of God or, more generally, for the people of Israel set aside from the mass of humanity to be the people of God, similarly Paul sees believers set apart from the unholy outside.[57] Certainly there is an ethical dimension to Paul's use of holiness language: being ἅγιοι implies abstention from vice.[58] However, as we have consistently argued in this study, ethical implications cannot be separated from identity: ontology and behaviour are indivisible in Paul's schema. To be ἅγιος is not only to be called out of the identity of outsider, it is to cease to behave in the manner that defines the outsider.[59]

There can be no getting around the fact that we are dealing here with anomalies: the unbeliever married to a believer is incongruously described as being made ἅγιος, and there are no real precedents for such a move on Paul's part. But then the situation itself is an anomaly, for the instance of a mixed marriage throws up particular concerns for the apostle. As we have seen, the ethical/ontological barrier between insiders and outsiders does not prevent social interaction per se (5.9–11), but it does prevent exogamous marriages (7.39). But what of when such a marriage has occurred, either prior to the believer's conversion, or despite the Pauline prohibition?[60]

For Paul, quite evidently, such a marriage is to be preserved by the believer if at all possible. Like in the case of the endogamous marriage, divorce is to be avoided. However, Paul treats exogamous marriages quite

56. Note the close relation between the calling of believers and their status as ἅγιοι (Rom. 1.7; 1 Cor. 1.2).

57. This is made clear in 1 Cor. 5.6–8, where, as we saw in section 4.3.2, outsiders correspond to the ritually unclean elements of the Passover, and believers to the pure unleavened bread.

58. Cf. 1 Thess. 4.3, 4.7 and 5.23. Fee (1987: 32–33) argues that such may be implied by 1 Cor. 1.2.

59. Murphy-O'Connor's (1977) suggestion falters on this point. He argues that Paul generally uses holiness in two distinct senses: first as an attribute of the Christian, marking his separation from the world and devotion to God; secondly in its ethical dimension, sometimes exhibited by the Christian and sometimes lacking. Thus, the reason the unbeliever can be described as sanctified is that by remaining in the marriage and rejecting divorce, he exhibits the ethical 'subjective disposition' that Paul would hope for in a believer, and this renders the marriage operable. (Murphy-O'Connor bizarrely asserts that although Paul cannot know the unbeliever's motive for remaining in the marriage he 'assumed the best' and attributed it to love!) Such an argument neither does justice to the constant linking of ethics and ontology in Paul's thought, nor to the fact that Paul consistently labels ἄπιστοι as ἄδικοι stereotyped by their vices. Why would he here consider their individual 'subjective disposition' and assume the best? Stereotypes rarely allow such luxuries.

60. It is invariably assumed that Paul is addressing believers who married unbelievers before their own conversion, but it must be possible he includes those who have subsequently married unbelievers, either ignoring Paul's prohibition, or because they have had little choice in the matter.

differently from those between believers. We must account for the fact that when Paul delivers the Lord's command to the married (τοῖς δὲ γεγαμηκόσιν) in 7.10, he does not consider this sufficient to apply to the 'rest' (τοῖς δὲ λοιποῖς) in 7.12, evidently those in mixed marriages, but requires to issue his own, parallel counsel. Why does the Lord's prohibition of divorce not hold good for mixed marriages? To contend that 'such concerns [i.e. mixed marriages] lay outside the province of Jesus' own life setting' is no answer.[61] Jesus' prohibition of divorce, as recorded in the Synoptics, is certainly issued in the context of the Jewish community, but then so is all of his teaching. To limit it to believers, or to extend it as a universal norm, is an interpretative decision. Why does Paul consider the dictum to be insufficient to cover the case of mixed marriages?

The answer must be that, despite the fact that Paul wishes believers to remain in mixed marriages, and like their counterparts in endogamous marriages not to instigate divorces, he accepts that there is a categorical difference between the two types of marriage. He asserts, on the Lord's authority, that endogamous marriages are to be preserved, and that is the end of the matter. However, the exogamous union is subject to a different logic. The Dominical logion does not apply and Paul is required to argue his case. This difference would seem to be indicated in 7.14, with the suggestion that the unbelieving spouse may be in some sense 'unclean'. The only other place where Paul appears to use the language of uncleanness of unbelievers is in 2 Cor. 6.14–7.1.[62] Here ἀκαθάρτου μὴ

---

61. Fee 1987: 298; similarly Barrett 1971: 163–64.

62. We are assuming here that 2 Cor. 6.14–7.1 is Pauline. Substantial objections to its authenticity have been made on grounds of a perceived linguistic and theological distance from Paul. However, these can satisfactorily be overcome (see Thrall 1994: 29–36). More problematic is the decision as to the relation of the section to its current epistolary context. Again, Thrall (1994: 25–29, 472–82) demonstrates the 'possibility' of understanding the passage in situ (and perhaps, since the balance of proof must be on those seeing an interpolation, this should be sufficient). However, what Thrall fails to consider is the likelihood of Paul writing in such a manner to the Corinthians after the misunderstandings evidenced in 1 Cor. (over relations with outsiders, 5.10 and sex with outsiders and pollution, 7.14) without qualifying and explaining his somewhat ambiguous remarks in light of those previous misunderstandings. Even if we can reconcile the passage with Paul's language and theology, can we reconcile it with Paul as pastor and rhetorician writing to Corinth? When this consideration is laid alongside the other difficulties, the burden of proof for an interpolation is perhaps closer to being discharged.

If the passage does not belong in its present context, but is plausibly Pauline, then the suggestion that it might be part of the previous letter (as Hurd 1965: 235–37) becomes somewhat tempting. The similar ethos to the letter of 5.9 (as misunderstood by the Corinthians), and the possible linguistic and ideological connections with 7.1b and 7.14 lend some support. However, since nothing in 2 Cor. 6.14–7.1 matches the reference at 1 Cor. 5.9, and there remains the problem of explaining how the letter became enmeshed in 2 Cor., there is finally insufficient evidence to make the case.

ἄπτεσθε (6.17) uniquely infers that certain types of 'touching' can pollute the believer. Given that this statement is in a section that begins μὴ γίμεσθε ἑτεροζυγοῦντες ἀπίστοις, which probably has the contracting of marriages in view (although perhaps not exclusively so),[63] it would seem that one function of this uncleanness is to render the outsider an unfit marriage partner.[64]

Thus it seems the same type of logic that serves to render the contracting of mixed marriages illicit in 2 Cor. 6.14–7.1 is being applied in 1 Corinthians 7 to question the validity of pre-existing mixed marriages. Paul affirms the marriages. He does not, however, reject the notion that unbelievers are intrinsically unclean (and thus unfit to marry believers), but suggests that the pre-existing marriage serves to transform the 'unclean' status of the unbeliever. Whereas believers are not to form sexual unions with outsiders and are not to become members of a πόρνη, here the marriage serves to alter the status of the outsider, from that of ἄδικος/ἄπιστος/πόρνος towards that of ἅγιος.

But who has raised the question of the holiness of the unbelieving spouse, and thus whether a marriage to him/her can persist? There must be three possibilities:

1. The Corinthians could have raised the matter as an objection to Paul's teaching. As μὴ συναναμίγνυσθαι πόρνοις was pushed to its logical extreme in 5.9, so the same Corinthian arguments could be echoed here: If, Paul, you require us not to associate with πόρνοι (interpreted as the πόρνοι τοῦ κόσμου) then we must divorce our unbelieving spouses. Or alternatively, if Paul has articulated a prohibition on contracting exogamous marriages using the language of purity (as he seems to do in 2 Cor. 6.14–7.1) then the Corinthians may have pushed this to its extremes. 'If, Paul, we are not to marry "unclean" unbelieving spouses, then surely we should divorce such'. In either case, Paul then retorts with the same style of *reductio* as in 5.10b-11: (ἐπεὶ ἄγα ... νῦν δέ). He is effectively saying: 'If I meant you should withdraw from unbelieving spouses as "unclean", then I would also have been saying that your children are "unclean" and thus you should withdraw from them, but we all accept that this is not the case'.[65]

2. It could be that, in response to the Dominical prohibition of divorce, some Corinthians have suggested that mixed marriages are

---

63. See Thrall 1994: 473.

64. Thus holiness has become a type of physical purity, rendering the holder fit for sexual union with the believer: fit, unlike the πόρη of 6.12–20, to 'enter' the temple of the Holy Spirit, which is the body of the believer. (The fact that such holiness is not salvific is irrelevant, *pace* Barrett 1971: 165.)

65. There seems no good reason to think that the attribution of holiness to the children assumes their baptism. The unbelieving spouse is holy – but has certainly not been baptized.

a special case, and that here divorce is justified by virtue of the status of the unbelieving spouse. Such is unlikely to have occurred for ideological reasons. The socially integrated Corinthians have been slow to take up Paul's sectarian division of the world. A group unconcerned with social withdrawal from πόρνοι, either inside or outside the church, is hardly likely to develop an aversion to unbelieving spouses as 'unclean'.[66] The Corinthians, however, appear quite adept at finding devices to defeat the counter-cultural imperatives that Paul attempts to foist upon them in light of their new Christian identity. It must be at least a possibility that the separation of the Lord's command from the mixed marriage has been an attempt on their part to justify some divorces by Christian reasoning, to distinguish a particular case from an already formulated rule.[67] If some Corinthians can take Paul's dicta to extremes in order to defeat them, perhaps others can utilize them as they stand in order to justify their own purposes. Perhaps συναναμίγνυσθαι πόρνοις or language similar to that in 2 Cor. 6.14–7.1, or the prohibition of contracting exogamous marriages, has been used to justify divorcing an unbelieving spouse unwanted for whatever 'normal' reason. To what lengths of ingenuity might a person stuck in an unhappy marriage go? How might someone who has divorced seek to justify his or her action?

This would also make sense of Paul's response in 7.14: citing the case of the children. It is not that the Corinthians have some doctrine of the holiness of the believer's offspring, but that Paul is pointing out a basic flaw in their justification of divorce: they are using 'uncleanness' as a ground for separating from an unwanted spouse, but are not applying the same logic to their children. If the spouse, as an unbeliever, is unholy, and if such demands that the believer separates himself from her (or herself from him), then the children, if also unbelievers, are unholy and the same separation should occur. Paul now engages in a *reductio*: by virtue of their own argument, their children would be unholy and socially intolerable, a thought that is as unthinkable to the Corinthians as to Paul himself.

3.   It is possible that, given the logic of 6.12–20 that believers should not be members of a πόρνη, the issue of pre-existing marriages has occurred to Paul independently. He sees the need to reconcile a prohibition of divorcing unbelieving spouses with the conviction that such unions should not be constructed in the first place.

---

66. Barrett is typical of many in suggesting that the Corinthians genuinely fear that marriage to an outsider will pollute their children. However, the evidence is that Paul is more prone to fear of pollution than are the Corinthians; cf. D.B. Martin's (1995) thesis.

67. Meeks (1983: 101) argues that the saying of Jesus against divorce is likely to be widely known in the Pauline churches. Cited twice in Matthew and once in the other Synoptics, it is certainly one of the best attested of Jesus' sayings.

Whatever the background, what Paul does *not* do is revealing. He does *not* attempt to apply the Lord's words to the case. He does *not* deny that 'uncleanness' would be a bar to the persistence of marriage. He does *not* deny that unbelievers are unclean in this regard. This is all evidence of the strength of the categorical distinction between believers and unbelievers, and evidence also of how much Paul is a victim of his own logic as he tries to distance pre-existing mixed marriages from the basic conviction that those in the category of believer should not be in a sexual relationship with those in the opposite category. Paul's solution betrays a basic tension between a belief in the permanence of marriage, and a belief in the abomination of sexual unions across the group divide. The unbelieving spouse is thus awkwardly reclassified as one differentiated from the general class of outsider. Paul's desire to preserve existing marriages overcomes his objection to exogamy. Of course the logic breaks down if pushed: if the sanctification of the unbelieving spouse is the result of (marital) union with a believer, then what objection can there be to a believer marrying one who is not 'in the Lord'?

9.6. *Remain As You Are: Principle and Paradox (7.17–24)*

9.6.1. *A Universal Rule?*
At first it appears that Paul engages in a *digressio* here, focusing on circumcision and slavery as analogies to marriage only in order to draw out the general principle 'remain as you are' (7.17, 20 and 24).[68] This principle has a double utility: it supports Paul's case against both divorce and separation in 7.10–16, and seeking marriage in 7.25–27. Further, as an argument for remaining single, it has a number of advantages, for, unlike 7.1b, it cannot be taken as an attack on existing marriages, or used as a justification for divorce. On the contrary, it allows Paul to counsel against marrying while explicitly upholding existing marriages, and to present himself as totally consistent in so doing. Neither the married nor the single should seek a change in status (7.27b), but there is no specific aversion to marriage or sex. Indeed the phrasing of an apparently general rule, applicable to a variety of social circumstances, and introduced as a universal 'rule in all the churches' (7.17) may be an attempt to present a constant principle, which is now only incidentally being applied to marriage.

7.26b (καλὸν ἀνθρώπῳ τὸ οὕτως εἶναι) applies this principle to the παρθένοι. 7.27 formally parallels 7.18 (with only a change in person); thus

---

68. Dawes (1990: 683) sees here a rhetorical device where 'if the speaker deals with another topic, it is only in order to illustrate or further explain the matter being discussed', and where 'what appears at first to be something of a distraction turns out in fact to be part of the argumentation'.

implicitly comparing marriage to circumcision. They are presented as similar situations to which the same general principle applies.

v. 18   v. 27

Περιτετμημένος τις ἐκλήθη;   δέδεσαι γυναικί;

μὴ ἐπισπάσθω   μὴ ζήτει λύσιν

ἐν ἀκροβυστίᾳ κέκληταί τις;   λέλυσαι ἀπὸ γυναικός;

μὴ περιτεμνέσθω   μὲ ζήτει γυναῖκα

On the face of it, then, Paul seems to have an overarching principle, expounded in 7.17–24, and then applied consistently to the marriage issues of 1 Corinthians 7. Indeed Yarbrough goes as far as to say that 7.17–24 'demonstrates that Paul's emphasis in chapter 7 is on remaining as you are, not on abstinence from sexual intercourse'.[69] The argument thus appears not so much as valuing celibacy over marriage, but as 'remaining' over changing: changing being rejected on the basis that both states, in each of the three social pairings, are finally irrelevant.[70]

However, appearances can be deceptive. We shall suggest that a closer reading reveals that the argument for singleness *is* the primary purpose of 1 Corinthians 7: the 'remain as you are' principle is developed and applied where it suits this purpose, but is constantly in tension with Paul's valuing of singleness over marriage. This tension will be seen when Paul applies the principle to marriage, but also in 7.17–24 itself, where the principle is in inherent tension with the convictions about slavery from which Paul appears to draw it.

9.6.2. *Tension in the Principle*
Let us begin by examining 7.25–31. There are a number of tensions here, which prevent 7.25–31 being a simple application of the 'remain' principle to marriage and divorce. First, there are exceptions to the principle. Marriage, although inadvisable, is permitted: the believer is not morally obligated to remain as he or she is. This does not in itself necessarily detract from the principle (remaining is still the ideal); it merely softens the application. However, more important is the fact that, despite 7.27, 7.25–31 is not applying the principle even-handedly to marriage, but using it, in combination with other (not totally consistent) arguments, specifically to dissuade the single from marrying.

7.25 opens with reference to the virgins (περὶ δὲ τῶν παρθένων),

69. Yarbrough 1995: 94. Fee (1987: 268) speaks of a 'controlling motif'.
70. Hence Wimbush 1987: 16, 'Paul wants to emphasise the *relative* unimportance of "worldly" relationships and conditions vis-à-vis Christian faith and existence' (cf. Bartchy 1973: 138).

indicating from the outset that Paul's interest is in the application of the principle to those currently single, rather than abstractly to marriage. 7.26 does not merely recommend 'remain as you are' as a value in itself, but in light of the 'present distress' (ἐνεστῶσαν ἀνάγκην). This distress can only be a reference to the θλῖψις of the married (7.28). Thus the general principle, the 'rule in all the churches', presented as applicable in all social circumstances, evolves in 7.26 into a suggestion, which needs underpinning by an additional argument: an argument which is specific to marrying! The universal argument against any social change is readily combined with a particular argument against one specific type of social change. However, the particular notion of the θλῖψις of the married, and the general principle of 'remain' stand in uneasy relationship, for the θλῖψις logically pushes towards a desire for the termination of marriages, a notion which the 'remain' principle prohibits. The unity of the two notions only exists in that both serve to dissuade the single from marrying. Thus the desire to dissuade from marrying, rather than the desire that believers remain as they are, proves to be the basic intention of the passage. The 'remain' principle is merely a convenient argument. When we turn to consider the slavery analogy we shall observe the same tension.[71]

9.6.3. *The Slavery Analogy*
The 'remain' principle has often been used to portray Paul as a social conservative concerned to reverse the Corinthians' more radical rejection of social norms. However, as far as marriage is concerned, to recommend 'remaining' is, as we have already seen, precisely to overturn the normal social expectations and aspirations of the Corinthians, who would have assumed marriage and divorce as inevitable and desirable parts of social existence. Paul thus does not seek to canonize but conversely to repudiate the status quo.

When we turn to slavery, the decision as to whether Paul's μᾶλλον

---

71. Another tension appears to exist in the *digressio* itself. For the maxim 'remain as you are' appears to be grounded simultaneously on the relativization of social status in view of a transcending obedience to God, and the sanctification of the social status in which the believer is at the time of his or her calling. 7.18–19 rationalizes the avoidance of circumcision or epispasm as circumcision and uncircumcision οὐδέν ἐστιν, compared with τήρησις ἐντολῶν θεοῦ. However, the inference in all three statements of principle flows in another direction. 7.17 commands the believer to live (περιπατέω) in the social position in which they were when God called them (ὡς κέκληκεν ὁ θεός), and denotes this as assigned by the Lord (ἐμέρισεν ὁ κύριος). Likewise 7.20 asks the believer to remain in the 'calling' (κλῆσις) in which he or she was called. Thus God's calling on the believer serves not to relativize the importance of the outward circumstances, but to sanctify them. Again, the unity of the principles is only in the social effect. Both arguments undermine any desire for a change in social status.

χρῆσαι injunction indicates that slaves should seek to 'remain' in slavery (use slavery) or accept any offer of manumission (use freedom), has been used to portray Paul respectively as a social conservative or social realist. But, given that the social aspiration of a slave would be for manumission, and the expectation of society would be that slaves desire, and sometimes attain, freedom, then any call for slaves to 'remain' in slavery would not be socially conservative but rather would overturn the expected social ethos.[72] Given that Paul overturns social conventions on marriage, then we might expect him to run counter to social expectations here also. This could justify interpreting μᾶλλον χρῆσαι as an injunction to remain in (the calling of) slavery.

Such a view would be consistent with the 'remain' principle being a universal Pauline social dogma. Indeed, it has been observed that those who look to the wider context of 7.17–24 as a guide to the meaning of μᾶλλον χρῆσαι are invariably driven to the 'use slavery' option.[73] However, as we have already seen, the consistency by which Paul applies the principle is open to question. How far it drives his social ethos, and how far it is an argument merely driven by his desire to counsel against marrying, is debatable on the basis of 7.25–31. Once we have compared the argument derived from slavery to that from circumcision, we shall see that the 'remain as you are' principle is not so overarching.

The analogies of circumcision and slavery are not identical. They are not examples of the general rule, which is then applied to marriage, but rather 'each of them has a particular purpose in the context of the

---

72. As Harrill (1995: 74) states, these 'pictures of Paul are anachronistic since they wrongly assume that opposition to manumission was a sign of "social conservatism"'. Roman social conservatives did not oppose the notion of manumission.

73. 'Most of those scholars who stress the grammatical considerations prefer the "take freedom" interpretation, and most of the scholars who stress the importance of the context prefer the "use slavery" interpretation' (Bartchy 1973: 23). For 'use slavery' based on context see e.g. Weiss 1910: 187–88; Barrett 1971: 170; Bartchy 1973: 23; Conzelmann 1975: 127 and Dawes 1990: 689. For 'use freedom' see Robertson and Plummer 1914: 147–48; Fee 1987: 317; Witherington 1995: 181–85; Harrill 1995: 118–20 and Schrage 1995: 139–40.

The contextual argument is that Paul's 'remain' principle would not favour manumission. However, the point is often made that the apostle consistently allows exceptions to his rule (marriage is no sin, deserted spouses in mixed marriages are not bound) so there may be a similar concession for manumission in the case of slavery (so Bartchy 1973: 9–10; Fee 1987: 318; Harrill 1995: 123–26). However, the three 'concessions' are not at all similar. Paul *prefers* the believer remains single, but *concedes* marriage as an option. Paul *prefers* that the married believer remains married, but *concedes* an exception for a deserted partner. But if μᾶλλον χρῆσαι meant 'use freedom' this would not be a *concession* permitting freedom, but a direct encouragement to change (cf. μᾶλλον). If 'use freedom' means choose freedom (an imperative) then the 'exception' has swallowed the rule.

argumentation of this chapter'.[74] This argumentation is finally against the believer seeking to marry. Thus, as we shall see, the linkage of the two analogies is in the light they shed for Paul on marriage, rather than their use in drawing out some universal principle. This becomes evident when the dissimilarities of the two are noted.

The discussion begins (7.18) with a balanced description of the states of circumcision and uncircumcision and the mutual command that those in neither category should seek a change in identity. Paul then proceeds to relativize both states in light of the commands of God (v. 19): here neither Jewish nor Gentile identity is of advantage. The believer's allegiance to God transcends such social identity: obedience is equally possible for those in either social situation. The principle is then drawn out (7.20) that each should remain in the social circumstances in which he or she was called.

The slavery discussion appears at first to parallel the previous example. The question 'were you called as a slave?' (7.21) echoes 'was anyone circumcised when called?' (7.18) and flows from the command to remain in your calling (7.20). This leads us to anticipate the equation of the social states of slavery and freedom with those of circumcision and uncircumcision. However, we are immediately aware of the difference in the argument. First, the enslaved state alone, and not the free state, is under discussion in 7.21a. Secondly, the 'never mind' of 7.21a, grounded in the paradox of 7.22, falls short of the confident relativization of circumcision in 7.19. The expected pronouncement that both slavery and freedom οὐδέν ἐστιν is conspicuous by its absence. The believer's identity is not seen as transcending slavery in the same way that it does circumcision.

One could begin to argue for the similarity of Paul's attitude to circumcision and slavery, by reading 7.22 as a relativization of states – in the Lord, the slave is a freedman, the freeborn a slave – and by viewing the command to the free not to become slaves (7.23) and the command to the slave to use his slavery (reading μᾶλλον χρῆσαι as 'use slavery'), as equivalent to the balanced imperatives of 7.18. There are, however, two problems with this. First, it requires a reading of μᾶλλον χρῆσαι that is at least uncertain.[75] Secondly, it ignores 7.23a, which, as we shall argue, prevents us viewing slavery and freedom as indifferent states, and as reading Paul even-handedly counselling 'remain as you are' to both.

9.6.4. *An Alternative Principle: The Lord's Ownership of the Believer*
The indicative 'You were bought at a price' (τιμῆς ἠγοράσθητε) has been variously read as a metaphor of Christ manumitting the believer from

---

74.   Dawes 1990: 689.
75.   See n. 73.

slavery (redemption),[76] or as a metaphor of Christ purchasing the believer for his own possession.[77] On this choice hinges how we interpret the imperative of 7.23b (μὲ γίνεσθε δοῦλοι ἀνθρώπων). If manumission is in view then the emphasis of the imperative lies on the 'do not become *slaves*': those freed by the Lord have not to enter into slavery. If the Lord's ownership is in view then the emphasis lies in 'do not become slaves *of men*': those who are now slaves of the Lord should not enter into the slavery of a human master. 7.22 can offer support for either reading. The notion that the one called as a slave is now the freedman of the Lord (ἀπελεύθερος κυρίου) supports a manumission reading. The notion that the one called as free is now a slave of Christ (δοῦλος Χριστοῦ) supports a notion of purchase into the Lord's slavery.

However, the notion of a purchase metaphor is, in the end, to be preferred to that of manumission, for the following reasons. First, the imperative not to become[78] slaves makes best sense as a command to those literally free. To read it as a more general injunction, applicable even to those in slavery, requires a totally metaphorical reading of the concept of enslavement (how else can slaves be in danger of becoming slaves?). Certainly slavery is introduced for its analogical value in the wider debate, but the analogy only functions properly if its logic makes literal sense in the context of actual slavery. Secondly, however we read μᾶλλον χρῆσαι, 7.21 offers two imperatives (one being 'never mind') to the slave regarding what their attitude to their social situation should be. The rationale for these imperatives is grounded in the indicative of 7.22 'for (γάρ) he who was called in the Lord a slave is the freedman of the Lord'. Given this, it makes best sense to read 7.23 as the corresponding imperative to the free, flowing from the indicative of 7.22b, which declared the freeborn as the slave of the Lord. Thirdly, the verb ἀγοράζω is used of the purchase transaction, but never in the Delphic manumission inscriptions;[79] as Fee notes, 'the verb "bought" with its corresponding genitive of quantity, "at a price", places it squarely in the slave market'.[80] Fourthly, the same

76. As found elsewhere in the NT (Gal. 3.13; 4.5; Rev. 5.9; 14.3).

77. D.B. Martin favours the slave-trade analogy (1995: 178) but most commentators favour redemption (e.g. Barrett 1971: 152, 171; Conzelmann 1975: 128), while some have held out for both (e.g. Robertson and Plummer 1914: 149; Fee 1987: 320).

78. Dawes (1990: 691 n. 35) argues that μὴ γίνεσθε is an injunction to all Christians, slave or free, and thus 'do not be' or even 'do not remain' are preferable translations to 'do not become'. This appears unwarranted, as the indicative would then stand in blatant contradiction to that of 7.24.

79. A point, which, as Bartchy (1973: 124) notes, is fatal to Deissmann's suggestion that these influenced Paul's thinking.

80. Fee 1987: 264–65. Fee actually makes this comment of 6.20, insisting that redemption is not in view, but then strangely proceeds to insist that 7.23, which has the same verb and genitive, carries a 'full double nuance' of becoming someone's slave through purchase and the 'purchase for freedom' (Fee 1987: 320).

phrase τιμῆς ἠγοράσθητε has already been used at 6.20 as a grounding for an imperative. On that occasion, the manumission interpretation is quite impossible, for τιμῆς ἠγοράσθητε provides the evidence for Paul's declaration 'you are not your own' (6.19), which precludes the notion of the believer as free. It is certainly possible that the second use of the language could carry a different nuance (as Fee), but this must be regarded as unlikely.

We thus have an imperative, based on the notion of the Lord's ownership of the freeborn believer, which prohibits his or her becoming a slave. Evidently, although such an imperative fits, and flows from, the immediate context, it is not designed for such. The Corinthians are hardly likely to desire to enter into slavery![81] Rather, like 'remain as you are', this imperative is drawn out of the slavery analogy for a more general application. To enter into slavery is incompatible with the Lord's ownership of the believer. The same principle, based implicitly on the same analogy, has already been used in 6.19–20. There the Lord's purchase for ownership of the believer led to the imperative 'glorify God in your body'. The Lord's ownership constrained the activity appropriate for a believer, and explicitly denied the possibility of allowing a πόρνη to have mastery over the believer's body. The one whose body is the Lord's shall not be mastered ὑπό τινος (6.12). The same notion is here: the Lord's ownership prevents the believer entering into obligations to another – he or she is not to become a slave of men.

In the context of the slavery analogy, the imperative 'do not become the slaves of men' serves to support, and is supported by, the 'remain as you are' imperative, drawn from circumcision, and reiterated at 7.24. Both preclude an entry into a new slavery. Both support the freeborn remaining free. But their grounding is at heart inconsistent. The 'remain' principle serves either to relegate social statuses as being equally unimportant (7.19) or to sanctify social statuses as being equally the place of the believer's calling. However, the notion of the Lord's ownership being inconsistent with entering into slavery implicitly rates literal freedom higher than slavery. To enter into slavery is said to be incompatible with the Lord's claim on the believer, in a way that could never be said of entering into freedom. Thus, just as, in 7.26, the 'remain' principle is only compatible with the notion of the θλῖψις of the married, since both are used to advise against marriage, so too the 'remain' principle is only compatible with the argument from the Lord's ownership, as both are used to advise against entering into slavery.

---

81.   *Pace* Witherington (1995: 185) who states, 'Paul is opposed to the trend of people, especially Christians, selling themselves into slavery to support their family' (cf. Winter 1994: 146). Even if Christians were doing so (and there is absolutely no evidence of this), it would hardly be a matter of choice, where Paul could act as dissuader.

But what is the slavery that Paul is advising the believer from entering into? As we have said, literal slavery cannot be the ultimate target. Fee, rightly maintaining the metaphorical use, concludes, 'Paul is probably reflecting once again on their [the Corinthians'] penchant to let merely human wisdom, disguised in the form of "spirituality", dictate their present anxieties about the need to be free from certain social settings, especially marriage. Don't come under such bondage he tells them'.[82] Thus, for Fee, the slavery of which Paul warns is the attempt to be *free* from marriage! The suggestion is as ingenious as it is unwarranted. There is no notion of bondage either to anxiety or to social change to be found anywhere in this passage. Rather the bondage that Paul has continually in view is the bondage of marriage. It is marriage that is constantly seen as placing the believer under obligation to another. Marriage deprives the believer of autonomy over their body by placing it under the ἐξουσία of another (7.4). To be married is to be obligated to a wife (δέω) while to be single is to be free from a wife (λύω) (7.27).[83]

Thus the imperatives, both against entering into slavery and to 'remain as you are', are designed to provide arguments against the single entering into marriage.[84] Circumcision and slavery both produce analogies to marriage, but the analogies differ. The circumcision analogy is used unequivocally to support the 'remain' principle.[85] The 'remain' principle applies to *entry* into slavery, while the slavery analogy develops the notion of the Lord's ownership, a notion which supports antipathy to slavery entered into (whether literal or metaphoric), but undermines any argument that one should 'remain' in slavery (whether literal or metaphoric). The

---

82. Fee 1987: 320.

83. Paul also implies that those obligated to marriage are δεδούλωται (7.15). Deming (1995: 148–50) seems correct in suggesting that this be translated 'enslaved' rather than 'bound' (although his suggestion, that Paul is refuting a Corinthian contention that saw specifically mixed marriages as enslavement, seems unjustified: on which see Horrell 1996a: 605–606). Paul often uses δουλόω for an extrinsic power having a hold over the believer (1 Cor. 9.19; Rom. 6.18, 6.22; Gal. 4.3).

84. Significantly, Patristic commentators are less inclined than modern ones to see 7.17–24 simply as a digression, which brings out the 'remain' principle, and more inclined to view circumcision and slavery as directly analogous to marriage (see E.A. Clark 1999: 299–303).

85. However, just as Paul's attitude to slavery is encapsulated better in the 'do not become slaves' principle rather than the 'remain' principle, the same could be said of circumcision. Is it really changing in general which would be Paul's concern here? Is Paul really as concerned with Jewish epispasm as Gentile circumcision? It is surely more probable that Paul has formulated his 'rule in all the churches' as a response to Gentile believers desiring to circumcise. We have enough evidence of how negatively Paul would view a Gentile Christian accepting circumcision, as opposed to the almost certainly hypothetical case of a Jew reversing his circumcision (Gal. 2.3–5; 5.1–5). The point is stronger when one considers that Paul in Gal. 2.3–5 suggests that to be circumcised is, for a Gentile Christian, a form of slavery – and as such an undesirable change.

unity of the 'remain' principle with the notion of the Lord's ownership and its prohibition on entering into slavery is then only in their rhetorical purpose. They are otherwise potentially inconsistent arguments.[86]

9.6.4. *Conclusion*

In conclusion, the so-called *digressio* of 7.17–24 is an integral part of the argument of the chapter as a whole. It does serve to underline the persuasion against separation found in the preceding section, and does so by developing a principle which is then to be utilized in the persuasion against marrying. However, it is the requirements of the later argument that drive this section, and account for the analogies that Paul has selected. 'Remain as you are' sits uneasily with the invective against slavery, indicating that that second instance is chosen for different reasons, and to draw out a different argument against marriage.

Thus, in the passage, Paul is arguing against changes in status, but what is primarily in view is the Corinthian desire to change status from single to married. The 'remain as you are' principle is a tool to fight such a desire for change, as is the 'do not enter into slavery' principle. However, the analogy of slavery appears to get us closer to the centre of Paul's argument and attitude to marriage.

Marriage is comparable to slavery: both the married and the enslaved lack autonomy over the body – it being mastered either by an owner or by a spouse. However, Paul's argument is in fact more complex than this. He does not simply liken marriage to slavery and singleness to freedom, and thus declare singleness preferable. Rather, in 7.14–21 he compares the Lord's ownership of the believer to slavery, and declares that the Lord's mastery renders entry into the slavery of a human master impossible: the Lord's slave is not free to obligate himself in such a manner. This then is the similarity to Paul's attitude in 6.12–20, where Christ-union was compared with marriage, and Christ-union renders entry into sexual union with another impossible: the Lord's 'spouse' is not free to obligate himself in such a manner. It is as inconceivable to be in two such unions, as it is to sell oneself into slavery, when one is the property of the Lord.

Possibly, Paul is pointing any Corinthian believer contemplating marriage to the example of his slave. In effect he is saying that, as slavery is compatible with identity in Christ, so too is marriage, but as no free believer should or would choose to enter into slavery, so none should

---

86. Although our reading operates regardless of how μᾶλλον χρῆσαι is read, it is possible to make a few observations. As we have noted (note 73), while grammatical considerations favour 'use freedom', the context has caused many to prefer 'use slavery': as Paul is thought to counsel slaves, as all other social groups, to 'remain'. But if the principle is, as we have argued, not being consistently applied then perhaps the grammatical considerations ought to prevail.

choose marriage, for both cause conflicts with the Lord's ownership of the believer. Thus slavery serves as an example of a social state like marriage, in which it is acceptable, although undesirable, to be, but into which it is unthinkable one would voluntarily enter.[87]

9.7. *Further Reasons for Remaining Single (7.25–40)*

There are three basic themes in this passage. First, there are repeated protestations of the legitimacy of marrying (for virgins, 7.28a; for the betrothed, 7.36, 7.38a; for widows, 7.39). Secondly, there are reasons for preferring singleness (the 'remain' principle, 7.26b-27; the ἐνεστῶσαν ἀνάγκην, 7.27a; the θλῖψις τῇ σαρκί, 7.28b; the divisions and anxiety, 7.32–35). Thirdly, there is an apparent relativization of certain activities in light of the nature of the καιρός and the κόσμος (7.29–31). The question is how to connect these various themes. What is the shape and thrust of Paul's argument? What is central and what is peripheral?

Generally, commentators reconstruct the passage along these lines. First, the thrust of Paul's argument is that marrying is permitted: a protest delivered in the face of over-enthusiastic ascetics. Secondly, the arguments for preferring singleness are attempts to agree with the ascetics' views while redirecting and supplanting their over-enthusiastic motivations. While they advocated celibacy as moral necessity, Paul presents it as (merely) expedient. Thirdly, Paul's relativization of 'worldly' activities is seen as an implied criticism of the ascetics' obsession with marital status. In the face of the Eschaton, the question of marital status is finally unimportant.

However, we suggest an alternative reading. First, the thrust of the argument is Paul's persuasion for singleness, presented to Corinthian Christians whom Paul knows to be a most reluctant audience. (He uses a number of rationales to promote singleness, which betray something of his concern with the compatibility of Christian identity and marriage.) Secondly, the protestation of the legitimacy of marrying is designed to

---

87. In view of Paul's insistence on the incompatibility of πορνεία with identity in Christ, one might ask whether his attitude to the compatibility of slavery with Christian identity is because the slave was legally unable to exercise control over his/her own sexual activity. Glancy suggests that Paul recommends 'choose freedom' for just such reasons (1998: 499).

However, there is nothing to connect the advice to slaves with concern for πορνεία. Paul nowhere considers the sexual ethics of slaves. (Glancy [1998: 499] rightly rejects Harrill's [1995: 123] contention that the λοιποί of 7.12 includes slaves.) Glancy makes too many assumptions. On the basis that the church was a cross-section of society (Meeks), she assumes that the church in Corinth (a) contained slaves and (b) contained slaves vulnerable to their unbelieving owners' sexual advances. The first assumption is reasonable, but the second is at least questionable. It is likely that the church would recruit the slaves of believers, but how far the church was able (or even sought) to recruit the slaves of outsiders is unknown. It is not until the Pastorals (1 Tim. 6.1) and 1 Pet. 2 that we have evidence of such a move.

rebut the Corinthian objections to Paul's previous commendation of singleness. Paul does not make marriage sin. Specifically he refutes an allegation that his teaching would compel the affianced believer to repudiate his obligations to his betrothed: if such a believer feels obligated to marry, he may do so. Thirdly, we will suggest that 7.29–31 is not a criticism of enthusiastic asceticism, but is an attempt to critique the socially integrated Corinthians' attitude to marriage (an attitude which affirms the Graeco-Roman social order). Marriage is part of the σχῆμα of a κόσμος which is passing. In light of the temporal nature of this world and its orders, the Corinthians' valuing of marriage and desire to marry is inappropriate. Investment in the world (and thus in marriage) is criticized.

9.7.1. *Paul's* γνώμη: *A Reformed Maxim? (7.25–26)*

At 7.25 Paul returns from the '*digressio*' of 7.17–24 to the topic of the desirability of marrying,[88] a topic he has already explicitly commented upon in 7.2 and 7.6–9. Indeed, since we have demonstrated that 7.17–24 is integral to Paul's instruction on marrying, we might rather see 7.10–16 as the digression, where Paul deals with divorce in response to Corinthian objections, before returning to the main issue of marriage and singleness.

What is immediately noticeable is Paul's tone. There appears to be a certain hesitancy on the apostle's part: 'this is not your standard Paul'.[89] He concedes from the outset that he has no ἐπιταγὴ κυρίου on this matter, but is merely, as one 'who by the Lord's mercy is trustworthy', offering his γνώμη (7.25). Paul may think it inadvisable to marry, but since the Lord has not spoken on this matter, he cannot compel anyone. Indeed, he has already accepted that in certain circumstances, because of human weakness, marriage is advisable. Thus marriage is not sin – Paul simply seeks to promote singleness as advantageous.

However, we should not overly stress Paul's hesitancy. The same formula – opening by conceding that there is no word of the Lord – is

---

88. Granted he addresses the παρθένοι, but the principles are evidently applicable also to ἄγαμοι (who presumably include divorcees 7.32–35) and to widows (7.39). The singling out of παρθένοι may be because Paul especially wishes to advise such against marriage, and/or because they are the group on whose behalf the Corinthians have particularly objected to Paul's previous teaching.

As to their identity, our sympathies may well be with Conzelmann (1975: 131) when he contends that 'what is meant by the term παρθένοι is – superfluously enough – hotly disputed: it means virgins'. The notion that *virgines subintroductae* (or 'spiritual marriages') are in view is to be rejected. We know Paul has little use for celibacy within marriage (7.3–5). Further, the notion that the consummation of marriages is what is under discussion can make little sense of the γαμέω/γαμίζω verbs in 7.36–38. The contention that παρθένοι refers specifically to the betrothed (as probably in 7.36–37) is possible but unnecessary. The NT elsewhere uses a designator in addition to παρθένος to denote betrothed (cf. Mt. 1.18 and Lk. 1.27; the meaning in Mt. 25.1–13 is disputed).

89. Fee 1987: 324.

used in 7.12 and neither there nor here does Paul refrain from offering strong imperatives and arguments for his preferred option. That it is his own opinion does not prevent him stressing his authority to advise (7.25b) and then mustering every argument for that advice. Fee's suggestion that the 'argument is advice only, and it reflects pastoral concern for them, not principles that would make singleness a better option'[90] is unjustified. For while Paul is unable (and unwilling) to compel the Corinthians, it is precisely from principles, derived from his convictions of how best to be committed to the Lord, that he will argue that singleness is 'a better option'. Translating γνώμη as 'opinion' may also be to underestimate the strength of Paul's advice. Various other words could be substituted – purpose, intention, mind, judgment, decision, declaration[91] – any of which convey a stronger urging on the apostle's part.[92]

Ramsaran[93] has gone so far as to suggest that 'maxim' may be a valid translation of γνώμη. Thus Paul alludes to a maxim that can be found in the next verse: καλὸν ἀνθρώπῳ τὸ οὕτως εἶναι. Given Paul's use of γνώμη elsewhere,[94] this may be too precise a translation, but it may be that Paul's 'counsel' of 7.25 is indeed articulated in the form of a maxim presented in 7.26.

Most commentators brush over the grammatical problem that is contained in 7.26, translating it something like 'I think that in view of the present distress it is well for a person to remain as he is' (RSV).[95] The Greek syntax is however more problematic; and translated literally, renders: 'Therefore, this I think to be good because of the present distress, that it is good for a man to be as he is'. Weiss, describing the grammar as it stands as 'nicht schön', goes so far as to suggest some form of interpolation.[96] However, the sense can be rescued if we take the last five words as a quotation, introduced by the ὅτι recitative. Most previous proponents of such punctuation have invariably viewed the quotation as being from the Corinthians' letter to Paul. However, there appears no

90. Fee 1987: 333.

91. BAGD 4th edn: 'γνώμη'.

92. Dolfe (1992: 115) argues that γνώμη has been translated 'advice' because here and at 2 Cor. 8.20 'the translators feel a contrast is required [to ἐπιταγή]'. Dolfe offers parallel instances where the implication is of an offer that cannot be refused, and thus suggests 'decision' is a better translation.

93. Ramsaran 1995: 531–40.

94. 1 Cor. 1.10 but esp. 2 Cor. 8.8–10. Ramsaran (1995: 533) points to the use of the word in the rhetorical handbooks, but damagingly omits a study of Pauline usage.

95. Similarly Robertson and Plummer (1914: 152) 'the construction of the verse is not regular, but quite intelligible'.

96. Weiss (1910: 193) suggests that τοῦτο refers to the Corinthians' question as to whether permanent virginity is recommended, and that the ὅτι καλὸν ἀνθρώπῳ τὸ οὕτως εἶναι is the 'glossierendes Zitat eines Abschreibers' designed to explain that enigmatic τοῦτο. However, there are no textual variants to support such a gloss.

good reason why this must be the case.[97] It may well be that we are dealing with Paul's advice (γνώμη), now articulated as a maxim.[98] Thus Paul commends the maxim 'it is good for a man to remain as he is' in light of the ἐνεστῶσα ἀνάγκη.

However we reconstruct the sentence, the final phrase bears obvious relation to both the maxim of 7.1b (καλὸν ἀνθρώπω . . .) and the 'remain' principle of the previous section (especially when the similarity of 7.18 and 7.27 is remembered). Thus it appears that Paul develops this maxim from the preceding section, and that he intends it to supplant the maxim of 7.1b. If we are correct in viewing 7.1b as Pauline, then it appears reasonable that 7.26 is designed as a reformulation or replacement of 7.1b, with the ambiguities removed. This new maxim can in no way be interpreted as a moral absolute; it carries no possibility of being understood as an ascetic aversion either to marriage or sex. It is simply advice not to marry: advice that is designed to be viewed as consistent with the 'remain' principle, which Paul presents as applicable to a variety of social settings. Indeed Paul's γνώμη may well be (or be part of) his 'rule in all the churches' (7.17b) now applied to the παρθένοι, just as he will identically advise the widow, to remain as she is, with the same γνώμη (κατὰ τὴν ἐμὴν γνώμη, 7.40).

9.7.2. Trouble and Strife (7.26–28)

Why does Paul think his γνώμη apposite? He advises it in the light of the ἐνεστῶσα ἀνάγκη. But how is this to be understood? Many link the ἀνάγκη to the θλῖψις τῇ σαρκὶ of 7.28b,[99] and then connect both to the overtly eschatological references contained in 7.29–31.[100] Commentators then note that ἀνάγκη and θλῖψις often appear in apocalyptic literature to describe pre-eschatological distress,[101] and thus suggest that Paul offers his pragmatic counsel as he believes marriage inexpedient at a time when he anticipates eschatological woes. Here Paul's advice is seen as akin to the warnings of Luke's Jesus who prophesies the distress of mothers during the end-time upheaval (Lk. 21.23).[102]

There are a number of problems here. First, 1 Corinthians 7 (unlike Luke 21) would appear to focus on the nature of the present, rather than

97. With Ramsaran 1995, against Hurd 1965: 178–79; Barrett 1971: 174–75; Fee 1987: 330 and Deming 1995: 110–12.

98. See n. 21.

99. Conzelmann (1975: 132) refers to ἀνάγκη and θλῖψις as 'synonymous terms'.

100. E.g. Barrett 1971: 175; Fee 1987: 328–30; Allison 1987: 62–63 and Deming 1995: 177–97.

101. E.g. Zeph. 1.15 (LXX); Lk. 21.23. Such pre-eschatological tribulation is a recurring belief in Jewish and early Christian literature (cf. Mk 13.7–8; 2 Bar. 10.13; 1 En. 99.5; Lk. 23.29).

102. See e.g. Bruce 1971: 74–75.

on an anticipated end or end-times. ἐνεστῶσα is best translated present rather than 'impending'.[103] This ties in with 7.31's assertion that the form of the κόσμος *is* passing away. So, if Paul were referring to eschatological woes, he would need to believe that the Corinthians were presently experiencing such. Secondly, as is now commonly admitted, neither ἀνάγκη nor θλῖψις are *necessarily* eschatological terms.[104] Paul nowhere uses ἀνάγκη in such a way. Where Paul does use it to indicate affliction it is an affliction against which he prevails, or to which he is reconciled, rather than one caused by the impending Eschaton.[105] Paul can also use the term in other ways, to indicate compulsion or divine necessity.[106] Thus ἀνάγκη must be seen as an oblique reference – its meaning to be taken from the wider context of the argument.[107]

7.28b finds Paul more explicit in what he is advising, and why. Marriage should be avoided so as to prevent the θλῖψις τῇ σαρκὶ. It is important to bear in mind what the logic is: those who utilize the concession of 7.28a and marry (οἱ τοιοῦτοι) will have (ἕξουσιν) θλῖψις τῇ σαρκὶ, but those who follow Paul's advice, and remain unmarried, will be spared that ordeal (ἐγὼ δὲ ὑμῶν φείδομαι). The θλῖψις then is the peculiar situation of the believer who marries, and is avoided by the believer who remains single.[108] The logic thus differs from that of 7.26. There the ἀνάγκη was apparently given as a general reason for one to 'remain' as he was; here on the other hand the θλῖψις appears as a particular reason to remain unmarried. Thus Morris's contention that 'when high seas are raging it is no time for changing ships'[109] (i.e. 'remain' is a general principle in light of the present circumstances) might work for

103. Fee (1987: 329), pointing to Paul's usage elsewhere, rightly insists that it 'invariably means what is already present in contrast to what is yet to come (see esp. 3.22 and Rom. 8.38)'. *Pace* translations such as 'impending' (RSV); 'imminent' (Conzelmann 1975: 132) and 'bevorstehenden' (Weiss 1910: 193).

104. As noted by Gager (1970: 331) and R.F. Collins (1999: 293). It is staggering how many commentators declare ἀνάγκη an eschatological term, on the basis of Lk. and Zeph., without considering Paul's usage (e.g. Allison 1987: 62; Deming 1995: 178).

105. 2 Cor. 6.4; 12.10; 1 Thess. 3.7 (the last two of these also refer to θλῖψις, yet there is no eschatological reference).

106. Rom. 13.5; 1 Cor. 9.16; 7.37; 2 Cor. 9.7; Phlm. 14.

107. Winter (1989) attempts to link the ἐνεστῶσα ἀνάγκη specifically to a famine in Corinth at the time Paul writes. However, even if there were famines in Corinth in the 50s, neither these nor Paul's letter can be securely dated (Winter's attempt is highly speculative). Further, there is no direct evidence to link the subject of marriage to *economic* distress, as Winter contends. Winter is forced into the highly unsatisfactory postulation that the Corinthians 'sought advice as whether to have further children' (93–94) in view of the economic climate.

108. *Pace* Fee (1987: 329) who argues that it is possibly the 'common lot of those who believe', i.e. the suffering of the church until the redemption, of which the community's own problems (cf. 11.30) are perhaps a part.

109. Morris 1985: 113.

7.26 but cannot for 7.28. 7.28 does *not* indicate that *all* believers experience high seas, and thus ship-jumping is inexpedient, but rather that the turbulence is reserved for those on the matrimonial boat, and that those sailing in the calmer waters of singleness should not seek to join their fellows in that choppy ocean!

One should take care not to ignore the particularity of the θλῖψις. It is exclusively the lot of the married, and can motivate only the single to 'remain' so, and not the married. Therefore one should not interpret θλῖψις in the light of the general reference to the ἐνεστῶσα ἀνάγκη, which apparently seeks to motivate every man to 'remain'. Indeed, given that the seemingly general advice of 7.26 is actually given quite specifically to παρθένοι, it seems better to interpret the ἀνάγκη in light of the θλῖψις experienced only by the married than the reverse.[110] It may not be 'remaining' in general that Paul has in view in 7.26–28; rather we have again an argument framed as general counsel, but actually aimed at those contemplating marriage.

But what is the θλῖψις τῇ σαρκὶ? Here we have an expression unique in Paul, and apparently unprecedented in the contemporary literature.[111] Paul can speak elsewhere of the θλῖψις that the believer experiences, but here alone we find the dative locative used with the term. Given this uniqueness it is perhaps inadvisable to be overconfident in offering any interpretation, but in light of the context we shall hazard a few observations. 6.12–20 discussed the physical implications of sexual union for believers. The body was an entity that participated in, or was owned by, Christ through the Spirit. But becoming μία σάρξ with a sexual partner was perceived as an alternative participation or ownership. Thus the choice between two allegiances was made precisely *in* the sexual body. The body was a location either sanctified by the Spirit's indwelling, or polluted by the πόρνη. Given this, perhaps Paul's dative locative in 7.28 should not too quickly be ignored. Married (unlike single) believers experience a physical conflict between two allegiances: their body 'for the Lord' and their body as the possession of the one with whom they have become μία σάρξ by marriage. Perhaps this is the 'pressure' (ἀνάγκη / θλῖψις) to which Paul is referring.[112] As we shall see, 7.32–35 supports this notion. The married believer again uniquely experiences an inevitable division of loyalties this time expressed as being between the κύριος and the κόσμος.

One could then understand θλῖψις τῇ σαρκὶ solely in terms of the

110. *Pace* Deming (1995: 178 n. 270) who states that 7.26 'speaks of ἀνάγκη as a reality for both the married and the unmarried alike'.

111. TLG provides us with no instances outside the NT. The nearest NT parallel is 2 Cor. 12.7, the infamous σκόλοψ τῇ σαρκί, which most interpreters view as a bodily affliction (Barrett 1973: 315; R.P. Martin 1986: 413).

112. Remembering that θλῖψις is derived from θλίβω to press, squeeze, constrain or restrict.

Pauline anthropology of 6.12–20, without recourse to eschatology.[113]
This, however, might go too far. In light of 7.29–31 it would appear that
Paul's apocalyptic convictions about the κόσμος give urgency to his
discussion. If Paul's beliefs concerning participation in Christ makes
marriage a problematic conflict of allegiances, then his cosmological
convictions about the nature of the present time serve to make the
question of allegiances critical. There is a 'pressure' on the believer to
decide *now* where his allegiance lies.

The allusive ἀνάγκη can then be seen as relating to this pressure on the
believer to choose allegiances. Perhaps it focuses on the anthropological
tension for the married believer: the θλῖψις τῇ σαρκὶ (cf. 7.32–35). But
perhaps, in view of its designation as the ἐνεστῶσα ἀνάγκη, it focuses
particularly on the nature of the present time in Paul's eschatological
schema (7.29–31). The nature of the present makes the need for decisive
allegiance critical and thus the divided loyalty of the married inadvisable.

9.7.3. *The Nature of this World (7.29–31)*
We observed in 8.1 that marriage was part of the assumed social order of
antiquity and tied to assumptions about the nature of the κόσμος. In
philosophy (with perhaps certain Cynic exceptions) marriage and the
social order were seen not merely as negotiated cultural norms, but as part
of the fabric of the universe itself. The divine order, the κόσμος, and social
order were all intrinsically related.

Throughout 1 Corinthians, Paul has been promoting a new social order
for believers, with values differing from those of Graeco-Roman society.
The Christian community is to supplant all else as the principal focus of
the believers' identity. The paradoxical values of the cross are to replace
the status evaluation common to the ancient πόλις. But, most significantly, while marriage may be expedient in certain circumstances,
singleness is to supplant it as the ideal and aspiration of the believer.
Such a contention brings Paul directly into conflict with the prevailing
cosmology. Is not the desire to marry always both natural and rational?

All through this epistle, Paul repeatedly refers to the κόσμος, and on
each occasion negatively. That which is τοῦ κόσμου, be it σοφία (1.20–25;
3.18–23) or πνεῦμα (2.12), is compared unfavourably, surpassed and even
condemned by that which is τοῦ θεοῦ. Both the evaluations of the κόσμος,
and those whom it values, are nullified by the paradoxical choice of God
(1.26–28; 4.9–13). Those τοῦ κόσμου τούτου are the immoral outsiders
(5.10). The κόσμος stands to be judged by (and is thus apart from) οἱ ἅγιοι
(6.2). In all of this, Paul seeks to break the chain that would have

---

113. Conzelmann (1975: 132 n. 19) argues that the use of the future tense 'will have'
indicates eschatological thought. This is ungrounded; the future rather reflects that the
consequences are conditional on marriage.

presented a harmony of the cosmic and divine orders. The world, its values and its people are set in antipathy to God and his choice of the cross, the Church and Paul's gospel of weakness. The κόσμος is 'defamiliarized' by Paul.[114] It is not the eternal and benign given of Stoic thought. Living in the light of true wisdom is not found in living in harmony with the κόσμος, but conversely in living in opposition to its false values and assumptions (i.e. choosing τὰ τοῦ κυρίου over τὰ τοῦ κόσμου).

However, there is perhaps a tension in Paul's use of the term κόσμος in 1 Corinthians 7. On the one hand it is most often negatively portrayed as that opposed to Christ, but on the other it is the sphere in which the believer is to live out his or her profession. Believers are, after all, not to withdraw from the κόσμος (5.9). This same tension we will find in 7.29–31.

7.29–31 begins by asserting that the time has been shortened (ὁ καιρὸς συνεσταλμένος ἐστίν).[115] Paul's focus, however, is not on the nature or chronology of the End (there is no allusion here to pre-eschatological woes), but on the implications of eschatology for living in the present time. As ever with Paul, while the eschatological judgment remains in the future (4.5; 6.3–4),[116] that judgment has been initiated and is in a sense anticipated in the Christ-event. Thus, for example, a dichotomy *currently* exists between the things of God, and the present order of the estranged world. In the cross, God's true wisdom and power have *already* been revealed to believers (2.9–10; 16). God has *already* selected the instruments that will nullify the current human order (1.27–28). So it may be said that the rulers of this age *are* doomed to pass away (2.6) and outsiders *are* perishing (1.18). Thus in 7.29 the imminent End and the future fate of the κόσμος impinge on the present age and on how the believer should evaluate and relate to it.[117]

7.31b (παράγει γὰρ τὸ σχῆμα τοῦ κόσμου τούτου) again indicates that the present order is moving to its terminus. κόσμου τούτου stands opposed to a world to come. Again we are concerned not just with future

114. See the insightful consideration of κόσμος in 1 Cor. by Adams (2000: 105–49). Adams concludes that in 1 Cor. Paul engages in a strategy of 'defamiliarization', whereby 'he "makes strange" a term which would have been familiar to his readers, a term which evoked a world-view and was impregnated (so to speak) with ideology. That ideology would have legitimated the Corinthians' social and cultural integration into the macrosociety ... he rejects the ideal of *integration* into the social order of the κόσμος and replaces it with that of *distinction* from the κόσμος' (147).

115. This is preferable to 'the time is short' (cf. Wimbush 1987: 26 and Witherington 1992: 27–30).

116. As Käsemann 1969a: 133–34.

117. As Adams (2000: 134) insists, the present tense here and at 7.31b 'functions not to de-eschatologise the apocalyptic belief in a coming cosmic change, but to indicate that the eschatological process ... has now been set in motion'. We might add that it also has implications for the present evaluations and existence of the believer.

eschatology (not *will* pass away) but the future impinging upon the present (*is* passing away).[118] That it is not the κόσμος itself but its σχῆμα which is said to be passing, indicates that Paul's focus is not on the nature of the physical world, but on the socio-economic order intrinsically linked with it.[119] 7.31b must be read in the light of 7.29b-31; thus what is passing is precisely that structure which demands and controls when and how one has a wife, rejoices, mourns or buys.[120] The invitation to reassess one's attitudes to these activities is being supported by the observation that the believer should know that the σχῆμα under which they are conducted is temporary. The result of this new Christian vision of cosmic reality is to be a radical readjustment of the believer's attitude to, and involvement with, the social order (σχῆμα). While the believer may, by necessity, engage in activities that are a valued part of that social order, the believer cannot share such evaluations. Again the κόσμος is defamiliarized.

But what is Paul counselling? What does it mean for those engaging in the five activities listed to live ὡς μὴ engaging in that activity? Once again, Paul appears to formulate a general rule or principle, but once again it is marriage in which Paul is solely interested.[121] What does it mean to live ὡς μὴ having a wife? It cannot mean divorce (7.12) or the refusal of matrimonial responsibilities (7.3–4). Yet, if Paul is counselling a new attitude for the married,[122] it is difficult to see what such might actually mean.[123]

118. Cf. Wimbush 1987: 34 and Witherington 1992: 28.

119.   Whether Paul implies the end of the spatio-temporal world (as Adams 2000: 133) or merely the end of the present socio-economic system can perhaps be left undecided. The focus is on the latter, but not necessarily to the exclusion of the former. Whether the physical world is destined for destruction or reformation, the point is that at the Eschaton the present social order will be swept away. (Deming's contention that the socio-economic order is being disrupted by the upheaval of the last days is insufficient.)

120.   As Deming (1995: 185) insists, we should take the meaning of σχῆμα 'from the admonitions in the preceding verses, since 7.31b both provides the rationale for 7.29b-31a, and appears to summarize and conclude this section of Paul's argument'.

121.   Wimbush (1987: 28) correctly insists that the focus is on the first statement; the others have no significance in the context and only 'serve a rhetorical function'. Thus we cannot look to the other statements to illuminate the meaning of ὡς μὴ (*pace* Barrett 1971: 177).

122.   Wimbush (1987: 29) seems correct when, noting the omission of the article in the second part of the statements, he argues that 'the exhortation calls for an equality or similarity not between persons in two different categories (those having x, those not having x), but between persons in whatever category (having x), and certain corresponding attitudes (being as though *not* having x)' (cf. Orr and Walther 1976: 219).

123.   Certainly there may be a parallel here with aspects of the Stoic ethic of 'inner detachment', but this should not be overstressed. Not only does Stoicism lack Paul's eschatological standpoint, Stoicism portrays its ethos as an appropriate way to live in accord with the κόσμος (of which the λογός is integral), and there is neither the antagonism to the κόσμος, nor an appeal to alternative cosmology and allegiance, such as we find in Paul.

Suffice to say that if the married believer is to adopt an attitude 'as if not' married, then Paul seems to suggest that the appropriate attitude to the social order, in light of Christian cosmology, is associated with singleness. If a believer is married he is to remain so, but he is to look to the example of the single for a model of the correct attitude to the world.

Crucial here is 7.31a: those using the world, as not over-using it (οἱ χρώμενοι τὸν κόσμον ὡς μὴ καταχρώμενοι). This is a summary of the previous statements,[124] but it is also an evaluation. Marriage is evaluated as a mode of 'using the world', while singleness is 'not over-using' it. Implicitly, then, marriage carries a danger of 'over-using the world' avoided by singleness. Indeed, perhaps singleness is presented as a mode of not 'using the world' at all (just as it does not carry a concern with τὰ τοῦ κόσμου in the next section). In view of what Paul is saying about the κόσμος as temporary and nullified in Christ,[125] 'over-using' it must be pejorative: an inappropriate response to Christian cosmological convictions. Granted, marriage as 'using the world' is not explicitly condemned, yet a danger of overuse seems to be implied, a danger that makes singleness a better option and a model for the married believer.

There is a tension here. The κόσμος and its social institutions are the sphere of existence in which the believer has to exist and live out his Christian calling, and is in this sense neutral. Using the κόσμος, providing the correct attitude is adopted, is permissible. However, the κόσμος and its institutions are also an alternative to allegiance to Christ, and in this sense using the κόσμος always carries the danger, perhaps even the necessity, of over-using it to the detriment of commitment to Christ, just as concern for τὰ τοῦ κόσμου will necessarily distract the believer from τὰ τοῦ κυρίου.

To return to the ὡς μὴ: these words perhaps make better sense if we ask not what Paul is saying *to the married* (since how one lives ὡς μὴ is most unclear), but what Paul is saying *about marriage*.[126] (Since 7.25, 7.28 and 7.36 explicitly address the question of whether the single should marry, it

---

124. An 'umbrella term' (Wimbush 1987: 28).

125. *Pace* Adams (2000: 131–32) it does not appear that κόσμος here means merely 'the physical environment which people inhabit'. Adams arrives at this conclusion by focusing on the objects of the buying and selling in the previous statements. However, if these statements are considered in their entirety, then the focus is not on the material which one may buy or own, but on the social order, which causes one to marry, weep, rejoice or purchase.

126. Commentators (e.g. Barrett 1971: 177) often deny that Paul's ὡς μὴ should be interpreted akin to the asceticism of the *Acts of Paul and Thecla*, where the ὡς μὴ also appear (*Acts of Paul and Thecla* 5). However, while Paul's ὡς μὴ in *Acts of Paul and Thecla* do incite Thecla to renounce her *intended* marriage, there is no indication in the text that they serve to undermine *existing* marriages (unlike in other apocryphal Acts).

is hardly fanciful to suggest that 7.29–31 concerns the same question.)[127] In Graeco-Roman thinking, marriage had generally been considered the ideal state and rational response to cosmological convictions but now, in the light of the Pauline reassessment of the social and cosmic order, singleness is to be regarded as the ideal. It is those who have chosen singleness who have properly responded to the current situation. While marriage is not condemned it is undesirable. Thus the *desire* to marry (other than to avoid πορνεία) must be an inappropriate response: an over-commitment to a perishing social order. Paul, then, critiques the assumptions of the socially integrated Corinthians. Their resistance to his advocacy of singleness is again essentially a 'worldly' response from those who claim to be spiritual.

Here we have offered a new reading of 7.29–31. It is worth, however, assessing the alternative view: that the passage addresses a church where celibacy is openly promoted. The traditional scenario leaves a number of questions unanswered. Why to a group that rejects marriage as part of the old order (especially if it has a 'realized' eschatology) would Paul write such things? Why would he invite them to live ὡς μὴ part of that order, or remind them of its transitory nature? The answer that they renounced marriage on the basis of *their* eschatological convictions but Paul sought to relativize the whole question of marriage and singleness on the basis of *his* eschatological convictions[128] has no basis in the text. While the married are invited to re-evaluate their existence in the world, there is no corresponding invitation to the ascetic.[129] Thus as a critique of enthusi-

---

127. We contend that 7.25–40 never leaves the question of whether the single should marry, despite the fact that, at times, Paul appears to speak more generally. 7.27's apparent address to the married and single, immediately gives way to the statement 'if you marry...' where it is simply assumed that the single are addressed. 7.29–35 again appears to address all ἀδελφοί on various aspects of social existence; however, it is probable that Paul is still concerned with the persuasion for singleness, seeking to bolster such by appearing to invoke a general principle (as indeed in 7.17–24). Again, without announcement, he returns to the question of the παρθένοι in 7.36–38.

Many scholars, accepting that Paul is addressing an ascetic problem in 1 Cor. 7, seem to bracket out 7.29–31 as a general principle rather than a response to the specific issue in hand (e.g. Adams 2000: 131). This may be because, if the ascetic hypothesis is assumed, it is difficult to see how this section with its cosmological critique fits into Paul's wider argument. It is submitted that the reconstruction of this study is able to explain precisely this.

128. As Fee, 'it is a general word that requires them to think of *both* marriage and celibacy in light of their new existence... Such things do not determine one's existence; Christ does' (1987: 337). Or again 'marriage thus belongs to the present scheme of things that is already on its way out. But so does their asceticism' (342).

129. The contention that Paul intends to relativize both marriage and celibacy, and is only impeded from so doing by the inability of the rhetorical form to support a call for the celibate to live 'as not' (so Fee 1987: 341 n. 21), is no answer at all. If the relativization of celibacy were the crucial point, Paul would surely have chosen a more adequate means of expression!

astic asceticism Paul's response would be at best overly subtle, and at worst counter-productive: it would seem to play into the hands of the ascetics, demanding that the married emulate the single. Are we really to believe that Paul expected the ascetics to read between the lines and see a veiled critique of their ethos?

It is easier to view the Corinthians here, as elsewhere, as committed to the expectations and values of Graeco-Roman social order (including marriage), and Paul, here as elsewhere, as viewing such commitment as essentially worldly. Thus Paul critiques marriage and the other activities as forms of using a world that is on the way out. ὡς μὴ is thus not a new mode of being which transcends marriage and celibacy, mourning/not mourning, rejoicing/not rejoicing, buying/not owning, using/not using, but a critique of the former activities as representing a potentially dangerous investment in the passing world.[130] The believer should not exhibit commitment to these activities but to the Lord. The believer who finds himself in such a position should emulate the attitude of the believer who is not in such a position, and thus in a more desirable position vis-à-vis the world. Further, if he who engages should emulate the attitude of the one that abstains, why should any believer seek to engage in such activities where they may be avoided? If the married believer is to aspire to the attitude of the unmarried, then why should the single ever aspire to be married?

9.7.4. *Divisions and Anxieties (7.32–35)*
In 7.28 Paul sought to deter the single from marrying by pointing out the θλῖψις experienced by the married believer. In 7.29–31 he critiqued the desire to marry, implying that such was an inappropriate response to the nature of the world. Now in 7.32–35 he combines both of these strategies. He presents the division and anxiety incumbent on the married believer, and suggests that, by following his counsel of singleness, the believer contemplating marriage might be spared such a fate (7.35). However, his description of the nature of that distress again serves to critique the desire to marry. The married believer's (necessary) commitment to the spouse is interpreted as a commitment to τὰ τοῦ κόσμου, and a commitment which necessarily detracts from commitment to the Lord. Thus to marry is not only to cause unnecessary distress to one's self, but again indicates an inappropriate attachment to world, and a lesser commitment to Christ.

---

130. For Wimbush, in 1 Cor. 7, Paul argues that 'one's condition or status in the world has no power to affect for good or ill status with God' (1987: 32–33). We might of course dispute this, but in any case the point is that status with God has implications for (a) one's attitude to the world's assessment of status, and (b) the social statuses one should aspire to (or not aspire to) (cf. esp. 7.22–23). In this sense, the world is not an ἀδιάφορον.

As in 7.29–31, there is no genuine intention to advise the married believer on how to behave in the light of his/her commitment to Christ. Even if the married believer were to live ὡς μὴ ἔχοντες (whatever that might entail), 7.32–35 indicates he/she can neither avoid the obligations to the spouse (as 7.3–4 already indicated), nor avoid the fact that this necessarily detracts from his/her commitment to Christ. The believer's interests simply are divided.

This is, of course, to assume the traditional interpretation of Paul's discussion of anxiety (μεριμνάω): although Paul states that he wishes the Corinthians to be free from anxiety (ἀμέριμνος, 7.32), he proceeds to use μεριμνάω first positively then negatively. The unmarried person's anxiety for τὰ τοῦ κυρίου and for holiness is commendable, whereas the married person's anxiety for τὰ τοῦ κόσμου and for the spouse is regrettable.[131]

Barrett, however, has argued that the verb should be taken as pejorative throughout.[132] Both the married and the unmarried are anxious, but neither should be. Thus Paul recognizes the problems of the married, but views the concern of the Corinthian ascetics to win favour with God also as the cause of undesirable anxiety. The problem with this interpretation is, as Barrett himself recognizes, viewing the phrase 'to please the Lord' in a negative light, when Paul commends the desire elsewhere.[133] Fee leans in the other direction, suggesting that the concerns of both the married and the unmarried be viewed positively.[134] It is legitimate to care for both τὰ τοῦ κυρίου and τὰ τοῦ κόσμου. The problem for this interpretation is that it can make little sense of 7.32a's desire that a believer be ἀμέριμνος.

Thus, in 7.32–34, μεριμνάω must be used in two senses. Consider the structure of the passage:

Single	*Married*
τὰ τοῦ κυρίου	τὰ τοῦ κόσμου
πῶς ἀρέσῃ τῷ κυρίῳ	πῶς ἀρέσῃ τῇ γυναικί
τὰ τοῦ κυρίου	τὰ τοῦ κόσμου
ἵνα ᾖ ἁγία τῷ σώματι καὶ τῷ πνεύματι	πῶς ἀρέσῃ τῷ ἀνδρί

That which is associated with singleness is unequivocally positive and, given that the negative meaning of κόσμος has already been established in

---

131. As Robertson and Plummer 1914: 157 and Adams 2000: 137–39.
132. Barrett 1971: 179–81 followed by Balch 1983: 434–35 and also Gundry Volf 1996: 535.
133. Rom. 8.8; 1 Thess. 2.15, 4.1; 2 Cor. 5.9.
134. Fee 1987: 344–45.

7.31, it is difficult to see here anything other than a positive/negative comparison. It is unimaginable that, for Paul, τὰ τοῦ κόσμου could be anything other than negative in comparison with τὰ τοῦ κυρίου.[135] Thus τὰ τοῦ κυρίου are expanded in the parallel statements πῶς ἀρέσῃ τῷ κυρίῳ and ἵνα ᾖ ἁγία τῷ σώματι καὶ τῷ πνεύματι and are set against τὰ τοῦ κόσμου expanded in the parallel statements πῶς ἀρέσῃ τῇ γυναικι / τῷ ἀνδρί.

Fee complains of this interpretation, 'how is the married man helped to be "free from anxiety" if his existence is subordinated to the celibate's in this way, so that he is indeed "anxious" about the things of the world while the celibate gets to "serve" the Lord in a pleasing way?'[136] But is Paul setting out to help the married to be free from anxiety? This assumes that 7.32a is an implied imperative addressed equally to the married and the single. But if 7.32–35 is read, as we suggest, purely as a commendation of Paul's advice for celibacy, then the answer is clear: the married, unlike the single, cannot be free from anxiety, cannot wholly be free to serve the Lord 'in body and spirit'.[137] It is for this reason that Paul promotes celibacy.

Consider Paul's other stated desire in this passage: that he might promote among the Corinthians 'undivided devotion to the Lord' (εὐπάρεδρον τῷ κυρίῳ ἀπερισπάστως, 7.35). How can the married man achieve such a level of devotion given that Paul has insisted that his interests are divided (μεμέρισται, 7.34)? Answer: he cannot. That is why Paul counsels celibacy. The same is true of anxiety.

But does this passage hint at Paul's deeper concern about marriage: a concern for the body as a particular object of holiness? What does Paul mean when he speaks of the unmarried as concerned ἵνα ᾖ ἁγία τῷ σώματι καὶ τῷ πνεύματι (7.34)? As Paul commands the holiness of all Christians, regardless of their marital state (Rom. 6.12; 12.1 etc.), and also declares that marriage can sanctify (1 Cor. 7.14), Barrett argues that he cannot be here implying that holiness is in any sense restricted to the unmarried. Thus, 'we have words quoted from the Corinthian ascetical party. Paul approves the sentiment, though he would not himself confine

135. Wimbush (1987: 51) rightly insists that the qualifying objects must govern the meaning of μεριμνάω. Adams (2000: 138) points out that the κύριου/κόσμος dualism here mirrors the θεός/κόσμος dualism elsewhere in the epistle (1.20–21; 2.12; 3.19) which is always a positive/negative comparison.

136. Fee 1987: 344.

137. Pace Wimbush (1987: 42–52) who suggests that although anxiety for τὰ τοῦ κόσμου is opposed to τὰ τοῦ κυρίου and that the goal is full devotion to the Lord, the married man 'is exhorted to relate to his wife in such a way that devotion to the Lord does not suffer', i.e. by living ὡς μή. 7.32–25 simply will not support this reading. Wimbush perhaps senses the difficulty when he complains of Paul's 'awkward manner' (53) here.

it to the unmarried'.[138] Gundry Volf concurs with this, 'unless Paul is simply inconsistent here, or unless he admits to a special bodily consecration of the unmarried which is different to the bodily consecration of all Christians'.[139] However, both of Gundry Volf's alternatives seem preferable to postulating a hypothetical quotation. Could Paul be inconsistent on the issue of holiness? If nothing else, 7.14 should alert us to this possibility. There, holiness was certainly being used in a manner inconsistent with Paul's usual restriction of it to those who are in Christ. Could Paul be admitting to a special bodily consecration of the unmarried? Given that singleness is being commended here precisely because the unmarried, unlike the married, believer is fully concerned for τὰ τοῦ κυρίου, such a conclusion seems rather obvious. Further, given the fact that Paul's argument in 6.12–20 served to indicate that τὸ σῶμα τῷ κυρίῳ was threatened by becoming 'one flesh/body' with any other (6.13–17), it seems reasonable to hold that the married believer's body, on which the spouse has a claim, is not fully devoted to the Lord.[140]

9.7.5. *Proper Behaviour (7.36–38)*

7.36–38 probably has to do with a believer deciding whether to marry his betrothed (παρθένος αὐτοῦ), although the possibility of a father deciding whether to 'marry off' his daughter cannot be excluded.[141] At any rate the suggestion seems to have been made by some in Corinth that a man in these circumstances who marries (or marries off) his παρθένος sins.

According to our reading, of course, the Corinthians would not actually hold such marriages sinful, but offer another *reductio* of Paul's καλὸν ἀνθρώπῳ γυναικὸς μὴ ἄπτεσθαι instruction. Paul is accused of making such marriages sin, and more precisely of thereby causing the man involved to behave improperly (ἀσχημονέω) towards his παρθένος. Paul denies this. If the marriage occurs in such circumstances it is not sin. Indeed, it can also be καλόν. However, singleness is still to be preferred (7.38).

Once again Paul's permission to marry is qualified. Marriage should only occur where: (a) the man believes he is otherwise acting improperly to

138. Barrett 1971: 181, followed by many (e.g. Fee 1987: 346; Wimbush 1987: 56; Gundry Volf 1996: 534–35; M.Y. MacDonald 1990: 174; 1996: 136; Wire 1996: 94). Deming (1995: 198) independently views 'holiness in body and spirit' as reflecting Corinthian concerns.

139. Gundry Volf 1996: 535.

140. The problem with Barrett's contention that this is a Corinthian notion, of which Paul only partly approves, is that Paul nowhere indicates his qualified approval: he neither counters nor modifies the notion.

141. Most modern commentators opt for the former (e.g. Barrett 1971: 184–85; Fee 1987: 349–52; Schrage 1995: 197–200; but cf. Conzelmann 1975: 134–36). The case for 7.36–38 relating to a 'spiritual marriage' can safely be discarded for lack of textual evidence, and in view of Paul's rejection of celibacy within marriage in 7.3–4 (see Fee 1987: 326–27).

his παρθένος (b) he (or she) is ὑπέρακμος (c) it 'has to be' (ὀφείλει γίνεσθε).

Being ὑπέρακμος is the most significant condition and the most difficult to fathom. It may be that this relates to the παρθένος who is said to be beyond (ὑπέρ) her prime. Certainly, if the section has to with a father-daughter relationship, the meaning must be something akin to this. Alternatively, if the section relates to a man's behaviour towards his betrothed, then ὑπέρακμος might relate to him. If so, it probably denotes his 'strong passions' (BAGD), which make marriage advisable. The parallels with lack of self-control as a motive for marriage in 7.2 and 7.9 would tend to support such a reading.

At any rate Paul sets conditions on marriage. He permits it only where to do otherwise would be unfair to the παρθένος, and (most likely) impossible for the man. If ὑπέρακμος is, as we suppose, related to the man's lack of self-control, then Thiselton is quite wrong to speak of 'Paul's desire not to offer a negative value judgment on those who wish to marry'.[142] For, like 7.7–9, Paul's permission to marry carries a condition that requires an admission of weakness on the part of the man. Even if ὑπέρακμος does not relate to the man, 7.37 supports the contention that Paul *does* offer a negative evaluation of those who marry. For, in speaking of the one who refrains from marriage, Paul lists a number of positive properties that implicitly the man who marries would have to lack. Singleness is for those who: (1) stand firm in their hearts; (2) have no compulsion (ἀνάγκη); (3) have control (ἐξουσία) over their own will; (4) and have decided in their hearts.

These properties are the antithesis of the man who marries. (And this does seem to indicate ὑπέρακμος is a lack of sexual control.) They suggest that the man who marries is unable to stand firm, resist compulsion, or exhibit self-control. Whereas it is possible that ἀνάγκη here relates to an external compulsion (the need to act properly towards the παρθένος), it is also possible that it relates to internal pressure, again a lack of self-control. This may well echo the absence of ἐξουσία over his own will exhibited by the man who marries. Whereas 7.36 allowed the man who wished to marry to do as he willed (θέλω), 7.37 declares that a man with a free will should choose singleness.

Thus once again we find Paul permitting marriage and denying that his advice for singleness forbids marriage or creates the intolerable situations (forcing a man to wrong his παρθένος) suggested by the Corinthian *reductio*. But once again we find Paul's permission to be qualified. Singleness is not only preferable: it is the option that will be chosen by the believer with any degree of self-control. 7.38 makes Paul's position clear. Marriage is also καλόν, legitimate and not sinful, but for the one who can

142. Thiselton 2000: 594.

exercise self-control, singleness is better, permitting a fuller and more complete devotion to the Lord.

9.7.6. *Blessed Widows (7.39–40)*

Here little need be added to what has already been said. In giving his advice to the widows, Paul begins by reiterating the prohibition of divorce – but asserting the freedom to remarry ('in the Lord') subsequent to the husband's death (7.39). Thus the notion that Paul either commands divorce or forbids marriage is excluded. However, Paul asserts that the widow is happier (μακαριωτέρα) if she remains as she is according to his γνώμη.[143] As we have noted, the mention of Paul's γνώμη may well serve to remind the reader of a particular form of words.[144] Perhaps he has in mind the maxim by which he originally advocated singleness (καλὸν ἀνθρώπῳ γυναικὸς μὴ ἅπτεσθαι), but qualified by the redirection of 1 Corinthians 7, or perhaps he draws the reader back to the γνώμη offered in 7.25–26 (καλόν ἀνθρώπῳ τὸ οὕτως εἶναι), a γνώμη which has essentially the same meaning as that cited in 7.1b, but without the potential for misunderstanding.

There remains Paul's closing appeal to his possession of the Spirit of God (7.40), which would seem to be some sort of authority for Paul's γνώμη. As we have noted, this appeal is often read by proponents of the ascetic hypothesis as Paul trumping the spiritual claims of his ascetic opponents.[145] But this can make little sense of the text. For a γνώμη that encourages singleness would surely be one that ascetics would support. Why then would Paul need to support this with an appeal to the Spirit? Paul's words make better sense if read as authority for a controversial statement: if he is advising, against both Graeco-Roman cultural norms and the inclinations of the Corinthians, that the widow should remain single.

9.8. *Conclusions*

9.8.1. *Corinthian Ascetics?*

We established in Chapter 8 that, given that the renunciation of marriage was a deeply anti-social phenomenon and given the evidence that the Corinthian church was largely at ease with its social environment (at least compared to Paul), the possibility of renunciation of marriage among the

---

143. Translations often reverse the word order of 7.40a (e.g. RSV 'In my judgment she is happier if she remains as she is') thus suggesting that the γνώμη *is* the assertion that the widow is happier if single. However, the word order makes it equally possible that the happiness is the implication rather then the content of the γνώμη, i.e. the happiness follows from the fact that singleness is καλόν.

144. See 7.7.1 above.

145. See 7.4.1 above.

Corinthians was *prima-facie* to be considered unlikely. We set out in this
chapter to ask whether, despite this, the text of 1 Corinthians 7 requires
such a reconstruction.

Our conclusion must be that it does not. The text can be explained in
terms of Paul's pro-singleness convictions, and his response to Corinthian
objections to these convictions (objections that our knowledge of their
social attitudes would lead us to anticipate). Indeed, we have demonstrated that at various points the ascetic hypothesis is unable to give an
adequate explanation of the text, and that the hypothesis of a Pauline
attempt to persuade reluctant Corinthians of the merits of singleness
provides a better explanation. Given, then, that both textual and
contextual considerations point away from the ascetic hypothesis, the
conclusion must be that it should be discarded.

9.8.2. *Paul and Marriage*

Viewing 1 Corinthians 7 as Paul's persuasion for singleness and as a
development, explanation and qualification of what he says and implies
about sexual/marital unions and Christ-union in 6.12–20, yields the
following conclusions:

(a) Marital union necessarily has implications for the individual. 6.12–
     20 speaks of believers becoming 'one body' with the sexual
     partner. 1 Corinthians 7 demonstrates that spouses have claims on
     their partners and in particular claims on their bodies. In marriage
     the individual relinquishes autonomous authority over the body
     (ἐξουσία) which is invested in the spouse – they are thus (like the
     slave) 'not their own'. This is an inevitable part of the marital
     union. It cannot, indeed must not, be avoided by the married: to
     ignore these implications is to sin.

(b) These effects of marital union have implications for union with
     Christ: they impede the believer's full devotion to the Lord. Paul
     can express this either in the language of participation and sanctity
     or that of ownership. 6.12–20 implied that the indwelling of the
     Holy Spirit in the believer's body precluded 'becoming one body'
     with another. 7.34 implies that only the believer who is not
     married is fully 'holy in body and spirit'. 6.12–20 insisted that the
     believer should not be mastered by another (ἐξουσιασθήσομαι ὑπό
     τινος, 6.12) and that the believer was not his own (6.19). 7.4 states
     that marriage gives mastery (ἐξουσία) over the body to another,
     and 7.23–24 hints that marriage, like slavery, places the believer
     under an obligation to another, an obligation that detracts from
     his ability to be fully the Lord's possession.

(c) It is in this light that Paul advises unmarried believers, where
     possible, to choose singleness. His preference for singleness is not
     based upon expediency in light of current circumstances (caused by

an imminent Eschaton or otherwise) but upon convictions valid in any and all circumstances, although made pressing by Paul's apocalyptic cosmology.

Thus, advice for singleness is the main focus throughout 1 Corinthians 7. For an unmarried believer to seek marriage (other than to avoid the sin of πορνεία or of offending against a betrothed to whom he is obligated) represents a failure. It is to choose marriage over Christ. Thus, to marry for 'Christian' reasons is permitted (although to utilize such reasons is to admit spiritual weakness and a lack of self-control), but to marry for 'normal reasons' (e.g. civic or family duty) is excluded.

(d)　Paul prohibits the married avoiding this conflict of commitment through divorce. The Lord's prohibition of divorce is a more fundamental norm than Paul's anxiety over the compromised commitment of the married believer. As problematic as it is for those in union with Christ to become 'one flesh' with another, the permanent nature of the marital union is not to be denied (this is also revealed in that the divorced believer is not free to remarry). Indeed, it is precisely because Paul takes marital union and its consequences so seriously that marriage becomes problematic.

(e)　Paul in no way attempts to mitigate the position of the married believer. His primary objective is to highlight the problematic nature of marriage in order to deter the single from seeking to marry. Whatever living ὡς μὴ does imply, it does not prevent the essential division of the married believers' commitment to the Lord. Nor is the married believer permitted to avoid the spouse's claims on the body (such is sinful, 7.4). Again the integrity of the existing marital union is a more fundamental norm than that which commends singleness.

While living ὡς μὴ does create space for the married believer, calling for a change of attitude towards the world rather than status within it, the attitude commended is unclear and its implications obscure, perhaps showing in itself the ambiguity of the situation of such believers. Paul's logic ties marriage to the order of the κόσμος, and yet perhaps due to fear of πορνεία, or the Lord's command against divorce, or some unstated missionary requirement for social engagement, Paul will not go the whole way and command a separation from the κόσμος in regard to marriage.

9.8.3. *Christ, the* κόσμος *and Marriage*

The question perhaps remains as to why Pauline cosmology and anthropology come together to make marriage such an ambiguous institution. Our study allows us to reject the possibilities favoured by most commentators. First, the suspicion of the body which later so influenced

Gnostic and early Christian asceticism is notably absent from Paul's thought. The body is not evil, nor even particularly inferior to the Spirit; rather it is intricately involved in the believer's participation in Christ. It is Paul's *high* view of the body, as being 'for the Lord' that drives his 'asceticism'. Secondly, we have rejected the notion that Paul's asceticism is essentially pragmatic. Paul is not akin to the philosophers of the middle-Stoa who weigh up the expediency of marriage and singleness. There are deeper than practical considerations for Paul's invitation to believers to reassess their commitment to marriage. Thirdly, we have excluded eschatology as the *main* factor in Paul's thought. Eschatological woes play no part in Paul's thought, and although eschatological convictions about the nature of the κόσμος are to the fore, they are not the sum of Paul's antipathy to marriage.

So with what are we left? Why does the 'body for the Lord' render its (sexual) involvement with another so problematic? It would seem that Paul thinks in terms of exclusive lordships. As we have seen, 1 Corinthians exhibits a marked dualism between the Lord and the κόσμος. These two spheres clash at every juncture. All knowledge, wisdom, status evaluations, power and indeed ethics pertain either to one or to the other. The believer, by baptism, has been dramatically delivered from one realm into the other. His identity as one who participates in the perishing κόσμος with its false wisdom and stereotypical immorality is transformed into one who by the Spirit participates in Christ, enjoying true spiritual power and wisdom, and living a life orientated to morality. Yet, and this is clearly seen in Paul's criticisms of the Corinthians, there is the constant danger of believers failing to seize hold of the wisdom, power and life that is a property of their Christian identity: of becoming 'worldly'.

This choice that the believer makes between the sphere of Christ and that of the κόσμος cannot be seen merely as a matter of ethics, or of existential decision. For, as the believer acts corporeally, so his actions place him corporeally in one sphere or the other.[146] His body is either 'for the Lord', or under the mastery of another. Here, with the caveats we expressed in Chapter 6, Dale Martin's insights prove helpful. For in the case of πορνεία, it is not simply a question of the ethical choice of the believer, but to whom he will surrender his body. Will his body participate in (be penetrated by) Christ or the πόρνη? That question becomes acute when the πόρνη is seen not just as an individual to which the believer relates, but as a representative of the 'corrupt cosmos', of that which stands outside and opposed to Christ. It is not (*pace* Martin) the purity of

---

146. Humanity is 'related, not to existence in isolation, but to the world in which forces and persons and things clash violently – a world of love and hate, blessing and curse, service and destruction, in which man is largely determined by sexuality and death and where nobody, fundamentally speaking, belongs to himself alone' (Käsemann 1969b: 21).

Christ that is at stake, but whether the believer participates bodily in the Lordship of Christ, or of this outsider.

However, Martin fails to connect Paul's abhorrence of a believer uniting with a πόρνη, to Paul's problem with marriage. For Paul's understanding of the Lordship of Christ excludes not only the believer being mastered by this obvious representative of the outside, but the believer being mastered by any other. Marriage is problematic not simply where it joins a believer to a member of the κόσμος but also because it is mastery by other than Christ.

We can see this operating at two levels. At one level Paul sees marriage as a commitment to an *institution* which is intrinsically linked to the sphere of the κόσμος. It is Graeco-Roman convictions about the natural and social order that place such a high value on marriage. Loyalty to that order is expressed in marrying. If the Corinthians share this high evaluation of marriage, rather than being prepared to consider Paul's prior commendation of singleness, this articulates a commitment to that order of the κόσμος, rather than to that of Christ. The world is not neutral ground, and how one relates to it expresses which sphere of Lordship dominates one.[147]

But at a second level, we cannot ignore the fact that Paul sees marriage as a commitment to, or a participation in, another *individual* which necessarily detracts from a believer's relationship to Christ. This is not a question of ethics, nor of personal relationships but of a demand for the Lord's sole ownership of, or mastery over, the 'body for the Lord'. Perhaps in the end we can only express this in terms of a need for loyalty or commitment to the Lord alone, aware that such categories only go so far in expressing Paul's understanding of participation in Christ.[148]

---

147. As Käsemann (1969b: 2) puts it, 'the faith in the God who justifies the ungodly which Paul proclaims so passionately does not merely burst apart the bounds of the law; it also breaks through the religious regulations and social ties or limits which had obtained before. In so far as these are still retained and recognized, they are merely the sphere in which the Christian has to prove his liberation from the forces which had once enslaved him, and with it the sole sovereignty of Jesus'. The paradox seems to be that marriage is both 'merely' the sphere in which the believer proves his allegiance, and also an alternative allegiance from which the believer needs to prove his liberation.

148. See 6.8.2 above.

CONCLUSION: THE BODY FOR THE LORD

We set out in this study to explore the part played by sexual ethics in the formation of Christian identity. To that end we asked a series of questions. (1) How far are Christian sexual ethics and behaviour viewed as different from that of the outside world? How far does this create a distinct sense of Christian identity? (2) How do Christian ethical convictions govern attitudes to and relations with outsiders? (3) How are Christian sexual ethics related to internal regulation? How is deviance to be dealt with? (4) How are Christians to relate to those social institutions (marriage and divorce) that normally govern sexual relations? What does the Christian attitude to these reveal about the attitude to the wider society? (5) How is the body constructed? How does this govern its sexual use? What might this indicate about the relationship between the individual, the Christian group, and the wider community?

In seeking answers to these questions from 1 Corinthians 5–7, we initially identified another question: can 1 Corinthians 5–7 be read as a sustained Pauline discourse on sexuality as opposed to a sequence of ad-hoc responses to a variety of situations within the Corinthian church?

i. *Unity*

To take the last question first, we have found 1 Corinthians 5–7 to be a coherent discourse. The unity of the chapters exists not only in the theme of πορνεία, but in a variety of thematic interconnections, and in the situational background presupposed. Throughout the chapters Paul presents a clear division between the immoral world and the sanctified church and invites believers both to conform to the moral stereotype presented and to base their behaviour towards others upon this dichotomy.

5.1–8 presented πορνεία as the antithesis of Christian identity. The commission of πορνεία identified the offender as a πόρνος and denied his claim to Christian identity. Such people are to be excluded from the church. 5.9–13 assumes that the κόσμος is pervaded by πόρνοι, and clarifies that the call to avoid πόρνοι is a call to maintain the integrity of the community, rather than a call for withdrawal from the κόσμος. 6.1–11 explores the implications of the ethical dichotomy for lawsuits. It demands that here believers *do* withdraw from outsiders (ἄδικοι), in that they should not allow them to judge between them. It also warns that the lawsuits themselves are evidence of believers committing ἀδικια, another vice incompatible with Christian identity, since believers are no longer ἄδικοι. 6.12–20 spells out why πορνεία is incompatible with Christian identity. It destroys the offender's participation in Christ. This section also serves to demand that believers withdraw from sexual relations with πόρναι, who pollute the believer's body-as-temple. 7.1–40 follows from 6.12–20, exploring the implications of its logic, and of the Christian antipathy to the κόσμος, for marriage. It also continues the exploration of relationships between believers and the outside world. One need not withdraw from sexual relations with ἄπιστοι spouses, but only because the marriage alters the identity of this outsider.

Although a reconstruction of the situation within the Corinthian church has not been our principal objective, we have made some important observations. We have rejected both the ascetic and the libertine hypotheses, and instead viewed the Corinthians as more socially integrated than Paul: resistant to many of the implications, for social and sexual behaviour, which he draws from Christian identity. This reconstruction has several advantages. First, and most importantly, it has aided reading Paul's discourse as a coherent whole rather than as separate responses to separate situations. Secondly, it has allowed us to present a coherent (and thus more plausible) view of Corinthian attitudes. Thirdly, it fits better with the evidence of Corinthian attitudes, to both Paul and society, found in the epistle as a whole.

ii. *Difference*

At the outset we noted that creating and sustaining a distinct group identity was not a function of 'objective' differences between groups in ethos or behaviour, but of how successful a group was in giving its members a positive social identity. To do this it needs to raise the 'cognitive, evaluative and emotive' investment in belonging by differentiating itself in positive ways from outgroups. In the case of the Roman moralists, although it is impossible to say that Romans were more moral than Greeks, and perhaps difficult to say where Roman morals differed in content from Greeks, the rhetoric of moral differentiation may still be effective. It serves to establish the positive social identity of the elite Roman male relative to the outgroup, thus making it important to belong. It also serves as a resource for controlling language: encouraging cohesion by relating deviant behaviour to the negatively evaluated outgroup.

In regard to attitudes to incest, we found little difference between Pauline and Graeco-Roman ethics: both condemn such. In practice, the Christian community can even be compared unfavourably to the outgroup, as incest is 'not found among Gentiles'. In regard to prostitution, Paul's condemnation is typically Jewish, and might even meet the approval of some Graeco-Roman philosophers. But this lack of difference is not what is significant. For, despite this, Paul is still able to promote a worldview in which all outside the church are stereotypically denoted by vice, and particularly by sexual vice. He presents a narrative whereby the Christian community does not and cannot include such people. Where once believers shared the identity of outsiders and were also to be identified by vice, now they have been 'washed, sanctified and justified' and thus share neither the negative identity, nor stereotypically immoral behaviour, of the outsider.

However, to say that the content of ethics *need* not be different is not to say that it *cannot* be. With regard to marriage, we have found Paul's ethos to be in stark contrast to that of his Graeco-Roman contemporaries. Here the claim is not that Christians exceed the moral righteousness of outsiders in regard to a mutually accepted ethical standard, but that Christians adopt a different response to marriage due to radically different convictions about the nature and value of the order of the κόσμος.

iii. *Social Relations*

Barth's work taught us that the persistence of a group's identity does not depend on social isolation. Indeed, the sense of identity may be at its strongest where it permits and governs interaction between groups. Social identity theory further indicated that, where the 'cognitive, evaluative and emotive' elements of belonging are important to individuals, social encounters tend to become intergroup encounters. Here individuals cease to be perceived and treated according to individual characteristics or inter-individual relationships, but are perceived and treated as undifferentiated members of a group, conforming to stereotypes held.

In 5.9–13 Paul rejects the notion that Christian identity entails a withdrawal from the κόσμος. But even while permitting interaction, Paul stresses the group divide and does so on the basis of ethics. Believers are to be aware of the difference between the church (where no πόρνος may be) and the κόσμος (infested by πόρνοι). Christian social identity and stereotypes of the outsider are relevant even where engagement is specifically permitted.

When it comes to lawsuits, the engagement of outsiders as judges is prohibited. Again the rules governing interaction are based precisely on the ethical stereotype. Outsiders are ἄδικοι and this inevitably carries ethical overtones. It is both membership of the outside group and that group's ethical stereotype that controls the believers' response to the judges.

Sexual interaction with outsiders falls somewhere between prohibition and permission. 6.12–20 forbids not only πορνεία but also specifically sex with any woman labelled a πόρνη. It is specifically her unethical identity that renders her unfit for sex. As we have seen, it is possible that such an identity and thus such a prohibition could be extended to all outsiders. 5.9–13 may imply that all members of the κόσμος can be stereotyped as πόρνοι. If so, sexual union with outsiders would be precluded on the basis of the unethical stereotype attributed to them. At any rate, the group divide *does* prohibit the contracting of marriages (and thus sexual relations) with outsiders: believers are to marry μόνος ἐν κυρίῳ.

But this leaves Paul with the anomaly of believers who *are* presently married to outsiders. Here Paul seems to accept that the spouse's status, as an outsider, should in theory preclude the relationship continuing. It is only by insisting that marriage to a believer somehow alters that status that the marriage can be preserved. But even here the status of the partner still governs the interaction. Unlike the believing spouse, the unbeliever is to be permitted a divorce, and unlike the believing spouse the unbeliever is to be seen as a potential convert. Group membership again determines social relationships. Believers are to relate to unbelieving spouses as people in the outgroup category who share outgroup attributes, rather than as individuals.

iv. *Deviance and Control*

With regard to πορνεία, Paul strictly enforces the ethical dichotomy. Deviance is not to be tolerated. The offender of ch. 5 is relabelled as a πόρνος and as such excluded from membership of the community. There is to be no question of internal discipline. There is no call for the individual to desist or repent, only a call for the community to exclude. The man's identity as insider has been rejected.

6.12–20 presents πορνεία as a unique sin: unique in the manner in which it destroys Christian identity. It alone is a sin εἰς τὸ σῶμα which terminates the believer's participation in Christ through the indwelling Spirit. 6.1–11 bears out this uniqueness. Believers are committing ἀδικία, a sin also incompatible with Christian identity (as believers are no longer ἄδικοι). But although endangering this identity, unlike πορνεία, ἀδικία does not automatically destroy it.

6.1–11 also serves as an example of what we have called 'controlling language'. Behaviour and attitudes to be discouraged are related to the already devalued outgroup (ἀδικία to the ἄδικοι). Those who fail to conform to the positively valued ingroup stereotype are presented as unlike 'us' and more like 'them', and are thus devalued among the ingroup (and even threatened with a loss of ingroup identity).

We observed that Paul uses such a tactic at various points in the epistle. In 1 Corinthians 1–2 he builds up a positive picture of the ingroup's epistemology compared with the outgroup only to relate the Corinthians' evaluations of his gospel to the devalued outgroup in 3.1–4. Also at 5.1 he compared the Corinthians' toleration of πορνεία unfavourably with that of the Gentiles. Now in 6.1–11 he labels the Corinthians' behaviour as ἀδικία, and thus associates it with the ἄδικοι who are then so negatively portrayed in 6.9–11.

We can see the same type of controlling language being used more subtly in 1 Corinthians 7. Although marriage is permitted for believers, singleness is commended for those who possess both the χάρισμα and ἐγκράτεια. The possession of χάρισμα has been presented throughout the epistle as an ingroup property. It is something outsiders lack and the Corinthians highly value. ἐγκράτεια is a virtue of which few in antiquity would wish to admit a lack. The lack of self-control (ἐγκράτεια or *continentia*) is an accusation proverbially made of one's opponents in ancient rhetoric. It is something 'we' have and in which 'they' are deficient. It explains why 'we' respond rationally in matters sexual when 'they' are driven by irrational desire. For the Latin writers the lack of self-control leads directly to *luxuria* and *licentia*. For Paul in 1 Thess. 4.4–5, Christian self-control in sexual behaviour (taking wives in 'holiness and honour') can be favourably compared to unrestrained pagan desire (ἐν πάθει ἐπιθυμίας).[1] Thus, in 1 Corinthians 7, those believers who choose to marry demonstrate their deficiency in attributes prized by the Christian ingroup. They lack both a spiritual gift and self-control. This is further compounded by the connection of marriage to the κόσμος; a term already negatively evaluated and connected to the outside.

Thus Paul's construction of a dualism, which ensures the positive social identity of believers on any pertinent scale, also serves to regulate inside behaviour. Certain deviant behaviour (πορνεία) deprives an offender of valued ingroup membership. Other behaviour (ἀδικία) may endanger this membership. But yet other behaviour (marrying), although not incompatible with ingroup identity, is presented as not conforming to the valued ideal. It thus devalues the participant in terms of the group norms, and associates him or her with the values and behaviour of the negatively valued outgroup.

v. *Social Institutions*

Paul's attitude to the social institutions of the surrounding society is ambivalent. According to 5.10, believers are not to withdraw from the

---

1. D.B. Martin (1997) has made much of this verse to argue that Paul sees marriage as an antidote to passion. However, he fails to consider that in antiquity most would rate rationality and order in sexual choices over motivations of passion and desire, and be content to claim the former for themselves while attributing the latter to their rivals.

κόσμος. They are to socialize (presumably including eating) with outsiders. Yet, on the basis of the differences in the respective ethical identities and eschatological fates of the ἅγιοι and κόσμος, they are to disengage from normal patterns of settling disputes. Here Christian values and institutions (internal arbitration) stand as direct alternatives to those of Corinthian society.

However, our most surprising conclusion is the clear break that Paul makes with Graeco-Roman practice and convictions with regard to the institution of marriage. Although marriage is not forbidden, the Christian ideal is to forgo such. Our study of Graeco-Roman attitudes to marriage (Chapter 6) clarifies how radical Paul's call for renunciation and singleness is. Previously, commentators have failed to recognize the shocking nature of Paul's call because, in the search for parallels for 1 Corinthians 7, they have emphasized those aspects of Graeco-Roman society that appear to renounce marriage. We, however, have shown just how rare, marginal and unacceptable such renunciation was, and thus the radical nature of Paul's suggestions.

We have also underlined the socially radical nature of Paul's prohibition of divorce. Rejecting the notion that Paul is concerned to prohibit 'ascetic divorces', we have shown that it is 'normal divorce' that Paul eschews. He is thus not putting limits on radical ascetics, but again introducing an ethos that flies in the face of the values of Graeco-Roman society, which saw divorce as an inevitable aspect of social life. Similarly, Paul's rejection of believers entering into exogamous marriages is likely to upset the normal marriage patterns of Corinthian society.

If Paul's call for the renunciation of marriage were to be followed by the Corinthian believers, then hostility from surrounding society would be the expected result. The Christian community would be seen as disruptive, presenting a direct challenge to the social and political order. Thus the comfortable position that the 'socially integrated' Corinthian Christians presently enjoyed would be threatened. But even without this, Paul's analysis of marriage seeks to alter Corinthian views of the social order. For part of Paul's problem with marriage seems to be precisely that it is an integral part of the present world order, and part of his criticism of the Corinthians' attachment to marriage seems to be precisely that it represents an over-commitment to that world order. If Paul's 'defamiliarizing' cosmology is accepted, then the whole of that order stands to be re-evaluated.

However, in the end, we are left with some ambiguity, for marrying is not actually forbidden to the believer, and existing marriages are strongly upheld. Even if undermined, the institution of marriage is still left standing. Perhaps this is due to the Lord's command against divorce and/ or the fear of πορνεία, but it perhaps also indicates a need for believers to continue living in (if in uneasy relationship to) the world as it is.

vi. *The Body for the Lord*

With the statement τὸ δὲ σῶμα οὐ τῇ πορνείᾳ ἀλλὰ τῷ κυρίῳ Paul offers the believer a radical choice. This is more than a choice of behaviour; it is a choice of identities: a choice of which realm and which lordship one will dwell under.

πορνεία is the sin of the outside. It is not only committed, but it creates an identity for the offender that symbolizes their belonging to the outside. He or she is a πόρνος/πόρνη and as such shall not inherit the kingdom of God. As we have noted, whether Paul stereotypes all outsiders as πόρνοι is ambiguous, but certainly the κόσμος is so pervaded by πόρνοι that to avoid the latter requires a withdrawal from the former. If all outsiders are not πόρνοι they are certainly all ἄδικοι, which also has ethical implications.

Believers also once shared the stereotypical ethics and identity of the outsiders. Once ἄδικοι, by baptism they were made ἅγιοι, and no longer may they be called πόρνοι or be denoted by other vice labels. However, with πορνεία the process of ethical transformation may be reversed. The ἀδελφός may become a πόρνος once again and, as such, he is excluded from the sanctified community of the Lord. His only possible way back is by being 'saved' once again (5.5) – his identity changing to that of a genuine insider. Thus the social 'body' of believers reflects the physical body – if it is 'for the Lord' it can have nothing to do with πορνεία or with the πόρνοι.

To say that the believer's body is 'for the Lord' is not simply to say that Christian identity has ethical implications. It is (as problematic as this may be) to speak of the believer participating bodily in Christ. The Spirit dwells *in* the believer's body-as-temple. The body thus becomes holy ground, and owned by God. Similarly, the dreadful alternative for the body, being 'for πορνεία', is not simply found in an unethical infringement of Christian norms, but is an alternative participation. This πορνεία is envisaged as a union with a πόρνη. The πόρνη is (as one of the πόρνοι) a stereotypical representative of the outside world who pollutes and destroys the body-as-temple. Thus the physical body of the believer reflects the social body – if it is 'for the Lord' it can have nothing to do with πορνεία or the πόρνοι.

But the 'body for the Lord' has further implications, for it not only means that the body cannot be for πορνεία, it means that the body can be for *no* other. For the body is thought of as a limited good. If someone has ἐξουσία over the body, it is denied to the believer (6.12; 7.4). If the believer is the Lord's, he is not his own (6.19). If he is the Lord's slave, he cannot become the slave of another (7.22). The body can only have one owner. If marriage too is a bodily participation in the other, it is thus problematic for the one whose body is 'for the Lord'. Particularly the focus is here on the spouse, who participates in the believer by marriage, but the problem is also with the institution of marriage itself, which is a participation in the cosmic order which lies outside Christ.

At the risk of reductionism, we might make a final use of the language of social identity. The choice of the 'body for the Lord' can be seen as a choice of an identity. Is the believer's identity to be derived from belonging to the Christian community or from other social ties and commitments (loyalty to a spouse and investment in the institutions and values of the πόλις)? Social identity theory suggests that social identities are not *normally* exclusive (one may be a Serb *and* a cafe manager, a Croat *and* a communist) but that the criss-crossing of identities normally serves to weaken both. For Paul, some other loyalty of, or claim upon, the believer cannot be permitted to weaken Christian identity. Thus although he can assert the priority of Christian identity, while allowing other social ties and identities to remain, albeit inferior in importance (as 5.9–13 and 7.12–16), he can also assert that the unique claims of Christian identity – the 'body for the Lord' – renders all other social identities and loyalties problematic.

In the end, we have a Paul with a radical notion of belonging. The Christ event not only opens up a new possibility of being 'for the Lord', but it also delivers judgment on the present order, its people, its values, its structures and its allegiances. All outside the sphere of Christ is negatively assessed. Thus to be 'for the Lord' is to commit every aspect of one's being, one's body and one's identity to Christ, and inevitably to reject all other possibilities for that being, body and identity.

BIBLIOGRAPHY

Original Texts

Lipsius, R.A, and M. Bonnet
   1891   *Acta Apostolorum Apocrypha* (Leipzig).
Hense, O.
   1905   *C. Musonius Rufi: Reliquiae* (Lipsiae: Teubner).
Jenkins, Claude
   1907   'Origen on 1 Corinthians', *JTS* 9: 500–14.

Translations and Editions

All ancient classical works are taken from the Loeb Classical Library, unless otherwise stated.

Elliot, J.K.
   1993   *The Apocryphal New Testament: A Collection of Apocryphal Christian Literature in an English Translation* (Oxford: Oxford University Press).
Ferguson, John
   1991   *Clement of Alexandria Stromateis, Books 1–3* (Fathers of the Church Series; Washington, DC: Catholic University of America Press).
Green, Peter
   1999   *Juvenal: The Sixteen Satires* (London: Penguin)
Le Saint, William P.
   1951   *Tertullian: Treatise on Marriage and Remarriage* (Ancient Christian Writers; London: Longmans and Green).
Walsh, P.G.
   1994   *Livy Book*, XXXIX (Wiltshire: Aris and Phillips).

Secondary Literature

Adams, Edward
   2000   *Constructing the World: A Study in Paul's Cosmological Language* (Edinburgh: T&T Clark).
Alföldy, Géza
   1988   *The Social History of Rome* (London: Routledge).
Allison, Dale C. Jr.
   1987   *The End of the Ages has Come: An Early Interpretation of the Passion and Resurrection of Jesus* (Edinburgh: T&T Clark).

Allo, P.E.-B.
 1934   *Saint Paul Première Épitre aux Corinthiens* (Paris: Ecole Bib).
Bailey, D.S.
 1959   *The Man-Woman Relation in Christian Thought* (London: Longmans).
Bailey, Kenneth E.
 1980   'Paul's Theology for Human Sexuality: 1 Cor. 6.9–20 in the Light of
     Rhetorical Criticism', *NETR* 3.1: 27–41.
Balch, David L.
 1971   'Backgrounds of I Cor. vii: Sayings of the Lord in Q; Moses as an Ascetic
     ΘΕΙΣ ΑΝΗΡ in II Cor. iii', *NTS* 18: 351–64.
 1981   *Let Wives be Submissive: The Domestic Code in 1 Peter* (Michigan: Scholars
     Press).
 1983   '1 Cor. 7.32–35 and the Stoic Debates about Marriage, Anxiety, and
     Distraction', *JBL* 102.3: 429–39.
Balsdon, J.P.V.D.
 1979   *Romans and Aliens* (London: Duckworth).
Barclay, John M.G.
 1987   'Mirror-Reading a Polemical Letter: Galatians as a Test Case', *JSNT* 31: 73–
     93.
 1992   'Thessalonica and Corinth: Social Contrasts in Pauline Christianity', *JSNT*
     47: 49–74.
Barrett, C.K.
 1971   *The First Epistle to the Corinthians* (London: A&C Black [1968]).
 1973   *The Second Epistle to the Corinthians* (London: A&C Black).
Bartchy, S. Scott
 1973   *ΜΑΛΛΟΝ ΧΡΗΣΑΙ· First Century Slavery and 1 Corinthians 7.21* (Missoula:
     Scholars Press).
Barth, Fredrik (ed.)
 1969   *Ethnic Groups and Boundaries* (London: George Allen and Unwin).
Barton, Stephen C.
 1994   *Discipleship and Family Ties in Matthew and Mark* (Cambridge: Cambridge
     University Press).
 1997   'The Relativisation of Family Ties in the Jewish and Graeco-Roman
     Tradition', in H. Moxnes (ed.), *Constructing Early Christian Families: Family
     as Social Reality and Metaphor* (London: Routledge): 81–102.
Baur, F.C.
 1831   'Die Christuspartei in der korinthischen Gemeinde, der Gegensatz den
     petrinischen und paulinischen Christentums in der ältesten Kirche', *Tübinger
     Zeitschrift* 4: 61–206.
Bernard, John Henry
 1917   *Studia Sacra* (London: Hodder & Stoughton).
Betz, Hans Dieter
 1979   *A Commentary on Paul's Letter to the Churches in Galatia* (Philadelphia:
     Fortress Press).
Billerbeck, M.
 1996   'The Ideal Cynic from Epictetus to Julian', in R.B. Branham and M.O.

Goulet-Cazé (eds.), *The Cynics: The Cynic Movement in Antiquity and its Legacy* (Los Angeles: University of California Press): 205–21.

Boyarin, Daniel
1994   *A Radical Jew: Paul and the Politics of Identity* (London: University of California Press).

Branham, R. Bracht
1996   *The Cynics: The Cynic Movement in Antiquity and its Legacy* (London: University of California Press).

Broek, R. van den
1983   'The Present State of Gnostic Studies', *VC* 37: 41–71.

Brown, Peter
1988   *The Body and Society: Men, Woman and Sexual Renunciation in Early Christianity* (London: Faber and Faber).

Brown, Rupert
1996   'Tajfel's Contribution to the Reduction of Intergroup Conflict', in P. Robinson (ed.), *Social Groups & Identities: Developing the Legacy of Henri Tajfel* (Oxford: Butterworth Heinemann): 169–89.

Brown, Rupert, and John Turner
1979   'The Criss-cross Categorisation Effect in Intergroup Discrimination', *British Journal of Social and Clinical Psychology* 18: 371–83.

Bruce, F.F.
1971   *1 and 2 Corinthians* (NCB; London: Marshall, Morgan and Scott).

Brunt, P.A.
1971   *Italian Manpower 225BC–14AD* (Oxford: Oxford University Press).

Bultmann, Rudolf
1952   *Theology of the New Testament*, I (London: SCM Press).
1964   'γινώσκε, γνῶσις ...', *TDNT*, I: 689–719.

Burkill, T.A.
1971   'Two into One: The Notion of Carnal Union in Mark 10: 8; 1 Kor. 6.16; Eph. 5.31', *ZNW* 62: 115–20.

Byrne, Brenden
1983   'Sinning against One's Own body: Paul's Understanding of the Sexual Relationship in 1 Corinthians 6.18', *CBQ* 45: 608–16.

Caird, G.B.
1980   *The Language and Imagery of the Bible* (London: Duckworth).

Calvin, John
1960   *The First Epistle of Paul to the Corinthians* (Edinburgh: St. Andrew's Press [1546]).

Caragounis, Chrys C.
1996   'Fornication' and 'Concession', in R. Bieringer (ed.), *The Corinthian Correspondence* (Leuven: Leuven University Press): 543–99.

Carter, Timothy L.
1997   '"Big Men" in Corinth', *JSNT* 66: 45–71.

Cartlidge, David R.
1975   '1 Corinthians 7 as a Foundation for a Christian Sex Ethic', *JR* 55: 220–34.

Catchpole, D.R.
   1974   'The Synoptic Divorce Material as a Tradition-historical Problem', *BJRL* 57:
           92–127.
Chadwick, H.
   1955   'All Things to All Men', *NTS* 1: 261–75.
Chester, Stephen J.
   2003   *Conversion at Corinth: An Exploration of the Understandings of Conversion
           Held by the apostle Paul and the Corinthian Christians* (Studies of the New
           Testament and its World; Edinburgh: T&T Clark).
Chow, John K.
   1992   *Patronage and Power: A Study of Social Networks in Corinth* (Sheffield:
           Sheffield Academic Press).
Clark, Elizabeth A.
   1999   *Reading Renunciation: Asceticism and Scripture in Early Christianity* (New
           Jersey: Princeton University Press).
Clark, Gillian
   1989   *Women in the Ancient World* (Oxford: Oxford University Press).
Clarke, Andrew D.
   1993   *Secular and Christians Leadership in Corinth: A Socio-Historical and
           Exegetical Study of 1 Corinthians 1–6* (Leiden: E.J. Brill).
Collins, A.Y.
   1980   'The Function of Excommunication in Paul', *HTR* 73: 225.
Collins, Raymond F.
   1999   *First Corinthians* (Sacra Pagina; Minnesota: Michael Glazier).
Conzelmann, Hans
   1975   *Commentary on the First Epistle to the Corinthians* (Philadelphia: Fortress
           Press).
Corbeill, Anthony
   1996   *Controlling Laughter: Political Humour in the Late Roman Republic* (New
           Jersey: Princeton University Press).
   1997   'Dining Deviants in Roman Political Invective', in Hallet and Skinner (eds.):
           99–128.
Countryman, William L.
   1988   *Dirt Greed and Sex: Sexual Ethics in the New Testament and their Implications
           for Today* (London: SCM Press).
Dahl, N.A.
   1967   'Paul and the Church at Corinth according to 1 Corinthians 1: 10–4: 21', in
           W.R. Farmer, C.D.F. Moule and R.R. Niebuhr (eds.), *Christian History and
           Interpretation* (Cambridge: Cambridge University Press): 313–35.
Dawes, Gregory W.
   1990   'But if you can Gain your Freedom (1 Corinthians 7.17–24)', *CBQ* 52: 681–97.
De Vos, Craig S.
   1998   'Stepmothers, Concubines and the Case of Πορνεία in 1 Corinthians 5', *NTS*
           44: 104–14.
   1999   *Church and Community Conflicts: The Relationship of the Thessalonian,
           Corinthian, and Philippian Churches with their Wider Civic Communities*
           (Atlanta, GA: Scholars Press)

Deissman, A.

1927 *Light from the Ancient East: The New Testament Illustrated by Recently Discovered Texts of the Graeco-Roman World* (London: Hodder & Stoughton).

Deming, Will

1995 *Paul on Marriage and Celibacy: The Hellenistic Background of 1 Corinthians 7* (Cambridge: Cambridge University Press).

1996 'The Unity of 1 Corinthians 5–6', *JBL* 115: 289–312.

Deschamps, J.-C., and W. Doice

1978 'Crossed Category Memberships in Intergroup Relations', in Tajfel 1978: 141–59.

Dodd, Brian J.

1999 *Paul's Paradigmatic 'I': Personal Example as Literary Strategy* (Sheffield: Sheffield Academic Press).

Dolfe, K.G.E.

1992 '1 Cor. 7,25 Reconsidered (Paul a Supposed Advisor)', *ZNW* 83: 115–18.

Douglas, Mary

1966 *Purity and Danger: An Analysis of Concepts of Pollution and Taboo* (London: Routledge).

1973 *Natural Symbols: Explorations in Cosmology* (London: Barrie and Jenkins).

Dungan, D.

1971 *The Sayings of Jesus in the Churches of Paul: The Use of the Synoptic Tradition in the Regulation of Early Church Life* (Oxford: Blackwell).

Dunn, J.D.G.

1995 *1 Corinthians* (Sheffield: Sheffield Academic Press)

Edwards, Catherine

1993 *The Politics of Immorality in Ancient Rome* (Cambridge: Cambridge University Press).

Ellis, E. Earle

1974 'Christ Crucified', in R.J. Banks (ed.) *Reconciliation and Hope: New Testament Essays in Atonement and Eschatology Presented to L. L. Morris* (Exeter: Paternoster Press): 69–75.

Engberg-Pedersen, Troels

2000 *Paul and the Stoics* (Edinburgh: T&T Clark).

Esler, Philip F.

1996a Review of Deming (1995), *ExpTim* 107: 184.

1996b 'A Social Identity Approach to Paul's Letter to the Galatians: The Examples of Righteousness and the Mosaic Law' (Paper delivered to the British New Testament Conference, Glasgow).

1998a *Galatians: New Testament Readings* (London: Routledge).

1998b Review of Horrell (1996a), *JTS* 49: 253–60.

2000 'Jesus and the Reduction of Intergroup Conflict: The Parable of the Good Samaritan in the Light of Social Identity Theory', *BibInt* 8.4: 325–57.

Fee, Gordon D.

1987 *The First Epistle to the Corinthians* (Grand Rapids, MI: Eerdmans).

Fiorenza, Elizabeth S.

1983 *In Memory of Her: A Feminist Theological Reconstruction of Christian Origins* (London: SCM Press).

Fisk, Bruce N.
　1996　'ΠΟΡΝΕΥΕΙΝ as Body Violation: The Unique Nature of Sexual Sin in 1
　　　　Corinthians 6.18', *NTS* 42: 540–58.
Forkmann, Goran
　1972　*The Limits of the Religious Community: Expulsion from the Religious*
　　　　Community within the Qumran Sect, within Rabbinic Judaism and within
　　　　Primitive Christianity (Lund: Gleerup).
Foucault, Michel
　1986　*The Care of the Self: History of Sexuality*, III (London: Penguin).
Fox, Robin Lane
　1986　*Pagans and Christians in the Mediterranean World From the Second Century*
　　　　AD to the Conversion of Constantine (London: Penguin).
Gager, John G.
　1970　'Functional Diversity in Paul's Use of End Time Language', *JBL* 89: 325–37.
Garnsey, Peter, and Richard Saller
　1987　*The Roman Empire: Economy, Society and Culture* (London: Duckworth).
Glancy, Jennifer A.
　1998　'Obstacles to Slaves' Participation in the Corinthians Church', *JBL* 117.3:
　　　　381–501.
Godet, Frédéric
　1886　*Commentary on St. Paul's First Epistle to the Corinthians* (ET; Edinburgh:
　　　　T&T Clark).
Gooch, P.W.
　1993　*Dangerous Food: 1 Corinthians 8–10 in its Context* (Ontario: Wilfrid Laurier
　　　　Press).
Gordon, J. Dorcus
　1997　*Sister or Wife? 1 Corinthians 7 and Cultural Anthropology* (Sheffield: Sheffield
　　　　Academic Press).
Goulder, Michael D.
　1991　'ΣΟΦΙΑ in 1 Corinthians', *NTS* 37: 516–34.
　1999　'Libertines? (1 Cor. 5–6)', *NovT* 41: 334–48.
Grant, Robert M.
　1981　'Charges of "Immorality" against Various Groups in Antiquity', in R. van
　　　　den Broak and M.J. Vermasern (eds.), *Studies in Gnostic and Hellenistic*
　　　　Religions (Leiden: E.J. Brill): 161–70.
　1983　'Early Christians and Gnostics in Graeco-Roman Society', in A.H.B. Logan
　　　　and A.J.M. Wedderburn (eds.), *New Testament and Gnosis: Essays in Honour*
　　　　of R McL Wilson (Edinburgh: T&T Clark): 176–83.
Grundmann, Walter
　1964　'ἐγκράτεια, ἀκρασία …', *TDNT*, II: 339–42.
Gundry Volf, Judith M.
　1990　*Paul and Perseverance: Staying In and Falling Away* (Tübingen: Mohr Paul
　　　　Siebeck).
　1994a　'Celibate Pneumatics and Social Power: On the Motivations for Sexual
　　　　Asceticism in Corinth', *USQR* 48: 105–26.
　1994b　'Male and Female in Creation and New Creation: Interpretations of Galatians
　　　　3.28c in 1 Corinthians 7', in Thomas E Schmitt and Moises Silva (eds.), *To*

Tell the Mystery Essays on New Testament Eschatology in Honour of Robert H. Gundry (Sheffield: Sheffield Academic Press): 95–121.

1996 'Controlling the Bodies: A Theological Profile of the Corinthian Sexual Ascetics', in R. Bieringer (ed.), *The Corinthian Correspondence* (Leuven: Leuven University Press): 519–41.

Gundry, Robert H.

1976 *Soma in Biblical Theology: With Emphasis on Pauline Anthropology* (Cambridge: Cambridge University Press).

Haaland, G.

1969 'Economic Determinants in Ethnic Processes', in Barth 1969: 58–73.

Hallett, Judith P., and Marilyn B. Skinner (eds.)

1997 *Roman Sexualities* (New Jersey: Princeton University Press).

Harrill, J. Albert

1995 *The Manumission of Slaves in Early Christianity* (Tübingen: Mohr Siebeck).

Harris, Gerald

1991 'The Beginnings of Church Discipline 1 Corinthians 5', *NTS* 37: 1–21.

Hauck, F., and S. Schulz

1968 'πόρνη ....', *TDNT*, III: 579–95.

Hays, Richard B.

1997 *1st Corinthians* (Louisville: John Knox).

Héring, J.

1962 *The 1st Epistle of Paul to the Corinthians* (ET; London: Epworth).

Hogg, Michael A.

1987 'Social Identity and Group Cohesion', in John C. Turner *et al.* (eds.), *Rediscovering the Social Group: A Self-Categorization Theory* (Oxford: Blackwell): 89–116.

Hogg, Michael A., and Dominic Abrams

1988 *Social Identifications: A Social Psychology of Intergroup Relations and Group Processes* (London: Routledge).

Hooker, Morna D.

1991 *The Gospel According to St. Mark* (London: A&C Black).

Horrell, David G.

1996a *The Social Ethos of the Corinthian Correspondence* (Edinburgh: T&T Clark).

1996b Review of Martin (1995), *JTS* 47: 624–29.

1999 *Social Scientific Approaches to the New Testament* (Edinburgh: T&T Clark).

2000 'Models and Methods in Social-Scientific Interpretation: A Response to Philip Esler', *JSNT* 78: 83–105.

Horsley, Richard A.

1979 'Spiritual Marriage with Sophia', *VC* 33: 20–54.

Hospers, John

1967 *An Introduction to Philosophical Analysis* (London: Routledge).

Hurd, John C. Jr.

1965 *The Origin of 1 Corinthians* (London: SPCK).

Hurley, J.B.

1972 'Did Paul Require Veils or the Silence of Women', *WTJ* 35: 190–220.

Ignatieff, Michael
1998   *The Warrior's Honor: Ethnic War and the Modern Conscience* (Guernsey: Vintage Books).
Jaquette, James L.
1995   *Discerning What Counts: The Function of the Adiaphora Topos in Paul's Letters* (Atlanta, GA: Scholars Press).
Jenkins, Richard
1996   *Social Identity: Key Ideas* (London: Routledge).
Jensen, Joseph
1978   'Does Porneia Mean Fornication? A Critique of Bruce Malina', *NovT* 20: 161–84.
Kahl, Brigitte
2000   'No Longer Male: Masculinity Struggles Behind Gal. 3.28?' *JSNT* 79: 37–49.
Käsemann, Ernst
1969a   *New Testament Questions of Today* (London: SCM Press).
1969b   *Perspectives on Paul* (London: SCM Press).
Kempthorne, R.
1967   'Incest and the Body of Christ: A Study of I Corinthians VI. 12–20', *NTS* 14: 568–74.
Kerr, Donald P.
2000   'Paul and Apollos: Colleagues or Rivals?' *JSNT* 77: 75–97.
Kirchhoff, Renate
1994   *Die Sünde gegen den eigenen Leib: Studien zu πόρνη und πορνεία in 1 Kor 6: 12–20 und dem sozio-kulturellen Kontext der paulinischen Adressaten* (Göttingen: Vandenhoeck & Ruprecht).
Long, A.A
1986   *Hellenistic Philosophy: Stoics, Epicureans, Sceptics* (Berkeley: University of California, 2nd edn).
Lütgert, W.
1908   *Freiheitspredigt und Schwarmgeister in Korinth: Ein Beitrag zur Charakteristik der Christuspartei Beiträge zur Förderung christliche Theologie*, XII, Part 3 (Gütersloh: C. Bertelsmann).
MacDonald, D.R.
1987   *There is no Male and Female: The Fate of a Dominical Saying in Paul and Gnosticism* (Philadelphia: Fortress Press).
MacDonald, Margaret Y.
1990   'Women Holy in Body and Spirit: The Social Setting of 1 Corinthians 7', *NTS* 36: 161–91.
1996   *Early Christian Women and Pagan Opinion: The Power of the Hysterical Women* (Cambridge: Cambridge University Press).
Malina, Bruce
1972   'Does Porneia Mean Fornication?' *NovT* 14: 10–17.
1981   *The New Testament World: Insights from Cultural Anthropology* (London: SCM Press).
Malina, Bruce, and Jerome H. Neyrey
1996   *Portraits of Paul: An Archaeology of Ancient Personality* (Louisville: Westminster John Knox Press).

Marshall, P.
1987   Enmity in Corinth: Social Conversions in Paul's Relations with the Corinthians (Tübingen: JCB Mohr).

Marshall, I. Howard
1978   The Gospel of Luke: A Commentary on the Greek Text (Grand Rapids: MI: Eerdmans).

Martin, Dale B.
1995   The Corinthian Body (Yale: Yale University Press)
1997   'Paul Without Passion: On Paul's Rejection of Desire in Sex and Marriage', in H. Moxnes (ed.), Constructing Early Christian Families: Family as Social Reality and Metaphor (London: Routledge): 201–15.

Martin, Ralph P.
1986   2 Corinthians (WBC, 40; Waco, TX: Word Books).

Martin, W.J.
1970   '1 Corinthians 11.2–16: An Interpretation', in W.W. Gasque and R.P. Martin (eds.), Apostolic History and the Gospel: Biblical and Historical Essays Presented to F.F. Bruce on his 60th Birthday (Exeter: Paternoster): 231–41.

Massie, John
1901   'Did the Corinthian Church Advocate Universal Marriage? A Study in Interpretation', JTS 11: 527–38.

Massingberd Ford, J.
1964   'St Paul, The Philogamist (1 Cor. VII in early Patristic Exegesis)', NTS 11: 326–48.

Maxwell, Marcus
1992   'Creation, Redemption and Sexuality in 1 Corinthians', in George G. Brook (ed.), Women in the Biblical Tradition (Lampeter: Edwin Mellen Press): 257–77.

Meeks, Wayne A.
1974   'The Image of the Androgyne: Some Uses of a Symbol in Earliest Christianity', HR 13: 165–208.
1979   ' "Since then you would need to go out of the world": Group Boundaries in Pauline Christianity', in Thomas Ryan (ed.), Critical History and Biblical Faith (Pennsylvania: Villenova University Press): 4–29.
1983   The First Urban Christians (London: Yale University Press).

Meggitt, Justin J.
1998   Paul, Poverty and Survival (Edinburgh: T&T Clark).

Meyer, H.A.W.
1877   Critical and Exegetical Handbook to the Epistle to the Corinthians, I (Edinburgh: T&T Clark).

Miguens, M.
1975   'Christ's "Members" and Sex (1 Cor. 6, 12–20)', The Thomist 39: 24–48.

Mitchell, Alan C.
1993   'Rich and Poor in the Courts of Corinth: Litigiousness and Status in 1 Corinthians 6.1–11', NTS 39: 562–86.

Mitchell, Margaret M.
1989   'Concerning ΠΕΡΙ ΔΕ in 1 Corinthians', NovT 31: 229–56.
1991   Paul and the Rhetoric of Reconciliation: An Exegetical Investigation of the

Language and Composition of 1 Corinthians (Louisville, KY: Westminster/
John Knox Press).

1997 Review of Martin (1995), *JR* 77: 290–92.

Mitton, Leslie

1973 'New Wine in Old Wine Skins: IV Leaven', *ExpTim* 84: 339–43.

Moffatt, James

1938 *The First Epistle of Paul to the Corinthians* (London: Hodder & Stoughton).

Morris, Leon

1985 *1 Corinthians* (Tyndale NT Commentaries; Leicester: Inter-Varsity Press).

Moule, C.D.F.

1953 *An Idiom Book of New Testament Greek* (Cambridge: Cambridge University
Press).

Munck, J.

1959 *Paul and the Salvation of Mankind* (London: SCM Press).

Murphy-O'Connor, J.

1977 'Works without Faith in 1 Cor. VII, 14', *RB* 84: 349–61.

1978 'Corinthians Slogans 1 Cor. 6.12–20', *CBQ* 40: 391–96.

1980 'Sex and Logic in 1 Corinthians 11.2–16', *CBQ* 42: 482–500.

1981 'The Divorced Women in 1 Cor. 7.10–11', *JBL* 100: 601–606.

1983 *St. Paul's Corinth: Texts and Archaeology* (Delaware: Michael Glazier).

Murray, Gilbert

1925 *Five Stages of Greek Religion* (Oxford: Clarendon).

Neirynck, F.

1996 'The Sayings of Jesus in 1 Corinthians', in R. Bieringer (ed.), *The Corinthian
Correspondence* (Leuven: Leuven University Press): 141–76.

Nejsum, Peter

1994 'The Apologetic Tendency in the Interpretation of Paul's Sexual Ethics', *ST*
48: 49–62.

Newton, Michael

1985 *The Concept of Purity at Qumran and in the Letters of Paul* (Cambridge:
Cambridge University Press).

Neyrey, Jerome H.

1986 'Body Language in 1 Corinthians: The Use of Anthropological Models for
Understanding Paul and his Opponents', *Semeia* 35: 129–70.

Omanson, Roger L.

1992 'Acknowledging Paul's Quotations', *BT* 43.2: 201–13.

Oropeza, B.J.

1999 'Apostasy in the Wilderness: Paul's Message to the Corinthians in a State of
Eschatological Liminality', *JSNT* 75: 69–86.

2000 *Paul and Apostasy: Eschatology, Perseverance and Falling Away in the
Corinthian Congregation* (Tübingen: Mohr Siebeck).

Orr, William F., and James A. Walther

1976 *1st Corinthians* (Anchor Bible; New York: Doubleday).

Ortner, S.B., and H. Whitehead

1981 *Sexual Meanings: The Cultural Construction of Gender and Sexuality*
(Cambridge: Cambridge University Press).

Pagels, Elaine
    1988   *Adam, Eve and the Serpent* (New York: Vintage Books).
Parker, Holt N.
    1997   'The Teratogenic Grid', in Hallet and Skinner (eds.): 47–65.
Parker, Robert
    1983   *Miasma: Pollution and Purification in Early Greek Religion* (Oxford: Clarendon Press).
Pascuzzi, Maria
    1997   *Ethics, Ecclesiology and Church Discipline: A Rhetorical Analysis of 1 Corinthians 5* (Tesi Gregoriana Serie Teologia, 32; Rome: Editrice Pontificia Universita Gregoriana).
Phipps, William E.
    1981   'Is Paul's Attitude Towards Sexual Relations Contained in 1 Cor. 7.1?' *NTS* 28: 125–31.
Pickett, Raymond
    1997   *The Cross in Corinth: The Social Significance of the Death of Jesus* (Sheffield: Sheffield Academic Press).
Pogoloff, Stephen
    1992   *Logos and Sophia: The Rhetorical Situation of 1 Corinthians* (Atlanta, GA: Scholars Press).
Poirier, John
    1996   'Celibacy and Charism in 1 Cor. 7.5–7', *HTR* 89: 1–18.
Proudfoot, C.M.
    1963   'Imitation or Realistic Participation?' *Int* 17: 140–60.
Ramsaran, Rollin A.
    1995   'More Than an Opinion: Paul's Rhetorical Maxim in First Corinthians 7.25–26', *CBQ* 57: 531–41.
Ramsay, W.A.
    1900   'Historical Commentary on the Epistles to the Corinthians', *The Expositor* 6.1: 19–31, 91–111, 203–217, 273–89, 380–87.
Richardson, Peter
    1983   'Judgment in Sexual Matters in 1 Corinthians 6.1–11', *NovT* 25.1: 37–58.
Riches, John K.
    1993   *A Century of New Testament Study* (Cambridge: Lutterworth Press).
Robertson, Archibald, and Alfred Plummer
    1914   *The First Epistle of Saint Paul to the Corinthians* (ICC; Edinburgh: T&T Clark).
Rordorf, Willy
    1986   'Tradition and Composition in the Acts of Thecla: The State of the Question', *Semeia* 38: 43–52.
Rosner, Brian S.
    1992   '"ΟΥΧΙ ΜΑΛΛΟΝ ΕΠΕΝΘΗΣΑΤΕ" Corporate Responsibility in 1 Corinthians 5', *NTS* 38: 460–73.
    1994   *Paul, Scripture and Ethics: A Study of 1 Corinthians 5–7* (Leiden: E.J. Brill).
    1998   'Temple Prostitution in 1 Corinthians 6.12–20', *NovT* 40.4: 336–51.
    1999   ' "Drive out the wicked person": A Biblical Theology of Exclusion', *EQ* 71.1: 25–36.

Rousselle, Aline
  1989   'Personal Status and Sexual Practice in the Roman Empire', in M. Feher (ed.), *Fragments for a History of the Human Body*, Part 3 (New York: Orzone): 301–31.
  1988   *Porneia: On Desire and the Body in Antiquity* (ET; Blackwell: Oxford).
Rudd, Niall
  1986   *Themes in Roman Satire* (London: Duckworth).
Sanders, E.P.
  1977   *Paul and Palestinian Judaism: A Comparison of Patterns of Religion* (London: SCM Press).
  1983   *Paul, the Law and the Jewish People* (Philadelphia: Fortress Press).
Schmidt, Karl L.
  1964   'ἔθνος, ἐθνικός', *TDNT*, II: 364–76.
Schmithals, Walter
  1971   *Gnosticism in Corinth* (ET; New York: Abington Press).
Schrage, Wolfgang
  1991   *Der Erste Brief an die Korinther*, I *(1Kor 1: 1–6: 11)* (Solothurn: Benzigerr Verlag).
  1995   *Der Erste Brief an die Korinther*, II *(1Kor 6: 12–11: 16)* (Solothurn: Benzigerr Verlag).
Schweizer, E.
  1969   'πρεῦμα, πνεῦματικός', *TDNT*, VI: 332–455.
Scroggs, Robin
  1972   'Paul and the Eschatological Women', *JAAR* 40: 283–303.
  1974   'Paul and the Eschatological Women: Revisited', *JAAR* 42: 523–77.
Shillington, V. George
  1998   'Atonement Texture in 1 Corinthians 5.5', *JSNT* 71: 29–50.
Skinner, Marilyn B.
  1997   'Quod Multo Fit in Graecia…', in Hallet and Skinner (eds.): 3–29.
Sollors, Werner (ed.)
  1996   *Theories of Ethnicity: A Classical Reader* (New York: New York University Press).
South, James T.
  1993   'A Critique of the "Curse/Death" Interpretation of 1 Corinthians 5.1–8', *NTS* 39: 539–61.
Tajfel, Henri
  1978   *Differentiation between Social Groups: Studies in the Social Psychology of Intergroup Relations* (London: Academic Press).
Tajfel, Henri, and John Turner
  1979   'An Integrative Theory of Intergroup Conflict', in W.G. Austin and S. Worchel (eds.), *Social Psychology of Intergroup Relations* (Monterey, CA: Brooks Cole): 33–47.
Theissen, Gerd
  1982   *The Social Setting of Pauline Christianity* (Edinburgh: T&T Clark).
Thiselton, Anthony C.
  1973   'The Meaning of ΣΑΡΞ in 1 Corinthians 5.5: A Fresh Approach in Light of Logical and Semantic Factors', *SJT* 26: 204–28.

1977 'Realized Eschatology at Corinth', *NTS* 24: 510–26.
2000 *First Epistle to the Corinthians* (NIGC; Grand Rapids: Eerdmans).
Thrall, Margaret E.
1994 *The Second Epistle to the Corinthians* (ICC; Edinburgh: T&T Clark).
Treggiari, Susan
1991 *Roman Marriage: Iusti Conjuges from the Time of Cicero to the Time of Ulpian* (Oxford: Oxford University Press).
Tuckett, C.M.
2000 'Paul, Scripture and Ethics: Some Reflections', *NTS* 46.3: 403–24.
Turner, John C.
1978 'Social Categorization and Social Discrimination in the Minimal Group Paradigm', in Henri Tajfel (ed.), *Differentiation between Social Groups: Studies in the Social Psychology of Intergroup Relations* (London: Academic Press): 101–40.
1987 *Rediscovering the Social Group: A Self-Categorization Theory* (Oxford: Blackwell).
1996 'Henri Tajfel: An Introduction', in W. Peter Robinson (ed.), *Social Groups & Identities: Developing the Legacy of Henri Tajfel* (Oxford: Butterworth Heinemann): 1–24.
Veyne, Paul
1978 'La Famille et l'amour sous le Haut-Empire Romain', *Annales: Economoes, Societes, Civilisations* 33: 35–63.
1987 'The Roman Empire', in Paul Veyne (ed.), *A History of Private Life: From Rome to Byzantium*, I (London: Belknap/Harvard University Press): 5–235.
Walsh, P.G.
1970 *The Roman Novel: The Satyricon of Pertronius and the Metamorphoses of Apuleius* (Cambridge: Cambridge University Press).
Walters, Jonathan B.
1997 'Invading the Roman Body: Manliness and Impenetrability in Roman Thought', in Hallet and Skinner (eds.): 29–47.
Watson, Francis
2000a *Agape, Eros, Gender: Towards a Pauline Sexual Ethic* (Cambridge: Cambridge University Press).
2000b 'The Authority of the Voice: A Theological Reading of 1 Cor. 11.2–16', *NTS* 46: 520–36.
Watson, Patricia A.
1995 *Ancient Stepmothers: Myth, Misogyny and Reality* (Leiden: E.J. Brill).
Wedderburn, A.J.M.
1987 *Baptism and Resurrection: Studies in Pauline Theology against its Graeco-Roman Background* (Tübingen: J.C.B. Mohr [Paul Siebeck]).
Weiss, Johannes
1910 *Der erste Korintherbrief* (Göttingen: Vandenhoeck & Ruprecht).
Welborn, L.L.
1987 'On the Discord in Corinth: 1 Corinthians 1–4 and Ancient Politics', *JBL* 106: 85–111.

Williams, Craig A.

    1999   *Roman Homosexuality: Ideologies of Masculinity in Classical Antiquity* (Oxford: Oxford University Press).

Wilson, Robert McL.

    1972–73 'How Gnostic were the Corinthians?' *NTS* 19: 65–71.

    1983   'Gnosis at Corinth', in M.D. Hooker and S.G. Wilson (eds.), *Paul and Paulinism: Essays in Honour of C.K. Barrett* (London: SPCK): 102–14.

Wimbush, Vincent L.

    1987   *Paul the Worldly Ascetic: Response to the World and Self-Understanding according to 1 Corinthians 7* (Mercer: Mercer University Press).

    1993   'The Ascetic Impulse in Ancient Christianity', *TTod* 50: 417–28.

Winkler, Martin M.

    1983   *The Persona in Three Satires of Juvenal* (Hildesheim: Georg Olms).

Winter, Bruce W.

    1989   'Secular and Christian Responses to Corinthian Famines', *TynBul* 40: 86–106.

    1991   'Civil Litigation in Secular Corinth and the Church: The Forensic Background to 1 Corinthians 6.1–8', *NTS* 37: 556–72.

    1994   *Seek the Welfare of the City: Christians as Benefactors and Citizens* (Carlisle: Paternoster Press).

    1997   '1 Corinthians 7.6–7: A Caveat and a Framework for "The Sayings" in 7: 8–24', *TynBul* 48.1: 57–65.

Wire, Antoinette C.

    1990   *The Corinthian Women Prophets: A Reconstruction through Paul's Rhetoric* (Minneapolis: Fortress Press).

Witherington III, Ben

    1992   *Jesus, Paul and the End of the World: A Comparative Study in New Testament Eschatology* (Exeter: Paternoster).

    1995   *Conflict and Community in Corinth: A Socio-Rhetorical Commentary on 1 and 2 Corinthians* (Carlisle: Paternoster).

Yamauchi, Edwin

    1973   *Pre-Christian Gnosticism: A Survey of Proposed Evidence* (London: Tyndale).

Yarbrough, O. Larry

    1995   *Not Like the Gentiles: Marriage Rules in the Letters of Paul* (Atlanta, GA: Scholars Press).

Zass, Peter S.

    1984   'Cast out the evil man from your midst (1 Cor. 5.13b)', *JBL* 102.3: 259–61.

    1988   'Catalogues and Context: 1 Corinthians 5 and 6', *NTS* 34: 622–29.

INDEXES

INDEX OF REFERENCES

BIBLE

OTHER EARLY JEWISH LITERATURE

Index of Modern Authors